The Next War

The Next War

Caspar Weinberger
and Peter Schweizer

REGNERY PUBLISHING, INC.
Washington, D.C.

Library of Congress Cataloging-in-Publication Data

Weinberger, Caspar W.
    The next war / Caspar Weinberger and Peter Schweizer.
        p.   cm.
    Includes index.
    ISBN 0-89526-447-1 (acid-free paper)
    1. War—Forecasting. 2. Twenty-first century—Forecasts.
I. Schweizer, Peter, 1964-   . II. Title.
U21.2.W394   1996
355.02'0112—dc20   96-30749
                                             CIP

Published in the United States by
Regnery Publishing, Inc.
An Eagle Publishing Company
One Massachusetts Avenue, NW
Washington, DC 20001

Distributed to the trade by
National Book Network
4720-A Boston Way
Lanham, MD 20706

Designed by Dori Miller
Maps by Chris Capell Computer Graphics

Printed on acid-free paper.
Manufactured in the United States of America

10 9 8 7 6 5 4 3

Books are available in quantity for promotional or premium use. Write to Director of Special Sales, Regnery Publishing, Inc., One Massachusetts Avenue NW, Washington, DC 20001, for information on discounts and terms or call (202) 216-0600.

Contents

Acknowledgments

A great deal of credit and appreciation goes to Rochelle Schweizer, who helped in the edits and rewrites for this volume. In a very real sense, this book is as much her creation as it is ours.

Beverly Danielson provided much-needed support for this project. Our thanks go to both her and Liz Derby. We were also blessed with three wonderful researchers: Erwin Schweizer, Frank Keuchel, and Steve Slivinsky. Stanislav Lunev, a colonel in the Russian GRU who defected in 1993, provided helpful insights into the functioning of Russian military intelligence.

We are grateful to Ambassador Rich Armitage, who provided more of the expert advice and knowledge he always gave in the Pentagon and since. And a special word of thanks to Dr. David Larson of the Mayo Clinic for technical medical advice.

Additionally, a big thank you once again to our longtime friends at the Defense Department for their unfailing support and particularly their help in providing the excellent photographs.

The team at Regnery was outstanding. This project was originally conceived by Richard Vigilante, and he helped us to shape and focus the text. David Dortman offered tremendous help in the editing phase and in piecing the manuscript together. Dori Miller's creative flare and layout added another dimension to the book.

The authors alone are responsible for the contents of this book.

Foreword
by Margaret Thatcher

C ap Weinberger and Peter Schweizer have written an important book, whose provocative title might usefully remind today's political leaders about the dangers we constantly face. My old friend—and one of Britain's greatest friends—Cap Weinberger is well placed to provide salutary advice in the matter. As President Reagan's brilliant defense secretary, he had direct responsibility for the American defense buildup in the 1980s without which the Cold War could not have been won so swiftly and relatively painlessly. Indeed, if the Reagan/Weinberger/Thatcher critics of the time had prevailed, it might never have been won at all.

Agreed: the Communist system contained within it the causes of its own ultimate destruction—its denials of human rights, its crushing of innovative thought, its suppression of nationhood. But only the competitive pressure of Western military might, particularly the technological pressure brought to bear by Ronald Reagan's Strategic Defense Initiative (SDI), made the Soviets realize that they could not get away with military adventurism to compensate for their system's economic and social failure. At this point they finally understood they had met their match. And so, after vainly seeking to reform the unreformable, the Evil Empire crumbled.

In some quarters, the past few years have been spent rewriting that history. Those who once warned of the dire consequences of daring to stand up to the Soviets can now be found explaining that the Kremlin was never in any case more than a zoo for paper tigers.

This folly would be of little importance if such distorted analysis of the past did not risk leading to policy failure in the present. For there has been too much emphasis on the differences between the Cold War and the post–Cold War worlds.

The first similarity is so simple and obvious that only experts could ignore it: it is that there is never any lack of potential aggressors. Of course, the identity of the source of the threat changes. Yesterday, we could have said with reasonable confidence that at its root would be some degree of Soviet mischief-making. But today, Islamic extremists, ethnically driven terrorist groups, rogue states no longer disciplined by powerful patrons—all of these have assumed a new importance, alongside the age-old problem of the dictator in charge of an unstable, bankrupt, expansionist state along the lines of Saddam Hussein's Iraq.

The second similarity between the Cold War and now is that the only way of securing peace and freedom is to ensure that the peaceful, democratic states—at the core of which are still the United States and her allies—have military superiority over the aggressive troublemakers. No amount of multilateralist high-mindedness can get away from that fact.

The third similarity is that the most important element of that military superiority, which America and her allies must possess, is technological. I have already mentioned SDI and its importance in winning the Cold War. But defense spending was cut back too far in the post–Cold War years of utopian euphoria. Moreover, whereas it is relatively simple (if there is the will to do so) to rebuild a country's military strength by increasing the numbers under arms or by purchasing already-developed weaponry, the crucial advances in sophisticated defense technology require a continuing large investment over a number of years. The West's technological lead has never been more important than now as we confront the immense dangers resulting from the proliferation of nuclear and missile technology.

There are a number of imponderables in assessing the precise timescale. It is likely that the United States will be subject to threat from such missiles early in the next century, and, once missiles are available in the Middle East and North Africa, so will all the capitals of Europe. Although diplomacy has a role to play—and although more effective action against the main source of the problem, North Korea, should have been taken—it is only the building of a global ballistic missile defense system that provides an adequate response. This should be a top priority—and America's allies should help foot the bill. Let me add that it is not only the terrible consequences of these weapons' actual use, but also the implication of their *threatened* use, that are so serious. For that threat also casts significant doubt on our ability to protect Western interests around the world.

War can occur in many different ways. But the worst ones usually happen because one power believes it can advance its objectives, either without a war at all or at least with only a limited war that it can quickly win—and, consequently miscalculates. Both psychology and cold steel therefore always have a part to play in a rounded and coherent security policy. I hope that the "war games" outlined in this book—and Cap Weinberger's well-trained wisdom that lies behind them—help ensure that the reality of war can continue to be kept at bay.

Introduction

"Security against foreign danger is one of the primary
objects of civil society. It is an avowed and essential
object of the American union."

James Madison, *The Federalist*

I n these budding years of the post–Cold War era it has become
fashionable to focus on "domestic issues" to the exclusion of
national security affairs. Internal decay, this argument goes,
poses the greatest danger to the republic while "far-off" events in
distant lands are seen, at best, as distractions. As a consequence, the
defense budget has been slashed and funds diverted to myriad
social programs.

It is very convenient to divide neatly "domestic" and "national
security" issues into separate categories. But in reality this
dichotomy is false. As Alexander Hamilton put it, "No government
could give us tranquility and happiness at home, which did not possess sufficient stability and strength to make us respectable abroad."

The rise of a global economy and technological change have
firmly linked our fate with peace and stability in the world. Consider these economic facts from 1993: More than 10 percent of our
gross domestic product (GDP) depended on international trade;
one in six manufacturing jobs was export dependent; America
exported $580 billion worth of goods—more than car-making and
home-building combined; and each billion dollars in exports

created twenty thousand jobs. The fate of American prosperity is unambiguously tied to international stability, and as the world's lone superpower (for now), America is the only nation that can keep the peace. As Sisyphus was condemned to roll the rock up the hill again and again, for the United States there is no one else at present who can carry the burden that peace and freedom require.

Our interests in world stability, moreover, extend beyond mere dollars and cents to include the physical security of the nation itself. Once, geography protected us in "splendid isolation." The United States was unprepared for war in 1941, but Germany and Japan could not threaten the American continent. While it was quite a shock to some on the West Coast when a stray Japanese sub lobbed a shell into Oregon, no one felt it was a real threat.

Today, technology has grabbed America by the lapels and pulled her into the crowded elevator of nations. Enemies halfway around the world could now visit destruction on the United States thanks to new weapons such as ballistic missiles carrying nuclear, biological, or chemical (NBC) warheads. Twenty-five nations already possess ballistic missiles, and the list is likely to grow during the next decade. The Department of Defense (DoD) estimates that by the year 2000, nine developing countries could have nuclear weapons, up to thirty could have chemical weapons, and ten could possess biological weapons. The Central Intelligence Agency (CIA) estimates that by the end of this decade, five more states may be nuclear powers.

These projections might be optimistic. American intelligence agencies have traditionally underestimated the progress countries have made in the production of nuclear, biological, or chemical, weapons. Consider the case of Iraq: prior to the Persian Gulf War, the CIA believed Saddam Hussein was still seven years away from developing a nuclear weapon's capability. After the war, however, when experts with the International Atomic Energy Agency (IAEA) got a closer look, they discovered that Baghdad was probably only three years from a nuclear breakthrough. Even with the spy satellites, we failed to grasp the extent of the Iraqi weapons program.

When the Gulf War began, American military planners had only two Iraqi nuclear targets on their hit list. But after the war, IAEA inspectors identified sixteen main facilities that should have been destroyed. What else is going on in the darkened corners of the world that we don't know about?

As time goes on, the threat posed by NBC weapons will only get worse—so get used to it. As Charles de Gaulle once dryly put it, "The future lasts a long time." We must also remember that right now—not three to five years or a decade away—a Russia with twenty-five thousand nuclear warheads could destroy the United States in an afternoon.

A Dangerous Past and a Dubious Present

Despite these threats, the United States has embarked on a massive disarmament. Since fiscal year (FY) 1985, military budgets have declined 35 percent. Spending on research and development has been slashed 57 percent, and procurement by a whopping 71 percent. Although some reduction was in order following the demise of the Soviet Union, we risk going beyond the danger point:

- Today, the Pentagon is spending less on new weapons and equipment than at any time in the past forty years.

- By 1999, the navy will have only 346 ships, the lowest number since 1938 and down dramatically from nearly 600 in 1991.

- For the first time in seventy years, the navy does not have a single new-design aircraft in the development or production stage.

- Projected defense budgets will account for less than 3 percent of the country's GDP in 1999, a smaller percentage than any time since 1940.

- Tank procurement has disappeared almost entirely.

- Thirty-three percent of all military personnel will be cut by 1999.

By 1997 U.S. Navy end strength will have been reduced 34 percent since 1988, to 390,000 active duty sailors. The number of ships and submarines will be off 41 percent, from 565 to 331; and aircraft will be down by 23 percent. Today, defense spending consumes less than 20 percent of the total federal budget, compared to 50 percent in 1962 (before Vietnam). Even in 1978 during the years of the so-called "hollow military," defense comprisd 23 percent of federal outlays. What we face today is a crisis. Both the General Account-ing Office (GAO) and the Congressional Budget Office (CBO) pro-ject a shortfall of $50 billion to $100 billion during the next five years simply to maintain our current force levels!

The intelligence budget has also been cut and personnel shifted to diverse (some might even say bizarre) tasks that have little to do with national security as it is traditionally understood. In 1993 the CIA had only 9 analysts left watching the Russian military—down from 125. Other resources designed to detect threats to America have also been cut. So what exactly is the CIA spending its time monitoring? The bulk of its resources have been shifted to "global issues" that include pollution, health, natural resources, and endan-gered species. Senior Clinton administration official J. Brian Atwood recently noted with pride that the Defense Intelligence Agency (DIA) was spending considerable resources examining the ecological deterioration of Lake Victoria in East Africa.

After every major war this century, the size of the armed forces was reduced and budgets slashed. Unfortunately, the price of neglect had to be paid in the next war, often with the blood of American soldiers.

The United States entered the First World War ill-prepared for the rigors of battle. In 1917 then-Major George C. Marshall recalled the dangers our soldiers had to endure because of this neglect. "American soldiers experienced something like Valley Forge over in France in the fall of 1917. I have seen soldiers of the 1st Division without shoes and with their feet wrapped in gunny sacks marching ten or fifteen kilometers through the ice and snow. I have seen so many horses of the 1st Division drop dead on the field from starvation, that we had to terminate movements in which they emerged." American casualties were high in the "war to end all wars," because our soldiers were put in harm's way without adequate equipment or training to perform their duties.

Washington, however, failed to learn the lessons from the war, and in 1918 there was a massive demobilization and large budget cuts. In 1941 when the United States was again thrust into war, our ill-equipped, ill-prepared forces suffered heavy losses at Pearl Harbor, Bataan, Corregidor, and Kasserine. The great arsenal of democracy did finally prevail, but not before many U.S. soldiers needlessly died on the battlefield in the face of a better-equipped enemy.

After the Second World War, President Harry Truman again dramatically reduced the military budget. And just five years later when the first ground units were committed to action in Korea, the 1st Battalion, 24th Infantry Division was routed by a better-equipped North Korean army. American tanks could not match the North Korean T-34s.

The United States prevailed in all of these conflicts because we could spend our way out of danger. When a threat emerged, we bought time until we were mobilized and able to respond. But that strategy will no longer work. Ballistic missiles and weapons of mass destruction have not only compressed geographical distances, but may also prevent U.S. forces from ever reaching the battlefield. The next war could be over by the time America is fully mobilized.

Victory Disease

The overwhelming victory by U.S. forces in Desert Storm has, if anything, even increased the danger of overconfidence and rapid disarmament. After all, a large portion of the Iraqi army was wiped out with only minimal allied casualties in a ground war that lasted one hundred hours. The victory was a testament to the will and determination of our troops and the superiority of our weaponry. It would be illogical for a town to cut the budget of a fire department that douses fires too quickly; but we are doing much that same thing that we are punishing our men and women in uniform for doing their jobs too well. James F. Dunnigan and Raymond Macedonia call this the "victory disease." "The Gulf War merely reinforced the feeling that America did not need such large forces," they write. "Moreover, it was a surprise to most Americans to find out how competent their armed forces were. So when victory celebrations were staged, the cheering crowds could not help but think, 'We don't need as many of these really dynamite troops now that peace has broken out.'"

The trouble with victory disease is that it ignores the valuable lesson learned from Desert Storm: victory in the gulf was the result of more than a decade-long commitment to excellence in the armed forces. "These accomplishments were not achieved by accident," General Gordon R. Sullivan, chief of staff of the Army, reminds us. "They are the product of twenty years of dedication, planning, training, and just plain hard work. The war-fighting edge of our military is the result of quality people, trained to razor sharpness, outfitted with modern equipment, led by tough competent leaders, structured into an effective mix of forces, and employed according to up-to-date doctrine."

While in no way minimizing the bravery of our soldiers, we need to remember that Desert Storm was in many ways a strange war. In short, the logistics were ideal and the enemy was frankly stupid. Saddam Hussein sent his army into the desert without air cover. He did not strike at U.S. bases and waited patiently for nearly half a year for the United States to build up its ground forces. Then he sat by as America put in place nearly two-thirds of all its tactical aircraft, which eventually were able to pound Iraqi ground forces in Kuwait, as one air commander noted, "like a tethered goat." So when General Norman Schwarzkopf was asked to rate Hussein as a strategist, there was little surprise when he accurately reported that the Iraqi president "did not understand strategy."

The United States did learn valuable lessons from Desert Storm, which are presently being incorporated into planning, doctrine, and training. But remember—current and future adversaries also took notes and drew conclusions about the Gulf War. The smart ones will not make the same blunders as did Saddam Hussein.

Even if the next war were a replay of Desert Storm, it would be substantially more difficult to fight and win today than it was in 1991. The U.S. force that defeated Saddam Hussein no longer exists. What we have today is a military that is a shadow of its former self. The Gulf War was fought with two Marine divisions, seven active Army divisions, and combat brigades of two additional divisions. Today, that commitment alone would exhaust all of the army's ten active divisions, including those now deployed in Europe and Korea. "If we had to match the force we sent to Desert Storm," says Lieutenant General Paul E. Funk, commanding general of the Army's II Corps in Fort Hood, Texas, "we wouldn't have anything left in this country." Funk estimates that half the Army's 1990 combat power has disappeared.

Air power so critical to victory in the Gulf War is also a fraction of its former size. During Desert Storm, the Air Force could draw from thirty-four fighter wings to keep ten wings at full combat strength. Currently, the number is being reduced to twenty-one fighter wings, barely enough to field the full-strength force needed for a similar conflict today and once again leaving us without reserves in the United States or elsewhere in the world.

Naval air power is also experiencing a decline. The average age of naval aircraft will increase 54 percent in the next ten years. Commander Daniel Moore, air operations officer for the USS

Enterprise Battle Group, warns that present procurement rates will not provide the number of combat aircraft needed to supply current forces.

The United States Marine Corps is not immune to these cuts. Major David Anderson, commanding officer of Combat Service Support Detachment at Cherry Point, North Carolina, complains, "we are approaching our threshold of effectiveness.... [T]he Marine Corps procurement budget is averaging only 50 percent of the $1.2 billion it needs annually. Pre-positioned war reserves have been depleted to offset nonreplaceable equipment."

The Lost Imperative

Since German reunification in 1989, the U.S. Army alone has awarded six hundred Purple Hearts for personnel killed or wounded in action. We place demands on our soldiers, but budget cuts are already depriving troops of training and equipment. Actually, the troubling signs began appearing as early as 1994:

- U.S. Army helicopter flying hours declined from 14.5 to 11.5 hours.

- There was a 10 percent reduction in the time new soldiers spent on advanced, individual training programs for combat support and services support.

- Air Force personnel were regularly deployed overseas for as many as 150 to 180 days a year, well beyond the recommended 120-day maximum.

- At Camp Pendleton, California, Marines trekked seventeen miles to training ranges to conserve costly truck fuel, tires, and maintenance and drilled outside of their office windows instead of in the field to avoid using expensive equipment.

- At Whidby Island Naval Air Station, five aircraft carrier squadrons were fully or partially grounded because the Navy couldn't afford both training flights and foreign operations.

- The 24th Infantry Division that went to Kuwait in October 1994 to deter Saddam Hussein suffered major training deficiencies—some platoon leaders had never taken their platoons into the field for training exercises; tank crews had not completed their crew-drill evaluations; and platoons had not been evaluated in a live-fire exercise.

- Tank crews in the 2nd Armored Division's 1st Battalion, 67th Armor were reduced to parking their tanks and conducting their platoon training dismounted, with soldiers walking the ranges and pretending to be tanks.

Concerns about readiness led the Defense Science Board's Task Force on Readiness to warn in 1994 that "pockets of unreadiness" existed. "The Department [of Defense] should... take careful notice of anecdotal readiness problems which collectively may foretell broad trends toward hollowness within units."

The downward spiral in capabilities has in turn affected recruitment: in 1994 the U.S. Marine Corps failed to meet its recruiting goal for the first time in fifteen years. Poorly funded forces are the greatest impediment we face in retaining the best and brightest in the armed services. As former Congressman David McCurdy has put it, "It takes just as long to develop a lieutenant-colonel as it does to design and build a new weapon system; keeping our forces modern and ready is a critical component of preserving a core of talented leaders."[1]

---

[1] David McCurdy, "And What To Do About It," *Washington Quarterly*, Winter 1996, 115.

But budget cuts explain only part of the reason that "hollow military" is back in the national vocabulary. How funds are being spent is also a problem. During the past several years, the Pentagon has had to sacrifice operations and maintenance programs to pay for a variety of nondefense programs. Pentagon funds have been used to fund United Nations peacekeeping operations in Haiti, Bosnia, Iraq, and Somalia. These operations may or may not contribute to our foreign policy goals, but they have little to do with national defense. Some $28 billion is to be spent through FY 1999 by the DoD on environmental compliance and cleanup, and other funds are to be used for a jobs program that, among other things, would upgrade the San Francisco Bay Area Rapid Transit system. These may all be worthwhile programs, but should they be funded with scarce defense resources?

Even those Pentagon funds which are devoted to military programs go less to muscle than support. Harlan Ullman distinguishes between the "teeth" and the "tail" of the armed forces budget. The teeth include strategic and general-purpose forces—the fighting force that constitutes our military capability. The "tail" includes all other accounts. Ullman notes that "teeth" are receiving a much smaller portion of the budget than ever before. In 1962, for example, the teeth accounted for approximately 55 percent of the budget. But by 1994 the teeth had declined to only 38 percent.[2] Weapons stockpiles will eventually run low. Will we have the funds to replenish them?

Nuclear Forces

Most of the discussion these days concerns conventional forces. Nuclear weapons are often dismissed as an anachronism of the Cold War. When the subject does come up, it is usually in the context of

---

[2] Harlan Ullman, In Irons: *U.S. Military Might in the New Century* (Washington, D.C.: National Defense University Press, 1995)

arms control or the efforts of nuclear aspirants striving to deploy their own arsenals somewhere in the developing world.

Yet nuclear forces are still central to our security. A Russia with an uncertain political future possesses an immense nuclear arsenal, and an increasingly assertive China adds to its force every year. As the list of nuclear powers expands, our nuclear weapons will take on even greater importance. Unfortunately, during the past several years, the United States has begun shutting down the infrastructure for maintaining its nuclear force. We now face a situation where not only can we not add to our stockpile, but even more important, the integrity of the current force may be threatened over the course of the next decade.

In March 1993 the Department of Energy (DOE) formally closed the Office of New Production Reactors, a body charged with ensuring the nation's long-term need for tritium. This action is typical of the Clinton energy department's publicity-seeking approach—a department that demonstrates more interest in releasing classified information than in keeping our nuclear arsenal reliable.

Tritium is a radioactive gas critical to the proper operation of every modern nuclear weapon in the American arsenal. Without this gas, these weapons will not perform reliably and as specified. Tritium decays very rapidly, losing 50 percent of its radioactive charge over a twelve-year period. And unless it is periodically replaced, nuclear weapons become inoperable and useless. Because of the Clinton administration's shutdown of our tritium program, we may be incapable of securing adequate supplies for at least a decade or more. Imagine—a U.S. president may face a nuclear crisis in 2007 and be uncertain as to whether he can truly respond to a nuclear strike. Even worse—imagine that the enemy knows about this unreliability problem!

The Next War

The Pentagon regularly conducts fictional war games as part of an intellectual exercise to better determine the threats we might face and the shortcomings in our armed forces. They use a wide variety of factors when conducting these exercises. Geography, the psychological traits of leaders, troop morale, weapons capabilities, allies, and political interests are just some of the ingredients that go into the war-game recipe. And while no senior military officer would stake the future on these computerized "games," they are useful in trying to unlock some of the mysteries of the "next war"—chiefly, how and where it might be fought.

In March 1982 President Ronald Reagan participated in a war game—the first president to do so since Eisenhower involved himself in 1957. Former Secretary of State William P. Rogers acted as the president while Reagan looked on. It was a five-day computerized exercise involving a hypothetical Soviet conventional attack against American troops in Europe, Korea, and Iran. The United States responded with conventional forces, and the Soviets escalated to tactical nuclear weapons against the U.S. Navy and chemical weapons against ground forces. American field commanders countered with small-yield nuclear weapons. In the end, the Kremlin let loose with an all-out nuclear strike that destroyed Washington and killed the president.

What follows is a collection of literary war games, developed in the spirit of the Pentagon's computerized scenarios. Those who read these scenarios as a prediction of future events will be missing the point. The authors do not view themselves as prophets. Instead, we simply hope to lay bare some possible (and some unlikely) threats that we may face in the not-too-distant future. When the Pentagon conducts its computerized "war games," it pits the United States against a variety of adversaries under multiple conditions. Sound strategic thinking requires understanding a broad range of challenges—not simply the most obvious. Scenarios are helpful in both understanding threats, as well as exposing our own limitations.

To avoid confusion, we have chosen to outline five scenarios that happen in isolation. But remember, the Pentagon hopes to be able to fight two regional conflicts at once!

The other group of readers who may be disappointed are those who hope to find an action-packed novel between these covers. This is not a novel. We make use of fictional characters to outline the type of tough strategic decisions that leaders are likely to wrestle with in the face of war. We also hope the characters will demonstrate the human and psychological dimensions of conflict. But you will find little of what novelists call "character development" in this work or the level of detail associated with fiction.

The reader should note that the effects of the scenarios are not cumulative: although many of the lead characters do not change, the later scenarios do not presuppose that the earlier ones actually occurred. And, of course, despite President St. John's apparent political longevity, U.S. Presidents are limited to two elected terms, or one in the event that they succeed to office during the first two years of a prior president's uncompleted term.

We have tried to portray accurately current American and foreign weapons systems. However, because these scenarios are all about the future, we have made some adjustments which we believe reflect current trends. For example, we have used information from current military research when describing the weapons of tomorrow. Historical (pre-1996) references are all real except as they relate to the lives of fictitious characters. Of course, any character that might resemble real or actual individuals is pure coincidence.

Part One

North Korea and China
April 6, 1998

Chapter One

Lieutenant Choe Kwang hoisted the sixty-pound canvas pack over his shoulders using his stout, rugged arms. He let out a grunt as the full weight of the bundle fell on his back. The young lieutenant looked toward the dark, imposing woods and checked his wristwatch: it was 4:18 A.M. A truck had dropped Choe and seven comrades at a desolate spot along the Korean Demilitarized Zone (DMZ). It was a cool, moonless night, and the air was heavy and damp. As the hulking truck sped off down the dirt road behind, Choe signaled his comrades with a simple hand gesture to follow him into the undergrowth. They worked their way through the thick bushes and weeds to the hillside only a quarter mile away. Once at the face of the incline, Choe and his men began their frantic but silent search for a secret passageway that was well shrouded, even to those who knew of its existence. The lieutenant checked behind both the brush and trees and in the crevices in the large volcanic rocks. After ten minutes of scouring the side of the hill, Choe pushed his arm through a thicket of bushes, and his hand found the emptiness of a tunnel. He gestured to his comrades and took one more look at the stars above before moving into the cavernous, underground passage.

As the group began its journey through the entrails of the tunnel, a storm of anticipation continued to build inside the young

3

lieutenant. This was a mission Choe had literally spent a lifetime training for. Born an orphan in the North Korean city of Sinuiju along the Chinese border, he might have ended up on the streets had he not been selected from a group of infants by a very important hand. Kim Il Sung, then supreme leader of North Korea, had made it a practice throughout his more than four decades in power to visit orphanages to select recruits for his intelligence services and special forces. The idea was brilliant—if Orwellian. Since orphans didn't have parents or family, they would be loyal to no other human being other than the supreme leader. Kim would, in a very real sense, become their father and the military their nursemaid.

Choe was one of the People's children. At age two he was enrolled in the Nampo Military and Political School where he received ideological training. Paramilitary war games began at age six. The incredible strength and endurance Choe demonstrated lead to a prized slot at the famed Mangyongdae, the specialized elementary school for orphans and children of the elite. After a four-year interval at that institution, he attended the Kanggon Military Academy, where he received training in special operations. Following graduation, the Korean People's Army (KPA) became his life.

This hazardous mission was Choe's first. Inside the long, snakelike shaft, it was stuffy and dank as water dripped from the dark brown volcanic-rock ceiling. It was pitch black, and the darkness was pierced only by the beams emanating from a couple of small flashlights. Each step sounded like sandpaper on wood, and the men in the unit occasionally scraped their legs on the scabrous walls. The mile-long tunnel had been dug by North Korean soldiers during the decades, each foot carefully and secretly chiseled by hand. There were dozens of other parallel tunnels, expertly constructed and woven together to form a tapestry of subversion. Choe wondered who else might be traveling the other tunnels that night.

After twenty minutes of walking, a marker signaled the midway point. The lieutenant stopped and gazed at the ceiling. "There it is," he said softly. It was the border, and the next steps put the unit in enemy territory.

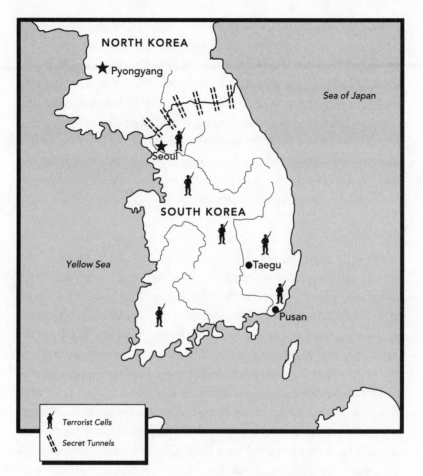

**North Korean Secret Tunnel Network
and Terrorist Cells**

The men continued, and at the southern end of the passageway, Choe began moving more cautiously. Sound was now extremely important because Republic of Korea (ROK) forces might be on patrol nearby. Choe turned off his flashlight and approached the mouth of the tunnel with heedful strides. With his semiautomatic pistol in hand, the lieutenant listened and then peered through a thin crevice in the rock. Nothing stirred outside. There was only a haunting stillness. He waited another moment and then went out into the night to the safety of a large thicket of bushes. Welcome to South Korea, he thought to himself.

In the early morning hours of April 7, North Korean dictator Kim Jong Il looked out his bedroom window and over the ornate, stone balustrade onto the lush, green valley below. The Special House on Jamo Mountain, north of Pyongannam, was his dead father's great monument, and the younger Kim went there often for solace from the turbulence pervading the country. The house was a marvelous structure, forged from a mountain. Kim Il Sung had made certain it was constructed to his precise specifications. Even nature would not deny him. A whole mountain in the Jamo Ridge was leveled by millions of pounds of explosives in order to erect the massive structure at the precise altitude desired by the Great Leader. After removing tons of volcanic rock, the palace was built and the rolling hills and plateau were remade and sculpted to Kim's exact measurements. Since the Great Leader thought of himself as a god, he set about creating his own natural scenery. A dense forest was planted and a lake was dug. It was supposed to be a testament to his immortality. But in an ironic twist, it was completed just two months before he died. The compound was so large that it took several hours to drive around the perimeter.

Kim Jong Il was dressed in a simple, white, Mao-style jacket and slacks. His whitish, pasty face and globule stomach hardly fit the image of iron and steel he tried to project to his people and to the outside world. The core inside this physical softness, however, was hard and cruel as he carried on the tradition of brutality his father had begun. Still, the young Kim longed for more, to step out of his father's penumbra, which still cast a powerful shadow over the country. To do so, Kim looked to succeed where his father had failed. As he drank some tea, he thought about his houseguest. This was perhaps the one individual who could help him.

General Hu Shih was powerful in both physique and stature. He was chief of China's Central Military Commission (the country's highest military command). In this position, Hu dictated China's military policy and, increasingly, its foreign affairs. He also happened to view Pyongyang as a strategic asset.

The general was bent on changing the strategic equation in Asia. Using Malthusian calculations, Hu saw a gloomy future for his country due to shortages of natural resources. He believed that unless the political order in Asia was recast, China's economic and military power would erode. He carried with him everywhere a chart outlining his country's resource crisis:

China's and the World's Per Capita Resources

	per capita China	per capita the world
Arable Land	946 square meters	3,200 square meters
Forests	1,100 square meters	9,333 square meters
Grasslands	866 square meters	3,466 square meters
Fresh Water	2,800 cubic meters	11,000 cubic meters
Coal (geological deposits)	1,500 tons	3,400 tons
Oil (geological deposits)	35–55 tons	90–110 tons

Strong economic growth and an aggressive (or brutal) family-planning program did nothing to change these realities. China was losing some eleven billion square meters of arable land per year, while its population was increasing by almost fourteen million annually. In 1996, for the first time since 1949, Beijing became a net importer of both oil and grain. In the minds of both General Hu and a growing segment of the Chinese officer corps, expansion was the solution.

An assertive China should lay claim to the abundant natural resources in the Pacific theater. This view had been first publicly expressed by Zhang Xusan, the deputy commander in chief of the Chinese navy, in 1992 when he noted that "the country's available land resources can hardly shoulder the heavy population. It is high time for China to readjust its marine strategy and make more efforts to recover the oil and gas resources of the South China Sea."

Exactly who owned these deposits was open to dispute. Half a dozen countries declared sovereignty over the oil- and gas-rich beds in the area. In 1992 Chinese energy experts estimated that the South China Sea may possess more than sixty-five billion tons of oil and gas reserves. They openly referred to the region as the "Second Middle East." As Liu Hauqing, the deputy secretary general of the Central Military Commission, put it in 1987, the South China Sea was "the last opportunity for China to advance."

Kim and Hu met for breakfast at a large glass table amid the sweeping branches of several grand cyprus trees which lined the edge of the garden. Hu was dressed in a khaki military shirt, stirrup pants, and black boots. In his mid-fifties, but looking much older, he had a wide, plump face with high cheekbones and square, white teeth. A stern look seemed permanently chiseled on his face.

Hu was a key figure in the development and modernization of the People's Liberation Army (PLA). For decades the PLA's doctrine called for fighting a Maoist "People's War." This approach was characterized by luring the enemy deep into the country and annihilating them through attrition. Mao and his compatriots elected to keep the PLA large and avoided the acquisition of advanced conventional weapons. Today, however, the cry from the PLA was for waging a "People's War Under Modern Conditions." The military budget saw double-digit growth during the 1990s, and the PLA purchased high-tech weaponry from Russia. Advanced weapons— fighter aircraft, a blue-water navy, and precision-guided munitions—were now the building blocks of Hu's army.

The two men shared a simple breakfast and herbal tea. Like his father, Kim was obsessed with his health and ensuring his longevity. An army of horticulturists and dieticians planned his meals. One thousand experts at the Ponghwa Health Research Institute carefully recommended a special diet of natural and traditional Korean health foods pulled from special farms across the country.

Kim and Hu discussed their mutual fondness for horses and military history and glossed over the general strategic situation in the Pacific. After letting the meal settle, they went to the side entrance of the main building and jumped into a black Mercedes sedan which had been modified to include a retractable roof and slits in the windows. Two hunting rifles were in the back seat.

The driver quickly sped off into the woods. Since the North Korean president was an ardent but inept hunter, he raised a select population of specially adapted wild boar, deer, and pheasants in the nearby forest. They were fed by staff and were not afraid of people or cars. The hunt was not particularly challenging, but was rather like shooting cattle at a theme park.

For several hours Kim and Hu took turns standing in the back seat, firing on the docile animals they encountered. As the game fell to the ground, guards on foot would collect them and toss the carcasses into a waiting truck. Kim enjoyed the outing, and the general was soon bored.

After the hunt, they returned to the impressive villa and were joined by aides for a series of formal discussions. The meeting room was a stately but unpretentious chamber, with silk wall hangings and a simple table covered with green felt. Kim sat in a large, ornately carved chair at one end of the table, while General Hu selected a smaller seat at the center.

The general started the meeting, as if to remind his host that Korea was the junior partner in any strategic marriage. His olive-complexioned face was stern as he spoke in perfect Korean. He bluntly expressed his concerns about the stability of Kim's Korea. And while the general offered to assist his friend, he made it clear that if present trends continued, the Kim government would soon find itself on the ash heap of history. Throughout the discourse, Kim cavalierly sat back and listened until General Hu finished.

After an interval of silence, Kim began, "I agree that the country is plagued with difficulties largely perpetuated by our enemies. But these are temporary nuisances to my government. I do not wish to dwell on present circumstances but would rather discuss immediate opportunities. General Hu, you have expressed to me in the past, rather forcefully, the aspirations of your people to extend their power and reclaim the Chinese territory now under foreign control." Hu nodded. "We in Pyongyang are now prepared to reclaim the southern portion of our peninsula from the imperialists. I believe that by working in unity we will find a strength greater than the sum of our parts."

General Hu squinted, his bushy eyebrows momentarily concealing his eyes as he descended into deep thought. "Tell me," he asked, "what exactly are your plans?"

Kim turned to the taciturn senior military officer seated by his side. The KPA leader had remained silent throughout the discussion. "General," said Kim, "tell our comrade what you have in mind."

General O Kuk-Yul rose from his chair and walked to an easel at the head of the table. He was a rotund, powerful man with small eyes and a narrow chin. There was an aura of arrogance about him. A young aide brought out a map and placed it on the wooden easel. "This is the current strategic situation on the peninsula," the general began with the tone of a schoolmaster. "The Americans are deployed near Seoul and in the central region of the demilitarized zone (DMZ). South Korean forces span the entire line. We now have 65 percent of the weapons needed for the first phase of an assault within one hundred kilometers of the DMZ. And we are continuing to move systems south toward the DMZ through the extensive tunnel network we have developed. This will allow us to fully mobilize within six hours."

Hu nodded slightly. "Tell me, what of your special services?"

General O Kuk-Yul pulled out another map detailing the extensive tunnels built along the DMZ. "These are our routes for infiltration.

We have revolutionaries passing through them on a regular basis. At this point, we have more than ten thousand fighters already placed in South Korea. They will cause enormous disruptions behind enemy lines, particularly in the first phase of the war."

Hu wrote a few notes to himself on a small pad. "What are the chances of achieving surprise?"

O Kuk-Yul rubbed his petite hands and paced in front of the map. "Of course surprise is desirable but not essential. The incitement of revolutionary warfare will generate chaos and terror throughout South Korea. The enemy's attention will be turned inward, and their ability to mobilize restricted. Our forces will overrun them in a matter of days. We expect to seize control of Seoul within forty-eight hours."

"And what of the Americans?" asked the visiting general in a skeptical tone.

"They can be overcome quite easily, their forces near Seoul posing little difficulty. They have only one infantry division in Korea, and, as you know, their forces have not carried nuclear shells since 1991. We will have a clear numerical advantage on the ground. While their air force is quite powerful, we expect to seize control of their air bases and disrupt the ground support operations which keep those planes flying. The central issue is reinforcements. The ability of the imperialists to reinforce their forces on the peninsula is what made the difference in our defeat during the 1950 to 1953 war of liberation. Our strategy is to initiate a surprise attack on the south and occupy the peninsula before substantial U.S. forces arrive. If we succeed, Washington will be faced with a tough choice: negotiate a settlement on our terms or fight their way onto the peninsula, which would be extremely costly. We expect them to negotiate. And of course, if we need to, we can resort to our ultimate weapon."

Hu grimaced and wrote more notes. He was not convinced that his ally would succeed, but he did sense opportunity in the maelstrom which was about to be unleashed on the peninsula. "Well gentlemen, you have presented my government with some very interesting information."

"Thank you, General," quipped Kim with a grin. "But we hope that this meeting might be more than informative. We both know that dual action by our countries to recover national territories dominated by imperialist forces is the best guarantee of success. The Americans cannot deal with both of us." Rubbing his chin and nodding, Hu said nothing.

The meeting broke up by early evening as the sun dropped below the tree line. General Hu said a brief farewell to Kim before taking his motorcade to the nearby airstrip. Walking slowly, he boarded the Russian-built Il-76 heavy-lift transport aircraft for the flight home. Inside the cabin, he settled into a comfortable chair and began reading through his notes as the plane's engines growled. Within minutes he was airborne.

As the giant craft soared over the Yellow Sea back to Beijing, Hu reflected on the changing geostrategic position in the Pacific. If Kim was really moving on the South, this might be an opportune time for China to fulfill her ambitions. A vacuum had existed since the American military reduction and the Soviet collapse. The western Pacific lay waiting to be dominated by a regional power. Hu ran his hand through his black, threadlike hair and thought deeply about his country's checkered history. China was the rightful owner of a treasure trove of resources in the Pacific. But he wondered about the Americans. There was no doubt in his mind that Washington was the chief adversary, the one power that could stand in his way. This view had become official army policy in June 1993 when the PLA High Command published a textbook titled *Can the Chinese Army Win the Next War?* The United States was identified as the "principal adversary," and most of the war-fighting scenarios centered around conflicts with the superpower. Would they come to blows in the Pacific?

As his plane arced through the cloud-heavy skies, the Korean peninsula fading into the darkness behind him, Hu remembered that the formal translation of Korea meant "the land of morning calm." He couldn't help but laugh to himself at the irony in light of what might happen next.

The following morning General Hu exited his Mercedes sedan

at the secret side entrance of PLA headquarters and headed immediately for the general staff room. This was the most secure building in all of China, a well-protected, ancient structure clothed in
grayish concrete and guarded by a plethora of soldiers. The PLA
had emerged as the new throne of power in China as the old guard
of the Communist party passed away. A leadership-succession crisis
had burgeoned with the death of Deng Xiaoping. And as a result,
the PLA became the kingmaker in Chinese politics. All civilian
political factions courted General Hu in the leadership struggle to
succeed Deng. Consequently, that gave the general a chance to
stake out control over Chinese foreign and military policy. He
grasped the reins most firmly when it came to Beijing's policy
toward Taiwan. China had always viewed the island as a renegade
province. When national elections were held in 1996, Taiwan made
a tacit move toward independence. But the very idea was out of the
question for Beijing. The general made his view clear by firing several warheads into Taiwan's territorial waters as a warning.

Beijing had also been aggressive in staking claim to territories in
the South China Sea. In 1992 the government asserted ownership
of the Spratly Islands, Senkakus, and Penghu. (Several countries in
the region rejected these declarations of ownership including the
Philippines, Vietnam, Taiwan, and Malaysia.) At the time it was an
empty claim because the PLA lacked the military capability to
extend its reach. But now it could project its power into these areas,
and General Hu was simply waiting for an opportune moment to
act. Had it finally arrived?

The commission meeting had a clublike atmosphere, each member having been personally selected by Hu. The military commission tended to serve as his rubber stamp, and now he wanted to act.
Puffing on a thin cigarette between sentences, he at once broached
the issue of Chinese territories. "The present circumstance is an
intolerable humiliation. For decades we have needed to endure
foreign control of Nansha [Spratly Islands], Xisha [Paracel],
Dongsha [Pratas Islands], and Zhongsha [Scarborough Shoals]. The
breakaway nationalists on Formosa have paraded our impotence

before the world. But I now believe, comrades, that we have reached a point of destiny. An opportune time has arisen for us to reassert our sovereign control over these parts of Chinese soil."

There was a murmur of voices. General Hu had never been so bold in his pronouncements. "What about the international situation—Japan and the Americans?" asked someone at the table.

Hu took a drag on his cigarette and blew a wisp of whitish-gray smoke over the table. "You ask a very good question, comrade. Both of these countries could present a problem, but they will soon have more than they can possibly handle."

There were more murmurs around the table. "What are you referring to, Comrade Chairman?" inquired a bespectacled octogenarian.

General Hu put the stick of tobacco to his walnut-shaped face and then pulled it away, expelling another cloud of smoke. "There will be immense conflict in the Pacific theater within the next month." Members shifted in their seats. "But it will present no direct security threat to us. On the contrary, it will present opportunity. As the world gazes on this coming storm, we can achieve our objectives amidst the chaos. But only if we act decisively." Although Hu did not go beyond his veiled suggestion of a coming war on the peninsula, he sought and received support to prepare the PLA for offensive military operations in the Pacific.

On April 9, an unusually bright spring day, the capital city of Seoul, South Korea, was a hivelike frenzy of activity. After a long, cold winter, residents were out on the streets shopping, the main arteries of the city were packed with commuters, and the sidewalks teemed with pedestrians. The warm weather also rejuvenated antigovernment protesters, who zealously contested the government each spring. While some were naive students caught up in the furor, many were hard-core revolutionaries who favored a unified Korea under Pyongyang's control. These student radicals were committed Marxists willing to provoke a clash with police in order to create a "revolutionary environment."

More than ten thousand protesters had gathered for a rally near the Blue House, the presidential mansion, to demand reunification. They carried placards and chanted slogans while thrusting their fists into the air. Covering their faces with black plastic masks, riot police formed a line in front of the crowd and blocked any attempt to storm the presidential home.

The rally began with speeches and incantations. But as the rhetoric grew more incendiary, the crowd grew more boisterous. Amid the angry sea of protesters stood Lieutenant Choe Kwang and two men from his KPA unit. Wearing civilian clothes, which covered their thin, Kevlar bullet-proof vests, and donning dark glasses, they blended in perfectly with the throng. Sensing emotions were reaching a fever pitch, Choe calmly pulled a small device from his shirt pocket. With the precision of a major league baseball pitcher, he tossed it at the police line fifty yards away. There was a flash and a boom, sending four constables to the ground. The crowd cheered, but the riot police began firing into the mass. A stampede ensued.

On the 12th-story balcony of a nearby building, four others from the KPA Special Forces unit opened up with sniper rifles on the police line. More officers fell dead to the ground, causing the security forces to increase their rate of volley into the crowd. The crackle of weapons fire continued for several minutes.

Intrepid television news cameras captured the carnage on videotape, and within hours it was appearing on news broadcasts around the world. Washington, Tokyo, London, and Paris all filed diplomatic protests after viewing the footage. The following day, riots broke out in the South Korean cities of Pusan, Inchon, and Seoul as furious students demanded the government resign.

A dark cloud of political paralysis hung over the government. Many newspapers echoed demands for the cabinet to resign, and the opposition threatened to leave the parliament in protest. As South Korea shuddered under the weight of the political fallout, north of the DMZ, troops from the KPA were bringing war materiel through the subterranean tunnels. Using the labyrinth of passageways constructed during the past forty years, armor, trucks, and men were moved to the front line to gain maximum surprise. General O Kuk-Yul hoped to have 75 percent of his attack force within a few miles of the DMZ. The limited, overt mobilization necessary to execute the first assault would reduce warning time for the ROK and U.S. forces in the South to a minimum.

Regular KPA forces formed along the DMZ in preparation for a bold thrust to the South. Meanwhile, the silent flood of subversion continued as thousands of troops from KPA Special Forces continued to trickle into the South by way of the same subterranean routes used by Lieutenant Choe and thousands before him. Among these forces was Unit 124 from the 8th Corps.

The group traveled through the tunnels on the night of April 10 carrying two dozen sealed metallic cylinders over their shoulders. Although the cylinders looked like large, two-foot-long thermos mugs, they contained an electronically coded seal which could be opened only with the proper code. During the two-day trek, the unit traveled by nightfall and hid by day. In the early morning hours of April 12, they reached Tongpuchon, just northeast of Seoul and the home of the U.S. Army's 2nd Division.

Shrouded by darkness, the men of Unit 124 approached the fence of the base and donned gas masks and large, black rubber gloves. After testing the wind, the members of this sensitive biological weapons detachment opened the metal cannisters near the perimeter fence. When the task was complete, they fled north on foot.

It started with complaints of high fever, choking coughs, and difficulty in breathing. By April 14, a strange illness afflicted thousands of men of the 2nd Division. Strong, virile soldiers were doubled over in pain from blood poisoning, pleading like small children for relief from the malady. Many had coal-black malignant skin ulcers covering their bodies. The infantry was suddenly at half-strength. General Gary Evers, an ecclesiastical-looking, white-haired man, met with his senior medical officer to discuss the problem. Colonel Gloria Peyton, a sweet-faced but tough soldier, was the chief medical officer. She had never seen anything like it.

"What is it, doc?" asked Evers, seated behind his desk with an American flag on one side, the Texas Lone Star on the other.

Peyton spoke slowly and without emotion. "This is an anthrax outbreak."

"How could this get out of hand so suddenly? We're at half-strength over the course of just two days."

Peyton looked through her wire-frame glasses with an acute seriousness. "This is an unusual situation. It defies medical understanding that this sort of illness could spread so quickly by natural causes."

General Evers stood and crossed his arms. "What are you suggesting?"

"I'm not sure, General. But I do think I can say one thing with confidence. This was a manufactured bacteria—man-made. That is the only explanation for its rapid diffusion."

Chapter Two

April 15
the Chorwan Valley, South Korea

Lieutenant Choi Lui stared through his field glasses with horror, his eyes wide with panic. In the early dawn light he saw scores of armored vehicles moving rapidly through the Chorwan Valley toward him. He knew instantly what it was: the advanced guard of an attacking KPA tank formation. The image raced through his mind like a zephyr, and he was so startled he could hardly process it. He never thought he would see Korean fighting Korean. He shook the panic from his mind and reached for his communications link (COMLINK). Speaking into the handset with concise, punctuated words like a stuttering machine gun, he told his commander, "Alpha One, Alpha One, this is Delta Nine. Confirming a sighting of the following: large armored formation passing through the border at checkpoint 69. Approximate division size: composed of T-62 and T-64 tanks and APCs [armored personnel carriers]. Inform headquarters that we are engaging. Out."

Choi's regiment was an antitank unit, the first line of defense to slow up the advance. They were deployed smack in the middle of the Uijongbu Corridor, the strategic lane that provided the KPA a fast, direct route to Seoul. Their mission was simple—cause as many enemy casualties as possible. The U.S. Army 2nd Division was deployed just behind them.

Choi and his men scampered into the thick undergrowth where they immediately assembled their Dragon antitank missile launcher and placed the glass-fiber launch tube on the tripod. Choi could feel the ground rumble under the weight of the forty-ton beasts that were closing fast. They were an enormous pack—a column of maybe twenty working their way down the road. Each time the snaking line moved closer, another tank became visible. Fifty yards ahead, he heard only a smattering of gunfire. And then the spasmodic thunder of artillery began.

From across the DMZ, KPA forces were firing Frog-5 and Scud-B missiles in massive quantities. The ground shook so violently as shells rained down on their position that it gave the sensation of an endless earthquake. Lieutenant Choi somehow managed to stay focused on the enemy column. From their vantage point, he and his squad had a perfect trajectory onto the main road. The night air was brisk, and the visibility surprisingly good. Choi briefly looked at his four-man Dragon squad. A couple of the soldiers had a look of penetrating fear, glancing at the woods behind them as if to hint at fleeing. But Choi steadied their nerves by putting them through the Dragon firing routine they had practiced thousands of times.

As the first T-62 closed to within one hundred yards, Choi and his squad let loose with a missile. The projectile screamed toward the KPA lead tank and exploded, ripping through its metallic skin and creating an orb of fire which illuminated the cool morning air. Although the explosion was drowned out by the chorus of enemy artillery, it was a small victory for the 1st Squad. The men looked approvingly at each other, but Choi wasted no time. Another Dragon was attached to the launcher and leveled at the next tank in formation.

Three hundred yards behind, Choi heard several tremendous explosions. There was a flash in the sky and a thunderous bang. He figured it had to be concentrated rocket fire on the U.S. 2nd Division. A private looked at him with alarm in his eyes. "That's behind us—is there no room for retreat?"

Choi shook his head slowly and deliberately. "No. Our unit is the first line of defense. Retreat is not an option."

As the column of steel continued to move down the winding, dirt road in front of Choi, the 1st Squad fired another missile, this one missing a T-62 by just feet. The blast created a heavy, thick gray smoke and a fairly good-sized crater, but the tanks continued to rumble south. Suddenly, having located the squad in the trees, the T-62s opened up with machine guns, sending sinister chatter through the darkness. Choi and his men let go with their third and final Dragon missile, which slammed into the right track of the lead tank. The hulking mass rumbled off the road into the ditch where it continued to sputter and roar in a frantic effort to get back on the thoroughfare. With all of his Dragon missiles spent, Choi ordered a pullback to the ammunition depot several miles down the road.

The 1st Squad navigated their way through the dense woods, twigs and bushes cutting their faces on the mad dash south. Choi could smell the cordite in the air, and the ground continued to tremble under the storm of artillery.

At the ammunition depot Choi found nothing but death and mayhem. KPA Special Forces had already been there. The American soldiers at the facility never had a chance. Several were dead by a single bullet through the head. The fear of snipers sent Choi back into the trees searching for answers. The 1st Squad was now cut off.

News that the storm of war had swept over the DMZ sent American forces in South Korea on full alert. U.S. air power was critical

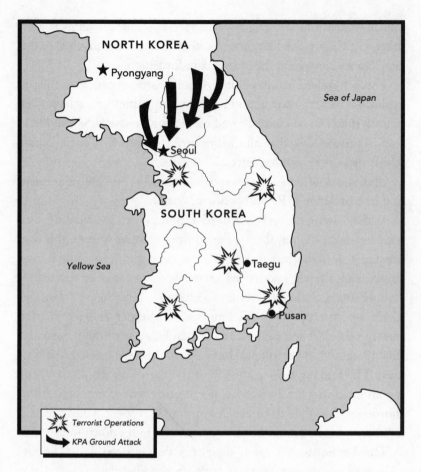

The North Korean Offensive Begins

if the advance was to be stopped. At Kunsan and Osan Air Bases there was a flurry of activity as ground crews and pilots prepared for takeoff to engage the enemy.

Above the main river valleys of central South Korea, almost two dozen Hughes 500 helicopters pushed west. Major Chu Chang-Jun sat in the pilot's seat of the lead helo, nervously scanning the horizon and tugging on the ill-fitting collar of his South Korean uniform. Surprise was everything for this mission, and, thus far, they had avoided suspicion. In the distance Chu caught his first glimpse of Osan Air Base. He climbed to one thousand feet, tightened his grip on the flight stick, and activated the weapons system.

Chu settled the formation over the treetops at the south end of the runway and briefly observed the activity below. American ground crews noticed the helos but, recognizing their South Korean markings, took little interest. The major then brought the craft in closer and spoke softly into the radio: "Commence operations." The helos closed quickly, diving at the airfield and opening up with machine gun and rocket fire. U.S. ground crews were stunned. More than seventy KPA commandos were dropped off on the tarmac, and an intense firefight erupted.

U.S. Air Force Colonel Mike Rickards ran into the hangar with the other pilots from his squadron. Outside, those that were still alive were scrambling for cover. "Those are ROK choppers!" a pilot screamed at Rickards. "What are they doing firing on us?!"

Rickards peeked out the door to get a better look with his rich, blue eyes. "Those have to be KPA Special Forces." He also knew that the longer they were grounded, the better the opportunity the KPA would have in achieving an early knock-out victory. "We've got to figure out a way to get up!" he bellowed, pounding his fist on the hangar's metallic door.

Up north along the DMZ, the American 2nd Division was seeking cover from the hail of ordnance falling on Camp Casey. The KPA had pushed its way through the first line of defense and was threatening to overrun the U.S. position. General Gary Evers fled from his office and leaped into the waiting Jeep at the center of the compound. Whistling and howling rockets seemed to be smashing everything in sight. Flames were crackling and smoke swirled through the base as fires spread. KPA Special Forces had generated an enormous amount of chaos and confusion behind the line. The 2nd Division was by now only at half strength due to the anthrax epidemic. South Korean front-line units were in a state of collapse.

The KPA was advancing on two main points: the Chorwan Valley and the Kaesong–Murasan Approach. Both offered a direct path to Seoul. Early intelligence indicated the bulk of KPA forces was concentrated north of Seoul. Clearly, Pyongyang was hoping to burst through the Uijongbu Corridor, capture the capital, and achieve a psychological, knock-out blow against U.S. and ROK forces in the initial stages of the war. The fast advance of KPA forces seemed to make this aim inevitable. General Evers was pulling the U.S. 2nd Division back to the suburbs of Seoul, where he hoped to mount a serious defense. The 1st Brigade, including two M1A1 Tank Battalions and one mechanized Bradley Fighting Vehicle Battalion, would remain behind to slow the North Korean advance.

General Evers raced south on the main highway toward Seoul in his Jeep. Most of his division was in tow, battered but still willing to fight.

As KPA ground forces continued their push south, the air war erupted overhead. The first wave of KPA fighters and bombers struck military installations along a one hundred–mile belt south of the DMZ. This action was designed to cut off reinforcements and complicate mobilization efforts in South Korea. By sheer numbers it was an impressive display—a cloud of more than five hundred aircraft took to the air. But soon U.S. and ROK aircraft joined in the battle for the skies.

It took Colonel Rickards and his men half a day to deal with the KPA Special Forces that had descended on the air base. By midafternoon, the F-15 Eagles were airborne and closing fast on the air corridor over Seoul. On radar, the mass of KPA fighters was a sight to behold—like a swarm of bees congregating on a victim. But once the dogfights began, their sting proved to be light. Rickards and his squadron made good use of their Sidewinders and AIM-120 advanced medium range air-to-air missiles (AMRAAMs), dropping dozens of KPA planes in the first several hours of combat. Despite being heavily outnumbered, American and ROK pilots inflicted huge casualties. Most of the KPA aircraft were vintage Soviet models, MiG-21s or SU-70s. Older Chinese and Soviet aircraft carried virtually no electronic countermeasures (ECMs) and were, therefore, extremely vulnerable to ROK and U.S. air defense missiles. The few advanced aircraft in the KPA arsenal (MiG-29s) were flown by pilots with little training and were no match for their enemies.

As Rickards banked over the Uijongbu Corridor to return to base for fuel and ordnance, he could see the billowing smoke and raging fires below. While he knew that the air war could be won, he worried about the situation on the ground. If ROK forces and the 2nd Division could not hold, allied air bases in South Korea would be overrun in a matter of days. That would compel the U.S. Air Force to retreat to Japan, seriously complicating air operations. Air power could help defeat the enemy, but it alone could not win the war.

During the early hours of the KPA push south, Kim Jong Il left his residence and raced down Kwangbok Street, past the high-rise buildings to a secret wartime command post. As his motorcade screamed down the boulevard, he could see the Reunification Expressway, a four-lane road including twenty-one tunnels and twenty-three bridges that connects the North Korean capital with the DMZ. It was the most direct route to Seoul and jammed with KPA units bound south.

The wartime operations command post was one hundred meters underneath the Sosong District of Pyongyang. It was a monstrous bunker. By 1990 it had been expanded to the point that Kim could both manage the country and conduct a war from the subterranean facility. More than 5,000 government administrators worked there, and 120 days worth of food and fuel was on hand. Made of concrete, wrapped with steel cords, and encased in rock, it was constructed to survive even a tactical nuclear weapons blast. Only air vents and communications cables were visible above the earth's surface.

Below, the hallways were narrow and connected hundreds of offices, meeting rooms, and bedrooms. President Kim Jong Il had a special wing of offices set apart from the others, protected by armed guards and several locked, steel doors.

The president arrived with an entourage carrying thousands of his personal items. He headed directly to his office. The decor was spartan and functional. Six phones allowed him to communicate with his military officers, his ministers, and Beijing. The rest of the room was occupied by a tumuli of tables and stacks of books. Some of the volumes were old, the spines worn to a dull sheen by decades of palms. Among the books was a collection of ancient stones and trinkets, supposedly from the tomb of King Wang Kong, one of the founders of the first unified Korean state. Kim sometimes rubbed them softly, hoping, perhaps, to conjure up mystical energy from the past or have the legitimacy of Korea's ancient monarchies rub off on him.

The bunker offered Kim a bizarre sort of solace, keeping him hermetically detached from the carnage and violence he had unleashed one hundred meters above. And he planned to remain in his underground fortress until the liberation of the South was complete.

Soon after his arrival, Kim picked up the receiver on a black phone by his side and placed a call to General Hu in Beijing. He tapped his fingers lightly on the mahogany desk until the general answered. Kim spoke with a seething arrogance, a broad grin evident on his face. "Comrade General, I bring you good news. Our forces have begun the liberation of the South. And we are experiencing tremendous victories on the battlefield. All is going as planned." Hu seemed pleased.

"We began with a massive missile and artillery barrage, and a wave of subversion spread throughout South Korea. Meanwhile, elite elements of the forward-territorial corps breached through the DMZ, overwhelming the defenders by vast numbers. Once the

Chinese South China Sea Fleet moves into the Strait.

DMZ was breached, elite armored and mechanized corps surged forward and advanced rapidly. Our army will occupy Seoul within the next thirty-six hours."

As soon as Hu set the receiver of the phone down in the cradle, he knew that if China were going to act to reassert control over its territories in the Pacific, now was the time. PLA forces were already on a higher state of readiness.

On April 16, under the cover of a fog-shrouded evening, China's South Sea fleet moved out of port. Vice Admiral Ou Zhenmou, the commanding officer, watched from the bridge of the destroyer *Xiaping*. His small, black eyes were scanning the armada of ten destroyers and six frigates bound for the Taiwan Strait. He took comfort in knowing that some two miles in front, seven Chinese attack submarines were moving quietly below the waterline to spearhead the deployment. Admiral Ou's orders were simple—blockade the islands of Quemoy and Penghu and force a showdown with Taipei's forces.

Penghu is a small archipelago west of Taiwan, and Ou deployed his forces between the two in a half-moon formation. If Taiwanese vessels wanted to move on Penghu, they would have to go through the Chinese fleet first. Barely two hours after Ou had established his line, two Taiwanese frigates appeared in the silky, blue waters due east of the archipelago. Admiral Ou knew that Taipei had sent the cruisers to demonstrate resolve and ensure access in territorial waters. For fifty years, Chinese and Taiwanese naval vessels had played a complex game of chicken with each other. Today Ou would end the game.

As the two Taiwanese frigates moved toward the line, two of the Chinese attack subs fired a volley of torpedos. The frigates took evasive action, but one torpedo managed to penetrate the light, gray, metal hull of the *Cheng-Kung*. A massive explosion rocked the vessel, which instantly began taking on water. The frigate *Cheng-Ho* responded by sending a quartet of antisubmarine torpedoes into the blue abyss. One found its target, damaging the rotor shaft on a Chinese sub.

Within minutes, the *Cheng-Kung* was a burning hulk of twisted steel with red flames licking the main deck. It began to list, soon slipping below the surface. The *Cheng-Ho* released a half-dozen surface-to-surface missiles before experiencing the same fate.

The attack on South Korea put U.S. forces around the world on full alert. The mobilization of forces to reinforce the battered 2nd Division soon followed. Hours after KPA forces had pierced the DMZ, members of the 82nd Airborne were on the "Green Ramp" along the main runway at Pope Air Force Base in North Carolina, meticulously checking their parachutes and harnesses. They were waiting to board the C-130 Hercules tactical transports and the C-141 Starlifters. Once airborne, they would fly straight to the Korean peninsula where they would provide some of the first American reinforcements.

At Scofield Barracks in Hawaii, General Eric Connerly was

preparing his 25th Infantry Division to ship out for Pusan. With his broad shoulders, strong arms, thick neck, refined nose, and solid jaw, Connerly fit the movie image of the tough army colonel. Before he boarded a transport, he met with the commander in chief, Pacific (CINCPAC), Admiral John Saunders.

Saunders had been up most the night with his planning staff and on the phone with General Evers in Seoul. Rail-thin, with a thick pile of white hair atop his sloping head, Saunders had a reputation for being erratic and unpredictable. Connerly knew of Saunders's reputation but also of his moments of brilliance. Saunders was like a volcano and could produce an incandescence unmatched by anyone when it came to strategic thought and courage. It just wasn't visible most of the time.

Connerly entered the room, and the two shared a pot of coffee as they sat in comfortable leather chairs in the lounge adjacent to the admiral's office. The room had a decidedly casual aura, and streams of light from the bright morning sun cascaded through the window. It seemed an unlikely place to discuss war.

"General, the 25th looms very large in our plans. You will be joined in Pusan by the 3rd Marine Division from Okinawa and the 82nd Airborne out of Fort Bragg. I want you to form a perimeter north of the city, just west of Taegu." Saunders slowly got up and moved to only a few feet in front of the general. "Eric, the success of our war effort will rest on your ability to hold the line. If you can't, we will not be able to reinforce the peninsula and that will force a perilous amphibious assault under fire."

Connerly nodded and swallowed, the nerves building in his throat. "Of course, Admiral. Did you say the 82nd Airborne would be there too?"

"Yes. Why?"

"My son is in that unit." Connerly had not seen him in six years. He shook off the temporary lapse into familial emotion. "Admiral, when can we expect reinforcements?"

"You will need to hold for ten days. Our airlift and sealift limitations make it virtually impossible to get anyone else there in the short term. War with China is a real possibility, and that is sure to stretch our naval-strike capabilities. The president has dispatched two carrier battle groups to the Taiwan Strait. We hope to have the 1st Mechanized Infantry Division, 2nd Armored Division, 1st Marine Division, and the 101st Airborne Assault Division in Taegu by May 1."

Connerly nodded. "What is the latest you hear from the ground?"

Saunders returned to his desk and pulled out the most recent cables from Seoul. "General Evers reports that we are taking quite a beating. The KPA is throwing everything at them. The fly boys are hitting them hard, but the advance continues. We expect Seoul to fall within the next day or so, and the KPA armored divisions to reach the Han-gang River by tomorrow—that's seventy-five miles south of the DMZ."

Connerly stroked the few strands of thinning hair on the top of his head. "Admiral, any evidence they have used nuclear, biological, or chemical weapons?"

Saunders raised his eyebrows. "Good question, Eric. That's where we get concerned. There is no evidence that nuclear weapons have been used. But we do believe that biological agents were used by KPA Special Forces near Camp Casey days before the attack. I'll be frank. You and your men are hanging on the horns of a dilemma. If you can't hold, you lose. But if your boys and the Marines do their job and hold the KPA, they may use nukes to try to bust the line."

A lump formed in Eric Connerly's throat.

Chapter Three

April 16
off the North Korean coast

A s the 25th Infantry Division and 3rd Marine Division headed for Pusan, the first elements of the U.S. Navy were positioned in the cold, dark blue waters of the western Pacific, just off the coast of North Korea. Admiral Joel Hatchett was commanding an element of the 3rd Fleet, including five destroyers and four cruisers. The group had been on maneuvers in the Sea of Japan when war broke out. Most U.S. Air Force planes in South Korea were fighting for control of the air, so it was Hatchett's job to strike the first blow at North Korea proper. A volley of Tomahawk cruise missiles were fired at the coast, directed at KPA command facilities and communication posts. It was a small but essential first step in bringing the war north of the DMZ.

Barely two days after its lightning strike on the South, North Korea was on a total war footing. Eight hundred thousand men in the armed forces were already at war, but the second wave, made up of reserves, was preparing to move to the front. A total of 4 million reservists were mobilized and organized into task force units, each 260,000 strong. Although inferior to the regular units in the KPA, the reserves were an important component in the war effort. The Pacification Units were prepared to form in 24 hours and included 26 infantry divisions and 18 infantry brigades. These divisions comprised 20- to 30-year-old reservists just released from military service. They numbered approximately 600,000. The Workers and Peasants Red Guard was made up of every able-bodied male citizen between the ages of 15 and 45. These reservists were organized into local units and were to guard their immediate neighborhoods and places of work, including air defense, construction, and communication missions. They were about

3.5 million in number. The final element of the mobilization reserves was the Red Youth Guards made up of close to 1 million 14- to 16-year-old schoolchildren. They received two months of military training each year at school and were expected to back up the regular units if an adverse situation developed on the front. A lack of human fodder was not something with which Kim Jong Il needed to concern himself.

By day two of the war, Seoul was in a panic as KPA forces approached the outskirts of the city. The outnumbered ROK regular army units were trying to hold as best they could, but the crushing force of the KPA was hard to bear. Operations by KPA Special Forces behind ROK lines had seriously hampered efforts to mobilize and form a coherent defensive position. Three amphibious brigades from the KPA Special 8th Corps had landed outside Inchon, and commandos were assassinating senior government officials in the capital. At the same time, the U.S. Army's 2nd Infantry Division was taking heavy casualties. It was down to only one-third of its pre-war strength, including the almost 50 percent of soldiers afflicted with anthrax.

From his temporary headquarters near the U.S. embassy, General Evers was contemplating what he thought he would never have to do—flee Seoul. It was a political horror but a military necessity. The 2nd Division's best hope was a retreat to Taegu. There they could link up with the American reinforcements. But withdrawal would not be easy. The roads leading out of the capital were jammed with escaping refugees. By midafternoon there was a hot sun and underneath it, an unbroken stream of humanity flowing south. The great bridge over the Han-gang River looked like a long, thin bread crust swarming with ants.

ROK forces were falling back and reforming in a desperate effort to stem the attack. Lieutenant Choi and his men from the 1st Platoon had managed to narrowly escape capture by racing through the hill country at night. They were now being redeployed from the Chorwan Valley to a position east of Seoul. The KPA's elite 820th Armored Corps was closing in on Seoul from the east. South

Korean commanders hoped that antitank units like Choi's might slow the advance. If they failed, Seoul would be surrounded and cut off from the rest of the country.

The truck ride to the eastern front was an amalgamation of visual horror as Choi and his men watched the refugees plodding from their homes, clutching personal items and desperately dodging trucks which drove at top speeds along the narrow roads. Thirty miles from Seoul, Choi and the rest of his platoon jumped from their vehicles to form a line in the foothills running north and south along the road. Intelligence put the 820th only ten miles due north and moving without opposition.

Choi and the other platoon commanders arrayed their antitank forces into small groupings. It was a risky strategy because it gave the enemy a concentrated target. Yet, it would also allow the antitank units to achieve a maximum concentration of fire.

The lieutenant wiped the gritty perspiration from his forehead and thought about his family. Somewhere in the torrent of humanity pouring out of the capital were his wife and two children. He wondered if they would make it out alive and if he would ever see them again.

Choi's platoon had not slept in three days, and it was only the frightful exhilaration coursing through their bodies that sustained them. There was no food, and their supply of Dragon antitank missiles was almost depleted. Most of the weapon depots had fallen to enemy hands by the time allied had forces organized. Each squad had three Dragon missiles, so each missile had to count.

By midafternoon, the rumble of the T-62s became audible over the bedlam in the countryside. Choi was with the 1st Squad when the lead armor battalion of thirty-one tanks became visible. He radioed the brigade commander and prepared his platoon for battle. Three squads from the platoon hid in the brush with a direct line of sight on the road. The plan was simple: Choi was to let the lead tank proceed forward until it was only twenty-five yards away. This would expose more vehicles in the advancing column and allow other squads to get a direct sight on other targets.

As the first T-62 roared around the crest of the hill, Choi could smell the diesel and the slight scent of spent gunpowder. The 820th had reportedly shelled a small village ten miles north in an effort to instill terror in the locals. Under the merciless glare of the hot sun, Choi could see the great treads tearing up the earth, throwing pieces of dirt into the air like a fountain. The column continued to move forward, and a young private looked at his lieutenant with anticipation. The tank was now barely thirty yards away. Choi finally gave the signal. In an instant, the missile was out of the tube. It found the side of a T-62, sending smoke billowing from the turret. Soon after, flames engulfed the large, metallic beast. The top hatch popped open, and the crew began to scramble from the innards. Though they nervously held their hands in the air, the 1st Squad opened up with small-arms fire.

By now all the squads had released their Dragons, and other tanks in the line were rocked by explosions. The four lead tanks were reduced to gasping metallic carcasses. Choi could hear voices in the distance, just around the bend. He knew that he had better prepare his men for the infantry. Each man grabbed his rifle and spread out in the thicket. After several anxious minutes, KPA regulars appeared through the black, billowing smoke. They walked cautiously and scanned the edge of the clearing, looking for the mysterious enemy. A quarter mile off, someone in the 2nd Squad panicked and opened up with his M-16. Although he dropped one KPA regular, the enemy now had their sights on Choi's men. The lieutenant had hoped that the KPA would get closer so that the South Korean forces could fire in unison.

The ROK antitank squads fought with the KPA regulars from the 820th Armored Corps for nearly two hours. Choi was the last to go, taking three regulars with him before hitting the ground, dead.

Word that the 820th was continuing to advance from the east reached General Evers in Seoul as he spoke by COMLINK with Admiral Saunders who was at Pacific Command (PACOM) in

Hawaii. "Admiral, I've just received intelligence from the front—the 820th Armored Corps has broken through. Within the next several hours, we will be cut off from any avenue of retreat."

"Can you pull back in time?" Saunders could hear the shelling in the distance over the line.

"John, it will take us at least six hours, bare minimum, to get the men ready. We need to load up the sick and wounded and pull back our men from the front. There are still some anthrax vaccines that need to be distributed. I think the KPA will beat us to the highway. And if they do, we'll have to fight our way out."

"What's your recommendation?"

General Evers paused. "Admiral, if we stay in Seoul, it's going to be a bloodbath. Our best bet is to take our chances with the 820th and try to fight our way out. If you can get us some air cover, I think we can make it."

"All right, Evers, get your men ready to move. I'll have the Air Force hit the 820th with everything they've got."

Two days after North Korean forces crossed the DMZ, Japan entered the war. Tokyo agreed to commit air, naval, and limited ground forces to the effort. Most important, the government granted the U.S. Air Force access to several air bases on the Japanese archipelago. U.S. air bases in South Korea at Kunsan and Osan were likely to be overrun in a matter of days. Two U.S. combat wings were deployed to Japan to supplement the war effort. They included the best the air force had—a squadron of B-2 bombers, F-117A stealth fighters, and a collection of B-1s and F-15s. It was a hefty concentration of firepower that had been in Japan for only three hours. But this was the arsenal Admiral Saunders hoped to rely on to rescue the 2nd Division. He called Air Force General Pete Merrill, who was on the Japanese island of Okinawa inspecting the combat operations.

"Pete, we need an Air Tasking Order (ATO) drawn up at once for the corridor southeast of Seoul. The 2nd Division is at half strength and has no avenue of retreat. I need your boys to hit the 820th Armored Corps, located east of Seoul, with everything you have. If we do nothing else this day, we need to get those boys out."

"What are we talking about in terms of time?"

"The 2nd Division wants to roll six hours from now."

Merrill grunted. "That's impossible."

"Pete, you're going to have to make it possible. We're all improvising with this."

Merrill set the receiver down and shook his head. His thick, red, bushy eyebrows furrowed with the thought that he was going to have to send his men up with minimal intelligence and no rest. The crews had been working nonstop for thirty-six hours, and he worried about fatigue.

The general arranged an emergency pre-mission briefing and, in his mild way, explained the desperate situation and the importance of the mission to the commanders. He threw together what intelligence he could and promised more from the airborne warning and control systems (AWACS) when it became available. The pilots were dismissed and within minutes were heading to the tarmac for pre-flight checks.

Eagles from the 366th Tactical Wing formed the lead squadron for the strike mission on the 820th. The flight from Okinawa, over the Sea of Japan and inland, went largely without incident as Colonel Wes Parker held firmly onto the stick of his F-15, surveying the skies in front of him. It was midevening, and as he checked the radar, he marveled at the job his fellow pilots had done. There were no KPA planes in the vicinity. The allies had gained a clear superiority of the skies. Still, Parker nervously scanned the area. This was his first combat mission. He had sat out the Persian Gulf War because of a leg injury during training. However, his weapons system officer (WSO), Major Hubert Alonso, had flown in Desert Storm, and Parker was happy to have an experienced friend only a few feet behind him.

The Eagles were packed full with every piece of ordnance they could carry. The latest electronic report from the AWACS directed the pilots to a valley southeast of Seoul. Parker's squadron flew at five thousand feet, low enough for a visual ID on any large formations below. The men slowly rotated their heads to either side of the canopy transparency, scanning the ground in the dark, clear night. As Alonso turned his head starboard, he located the 820th snaking its way through a valley 60 miles southeast of Seoul. The lights from the armored column blinked as they moved through the tree-lined valley. Parker immediately radioed the location to his wing mates and the other aircraft from the strike force. "Rascal Two, this is Rascal One: We have our snake. I repeat, we have our snake." The colonel then lined up his squadron of Eagles for the ground strikes.

Parker took the lead, gripping the stick tightly and banking his bird over the hills of central Korea before diving toward the tank column. Major Alonso used his forward-looking infrared (FLIR) system to lock onto the column's vanguard. Parker looked for the steering cue on the heads-up display (HUD) and brought the Eagle in at a 45-degree angle. Ten miles off, they released two Maverick missiles which went screaming toward the lead tanks. Parker and Alonso could almost feel the concussion as the warheads detonated. Parker kept the plane on course, and once over the column, Alonso released the gravity bombs and cut loose with the cannon. As they climbed back over the hills, Alonso looked over his shoulder and saw the red, burning rope of fire, growing as the other F-15s made their passes.

It was an awesome sight below: a chain, maybe two miles long, of burning vehicles. The 820th had failed to dim their lights for the advance on Seoul and paid dearly for the mistake. The fires in the valley turned the moon blood red, and smoke drifted down till it formed a canopy over the valley. As the last Eagle climbed over the hills, other aircraft arrived and joined in pounding the besieged column. Parker stayed as long as he could until low fuel forced him to return to Japan.

It was early evening when the 2nd Division, battered, yet brimming with revenge, made its way south, out of Seoul, and down the peninsula in full retreat. Two ROK infantry divisions, who were covering the left flank of the U.S. 2nd Division, held off the lead elements of the KPA 9th Corps. Generals Evers was hunkered down in his Humvee as the fighter planes continued to scream overhead, making their runs at KPA forces nearby.

Evers had slept only by fits and starts for the past three days, always expecting to be awakened by the noise of a violent explosion. He heard the rumble of artillery in the distance and wondered just how far off the enemy was. His men moved and acted like automatons, dirty and tired from nearly three days of constant fighting. Half the division was doubled over or dead from anthrax and stacked into trucks or onto jeeps. The 2nd Division moved south, through the town of Suwon, and then headed southeast for the almost two hundred–mile journey to Taegu. They hoped by the time they arrived, the 82nd Airborne, the 3rd Marine Division, and the 25th Infantry Division from Hawaii would have established a defensive perimeter.

Chapter Four

April 17
the Taiwan Strait

Admiral Ou pulled on the cuffs of his dark blue jacket and adjusted his naval cap, tilting it slightly on his head. He had not slept well the night before. The fire in his veins was burning strong. He wiped his face with a washcloth and then proceeded to the bridge.

The waters had been quiet since the exchange with two Taiwanese frigates a day earlier. Today, however, it would be different. Beijing believed it could control the strait if it became necessary. This would be a major test of Beijing's capabilities and signal a major shift for the Chinese navy. For decades the navy had operated under the restrictive Maoist *houfazhiren* principle: "Strike only after being struck." But now the fleet was guided by the doctrine of *xianfazhiren:* "Strike first."

The clouds were overcast, the seas choppy. Ou found the strategic calm disconcerting. The PLA had tightened the screws by shelling Taiwanese airfields with intermediate-range missiles. But the Taiwanese air force, with well-trained pilots and some top-flight aircraft, had yet to make an appearance in the skies above the strait. It was something the admiral had expected in the hours following the first engagement. The enemy's unpredictability was troubling: was Taipei planning to hit targets on the mainland?

By midmorning, Admiral Ou's fleet was joined by a massive armada of frigates, destroyers, and transports from the East Sea Fleet. Aboard the transports were members of the elite Rapid Reaction Force (RRF), highly motivated troops equipped with advanced weapons.

Ou's fleet approached the small, Taiwanese-controlled island of Quemoy, which was already under siege by land-based Chinese rocket launchers. PLA rocket batteries had been lobbing DF-3 missiles at the island for the past 12 hours. The 2,150-kilogram warheads violently shook the ground, killing civilians and soldiers alike. Out at sea, the PLA Luhu destroyers fired solid-fuel C-801 rockets, joining the chorus of destruction. Taiwanese forces on the island responded with artillery fire and antiship missiles, but the effort was futile. By early afternoon, Chinese amphibious forces hit the beaches of Quemoy. And by 5:00 P.M., the RRF had a strong foothold on the eastern shore of the island.

Chinese missile batteries near the city of Fuzhou also pounded the main island of Taiwan. The glare of rockets blanketed the skies over Taipei, as missiles directed at airfields and military installations sped toward their targets. The missile systems were older and not very accurate, but they served the chief purpose—to terrorize the civilian population and to restrict military operations.

From anywhere in the capital city, you could see fires and rising smoke. While Taiwan lacked any serious missile capacity, the island did possess one advantage—advanced air power. It fell to the brave pilots of the air force to knock out the missile batteries as soon as possible. A full tactical wing of F-16 Falcons took off from the main air base, each packed with the maximum load of ten tons of ordnance. Although the heavy load decreased performance, reduced maneuverability would have to be risked in favor of maximum firepower.

Air Force Major Li Fei-Kan served as the flight commander. Educated in the United States as an aeronautical engineer, he was very much the modern fighter pilot. A small man with a cherub face, Li hoped to retire and go into business in several months. Now he was wondering if his country would even survive.

Li flew the wing at ten thousand feet on a nearly straight, westward trajectory. The mission called on the Falcons to knock out the large number of PLA rocket launchers and heavy artillery hitting Quemoy and Taiwan from the mainland. As Major Li directed the Falcons through the cumulus clouds over the placid, blue water of the strait, he contemplated his fate.

About forty miles off the west coast of Taiwan, Li and his men spotted elements of Admiral Ou's armada streaming east for the main island. He looked through the bubble canopy of his fighter and saw an encouraging sign: no transports. That meant that the PLA was preparing for more harassment of Taiwanese shipping—an invasion of the island was not yet in the works. Li and his men still had time.

Since there were no PLA aircraft in the area, Li radioed headquarters and took one squadron in for a swift strike. Putting his Falcon into a steep, seventy-degree dive, Li let loose with two missiles twenty miles north of the PLA fleet. They closed the distance quickly and slammed into the gray, metal hull of a Jiangwei frigate. As he swung his plane out over the water, he could see a great orb of black smoke swelling from the ocean surface. The other fighters followed, each picking a different vessel in the fleet. Suddenly, two surface-to-air missiles (SAMs) surged skyward at Li. He jerked the controls violently and released several flares. Fortunately, the outdated missiles sped off aimlessly into the light blue sky. Li's emotions encouraged him to take another run at the fleet, but his mind told him he could not be diverted from the main mission.

As the Falcons approached the Chinese mainland from the east,

Quemoy looked like a cauldron, the ground erupting with flashes of light and fire. An enormous wall of thick ash smoke rose to the sky as death rained down on Taiwanese positions. Li knew that Quemoy must be an earthly hell for civilians and soldiers alike.

A cluster of PLA missile batteries across the channel spit out rockets at a furious rate. They had no great accuracy but by sheer quantity combined to create a fatal barrage. Li and the other pilots located the launchers by following the vapor trails from the rockets. The batteries were barely one mile from the coastline, and the bomb delivery computer software on his Falcon was optimized for low-level strikes. Li made his approach just a few hundred feet above the water. The hands-on-throttle-and-stick (HOTAS) controls on his F-16 allowed him to regulate the engine power settings and steering command with one hand, freeing him to prepare to drop his load of gravity bombs over the target.

Li's pulse surged as he saw the coastline in the distance. He gripped the controls a bit tighter and squinted his deep, brown eyes, as if to raise his level of concentration even higher. Now over the trees of the coastline, Li saw a grayish smoke hanging above the ground—evidence of a lot of launch activity. All at once the missile launchers appeared underneath him. He glanced at the look-down radar and released a load of gravity bombs on the targets below. As the bombs fell, he felt a slight shock and then let out a deep breath.

Li banked his Falcon over the green coastline for his return flight, when all of a sudden he felt several violent shocks, like someone kicking him on the buttocks. The displays in front of him started registering a blur of numbers. It took him only seconds to realize he had been hit by ground fire.

The avionics had been damaged, but he was also rapidly losing fuel. Once over the wind-swept waves of the strait, he leveled out his Falcon and glanced back at the coastline. He was transfixed momentarily as he watched his wing mates dive at the PLA batteries like predatory birds who had located their prey. It was a heart-warming sight to see the missile batteries silenced.

As his Falcon hiccuped for lack of fuel, his attention returned quickly to his perilous situation. He radioed his compatriots, "This is Dragon One. I repeat, this is Dragon One. We have won a great victory today. I am rapidly losing fuel and must eject. Return to base at once." The pilots behind him watched the glow of his engine dim as the fuel ran out.

Li reached to his side and activated the ACES II ejection seat. The transparent canopy popped off, and the explosion under his seat propelled him into the air. After the initial shock left his body, he rode the wind on his parachute and watched his beloved plane swan dive into the indigo blue sea. As it was swallowed by the ocean surface, disappearing forever, Li felt as if part of him went with it.

Only the roar of the Falcons returning to Taiwan broke the eerie silence of his parachute descent. Li braced himself and then fell into the water. The splashdown was a frightening experience as he was temporarily submerged by the mighty force of his drop. But once on the surface, he let out a deep sigh that he was at least alive and in one piece. Overhead, he saw his compatriots rock their wings in a sign of solidarity. Although his hands were numb, he managed to free himself from the chute and find the radio transmitter attached to his shoulder. He flicked the switch, realizing that all he could do now was wait.

The sun was getting hot, and Li's rhythmic rise and fall with the ocean waves was making him seasick. More than two hours passed before he spotted several helicopters fluttering in the distance. His heart began pounding rapidly and vigorously. Who were they? He reached for the revolver holstered under his arm. Li had decided in the minutes after splashdown that he would not let the PLA take him alive. The thought of torture was unbearable to him. As the helicopters moved closer, he could feel the wind generated by the rotor blades and the spray of seawater on his face. Then he saw it— the Taiwanese insignia. His heart leapt for joy.

In the empty skies over Taegu, South Korea, a group of enormous, green transports ambled loudly across the cloudless sky. While the trip seemed to take an eternity, once over the drop sight, huge crates spilled from the Starlifters and Galaxies. Large, green parachutes opened, and the cargo descended gracefully to the green-carpeted landing zone below. As the gigantic packages hit and skidded across the ground, hundreds of paratroopers descended from another group of transports. The last troopers came out of the aircraft before the first hit the ground. Once on the earth, troopers in green camouflage scrambled to unhook from their chutes. Within twelve minutes, this first echelon of the 82nd Airborne was moving.

The U.S. Marine Expeditionary Force (MEF) based on Okinawa was already en route from Pusan to Taegu. The 23,000-man MEF included two brigades from the U.S. 3rd Marine Division plus air units and support troops. General Connerly and the 25th Infantry Division from Honolulu could be expected tomorrow.

As the curtain of night fell on Seoul, brutal street fighting began as the KPA 820th Corps swept in from the east. Even though the South Korean infantry was heavily entrenched, indiscriminate rocket and artillery fire from KPA batteries spawned hysteria on the busy streets of the metropolis. Adding to the maelstrom were KPA Special Forces that had slinked into the city under the cover of nightfall.

Amid the tumult of scattering civilians, house fires, debris, and heavy bombardment, KPA Lieutenant Choe Kwang and three other men ran speedily through the dark, dusty, smoke-filled streets of the capital. Dressed in South Korean military uniforms and clutching M-16 rifles, they dodged the legions of souls, both civilian and soldier, who were scampering in the opposite direction. The quartet rounded the corner to the front of South Korean army headquarters, where there was a black staff car and two escort vehicles.

General Rhee Park Sam, chief of the army staff, exited the building with forceful strides and headed defiantly for the waiting black sedan. General Rhee was the most respected of the officer corps and was firmly committed to holding the line in Seoul. As the firm-lipped, brazen general reached the door of the car, he turned and immediately saw the four mysterious men raise their rifles and open fire. Within seconds, the general and two guards hit the ground. The perpetrators turned and dashed down the same street from which

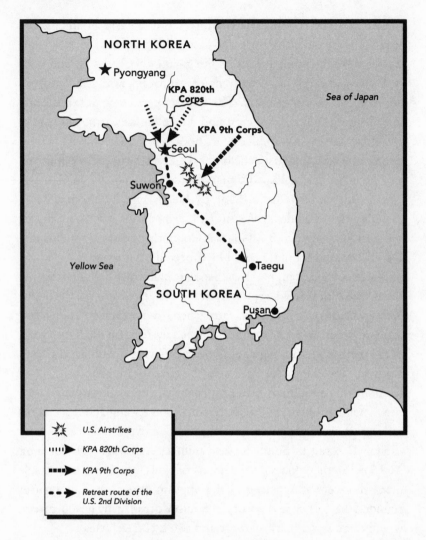

Retreat From Seoul

they had come. Several ROK officers ran in pursuit but failed to catch them. As the four zigzagged through the streets, they eventually located an abandoned office building in which they found refuge.

Lieutenant Choe and his men had remained in the capital since provoking the massacre in front of the Blue House on April 9. Spending nights sleeping in the squalid houses on the edge of the city, they had meticulously planned the assassination of General Rhee. As he leaned on the scarred walls of the abandoned building, Choe felt numb and worn from his week-long odyssey. Though battle-hardened, he felt a tinge of anxiety and fatigue as a river of doubt grew inside him. He had been raised to see the South as an oppressive place and Seoul as a decadent city with a small, tyrannical minority dictating to the masses. But he now realized that description was more appropriate for his homeland.

Choe and his men rested for several hours and then removed the military uniforms they were wearing. In their place, they slipped on civilian clothes and special wristwatches. The watches were evidence that they were KPA agents, a form of identification to incoming North Korean forces. By 4:30 P.M., the ROK position in Seoul had collapsed and the KPA 820th Corps swept through the city's broad boulevards and stormed the Blue House. The ROK 17th Division was the last to withdraw from the capital. For those civilians unfortunate enough to be left behind, it was the beginning of a nightmare.

The retreat of the U.S. Army 2nd Division to Taegu was brutal. General Evers and his men traveled more than two hundred miles through rough terrain and adverse weather conditions with KPA forces harassing them from behind. Fortunately, KPA forces were unable to keep up with the retreating American Army. When U.S. soldiers crossed the Naktong River on the evening of April 19, they were greeted as long lost brothers by entrenched Marines and Army grunts.

Evers knew it was only a matter of days before the KPA forces would be engaging the U.S. perimeter established north of Taegu. Crack KPA units, which had led the attack in the initial phase of the war, were being reinforced by a deluge of reserves pouring south. A combination of surprise and huge numbers had split the South Korean line, and now the KPA was set on taking control of Pusan.

Chapter Five

April 18
outside Taegu, South Korea

Seoul and Quemoy fell on the same day. Although Pyongyang and Beijing could celebrate important victories, their major strategic goals had yet to be achieved. Taiwan was stubbornly resistant, and its substantial air power posed a very real threat. On the peninsula, the KPA had pushed allied forces from north central South Korea, but enemy reinforcements were arriving.

In the fertile valley outside Taegu, General Connerly had arrayed his 25th Division in a defensive line running along the eastern shore of the river. The infantry was digging in, and artillery units and armor were deployed to provide support. Connerly did not quite know what to expect from the North Koreans. The KPA 10th Mechanized and 425th Corps were expected in one day. And while the enemy would enjoy a more than 4 to 1 advantage when the two forces met, Connerly still believed his men could hold the line in a conventional battle. What he did fear was the use of NBC weapons.

It was well-known that the KPA possessed a store of nuclear and chemical weapons. Pyongyang's erstwhile ally, the Soviet Union, concluded in a February 1990 KGB report that the country had already completed the development of its "first atomic explosive device." The KPA was undoubtedly carrying nuclear and chemical artillery shells. The horrible question was, would they use them?

Pyongyang also had numerous missile launch facilities in the north which could rain nuclear, biological, or chemical destruction down on the American defensive position. The deployment of KPA missile brigades was widespread: To-Kol along the DMZ just north of Seoul, Kangwon Province, north Hamyong, Munchon, and Chungan near the Chinese border. In addition, the KPA had mobile launchers which were moved by heavy Italian-made Iveco trucks.

The U.S. Army deployed Patriot missile systems with the 2nd Division in Korea. While they had proven successful against the Scuds in the 1991 Persian Gulf War, General Connerly and the other officers knew that the Patriots could be overwhelmed by a massive rocket barrage from the North Koreans.

The KPA's decision to use nuclear or chemical weapons would be determined by military expediency, not morality. The fact was, the KPA offensive had never been bogged down, so the weapons had not been necessary. Connerly feared that if his men did their job and halted the advance, the consequences might be cataclysmic. It could mean their annihilation by a frustrated KPA leadership frantically hoping to break the American line.

Elimination of North Korea's nuclear weapons capability was the most pressing concern for General Pete Merrill, head of U.S. Pacific Command Air Forces (PACAF). In the early hours of the war, U.S. aircraft had been committed to seizing control of the skies over South Korea. America had some 500 combat aircraft in the area, including 120 U.S. Air Force planes in Japan. The U.S. 7th Fleet, deployed in the Sea of Japan, had two carrier battle groups with a total of 116 strike and fighter aircraft. Air-superiority fighters such as the F-14 and F-15 took on KPA planes, and ground-strike aircraft such as the F-16 and F-18 devoted most of their energy to pounding KPA formations pushing south.

On day two of the conflict, U.S. aircraft ventured north of the 38th parallel to deal with the remnants of the KPA air force. As more American and Japanese air power became available, PACAF could start thinking about a sustained campaign to hit strategic targets north of the DMZ. The navy had already launched several strikes at KPA command centers using Tomahawk cruise missiles.

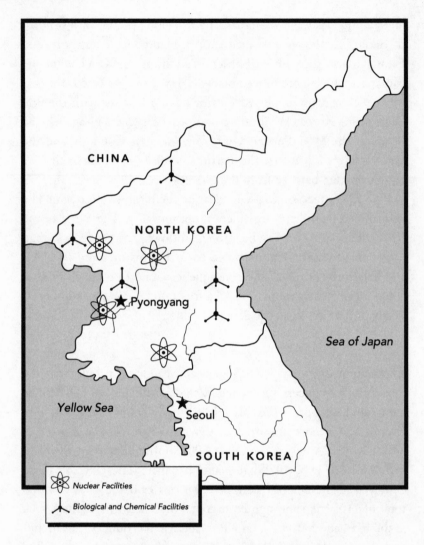

**North Korean Nuclear, Biological,
and Chemical Weapons Facilities**

Yet the frightening shadow of KPA nuclear weapons still hung over the peninsula. The KPA not only had missiles that could hit U.S. forces in South Korea, but they also possessed NoDong-X ballistic missiles that could strike Japan and even the West Coast of the United States and all of Alaska.

It was General Merrill's job to make sure that such a launch never happened. Since America had no defense against ballistic missiles, the only way PACAF could deal with the problem was to find the launch sites and hit them before they were used. This strategy assumed that U.S. intelligence could locate all the KPA launchers and that the massive air campaign could achieve surprise. It was, in many ways, an impossible mission. Merrill only hoped that Kim might be deterred by the prospects of a U.S. retaliatory strike.

A light rain fell as General Merrill met with Admiral Saunders, the CINCPAC back in Honolulu. The admiral appeared tired and worn, his shoulders drooping under the weight of command. In contrast, General Merrill was intense and full of energy. He was a powerfully built man with a face resembling a worn, weathered baseball.

"Well, Admiral, how does it look on the ground?" asked Merrill.

Saunders ran his fingers through his white hair. "I don't know. The KPA keeps pushing stubbornly in the west. With Seoul now occupied, they will be able to pour more units south. We expect their forces to meet our defensive positions near Taegu by tonight. If our boys can hold, we will have five more divisions there within the week. I expect to begin offensive operations in ten days." Saunders shifted in his seat and drank some coffee. "Now, General, tell me, what is your recommendation for the air campaign? Do we go after their nuclear facilities immediately?"

Merrill grinned slightly. He knew that whichever answer he gave, there would be criticism. "Admiral, I recommend we be cautious. We are assuming we have perfect intelligence. And with no defense, this is pretty much what we need. If we start hitting nuclear launch sites and don't get them all in the first blow, Pyongyang will be awfully tempted to strike. Use 'em or lose 'em."

Chinese Military Deployments

Admiral Saunders stood and rubbed his eyes. "You know, General, that will leave us exposed. It gives them the opportunity to make the choice on using their nukes. And if they get desperate—they will use them."

"I agree, Admiral. But we can only hope that they will be deterred by fear of retaliation."

Saunders nodded vaguely in agreement. "General, the president also wants us to draw up operations to support Taiwan. While this is mostly a job for the navy, your boys may be needed down there soon."

"Are we going to war with Beijing?"

"To be candid, I don't know. Two carrier groups are headed for the Taiwan Strait. Korea is obviously our first priority. But we could also come to blows with Beijing, so we need to be ready. We just forwarded the latest satellite intelligence to Taipei, and it looks ominous. Taiwan runs the real risk of occupation unless we support them."

During the past forty-eight hours, U.S. satellite intelligence had detected the concentration of PLA naval forces along the Chinese central seaboard. Attack vessels had congregated at naval facilities in Shanghai, Hangzhou, Santu, and Donchuan. At the same time, fighter aircraft on the mainland had been redeployed near Hangzhou and Guangzhou, putting them within striking distance of Taipei. All evidence indicated that this was a full mobilization of PLA forces. And it wouldn't take long for Beijing to use this unsheathed sword.

Rain fell lightly from an opaque sky as the combined forces of the Chinese navy and air force moved east toward Taiwan during the early morning hours. Crews could see the trajectories of dozens of rockets curling over the strait on their path to Taiwan. In the Gobi Desert, hundreds of miles west, PLA technicians had orders to sustain the rocket barrage for six hours. From the mainland port of Zhanjiang near Hong Kong to the bustling harbor of Shanghai, the menacing gray ships, bent on war, cut through the churning waters of the Pacific.

A number of squalls were rumbling through the Taiwan Strait, but General Hu did not want any delays. He ordered all operations to proceed as scheduled. Two U.S. carrier battle groups were off the coast of Thailand and bound for the strait. Hu wanted to begin his offensive before the carriers arrived. Then Washington would have to make the choice of war or peace, whether to join the fray or stay out.

As the Chinese armada cut through the rough waters and closed in on Taiwan, PLA pilots were receiving their final preflight briefings from commanders at air bases on the mainland. Wearing white helmets topped with painted red stars, the pilots listened to final orders and a brief address from General Hu. The PLA air force included five thousand combat aircraft. Most, however, were vintage aircraft from the 1960s and lacked the electronic warfare capability to counter Taiwan's air defenses. General Hu pinned his hopes on overwhelming numbers, spearheaded by several squadrons of SU-27 Flankers purchased from Russia in 1996. The Flanker had been constructed by the Sukhoi Design Bureau in Russia as a long-range air intercept and superiority fighter. Sweeping, curved lines and twin engines gave the plane a quickness and agility that could match up with most fighters in the world. The Flankers would engage ground-air defense systems and Taiwan's interceptors, as a vast conflux of MiG-21 Fishbeds conducted ground strikes on military and civilian targets. The Fishbed was already considered an antique at the end of the twentieth century, but Hu hoped that quantity would make up for quality.

Amid the rain and clouds of a mid-April morning, the aircraft lined up on the runway and propelled themselves into the heavy air. The Flankers went up first, cruising toward the island nation at ten thousand feet. This first wave, comprised of two squadrons, would engage Taiwan's interceptors. A second echelon of three more squadrons would act as a counterforce.

From their cockpits, the pilots in the Flankers could see the explosions rocking Taipei as massive numbers of Dong-Feng 15 and

Dong-Feng 11 solid-fuel rockets pierced the heart of the city. Fires raged, the tall, red flames dancing in the gray morning air. Thick clouds of black smoke floated toward the heavens.

From the capital city, the approaching Chinese aircraft looked like a swarm of locusts, covering the sky and blotting out the sun. It was the largest concentration of air power over one metropolitan area the world had ever seen: over one thousand aircraft in a single air operation.

Meeting this immense cloud of electronics and steel were three-dozen F-16 fighting Falcons. Major Li was again the flight commander, having been extracted from the lukewarm waters of the strait only hours earlier. Li's Falcons squared off against the Flankers while two-dozen Mirage 2000 attack fighters worked on whittling down the enormous swarm of MiG-21s diving on Taipei. The French-built fighters inflicted casualties but had trouble in compressed turns. The delta-wing design produced a high drag while turning during tight maneuvers, causing the plane to lose velocity.

Taiwan's air defense systems were not as advanced as Taipei wanted them to be. A key factor was the reluctance of the U.S. government to sell advanced military systems to Taipei for fear of offending Beijing. The sale of F-16s to the island had been approved in 1994, more than fourteen years after U.S. allies such as Israel had received them.

The PLA Fishbeds were essentially used as weapons of terror, toss-bombing indiscriminately on the streets of the capital. They approached Taipei at two thousand feet and then descended to one thousand feet, releasing their ordnance before climbing again. The bombing campaign lasted for two hours before Chinese fighters returned to the mainland. The spasm of violence left a groan of stark terror and suspense in the capital city that could not be put into words. Whistling and howling bombs smashed everything within several city blocks. The air was filled with the stench of the dead, and the smoke was choking those lucky enough to still be alive. Burning fuel threw flames fifty feet into the air.

At sea, the Chinese navy was intercepted by half a dozen

Taiwanese destroyers and three corvettes in open waters. Admiral Ou struck instantly, ripping the skies with dozens of antiship missiles directed at the blocking fleet. Next came Silkworm cruise missiles, skimming their way toward the endangered ships. The Taiwanese flotilla responded with a limited volley but could not match the sheer numbers thrown their way. (The navy had never been able to purchase top-of-the-line ECM systems.) As the missiles found their targets, they set off bursts of light in a gigantic splash of orange against a deep gray sky. Within minutes, many of the destroyers and corvettes were listing badly before sinking into the abyss of the sea.

News of the tremendous blows against Taipei reached General Hu in Beijing as he and some aides sat down to eat their afternoon meal. Despite the stunning victory, the latest reports did not seem to bring the general much joy. In fact, he was almost emotionless as he shoveled food into his mouth. Hu always ate with the speed of a small dog consuming meat in the presence of larger dogs. In a perfunctory manner he ordered an aide, "Have my secretary come in at once to draft a cable to Taipei."

The dispatch to President Chiang in Taipei was simple.

> Chiang Hu-San
> Taipei
>
> The armed forces of China have struck the rebellious province of Formosa with force. We demand your immediate and unconditional surrender. Failure to comply with this order will warrant further action by our forces.
> General Hu
> Chairman
> PLA Military Commission

President Chiang, a short, stout figure who was both reflective and impulsive, huddled with his cabinet in his private residence outside Taipei. The milieu was gloomy. Everyone at the meeting looked

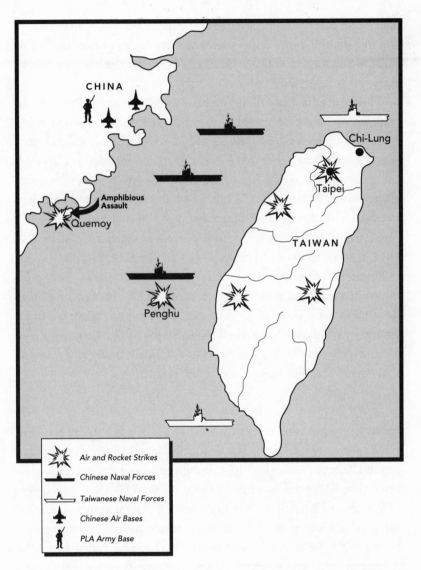

Chinese Assault on Taiwan

sullen and fearful, as if they had all been sucker punched and were still in a painful daze. Taipei was now a graveyard of burning buildings and scattered debris. Thousands of civilians were dead and many more injured.

The demands from Beijing came as no surprise. But how to respond was open to question. Continued resistance would bring more missile attacks, air strikes, and carnage. Taiwan did not possess a missile arsenal that could threaten the mainland. Capitulation, however, would mean absolute control by the central government in Beijing. Chiang faced the stark choice man had wrestled with throughout human history: peace or freedom?

Of course Chiang wanted both peace and freedom. But he also knew it was impossible to imagine that an island of 20 million could indefinitely defend itself against a country of 1.2 billion. The question remained, what would the Americans do? Were the carrier battle groups just a show of force, or was Washington prepared to go to war with Beijing? Since the United States had its hands full with a war raging on the Korean peninsula, Chiang had serious doubts that America would enter a war in the strait.

In the early morning hours of April 18, U.S. soldiers crouched in their protective positions as a cold mist hovered over the rugged ground. Throughout the night, intelligence and rumors had indicated that KPA guns had moved closer to the U.S. line near Taegu. While the KPA artillery had once been a distant murmur, it now sounded like a bass drum in an approaching parade. The vanguard of the KPA push south was barely twenty-five miles from the American line, and General Connerly knew that his men would soon stare straight into the grisly, ashen face of battle.

The KPA 10th Mechanized Corps lumbered along the narrow valley leading south. The unit included four mechanized infantry divisions and one armored division. It was supported by two artillery brigades and an anti-aircraft brigade. The mass of engines from the trucks and armored vehicles belched smoke and roared like angry tigers as U.S. fighter aircraft intermittently made an appearance in the skies to strike at the columns. But visibility was poor, and the U.S. Air Force was evacuating Osan and Kunsan, which seriously disrupted allied air operations.

The relief from air attacks could not have come at a more opportune time for the KPA. You could see vacant stares and battle-weariness on the hollow faces of the KPA regulars. There was no idle talk, only deathly silence. The 10th had engaged in hand-to-hand fighting with South Korean forces for four grueling days, and that had frayed the iron of even the most hardened soldiers. The constant downpour of steel from the U.S. Air Force had sapped the verve from their bodies. All that remained were robotic, young men with a fervent desire to go home.

Lieutenant Choe and his unit from KPA Special Forces had joined the colossal caravan of men and weapons just south of Seoul. They could be useful in performing valuable missions behind American lines. The eight-man team was distinct from the others, dressed in their forest green South Korean military attire.

As the 10th Mechanized Corps rumbled south, a few solitary figures, several miles off in the foothills, shadowed them, circling like cats. They rode on black off-road motorcycles with special mufflers to dim the noise. Army Ranger Lieutenant James Hope of the U.S. Special Forces was one of those circling. With broad shoulders and a compact body, he was built for endurance and durability. He wore black garments, and his face was covered with a black stocking mask. A riflelike device was slung over his back, and a small radio transmitter was attached to his hip. Hope journeyed through the rough terrain, keeping a watchful eye on the progress of the 10th Mechanized. He stopped occasionally to look at the huge column through his infrared field glasses. The Global Positioning System (GPS) transmitter attached to his waist and a small navigational computer on his hip informed General Connerly and headquarters of his position.

Twenty miles from the American lines, Hope received a message over his COMLINK: "Condition blue." He immediately brought his motorcycle to a halt and removed the riflelike device from his back. The young lieutenant leveled it and pointed at a truck one mile from the front of the KPA column. He then pulled the trigger, shooting a thin laser beam at the vehicle. Instantaneously, the laser designator relayed the precise location of the column via satellite to Major Frank Gribbon, who sat crouched in a task force commander's vehicle forty miles east. The data provided Gribbon with the precise latitude and longitude of the enemy column.

With his burly fingers, Gribbon hurriedly tapped the coordinates and a fire-mission order on his data message device (DMD) keyboard to the six multiple launch rocket systems (MLRS) in his unit.

The large-tracked MLRS vehicles were resting in a vacant field five miles behind the U.S. line when the orders came through. Inside each crew cabin, the gunner took the data and entered it on the fire-control computer keyboard. Within seconds, each of the units— miles apart—sprung to life in unison. The hydraulic-actuated launchers hummed as the rocket tubes were elevated to the correct angle. The rockets were hurled out of the tubes one after another in a momentary convulsion, their plumes lighting up the sky. Each MLRS sent twelve rockets screaming over the horizon. Shortly after the rockets departed the launch tubes, the MLRS vehicles began moving, plodding through the fertile valley along the riverbed. They hoped to avoid targeting by enemy artillery or aircraft.

Seventy-two missiles converged on the KPA column, a plummeting, steel swarm bent on annihilation. Packed inside were M-77 submunition warheads—small bomblets that explode like grenades. In all, forty-six thousand of these munitions rained down on the 10th Mechanized, covering a thirty-acre strip with death. In an instant, the first mile of the column was a graveyard of twisted steel and burning fuel. Thousands of KPA regulars were killed or wounded before they even had a chance to react.

The monstrous rocket strike brought the KPA column to a grinding halt. Panicked soldiers fled their vehicles. Commanders eventually organized a retreat but not before another swarm of munitions cascaded onto the ground. For U.S. troops in the trenches, the glare of rockets arcing over the U.S. lines brought cheers.

The massive firepower by U.S. ground units was a compelling problem for the KPA. They had encountered nothing like it in the early stages of the war. The accuracy of U.S. artillery and rocket fire was a result of reconnaissance patrols carried out by specialists like Lieutenant Hope. KPA commanders knew that locating and eliminating these spotters was essential, so they immediately dispatched infantry to comb the area. At the same time, the North Koreans put in place powerful artillery, based on the design of the South African G-5 with a range of twenty-five miles. As night fell, KPA spotters began moving slowly forward to scout the American lines. The two forces were deadlocked.

For General Connerly, the rocket strike could not have gone better. It inflicted heavy casualties. But more important, it had forced a KPA pullback, buying time for American forces. The general was tempted to advance and press his advantage, but he had orders to wait for reinforcements. Within five days, the U.S. armored divisions could be expected and American soldiers could rise from their defensive crouch and take the war to the North.

Word that the 10th Mechanized and 425th Corps were stopped dead in their tracks by American artillery sent Kim Jong Il into one of his uncontrolled furies. His face seethed with anger as he threw a batch of files across the conference table at General O Kuk-Yul. Kim's erratic mood swings sometimes left him unhinged for hours. In spite of his army's stunning victories, Kim became as impatient as a schoolchild. "I will not be denied!" he bellowed to his cabinet. The general did not quite know how to react, his emotions fluctuating between anger and embarrassment at the sight.

After a three-minute tirade, Kim calmed himself and returned to his chair at the head of the conference table. He stared deeply into the face of his general. "We must break through the American lines at once. The entire war will be lost if we fail to do so over the course of the next several days. If they are able to resupply, they will turn the tide quickly."

General O Kuk-Yul knew what the president was driving at, and the thought mortified him. He counseled patience, not wanting his country to act with temerity. "President Kim, the correlation of forces will favor us during the next two days. As our reserve troops push south, we will be able to bring overwhelming forces to bear on the American lines. They will be pushed into the sea."

Kim scowled, a crooked smile of skepticism marking his face. "General, can you guarantee that with the reserves in place the American lines will break?"

O Kuk-Yul shook his head in honesty, his eyes looking downward at the carpet. "Guarantee? No. Nothing in war is a guarantee."

Kim smirked again. "That is what I assume, General." The president stood, his protruding stomach rubbing the front of the table. With his hands clasped behind his back, he began a methodical pace. "All of us in this room know that only one thing can guarantee victory. And that is our nuclear capability." He stood still and shook his fist with each word. "Only with nuclear weapons can we break the Americans."

General O Kuk-Yul felt his heart sink.

Chapter Six

April 19
the American line in central Korea

The night was solemn and quiet as the soldiers of the 25th Division sat in their foxholes eating rations and swapping stories about home. There was a stillness in the night air, and the thunder of artillery was a fading memory. An eerie tranquility hung over the area like a gentle mist. The KPA had pulled back, out of range from American artillery. For days General Connerly had waited anxiously for word of his son. News finally came that he had arrived with the 82nd Airborne and was forward deployed with the infantry. Father and son planned to meet tomorrow morning. Connerly settled into a cot in his headquarters at 10:30 P.M., shortly after reviewing the last of the intelligence reports from the front. His eyes got heavy as he walked the tightrope between wakefulness and slumber.

Suddenly at 12:04 A.M., he heard a tumultuous whoosh, followed by an incredible flash of brilliant light poured out over the area. An intense, burning wind ripped through the darkness, throwing him from his cot. A few seconds later, those still alive heard a thunderous boom. Connerly felt it—an abstruse, searing agony that covered his entire body. Blinded by the blanched light that had filled his room, he slowly staggered to his feet. His eyes still blurred, he hazily viewed the sea of fire encompassing the area around him. It looked like a potent hurricane of fire had scorched the area west of him. Though his mind felt clouded, Connerly knew what had happened: The KPA had launched a nuclear strike.

North Korean crews outside Pyongyang had fired an M-11 single-stage missile topped with a twenty-kiloton warhead. The solid-fuel missile had been co-developed with Beijing and was the same size as a Scud missile. Once it had left the launcher, an inertial, mid-course guidance system kept it on course and a rounded top cone provided superior ballistic qualities. The twenty-kiloton fission bomb (equivalent to the bomb dropped on Hiroshima) was detonated fifty feet above the ground to maximize heat damage. A twenty-kiloton warhead will cause 50 percent casualties for twenty-three square miles to anyone in the open ground. Soldiers in trenches and foxholes within eleven square miles will experience 50 percent casualties.

General Connerly was fortunate to be in a fortified headquarters several miles from ground zero. Feeling a trembling numbness throughout his body, he went to the COMLINK on his desk. The gamma rays from the explosion had stunned the electronics, but after a few minutes, they worked. Connerly braced himself with the desk as he waited for Admiral Saunders to pick up.

Saunders was sleeping in his office at CINCPAC headquarters in

Hawaii when he was awakened by an aide. Word of the strike sent a furious wrath charging through his veins. He slammed his fist on the desk and threw the first object he could find—a paperweight—at the wall. He then picked up the COMLINK.

Connerly's speech was slurred and his voice monotone. "Admiral, we just took a hit from a nuclear warhead. I'm not sure, maybe twenty kilotons—about three miles west of here. I'm not sure of damage, but there are fires everywhere… "

"Dear God, Eric. Get on the NBC suits and prepare for a probable ground assault. I'm calling the president and recommending an immediate counterstrike."

Saunders slammed down the COMLINK receiver and placed an urgent call to President St. John, who was meeting with a small group of advisors. The admiral paced with forceful steps until the president picked up. "Mr. President, the KPA has just hit the 25th Division with a tactical nuclear strike. I strongly recommend that we hit them back at once. If we don't retaliate now, they may have another go at us."

"Dear God. The secretary of defense is right here. Let me put him on the extension."

Tom Bodine was thin and hawklike with intense, brown eyes and a keen mind. He had spent fifteen years in the navy before joining corporate America. "Admiral, this is Tom. What are you recommending?"

"Tom, we need to hit them now and hard. If we don't, they will take another shot at our boys. We're talking about the complete destruction of several divisions if we fail to do this now."

Bodine looked at the president and could see the stress on his telegenic face. Michael St. John, with smooth motions that were evidence of good breeding, closed his pained eyes and nodded his head in agreement. "All right, Admiral. We have a contingency in place for the immediate launch of a twenty-kiloton warhead at the main nuclear command post outside Pyongsan. And we will hit their other known nuclear production sites in Yongbyon, Hamyong, and Kangwon with conventional weapons."

St. John and Bodine set the receivers down. Both were dazed by the cataclysmic event. "Mr. President, you will need to call Moscow and Beijing and alert them to these launches. We don't want them to miscalculate on this."

The presidency was supposed to be the crowning jewel on a political career spanning more than forty years. From county commissioner in Florida, to the U.S. Congress and then Senate Majority Leader, President St. John had viewed the presidency as his chance to make the history books. But a nuclear strike is not what he wanted to be remembered for.

Only hours after the North Korean M-11 delivered a nuclear blast outside Taegu, a U.S. Air Force B-52G bomber took off from the main air base on Okinawa and flew north. Once out over the Sea of Japan, the Stratofortress released a single AGM-86B cruise missile. The slender, 250-inch-long projectile headed directly for central North Korea. Once over its target, the PBM-9502 high explosive ignited, creating a fusion reaction. In an instant, there was a holocaust belt north of Pyongsan. The military compound was leveled and life evaporated in a five-square-mile area.

While Pyongsan was the known location of a KPA nuclear missile launch facility, the United States had little intelligence on other probable weapon sites. General Merrill ordered a series of conventional strikes on nuclear production facilities. Chief among these was the military nuclear facility in Yongbyon. Ostensibly, it was a power-generating reactor, or at least that's what Pyongyang had told the International Atomic Energy Agency (IAEA). But there were no electrical wires leading from the site nor were there any transformer stations. All indications were that this was the heart of the North Korean nuclear weapons program.

The U.S. conventional strike package was basic—two dozen Tomahawk cruise missiles specifically designed to pierce through thick concrete and other hard substances. The navigational computers were programmed to hit "Building 500," the main research and management compound on the site. Selecting targets on a nuclear facility was a delicate matter. All structures that potentially housed plutonium were off limits. The object was to cripple the site's ability to produce weapons, not destroy the safety features that kept the plutonium secure. After only a few hours, the nuclear weapons facility at Yongbyon no longer functioned.

In Beijing, General Hu was at his desk reviewing battlefield reports from the air war over Taipei when he received word from the United States of the KPA strike and the American response. He found himself wondering aloud if Kim was mad. He had assumed that he was a cruel eccentric; but a nuclear strike against the Americans was in his mind the height of folly.

The general placed an urgent call to Kim, who was still in his bunker several hundred yards below the earth's surface. Hu tried to maintain a sense of controlled tension, speaking curtly on the phone. "President Kim, this is madness. What do you hope to accomplish in a nuclear exchange with the Americans? You fool, this could mean the destruction of us all."

Seated comfortably behind his desk and rubbing some of his ancient stones, Kim chuckled sinisterly. "General Hu, have you lost your nerve?"

Hu jumped to his feet in anger as if Kim were right in front of him. "Have you lost your mind?!" He slammed down the receiver.

Despite the anger brewing inside him, the general had other immediate concerns. Hu and the rest of the PLA leadership were waiting anxiously for word from Taipei concerning the ultimatum. And elsewhere in the Pacific, PLA units had already moved on several other Chinese "territories" Beijing believed to be rightfully theirs. Units from the 15th Airborne Army, supported by naval forces, began fortifying their positions on the Spratly Islands. Vietnam, the Philippines, Malaysia, Brunei, and Taiwan had all laid claim to the oil- and mineral-rich islands. But now Beijing was making her claim a reality.

General Hu knew that only one power could halt his imperial grab—the United States. He calculated that Washington would be emboldened by the North Korean nuclear strike since President St. John was unlikely to back down for fear of losing all credibility. War between the two great powers now seemed inevitable.

To those still fortunate enough to be alive after the strike, the air west of Taegu smelled and tasted like Armageddon. The 25th Division suffered 50 percent casualties and the 82nd Airborne lost one-fourth of its entire force. A plague of radiation sickness passed over the living like a dark rain cloud. The soldiers wandered through the wreckage covered by their standard-issue NCB suits and hoods, breathing through their respirators. Although the Marine 3rd Division farther south had sustained little damage, another strike might be imminent.

There was a frenzied rush at the field hospital in Taegu as doctors and nurses went about treating the living and the near-dead. General Connerly, nauseous with radiation poisoning, visited the young, bedridden soldiers. From the window of the radiation-sickness ward, he could hear the rumble of artillery. The KPA was once again shelling American positions, and that could mean only one thing: an offensive was near-at-hand. Intelligence indicated that the 10th Corps had now been joined by the 9th Corps, including two mechanized divisions and two infantry brigades. Connerly dashed from the hospital to his jeep and returned directly to headquarters.

The downpour of artillery was heavy but much of it wide of target, most of the shells falling well in front of the American line. Connerly radioed Gribbon, in command of the MLRS units, and ordered another barrage on the KPA position.

As he scanned the horizon, Connerly noticed that the low clouds and heavy rain had lifted. Minutes later he heard the welcome roar of U.S. fighter-bombers strafing the KPA. Air power was now less effective than it had once been because North Korean forces were dug in and making use of camouflage. While speaking with his forward commanders, a call came in from a forward observation post: "This is Red Rover, this is Red Rover. They are moving east at full strength. I repeat, they are moving east at full strength. We are pulling back."

Connerly had arrayed his forces in a way to raise the odds that the center of the line would hold. Much of the KPA command still adhered to Soviet military doctrine which called for a frontal assault that could be exploited by echeloned forces. There was no reason to expect the KPA would diverge from this script.

The 25th Division held the center of the line and Marines from the 3rd Division the left flank near the riverbed in the fertile valley west of Taegu. The 82nd Airborne held the right flank. The middle of the line had taken a nearly direct hit from the nuclear strike, so it was at only half strength. Connerly committed the remnants of the battered U.S. Army 2nd Division, fresh from its retreat out of Seoul, to plug gaps in the center. The general wondered what the nuclear strike had done to morale. Would the line hold?

Lieutenant Hope observed the KPA ground assault from a distance. It was an awesome sight: like tens of thousands of ants crossing a narrow strip of soil. Many of the KPA soldiers were on foot, but the long queue of vehicles extended for tens of miles. Hope fixed his laser designator on the KPA advancing echelons, guiding the rockets to their targets. It was amazing that KPA soldiers managed to approach the American lines in the face of immense air strikes and artillery fire.

In a two-mile belt five thousand yards in front of the American line, there was a surging torrent of exploding ordnance. The artillery and MLRS first fired to block enemy thrusts and then struck deep behind KPA lines to delay or prevent follow-on forces from arriving in the battle area. Still, KPA regulars emerged from the storm of cordite, shrapnel, and powder to attack U.S. forces. The American infantry responded with mortar and small-arms fire. The line held.

Hearing the chatter of machine gun fire and the percussion of artillery in the distance, Lieutenant Choe and his men from the KPA Special Forces spent the entire night prowling through the foothills south of Taegu. They were carrying South Korean M-16 rifles and were garbed in ROK military uniforms. They appeared as a straggling, lost South Korean unit—a common sight on the peninsula. Along the riverbed, they encountered a U.S. Marine foot patrol two miles behind American lines.

The Americans raised their weapons in caution, but Choe greeted an officer with an extended hand. "I am Lieutenant Choe of the ROK Army," he said in broken English. "We were separated from our unit when the KPA came. We became lost in the hills and hid. The villagers told us that you had set up lines here."

The American officer accepted Choe's hand and gave a compact nod. There were tens of thousands of ROK soldiers wandering the area, separated from their units. He wasn't particularly surprised. "Very good then, Lieutenant Choe. Why don't you and your men accompany me and the rest of the patrol back to headquarters."

Choe nodded eagerly. "Yes, of course. If I might speak to your commanding officer. I have valuable intelligence from the last several days spent behind KPA lines."

The men walked down the narrow paths of the hills, toward the command post. The raging battle in the distance seemed to have subsided by the time they reached the post. American soldiers were standing guard outside when they arrived. As they moved to enter the building, an American sentry blocked the entrance. "I'm sorry, gentlemen. You will have to leave your weapons outside. Strict orders."

Choe shook his head and looked at his men. With lightning-quick precision, they raised their weapons and opened on the Americans, cutting down the Marines in the area. The Americans were able to hit two of the imposters. Still standing, Choe and three of his comrades rushed directly for the front door. Inside, they were met by more soldiers and another brief fire fight took place. When it was over, only the redoubtable Choe was left standing. He pressed on, charging for what appeared to be the office of the commander. As he burst through the door, he was met by General Connerly aiming a

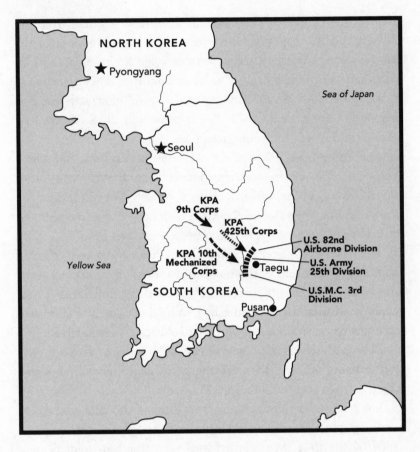

The Bloody Boundary Stalemate Outside Taegu

.45 at his head. In a second, a stream of bullets pierced Lieutenant Choe's body. He was dead before he hit the ground.

Connerly let out a sigh and slowly lowered his weapon. The U.S. Army had switched from the .45 to the 9 mm several years ago, but Connerly could not part with his. He always favored its stopping power.

In the misty waters of the South China Sea, the Taiwanese fleet slipped out of port and congregated on the southern tip of the island. The Chinese fleet was barely fifty nautical miles west, smack in the middle of the strait. President Chiang had made a decision to strike back at the Chinese fleet. If the fleet's strength could be cut, it would limit the threat to the main island.

Four F-16s took off from base and proceeded west toward the Chinese armada. Twenty miles from the vessels, they released several German MBB Kormoran tactical antiship missiles. The 600-pound thrust engines propelled the rockets toward the enemy. Primitive ECMs failed to divert the projectiles, which slammed into the port-side hulls of the destroyers *Xi'an* and *Yinchuan*. The 360-pound warheads sent a radial blast through the body of the craft.

Meanwhile, the Taiwanese flotilla pushed west past the southern tip of the island and into the open waters. The destroyers and frigates launched a bevy of missiles at the Chinese fleet which was now only thirty miles away. The slender rockets gave off a radar cross section the size of a sea gull on even the most advanced systems. On the basic Russian-designed systems, nearly twenty years old, they were invisible.

Back in Beijing, General Hu pounded his burly fist on his desk as news of the bold strike by Taipei sent him into a frenzy. He had not expected Taipei to retaliate. While the full damage report had not yet come in, Hu knew that the counterstrike would set his plans back at least one week. By then it might be too late to conduct offensive operations. Two U.S. carriers and a battle group were expected in the Taiwan Strait by early next morning. If the fleet remained in the strait—as expected—they would check any move on Taiwan and forever delay his plans.

The general decided to take a firm line, cabling Washington to declare that China considered large elements of the South China Sea to be its territorial waters. American vessels could use that body of water but only with the approval of Chinese naval authorities. He hoped that Washington would blink. He also reluctantly issued an order to his naval and air force commanders: if American vessels enter the territorial limits, they should be attacked on sight.

The American carriers were north of Singapore and closing at flank speed on the Taiwan Strait by midevening. Since Beijing's latest warning, Admiral Charles "Blip" Cheaney had put the entire armada on full alert. Cheaney was sitting in the *Nimitz* Combat Information Center (CIC), a small room in the bowels of the ship where all sensor and fire-control information was centralized. A gray-haired, fireplug of a man, Blip was smoking a cigar and staring over navigational maps. He twirled the cigar before letting out another globe of smoke. Blip was not going to take any chances on this mission. His instincts told him war with China was inevitable. Both powers had too much at stake in the rising Asian tempest.

Blip had divided the territory extending hundreds of miles from the carrier group into three zones. The primary, or vital zone, extended twenty-five to thirty-five miles from the carrier. This area was monitored by sensors aboard the aircraft carriers. The admiral was counting on ECMs, SAMs, and guns to defend this area. The middle zone was monitored by patrol aircraft from the carrier. They could spot surface warships 360 kilometers away and other aircraft within 700 kilometers. In this area, the Aegis cruisers reigned supreme, fending off attacks from enemy aircraft. Equipped with phased-array radars and active and passive countermeasures, the Aegis can handle saturated attacks by aircraft or missiles, including sea-skimmers. F-14 Tomcats were flying combat patrol missions in case enemy forces approached. An outer zone extended beyond 700 kilometers, making use of satellite information and P-3 patrol aircraft. This was the critical far reach of the battle group, providing early warning if an enemy was lurking.

Blip's orders to the men were simple: any military aircraft entering the area would be issued one warning and then shot down. Any surface vessels or submarines in the zone would receive the same instructions.

By the early morning hours, the American carrier battle groups were cutting a wake in the South China Sea, the spray from the stormy seas crashing into the gray, stalwart fleet of steel. The sentry for the armada was a vast network of surveillance aircraft. One American EC-2A surveillance plane cruised at twenty thousand feet above the water, one hundred miles south of Hong Kong. The crew detected the presence of several Chinese combat aircraft over the mainland, pressing south at a high speed—including eight SU-27 fighters flying at twenty-two thousand feet. The Flankers were heavily armed, each with a maximum load of ten air-to-air missiles.

Lieutenant John Carlson watched the gap close while he contacted the CIC on the *Nimitz* to alert Admiral Cheaney. He kept the aircraft on a steady, northerly course but felt as though he were an insect flying toward a Venus flytrap. Although the Flankers flew closer, Carlson took comfort in the fact that four F-14 Tomcats were scrambling to back him up. In an attempt to deter the attack, he gave the order to activate ECMs. But it was too much to hope for.

Two Chinese air-to-air missiles ripped the halcyon curtain, screaming toward the surveillance aircraft at Mach 2. Carlson put the bird into a slight climb while releasing chaff and flares. Fortunately, the missiles took the bait and flew off aimlessly.

But the Flankers were far from done. They closed rapidly like a predator hunting a defenseless prey. At 200 yards, they opened up with cannons. Carlson could hear the shells ripping into the fuselage, and he jerked the controls to the left to break out of the line of fire. The lieutenant then banked his plane hard, heading in the direction of the Tomcats still 150 miles away. But the Flankers stayed right with him.

Carlson radioed the *Nimitz*. Alarm was evident in his voice.

"*Nimitz*, this is Carlson. We have been attacked by PLA aircraft. I repeat, we have been attacked by PLA aircraft."

Blip Cheaney was still in the CIC when the word came in. He threw his cigar on the floor and grabbed the microphone. "This is *Nimitz*, what do you see?"

There was no answer.

"Carlson—are you there?"

The U.S. Navy F-14 Tomcats were now one hundred nautical miles south of Carlson, and, to their horror, they saw the EC-2A reconnaissance plane disappear from radar. Commander Mike Valentine kicked on his afterburners and immediately activated his weapons systems, ordering the rest of the squadron to do the same. The Flankers were still moving south toward the U.S. battle group. When the forces closed to within thirty miles, the Tomcats released a quartet of AIM-120 AMRAAMs. Three Flankers went down, plunging to the ocean; the others reversed course. Valentine was now only one hundred miles from the Chinese mainland, and he feared that even more Chinese aircraft might arrive.

Aboard the *Nimitz*, Admiral Cheaney ordered the launch of the full contingent of American fighter aircraft from both carriers. Soon, the skies over the South China Sea were likely to be littered with Chinese aircraft. The air incident one hundred miles south of Hong Kong dramatically changed the course of the war in the Pacific. The United States was now at war with China.

General Hu knew that in order for his plan of conquest to succeed, he would have to play to his strength and exploit American weaknesses. The Chinese navy was no match for the U.S. fleet. And in the air, Chinese pilots and planes were outmatched. But if America did have a weakness, it was sustaining an army for a full-scale ground war on the peninsula. The U.S. Army was down to ten divisions, and Hu believed that the Americans could not stomach a meat grinder.

Hu hesitatingly phoned President Kim, who was still concealed in his bunker beneath the capital. While the general considered

Kim neurotic, he realized China's fate was tied to a North Korean victory. On the phone, Kim was as garish as ever, still spouting about his victories on the battlefield. It took all the patience Hu could muster to listen to the sermon. He was only thankful that Kim did not discuss military details on the phone; for the Americans were most certainly listening. General Hu knew that talk of victory was premature: the war would be lost unless a breakthrough occurred near Taegu in the next twenty-four hours.

At the end of the candid conversation, Kim and Hu agreed to meet at a retreat in the Kangnam Mountains along the Chinese–North Korean border. While unspoken, both knew it was to discuss a formal alliance.

General Hu took an unmarked military transport northeast over the surprisingly serene Korea Bay, landing on a narrow, dirt airstrip along the North Korean border. There he was met by a PLA detachment which included four jeeps and twelve armed guards. Hu went directly from the plane to a waiting jeep and sped off into the twilight. The roads were narrow, unlit, and unmarked. He rode on the twisting, turning roadway for three harrowing hours. It was rough country that gave the appearance of a sea in a heavy gale preserved in ballast lava.

As his almond-shaped eyes watched the trees pass by, General Hu took time to think deeply about what was at stake. This was no doubt a defining moment for his career and his country. If his gambit succeeded, his ambition told him that China could rewrite the entire international political order. A humbled America would be supplanted by a fast-rising, expansive China eager to protect its interests. However, the consequences of failure would be just as revolutionary. Defeat would mean an overthrow of the Chinese domestic order, the likely dismembering of the Communist state, and the birth of a westernized regime.

As Hu proceeded south on his lonely, serpentine journey through the mountainous roads of the Kangnam Range, President Kim and General O Kuk-Yul were screaming up the motorway north of Pyongyang to Kanggye in an unmarked, Russian-built sedan. The old Russian Lada sedan vibrated energetically at high speeds, its driver clinging nervously to the wheel. The sound of jets in the skies overhead sent surges of anxiety through those in the car. Everyone knew that the Americans were again making bombing runs. And it was the fear of allied air power that provoked this decidedly austere mode of travel. Stealth was necessary since the typical Kim Jong Il motorcade of thirty cars was likely to draw attention from the air.

Kim and General O Kuk-Yul spoke very little during the trip. Kim skimmed a biography of Josef Stalin and an odd assortment of production statistics provided by his planning bureau. The general read through the latest military reports from the front. It was a grim read, both in terms of the casualty figures and battlefield prospects. With the latest front assault on the American lines quelled, he wondered how his forces would ever reach Pusan and cut off allied reinforcements.

The two parties finally converged at 3:00 A.M. as a full moon peered through the misty clouds. President Kim was unusually upbeat despite the eight-hour road trip. He was convinced that the grim realities of the day were simply trying obstacles on the path to a glorious future in which a unified Korea and a strong China would dominate the Pacific Rim. Wearing heavy overcoats to protect them from the near-freezing mountain temperatures, the three men sat with cups of hot tea in comfortable, leather chairs in front of a roaring fire. General O Kuk-Yul cradled the cup in his cold hands, occasionally drinking the warm contents. Kim seemed rather indifferent to the beverage even though he had gone eight hours without food or drink. He was instead totally engrossed in the immediacy of planning for his great victory.

Kim leaned back in his thick chair. "You see, my friend General Hu, it is as I said."

"What do you mean?" Hu asked wearily, raising the bone china cup to his face.

"We share a common fate. We will succeed—or fail—together. And in unity we can do nothing but succeed. It is, after all, our destiny."

General Hu nodded unenthusiastically in agreement. "Yes, President Kim, I agree. But destiny is not predetermined. Only if we make the correct decisions—think strategically—can we triumph. Defeating the United States is something that neither of our countries has succeeded in doing. We are hoping to accomplish what no one has been able to do: defeat the Americans in a conventional war. If we succeed, we will rewrite history and rearrange the world political order."

Kim motioned for General O Kuk-Yul to pull out the folders he had specially prepared for the meeting. The planning session began in earnest.

The killing fields west of Taegu were unlike anything even the most hardened veteran had seen in combat. Remnants of nuclear radiation still clung in the air. The walking ill were a common sight, easily recognized by their thinning hair, persistent vomiting, and heavy fatigue. The conventional assaults had added another hardship. While three KPA assaults on the main American position had all been pushed back with the North Koreans suffering heavy casualties, the KPA reservoir of men and equipment appeared endless. General Connerly began to wonder for the first time if his men could hold the line. He calculated that the KPA still had two or three frontal attacks left. And that was probably one more than his men could sustain. It was now only two days until the reinforcements arrived. But the KPA knew that too.

Connerly toured the front the midmorning hours of April 21, riding in his mud-covered Humvee which skidded along the narrow, miry roads. He traveled by foot through the reddish clay, ankle-deep mud visiting foxholes, trenches, and crude fortifications. Amidst it all he could see the worn eyes and hollow, marblelike faces of men broken by war.

For the first two hours, the front was mostly still, broken only by the occasional babble of gunfire. Then with the suddenness of an April thunderstorm, North Korean artillery began raining down on the American position, sporadic at first before settling into an unwavering, continuous rhythmic thunder. KPA Lieutenant An Myong-Chin could smell the burning oil as his unit sought protection behind the tanks for the advance east. His orders were simple: push toward the American line, feigning another assault. The real action would take place several miles north—at the American right flank.

Looking through his field glasses from the center of the line, General Connerly watched as the KPA units struggled through the wasteland of burned-out armored carcasses and bodies of men from prior assaults. Artillery shells continued to whistle down on the advancing troops, and the offensive appeared spent right after it got under way. Connerly sat back against the dirt barrier and sighed deeply. The North Koreans must be even more exhausted than we are, he thought to himself.

Suddenly, an urgent message came through on the COMLINK. A massive KPA force was bearing down on the 82nd Airborne. It now became evident: the frontal assault was a diversion; the main thrust was an attempt to turn the right flank. Connerly's heart sank at the thought of it. He had committed his reserves to shore up the center of the line. There was no one to reinforce the paratroopers. The 82nd Airborne would have to stand firm. If they broke, it could split the line and mean the encirclement of the entire U.S. position.

The North Koreans had shifted their big guns at night, moving them without the aid of noisy trucks. Artillery crews concentrated their fire on the American right flank. The shelling became so intense for the 82nd Airborne that there was a constant hum of concussion. Following the artillery barrage, most of the remaining North Korean armor surged forward to attack the American paratroopers as several U.S. Apache helos fluttered overhead, firing Hellfire missiles. There was only a dim hope of stemming the gigantic surge of rolling steel. The 82nd had only a few Sheridan light tanks deployed, and they lacked the punch of larger armor. The tank had all-aluminum construction and a welded, steel turret. It was widely regarded as a clunker. Yet, it was the only tank that could drop with the airborne.

The Sheridans went quickly. Behind them only a thin, green line of infantry remained. In desperation the paratroopers began the rapid fire of their 60-mm mortars at twenty rounds per minute, and the limited number of M202 FLASH four-barrel rocket launchers rapidly spit out incendiary rockets. Still, the North Korean armor continued to close in. The last breath of defense was a group of M-67 recoilless rifles which released 90-mm rounds until the T-62s broke the line.

The second echelon of KPA units broke through, and U.S. officers and enlisted men were forced to fight with grenades and small arms. Many of the paratroopers died fighting, including Lieutenant James Connerly, who had hoped to see his father later that day.

Once the line broke, General Connerly committed his ground forces north in a desperate attempt to contain the North Korean push. Although the move brought soldiers out of their fortifications and risked the entire line, the counterattack succeeded and the KPA offensive fizzled. American casualties were high—more than three hundred were killed or wounded.

For three days an unstable, bloody stalemate locked the war-scarred Korean peninsula. The North Korean offensive had stalled, and there had been no more nuclear launches. KPA forces dug in and used camouflage for protection from allied aircraft.

On April 24 at 7:00 A.M. the U.S. Army 1st Mechanized Infantry, 2nd Armored Division disembarked at Pusan shortly to be followed by the 1st Marine Division, the 101st Airborne Assault Division, and an international contingent. In addition to pilots already patrolling the skies over Korea, Japan contributed four brigades of infantry. France furnished the 1st Parachute Brigade and the 13th Dragoons Parachute Regiment. And faithful Great Britain provided an infantry division and a carrier.

To Admiral Saunders in Honolulu, the arrival of these forces was good news. Finally, he had the tools to do more than simply maintain a toehold on the southern tip of the peninsula. Yet, the latest satellite intelligence put him in an apprehensive mood. Thirty divisions of the Chinese army were on the move, some beginning to cross the Yalu River into North Korea. Like a weather forecaster interpreting satellite data, Saunders assumed the worst: Beijing was entering the Korean imbroglio. And China's commitment was substantial—three hundred thousand-plus troops and large quantities of artillery. National Security Agency (NSA) intercepts of encrypted Chinese messages pointed to a full alliance between the two countries.

How to respond to China was a perplexing subject. As the allied forces moved north from Pusan to Taegu, Saunders was planning a bold counterstrike to push back the KPA. But the allied forces risked getting bogged down in a swamp of carnage if Chinese forces reached the front. A protracted stalemate was the likely result, with qualitatively superior allied forces counterbalanced by enormous Chinese numbers. General Hu would settle for a stalemate. But Saunders knew that a long, tumultuous ground war in Asia would be impossible for the United States without the full commitment of all reserves and conscription. The admiral wondered, how could the dynamics of the war be shifted to the allies' advantage?

Saunders met with General Pete Merrill in his office on the afternoon of April 24 to discuss that very question. Merrill was back from a tour of Okinawa, and Saunders was eager to hear his views. The two shook hands and reclined in their familiar chairs. "Admiral, I met with the flight commanders and our people in logistics. We now have over three hundred aircraft in the area, and we are flying sorties twenty-four hours a day. Morale is good, but fatigue worries me. And so does the spare-parts problem."

The United States had consistently reduced the budget for logistics throughout the 1990s, so stockpiles of ammunition and spare parts were now lower than they had been for more than two decades. And with fewer aircraft in the American arsenal, "cannibalizing" planes for parts was not an option.

Admiral Saunders sat pensively with his hands folded. He was thinking about China. After Merrill finished, Saunders laid satellite photos out on the walnut coffee table. "Pete, these were taken during the past twenty-four hours. It is very clear that the Chinese intend to commit themselves to the war on the peninsula." His aged finger pointed to a black emptiness which represented the South China Sea. "Notice that they have begun redeploying their forces north. Some fighter aircraft, as well as a thin, gray line of naval vessels, remain in the central coastal region. But they have suspended all operations around Taiwan."

Merrill shook his head. "I don't understand, Admiral. Why have they abandoned their efforts without so much as a fight? It doesn't seem to fit."

"It does if they figure to first bleed us on the peninsula and then resume their plans for conquest once we have pulled back, worn and exhausted." He again ran his finger over the photo, pointing to the region along the North Korean–Chinese border. "These Chinese forces are some of the best in their army, and Beijing is committing them to the war in Korea. This is not going to be like the last war here, when they drew a line at the Yalu and then joined the war. They mean to fight right away, before we can push the North Koreans out of Seoul."

Merrill got up and headed for the French windows at the south end of the room. "Admiral, Beijing is putting us in the position of having to fight a three million–man army thousands of miles from our borders. They know that sooner or later the American people will tire of a protracted war."

Saunders stood and joined General Merrill at the windows. "Well, Pete, that is what we have to prevent. The question is, how are we going to do that?"

During the early morning hours of April 25, the heavy resonance of moving armor could be heard in the flatlands around Taegu. The tanks seemed to breath like giant beasts, belching forth smoke and carbon. When the beleaguered American soldiers who held Taegu heard the rumble of friendly armor in the distance, the sense of doom and foreboding that had held them captive for so long melted.

At 3:42 A.M. allied artillery began to fire with a sonorous boom. The U.S. Army 2nd Armored Division had traveled all night under a star-filled sky, looping around the foothills connecting the spine of the Taebaek Range. Just as the sun peeked over the horizon, they attacked the right flank of the North Korean position held by the KPA 10th Armored Corps. French paratroopers offered support. Farther west, the U.S. Army 1st Mechanized Infantry Division had slithered along the Naktong River, twenty miles north of the KPA's 9th Armored Corps, before striking the left flank of the line at 4:05 A.M. The 101st Airborne Assault Division, including a large contingent of attack helicopters, reinforced the offensive.

The sun had yet to appear in the skies as the engagement began. As the first platoons came upon the enemy units, an American gunner used the laser range finder to sight the lead enemy tank. The platoon commander then sent the contact position report over his Inter-Vehicular Information System (IVIS) to the other tanks. The data relayed the composition and position of the KPA tanks. Within half a minute the first high-explosive antitank (HEAT) rounds were fired. Most KPA armor lacked night-vision equipment and fought blindly, searching for muzzle flashes to locate the enemy. KPA gunners did not see the enemy until the sun rose at 6:20 A.M.

Back at command headquarters near Taegu, General Connerly waited anxiously for word. At 7:58 A.M. both divisions were reporting that the flanks had been turned and the enemy was in retreat. The general immediately ordered an advance on the center of the KPA line. He worried about morale—the American forces in Taegu were battle-weary. But when word spread through the rank that an offensive would begin, it was met with triumphant cheers. Marines from the 3rd Division led the assault, with support from Japanese and British infantry.

American artillery and allied fighter aircraft pounded the KPA, quickly turning the assault into a rout. North Korean regulars cowered in foxholes as the earth trembled around them. KPA commanders tried to embolden their men by telling them that their T-62 tanks and RPG-7 antitank rocket launchers could puncture the American

April 25, 1998: The Allied Counteroffensive Begins

M1A2 tanks with a single volley. On open ground, several North Korean squads tried to do just that. But when the first several rockets exploded, not causing any damage, the KPA soldiers looked at each other mystified. A stainless steel shell with a layer of depleted uranium, the Abrams armor is impervious to most antitank systems.

KPA T-62 tanks rolled forward to actively engage the U.S. Abrams tanks in an open field west of Taegu. The T-62s managed to fire the first round from their position just over the crest of a hill. But when the shells bounced off the armor, the tank crews knew they were in trouble. The Abrams returned fire with deadly accuracy, and the T-62s became metal caskets.

American fists of steel hammered the beleaguered North Koreans throughout the day. By midafternoon the entire KPA position had collapsed and both corps were in full retreat. The army of conquest became an army of hungry scavengers lost in the fog of war.

Word of the stunning defeat outside Taegu reached General O Kuk-Yul as he was perusing the mounting casualty lists. Large numbers of reserves streaming south would shore up the KPA position in Seoul. The reserves, however, were not as well-trained or equipped as the regulars, and they would likely wilt quickly under the weight of the allied advance.

For General O Kuk-Yul, the reversal at Taegu was an ominous turn in the war. He now knew that his earlier projections of an immediate KPA victory were flat out wrong. The defeat outside Taegu was more than a temporary setback. The 9th and 10th Corps were the KPA's best units. Apparently, the American nuclear counterstrike had deterred Kim from further use of his atomic arsenal, but in a desperate state he might return to such a weapon. Fearing Kim's reaction, General O Kuk-Yul walked reluctantly down the lonely, sterile hall to the Great Leader's office.

Inside he found the North Korean dictator rubbing a few of his mystic stones. The general waited silently by the door until Kim acknowledged his presence. "Yes, General, please come in." With a graceful gesture, he signaled him to a large, Gothic-style chair near his desk. General O Kuk-Yul sat down, a notepad resting on his solid thigh.

American Apache helicopters attack North Korean positions outside Taegu as the counterattack begins.

Kim leaned back in his leather chair, a confident grin painted on his face. "And what news do you bring me?"

The general hated being the bearer of bad news because Kim often equated the messenger with the message. Several government officials had actually been shot in 1994 when they reported the poor agricultural harvests in the country. Kim thought it was good for motivation, but somehow it did nothing to improve the 1995 harvest.

Slowly breathing air into his lungs, the general cautiously began, "The latest news from the front is grim. The Americans have indeed landed their heavy divisions and have attacked our forces on both flanks. They broke our lines outside Taegu, and our forces are in full retreat."

Kim shook his head and laughed heartily. General O Kuk-Yul was taken aback at the reaction. Yet, he could also detect Kim's anger. The president stood and began to pace, still clutching a stone in his right hand.

"General, " he paused, "did I not give strict orders to my commanders concerning engagement with the enemy?"

O Kuk-Yul lowered his head and stared at the notepad. "Yes, Mr. President."

"And what where those orders?"

"That under no circumstance were our forces to retreat."

Kim snickered. "And were those orders received by our commanders?"

O Kuk-Yul anxiously nodded in affirmation.

Kim continued to pace in a slow, well-defined, synchronized cadence. "Very well then. What we have here is a direct disobeying of orders. During war this is treason. So you are to find the commanders responsible and have them shot."

The general flinched. He attempted to throw Kim off course by changing the subject. "Mr. President, I believe that we can stabilize the front and hold south of Seoul. We can solidify our position there until our Chinese comrades arrive, at which point we can plan for a summer offensive."

President Kim took the bait and nodded in agreement. "Yes, General. What is the status of our Chinese comrades?"

"They have crossed the border at Sinuiju and are proceeding south. Their Rapid Reaction Force has landed airborne elements near Anju with no interference from the American air force."

By now President Kim was deep in thought, planning his next step. After a momentary silence, he returned to his chair. "What are your best estimates of our remaining nuclear capabilities?"

O Kuk-Yul felt a shiver run down his spine, and after a brief but pregnant pause, he began, "President Kim, I feel I must remind you that we have committed to General Hu that we will not use such weapons without consultation. That was part of our alliance agreement."

Kim began to grow impatient. "General O Kuk-Yul, I have asked you a question. It is I who am the commander in chief. The first units of Chinese forces will be at the DMZ in a matter of several days. Once they have tasted combat, Beijing cannot back down. Then we will be able to act as we see fit. So I ask you again—what capabilities do we still possess?"

The general nervously stood his ground. "President Kim, the Americans have already demonstrated that they fully intend to retaliate at even the most limited use of our capabilities…" His words trailed off as the glare from President Kim silenced him. The general shifted in his chair and then reluctantly told Kim what he wanted to know.

Chapter Seven

April 26
the skies over South Korea

In the predawn hours of April 26, Colonel Wes Parker made one final systems check on his plane before pushing his F-15 Eagle onto the runway and propelling it into the aphotic sky. Parker's Eagle was part of the more than fifty combat aircraft taking off from the new makeshift military air base outside Pusan. They would fly north across the quiet horizon and then through the dense air defense systems over North Korea. It was Parker's job, along with the other fighter pilots, to make sure that the four B-2s and half a dozen B-1 bombers made it to their targets.

Saunders and the military brass had elected to target Chinese forces moving south to reinforce the front. Two major air strikes were planned for tonight: the first on the Korean city of Sinuiju bordering China; the second on the Chinese military facility in Fushun. The strike on China was a major escalation in the conflict, but Saunders felt it was critical to winning the war. If Beijing was able to continually pour troops into Korea, the allies would eventually grow weary and withdraw. But how China would respond remained open to speculation.

The flight to Sinuiju went without incident. But once over the city, KPA anti-aircraft guns began to thunder. The flight crews could see the muzzle flashes from guns winking on and off as though people were lighting matches all over the hillsides. Two squadrons of B-1 Lancers flew in tight over the main military compound just south of the city, discharging tons of ordnance on the Chinese infantry below. The night sky was painted with angry light from exploding shells. Fortunately, no American planes went down.

Barely two hundred miles northwest in the skies over Fushun, China, a tempestuous air war had erupted. U.S. fighters—mostly Eagles and Falcons—were dueling with Chinese interceptors protecting the northeast sector of China. The defending aircraft—including Flankers and Fishbeds—were so numerous on radar that they looked like a swarm of fireflies on a spring evening. Several SAMs were launched, but ECMs sent them off course. The SAMs were old and relatively unsophisticated.

While the American fighters blew more than twenty Chinese MiGs from the heavens, B-2 stealth bombers slinked into the area to deliver their payloads. Using scores of fragmentation bombs, the B-2s devastated two PLA infantry divisions awaiting deployment in Korea. Parker saw the bombs hit the ground, and the base became faintly outlined in the glow from the livid red flames dancing and reaching into the midnight air. PLA casualties on both the ground and in the air were high. The Americans escaped with only one loss—an Eagle was shot down and plunged into Korea Bay.

It did not take China long to respond. The following afternoon, six rockets rose through the canopy of clouds above the Gobi Desert and climbed out over the water before descending on the Japanese island of Okinawa. In the computerized engagement control station of the Patriot mobile battlefield defense system, the phased-array radar detected the missiles several hundred miles away. The station tracked their flight until the fire unit was activated. A half-dozen slender Patriot missiles exploded out of their launchers, streaking into the sky at Mach 3 to intercept the incoming rockets. Patriots smashed into five of the missiles, knocking them from the sky and shattering them into thousands of metal fragments. One, however, managed to get through. At the main allied air base there was a tremendous flash followed by a deafening bang. As the wisping smoke cleared, a ten-foot crater became visible in the asphalt. Three dozen soldiers were dead and hundreds injured. Intelligence revealed that the missile carried a conventional warhead.

Admiral Saunders saw the Chinese response for what it was—a warning against further attacks on the mainland. Beijing wanted to keep the conflict contained to Korea because limiting the war to the peninsula would undoubtedly prolong it. But Saunders knew that this was a recipe for allied defeat, so he reluctantly concluded that the air strikes on the Chinese mainland would continue despite the inherent risks.

By the end of April, allied air power was beginning to stretch thin. Pilots had fought the air war over the South, conducted ground strikes against key targets in the North, and in recent days had landed blows against China. Air strikes on the bridges over the Yalu River had slowed considerably the advance of countless Chinese units. But they still continued to move south and were, by now, beginning to arrive at the newly established front on the outskirts of Seoul. Here the KPA hoped to make its stand. The allies formed a line along the south bank of the Han-gang River. Two American armored divisions held the center, with French paratroopers and the U.S. 25th Infantry Division on the left flank, and Japanese and Australian forces along with the U.S. 101st Airborne Assault Division on the right.

Connerly had hoped to avoid a pitched battle in the streets of the capital, but it now seemed inevitable. Artillery fire rocked the streets and buildings facing the Han-gang as allied forces took out KPA snipers and other units. Connerly was desperately looking for a way to push the KPA out of Seoul before more Chinese infantry arrived and further complicated matters.

General Connerly was not the only one concerned about the next phase of the war. The burgeoning allied force had Kim worried for the first time. A total of ten divisions were en route, including more American armor and Japanese and Australian infantry. General O Kuk-Yul noticed the first sense of doubt at a midafternoon briefing in the planning room in the bowels of the underground bunker. The trouble was, Kim's doubts were encouraging in him the view that only the use of chemical and nuclear weapons would ensure victory. The general knew otherwise. The use of such weapons would not only lead to eventual defeat in the South; it would also mean the decimation of the North.

Kim sat with his arms crossed and his head tilted slightly to the right. He seemed disinterested as his officers ran through the latest casualty lists. Midway through the report from Seoul, he raised his hand to halt the presentation. After a few moments of silence, he stood and began his customary pace at the front of the room. "General O Kuk-Yul," he began in a clipped tone, "have any of the retreating officers been shot as I instructed earlier?"

O Kuk-Yul felt the color fade from his face. "Not yet," he said defensively. "The chaos of the battlefield has precluded this so far."

Kim nodded as his mind seemed to be racing to other subjects. To O Kuk-Yul it was maniacal. "We all know that a conventional war now favors the allies," crackled Kim. "Beijing may help tip the scales, but of course General Hu is not a fool. He will extract a heavy price from us to defeat the Americans. No, it is clear to me that we must again use our weapons of mass destruction to win this great victory."

A hush fell over the room, and General O Kuk-Yul felt a horror come over him. It was as if he were witnessing madness unfold before him. But Kim continued.

"Look at this bunker," he said waving his arm in the air. "It was constructed for just such a situation as this. There will be high casualties for sure. As the French say, 'You must break eggs to make an omelette.' But in this bunker, we will survive. And a united Korea can position itself to influence the course of events as it did under the ancient kings of the past." While many eyes nervously darted around the room, no one apparently had the courage to halt a madman hatching his twisted plan. General O Kuk-Yul, however, knew that something had to be done. Taking silence as a sign of approval, Kim ordered his commanders to remove all safety locks on the full arsenal of North Korean nuclear, biological, and chemical weapons to prepare them for use.

O Kuk-Yul left the meeting with a cloud of despair hanging over him. Yet he knew that brooding would not eliminate the source of his grief. He returned to his office just down the hall and opened the top drawer of his desk. He reached in and pulled out a black, burnished automatic pistol. With delicate strokes, he used a cloth to clean the weapon before inserting the clip. Small beads of sweat formed on his face as he stood and moved toward the door, the pistol tucked into the back of his pants. He headed out the door and back down the hall. His heart was now pounding.

With careful strides, he turned the corner and proceeded stiffly down the long, lonely corridor to Kim's office. Recognizing that it was the general, the two ever-present guards paid him little attention. As he approached the door, the sentries stood to prepare for the mandatory search. Suddenly, the general pulled out his weapon. The guards' eyes grew large, and before they could utter a word, he fired twice at each, killing them instantly. O Kuk-Yul picked up his pace, bursting through the office door in a nearly full sprint. With the sound of gunfire, Kim's assistant was frantically reaching for his pistol. Just as his fingers touched the barrel, the general shot him. O Kuk-Yul now pivoted and headed for Kim's door.

Inside he found the Great Leader crouched in the corner, his hands in the air in an anguished plea for mercy. He whimpered softly. O Kuk-Yul did not consider himself a particularly cruel man, and he felt his stomach sear at the thought of shooting a defenseless man. But he knew Kim's brutality. If the president were allowed to live, he would do everything in his power to dispose of the general. So O Kuk-Yul raised his gun, shut his eyes, and pulled the trigger until the clip was empty. When he opened his eyes, he saw Kim lying motionless in the corner, his soft, porcelain-like hands clutching several small stones.

By now a crowd had gathered in the door with a mix of confusion and fear on their faces. Security officers felt the urge to arrest someone, but they were uncertain as to who was now in charge. Kim was generally despised by the officer corps, so O Kuk-Yul won the loyalty of senior officers. Although the general was in support of continuing the war, he was unwilling to use weapons of mass destruction. He knew that it would only bring widespread terror to his country.

As several officers dragged the limp body of the late president out of the office, O Kuk-Yul phoned General Hu in Beijing and alerted him to the leadership change in Pyongyang. Hu was surprised but elated and relieved. O Kuk-Yul, who had always been the reluctant warrior, committed himself to honoring the alliance between the two countries and hoped to adopt a strategy for victory.

Chapter Eight

May 3
outside Seoul

Allied strength had grown steadily in the aftermath of the counterattack and since the move north from Taegu to the southern suburbs of Seoul. The combined South Korean, American, Australian, Japanese, British, and French forces numbered more than twenty divisions. Even so, South Korean forces had proven their staying power, recovering from stinging defeats in the early days of the war.

While General Connerly was anxious to push the war north, intelligence pointed to a growing Chinese and North Korean army. General O Kuk-Yul held the 820th Corps in Seoul along with five other infantry divisions. Members of China's elite RRF had also taken up positions in the center of the city. There were now close to ten other divisions between Seoul and Pyongyang, and KPA forces continued to occupy portions of the South Korean west coast. (The 124th Army, including light infantry and special forces, held Kunsan with the help of a division of regular infantry.)

General Connerly decided to turn the massive size and immobility of the enemy to his advantage. As night fell on the peninsula, the two American armored divisions pushed northeast to move around Seoul and attack supply lines connecting enemy forces with Pyongyang. Cutting the force off from supply lines and support from the North would cause a terrible dilemma for Pyongyang. Without supplies, such a large army could not subsist for long. They would either have to surrender or attack the allied armies. And because the KPA and Chinese forces were mostly infantry, it would be extremely difficult for such an assault to succeed.

The U.S. Army 1st Mechanized Infantry and 2nd Armored Divisions began moving by darkness, with support from the 101st Airborne Assault Division. When they encountered the KPA lines ten miles west of Seoul, it was an entirely one-sided affair. North Korean forces lacked night-vision equipment and shot blindly into the Cimmerian expanse. With support from allied fighter bombers, the two divisions broke the KPA lines early and moved rapidly northwest on an axis, driving for the sea. Within three hours, they had cut off the enemy force in Seoul from any supply lines. When word reached Connerly of the breakthrough, he ordered allied artillery to pound the capital city. It was more for effect than anything else.

The allied sweep around Seoul put North Korean soil within reach of the U.S. Army. General O Kuk-Yul was enough of a realist to understand that the beleaguered and hungry masses of his country were likely to greet the allies as liberators—not conquerors. His earlier fears of a lost opportunity to conquer the South now turned to panic for his own political survival. Seated behind Kim's desk in his bunker officer, O Kuk urgently phoned General Hu.

The Chinese general was pacing in his cavernous office, plotting his next move when the call came. Hu was like his Korean colleague—mindful that military defeat would mean certain political

A U.S. Air Force B-2 bomber en route to the Pacific for a bombing run on a Chinese military facility outside Fushun.

demise if not execution. He had invested all of his political capital in the war, and he had precious little to show for his efforts.

"General Hu," began O Kuk-Yul nervously, "our forces are incapable of blunting the attacks of the Americans. Once the allies begin to press north, they are likely to build a momentum that cannot be stopped."

"I understand, Comrade," offered Hu contemplatively. "We must break the siege around Seoul. I will communicate my plans to you by courier." Hu always assumed that the NSA was tapped into North Korean communications.

Things had been quiet for the U.S. 2nd Armored Division for several days. Both KPA and Chinese forces were in the vicinity but had chosen to remain in the meager hills nearby. Orders from General Connerly at headquarters called for the division to hold its position along the main highway and intercept any efforts to supply enemy forces in Seoul.

On the morning of May 5 everything changed. Lieutenant General Paul Stewart was awaiting reports of reinforcements when allied intelligence aircraft radioed with an alarming message. But it came too late—only thirty seconds prior to disaster.

"Falcon One, Falcon One. We have condition red! Missiles incoming!"

In what seemed an instant, a flash of brilliant, white light enveloped the 2nd Armored Division. Intense winds carried a searing heat, which flattened most structures and scorched everything in a three-square-mile area. A deep-throated rumble followed shortly after, but General Stewart and most of the senior officers never heard it. The seventy-five–kiloton nuclear blast killed them instantly. The only survivors were crews fortunate enough be inside their tanks.

Word of the strike reached President St. John at Camp David. Seated in his favorite black leather chair, the president had just finished digesting a cable from General Hu.

> **President Michael St. John**
> **The White House**
>
> **Dear Mr. President:**
>
> **The Chinese government and the people of the Democratic People's Republic of Korea (DPRK) are willing to negotiate a cease-fire to end the hostilities in the Pacific.**
>
> **Beijing is fully prepared to vigorously protect its interests and will participate in such discussions only if its legitimate national interests are recognized.**
>
> **General Hu Shih**
> **Central Military Commission**

The startling news concerning the fate of the 2nd Armored Division led the president to cast the note aside in anger and frustration. Intelligence was still fuzzy and coming in slowly. National Security Adviser Jack Fowler spoke with Admiral Saunders on the secure phone for twenty minutes. He then hung up and crossed the room to join the president and Defense Secretary Bodine in the sitting area.

"What do we know, Jack?" growled the president.

"Mr. President, the intelligence is clear on two matters. First, this missile was fired by Beijing—not Pyongyang. And second, an analysis of the blast data indicates it was probably a one hundred–kiloton warhead."

"Dear God—it was the Chinese." President St. John leaned over to pick up the cable from Hu. "Why send this note if you are plotting to nuke our forces?" He rubbed his forehead with more than a hint of exasperation.

"Mr. President," grunted Tom Bodine, "they may be sincere in wanting to come to some sort of settlement, but we should ignore that note until we respond to this provocation. We have to respond. Then we can talk peace."

St. John rose from his chair and went to the north window. He looked out over the greenery. "You're right, Tom. I think we all agree on that. The question is—how do we respond? If we strike back at the Chinese mainland, Beijing may hit the continental U.S. But if the retaliatory strike is launched at Chinese forces in North Korea, Pyongyang might fire another tactical nuke or use more biological weapons. Any response seems to be a losing proposition."

Tom Bodine stood from his seat on the plush sofa and joined the president at the window. "But, Mr. President, we must also keep in mind that taking no action is also a choice—and one that might have enormous consequences as well. Beijing has crossed the threshold, and maintaining future deterrence requires that the culprit pay a price for its actions.

"There is also a less-abstract reason for retaliating: Allied forces along the Han-gang river south of Seoul are exhausted and short of supplies. Another offensive will have to wait at least a week. Soon we are going to have to commit reserve units to actual combat situations. With only ten regular army divisions available, things are getting thin on the ground." St. John nodded. "At the same time, General Merrill reports that he is going to have to scale back the number of air sorties our aircraft are running over North Korea. As you know, we have basically half the operational air force fighter wings that President Bush had in Desert Storm. We must suspend some operations to rest our pilots and to replenish our forces."

"What are you saying, Tom?"

The defense secretary let out a sigh. "We need to end this war as quickly as possible. This pause will give the KPA and the Chinese an opportunity to regroup and dig in. General Hu wants to negotiate because he believes that we can press our advantage. He may show less interest a week from now unless we show him how serious we are about the use of nukes."

St. John nodded again and lightly touched the window pane. "All right, Tom. I think you have convinced us." The president then turned and looked Bodine straight in the eyes. "Now, what do we target?"

U.S. intelligence satellites had been tracking the movement of Chinese forces through North Korea to the front. Allied aircraft had hit a fair number of them, particularly as they moved down Reunification Highway, which ran from the Chinese border in the north to the DMZ.

At 7:18 A.M. on the morning of May 8 President St. John placed U.S. nuclear forces on a DEFCON 4 alert, which means that American strategic bombers, nuclear submarines, and land-based missile silos are ready for launch at a moment's notice. In the Sea of Japan, a U.S. Los Angeles-class submarine received the final launch sequence codes and minutes later two Tomahawk cruise missiles burst through the waters and flew west for the Korean coast. They traveled quietly through the heavy spring air. At the end of their two-hour flight, both erupted in a storm of atoms and nuclei, generating two explosions the equivalent of fifty kilotons of TNT. The Chinese infantry division positioned beneath the blast was completely destroyed.

During the next several hours President St. John anxiously awaited any word of a response by Beijing. The president and Colonel Mark Bright, who was carrying the "football," or nuclear launch codes, exchanged occasional glances. As the hours drifted by, St. John could feel the tension ease. At 4:14 P.M. EST he cabled General Hu.

> General Hu Shih
> Central Military Commission
>
> Dear General Hu:
>
> The United States is willing to dispatch a team of nego-
> tiators to meet with a Chinese delegation at a neutral
> site. We await your reply.
>
> President Michael St. John
> The White House

On May 11 a delegation of American military officers arrived in the Russian far east port city of Vladivostock to meet a group of PLA officials. Admiral Saunders, CINCPAC, led the American team. His counterpart was General Wan Biao, a protégé of General Hu. The terms of a cease-fire were negotiated in the first six hours. All pow-ers were now permitted to move only units smaller than brigade size. Air operations were suspended, and both parties agreed to not move forces into zones they did not already occupy.

But negotiations over the fate of the North Korean government quickly bogged down. Beijing was insistent that the DPRK remain intact, with General O Kuk-Yul as the head of state. (This was the West's first hint that Kim was no longer in power.) General Wan used the occupation of Seoul as leverage. "We will never relinquish our occupation of Seoul," he bluntly told Saunders, "unless you rec-ognize the government in Pyongyang." To Admiral Saunders it was inconceivable that the aggressors might remain in power north of the DMZ, but he also understood well the American position. He cabled back to Washington General Wan's demands and waited for a response.

The president was grappling with the issue as he strolled amid the pine and maple trees of Camp David. Tom Bodine and Jack Fowler joined the president, respectfully avoiding the issue of a possible peace settlement until St. John broached the subject. "We've suffered more than eighteen thousand casualties in this war," he began, picking up a stone and tossing it into the woods. "Our men and women have been attacked with biological weapons and radiated by nuclear fallout. There may be an anthrax epidemic in Seoul, and Taipei has been pummeled from the sky. We have pushed the enemy back to the DMZ and now we are being told that the perpetrators of all this horror can remain in power?"

Both Bodine and Fowler knew it was a rhetorical question and did not answer. Besides, neither knew quite how to answer.

The president picked up another rock and hurled it into the forest. "I can't agree to this type of a settlement."

Bodine shook his head in agreement. He understood the injustice of the entire process. But the nagging military realities were of serious concern. "I agree with everything you said, Mr. President, but I think we need to sign this agreement."

St. John wheeled around and glared at his secretary of defense. "Tom, what are you saying? Don't you think we can handle the Chinese?"

"No, Mr. President. Victory is going to be very difficult indeed. As you already know, we don't have the same armed forces that won Desert Storm. We are smaller and lighter, and this enemy is stronger."

"But are you really suggesting that we have little alternative but to maintain the status quo and let this aggression go unpunished?"

Bodine nodded. "We are going to have to commit all our reserves to the Korean conflict. And unlike Desert Storm, the reserves will not be serving in a support role. We will have to put them on the front line."

The president began walking again, with both Fowler and Bodine following him. "Jack, what does the NSC [National Security Council] say about this?"

"Mr. President," Fowler said hesitatingly, "we agree with Defense."

On June 24 the United States and the Republic of Korea reluctantly signed a peace agreement with the Democratic People's Republic of Korea and the People's Republic of China at a solemn ceremony in Vladivostock. President St. John did not attend. Instead, he sent the secretary of state to sign on the dotted line as PLA officers gleefully watched.

After watching the ceremony on CNN, the president skimmed the postwar analysis by the Department of Defense.

June 24, 1998

Postwar Strategic Assessment of the Pacific Conflict

Summary: Failure to achieve U.S. war aims in the conflict is a direct result of fundamental deficiencies in American security policy.

Military Considerations: The United States suffered 18,124 casualties in the Korean conflict. Many of these deaths might have been avoided. For several years America has possessed the technological ability to develop and deploy theater missile defense (TMD) systems. However, the failure of the previous administration to develop and deploy these systems and our continued pursuit of this policy led directly to the loss of life. The 5,814 casualties resulting from the use of theater missile forces might have been prevented. The continued vulnerability puts U.S. forces at risk

wherever they might be deployed and makes conducting military operations extremely difficult.

The United States was compelled to negotiate the
present unfavorable settlement primarily because of
the shortcomings in our armed forces. Although
units proved capable, they simply lacked the numbers to fight a major power. Ten Army divisions is
simply too small a base to develop a force that can
deal with a major land-based threat. To conduct
operations in Korea, America essentially pulled all
active-duty ground forces from deployment around
the world into the Pacific theater. Had another crisis
developed, we would have been incapable of effectively dealing with it.

This conflict also exposed deficiencies in American policy toward Taiwan. Since the Taiwan Relations Act of
1978, the United States has elected to avoid selling
advanced weapons systems to Taipei that might tip the
military balance vis-à-vis the mainland. Events now
reveal that Taiwan is a critical factor in any effort to prevent future expansion by China. Containment of China
requires that America allow for the sale of advanced
aircraft, air defense systems, and naval vessels to
Taipei.

Long-Term Strategic Concerns: We should antici-
pate further conflict with China in the not-too-distant
future. The People's Liberation Army has stated since
the early 1990s that it views the United States as its
most likely adversary. PLA training and doctrine is
being crafted to deal with possible conflict with
America. The expansion of PLA capabilities has come
at a time when U.S. forces in the Pacific have been

dramatically reduced. Computer simulations conducted by the Naval War College in 1994 and the Central Intelligence Agency in 1995 predict that war between the United States and China in 2005 will lead to a probable victory for Beijing.

Conclusion: Failure to expand American military capabilities and support the procurement of advanced weapons systems by Taiwan will doom the United States to further defeat in Asia.

Part Two

Iran
April 4, 1999

Chapter Nine

April 4, 1999
Geneva, Switzerland

S audi Prince Abudulillah Salaam Abdul Rahman left the emergency Organization of Petroleum Exporting Countries (OPEC) meeting feeling dejected. Walking with his characteristically long, graceful strides, his thōbe—the long, shirtlike garment worn by Arabian men—flowed in the strong breeze. Waiting by the curb was a throng of press from around the world. Somehow, as he passed through the mob toward his waiting limousine, the prince managed to keep the anger from what had just transpired deep inside. But maintaining a calm, chiseled look on his face was hard work. After more than seven hours of fruitless negotiations over oil pricing and production quotas, the rough deliberations had taken a very ugly turn.

For the past twenty years, a schism had haunted the organization. Radical producers such as Iran and Libya wanted to use oil as a weapon against the West, to maximize profits and gain leverage over the major industrial powers. Moderate Arab states such as Saudi Arabia and the United Arab Emirates (UAE) favored a more balanced approach—modest oil prices and stable markets. While negotiating with the radicals was never a pleasant task, this time it had been unbearable for the prince.

Iran had embarked on a belligerent course, including a vicious campaign of verbal intimidation and threats. It began in January with inflammatory statements in public speeches and the Mideast press, as well as radio broadcasts designed to move the Arab masses. Now in Geneva, Iranian Oil Minister Hushang Akbar Mohtashemi launched a verbal barrage that insulted the moderates in every conceivable way. He accused Saudi Arabia, Oman, and the UAE of serving as the "handmaidens of the Satan West" and of involvement in a "Zionist conspiracy." The hope was to shake the moderate producers into submission. But Prince Abudulillah reacted otherwise, leading to a walkout by the moderates. The Iranian oil minister scowled as the prince left the room.

As he rode in his limousine down the elegant boulevards of Geneva, Abudulillah feared that Iran's diplomatic posture had grown more shrill and arrogant in recent months for a reason. Perhaps the much-rumored Iranian bomb had emboldened Tehran to take a more resolute stand. Drinking a club soda from a crystal glass, the prince gazed toward beautiful Lake Geneva as his mind replayed the course of events during the past two decades. Abudulillah was above all a strategist—a former Sandhurst student and one-time head of the Royal Saudi Air Force (RSAF).

A crisis was mounting in the gulf. The events at OPEC appeared to be only the latest kindling tossed on a slow-burning fire built and fed by Tehran. For the better part of two decades, Iran had been on a quest to transform both institutional Islam and all Muslim society as a whole with the hope of resurrecting an Islamic empire. It was a realistic ambition for the enormous country of mountains and plateaus, home to the world's largest population of Shiite Muslims. Dominion was a part of her history.

As a nation, Iran had a tradition of empire dating back to 1000 B.C. Persia could claim a national identity stretching back to the ancient empire of Cyrus the Great and Darius I, which by the fifth century B.C. extended from India all the way to what are now modern Greece and Libya. Later, the Panthian empire emerged and became the eastern rival to the Roman Empire. In 1979 this history of empire was fused with a raging Islamic fundamentalism. Islamic extremism provided an ideology to mobilize the masses and a younger elite willing to lead a revolution.

Calls for an Islamic Jihad had isolated Tehran from much of the world. But Tehran learned from that period and developed a more sophisticated strategy after the passing of the Ayatollah Khomeini. The new stratagem was characterized by a dual approach—combining aspirations for a global utopian Islamic empire with pragmatic, regional objectives. And powerful forces in the region were working in Iran's favor to rebuild the empire of old. The collapse of the Soviet giant removed a powerful military force from Iran's northern borders, expanding its zone of influence and putting a buffer (Turkmenistan) between Iran and Russia. This was the first time in more than a century that Iran and Russia did not share a common border.

Abudulillah had felt the chilling winds of Islamic extremism strengthen during the last decade of the twentieth century—a growing tempest that made him very anxious. Saudi Arabia was sitting on more than half the world's known oil reserves and had been able to hold the line. But whether the coalition remained was yet to be seen. With the lights of Geneva now fading behind him, Abudulillah's limousine proceeded to the airport where his private jet awaited. He would return to Riyadh immediately to brief his uncle, the king.

Iranian Oil Minister Hushang Akbar Mohtashemi met with the National Defense Council (NDC), his government's supreme decision-making body, on April 6. He had come back from Geneva empty-handed, so Tehran now had to decide on its next move. President Muhammad Montazeri sat at the head of the table, stern and taciturn. His cold, harsh demeanor was not reserved for enemies, as even his closest political allies were not immune to his temper. Heavyset, with a round face, Montazeri had long dreamt of building an Islamic empire. All Muslims, in his mind, constituted a "single nation" (*Ummah*), and his regime was the tool Allah would use to bring final unity to the people.

The NDC included the president's most trusted advisors. Yet he usually made the decisions of greatest consequence without counsel. To his left sat Ayatollah Ali Morteza'i. The cleric was a brilliant man, versed in both the Koran and political theory. He lived by Machiavelli's dictum that it is better to be feared than loved by the ruled. He had a medium build, and his bony, narrow face never appeared to change expressions. The ayatollah was President Montazeri's closest advisor.

Next to the cleric sat Defense Minister Akhar Shamkhani, who was an almost comical sight. The bold, flashy infantry officer, bedecked with metals and other military insignia, was a sharp contrast to the conservative ayatollah in his dark *Mishlah* robe. The two men symbolized the contrasting forces shaping Iran. While Morteza'i preached against the satanic West, the defense minister prided himself as a leader for the new Iran—committed to its Islamic roots while harnessing the power of Western technologies to advance the cause of Iran.

To the right of President Montazeri sat Foreign Minister Ali Habibi, the son of a university professor. Habibi had studied overseas at Oxford and the Sorbonne and consequently was the most cosmopolitan of the Iranian leadership. Shamkhani liked to joke that Habibi was "fitted" for the vocation of a diplomat: he favored Italian suits, English shirts, and French cologne. His dexterity in the game of diplomacy was highly valued by all, but his commitment to the cause was sometimes questioned. A tight, neat beard and intense, brown eyes made him an unusually dramatic figure.

Mohtashemi gave a brief report on the deliberations in Geneva. He said that he had exhausted every avenue. Hours of persuasion, followed by verbal threats and abuse, had yielded nothing. "They do not fear us, but rather assume that these are empty threats."

Montazeri looked pained as anger bubbled inside him. He shifted around in his chair, waiting to speak until the oil minister concluded his report. The president was clearly insulted by the refusal of the other gulf states to acquiesce to his heavy-handed demands in Geneva. "We will have to teach our brethren the seriousness of this matter." He turned to an aide, "Bring him in."

The young aide exited hastily, returning moments later with an elderly man dressed in a grayish suit. With blond, mussed hair and Slavic features, the man looked out of place. Nonetheless, he was treated with unusual respect and deference by those who knew him.

The defense minister rose at once to greet him. "My friend, it is so good to see you again." Shamkhani directed him to a seat at the table. "For those who have not had the privilege, let me introduce you to Igor Vladimorov. Although you do not know him, our history books will say great things of him."

Everyone instantly became curious about the elderly visitor. There had been persistent rumors in ruling circles about a nuclear weapons program, but the NDC had never discussed it. Only President Montazeri, Defense Minister Shamkhani, and Ayatollah Morteza'i knew of its existence. Tehran had brought in a handful of foreign scientists to work on the project, and chief among them was Vladimorov, a Russian expert in missile systems who had moved to Iran in 1992. The thin, calculating scientist was the son of Moscow schoolteachers. As a child, his early grasp of science and mathematics had been truly astonishing. When he was only twelve years old, he was selected by the schoolmaster for intensive study of physics and engineering, and by age twenty-one he was working for the Central Design Bureau on missiles and guidance systems for the Kremlin's burgeoning nuclear weapons arsenal.

Having studied under S. P. Korolev, the Soviet Union's most brilliant rocket designer, Vladimorov became a legend in Soviet nuclear missile design. He contributed substantially to the design of the first Soviet solid-rocket booster. Under communism he managed a decent life, receiving special privileges because he was part of the elite. But the dissolution of the Soviet Union brought his isolated world to an end. Life became hard, and his pay dissolved to the equivalent of $12 per month. Desperate, Vladimorov jumped at the chance for a move when Tehran began fishing for Russian scientists with promises of big money. Following him to Iran was a team of colleagues from the Central Design Bureau. That was 1992. Now, seven years later, his team had yielded results, and the Defense Council would finally hear about it.

Montazeri asked the elderly man to describe the status of the weapons program. In broken English (he spoke no Farsi), he described his progress in short, punctuated sentences. "We now have in place three missiles with a range of twenty-five hundred miles. The propulsion system is solid fuel, which allows us greater flexibility. We have developed an advanced fly-by-wire inertial guidance system, providing us with an accuracy of sixteen one-hundredths of a nautical mile. These systems are based on mobile launchers, which allow us to protect them more effectively. Each is equipped to carry either a singular nuclear warhead of a one hundred–kiloton variety or a chemical or biological agent. We have several warheads ready to be put in place."

Tehran's efforts to develop and deploy a nuclear arsenal were not unknown in the West. Unfortunately, the United States was never able to seriously impede the flow of nuclear-related technologies so critical to the Iranian weapons program. When both China and Russia sold nuclear and missile components to Tehran in 1994, Washington did little other than file a few diplomatic protests. German and French companies which had built nuclear reactors in Iran continued to provide technical support to these "nonmilitary" reactors and faced no sanction from America.

Montazeri, his pride rising in him like a cobra, was overjoyed by Vladimorov's report. He turned to his Defense Council, "We have named this new weapon Zulfiquar, after the legendary sword of the Shiite warrior Ali. Zulfiquar will change the Muslim world forever. Our ambitions may now be realized."

Foreign Minister Habibi was interested in the production schedule. "Tell me, Vladimorov, how rapidly will this force be able to grow?"

The emigrant scientist stroked his reddish, worn face. "We still encounter some technical difficulties in the process, so stable production is not easy to predict. What we lack most are components for more guidance systems. As of now, we are not able to replicate these systems internally, and until we can, we will continue to rely on illicit imports from the West and Russia. An additional three missiles can be produced during the next two months. We currently have four warheads."

The prospect of a nuclear arsenal made Habibi very nervous. He feared that it might provoke Iraq or Israel into military action. He also feared that it might lead to a recklessness by his own government. "President Montazeri, I suggest that we review this matter in several months when the size of the nuclear arsenal has grown. Extreme caution is in order."

President Montazeri moved gracefully from the table to his desk. There he poured himself a small cup of rich coffee. His gestures were refined as he took a drink and then returned to the discussion. "That is too much time. We must act now while we have the chance, before our enemies can prepare to deal with our potent new weapon. The current arsenal of four will have to do." He turned to the scientist, "But, Mr. Vladimorov, you and the team should continue to work accordingly." Vladimorov stood up from the Persian-carved chair, bowed, and then exited.

Montazeri smiled again. "We can become masters of the Persian Gulf. We must be prepared to act within the next thirty days."

By May 6 Commander Abbas Muhtaj had been on a hair trigger for days, awaiting final orders. For the past week he had sat in his spartan office in the port city of Bandar-e Bushehr expecting word that his 2nd Division of the Iranian Revolutionary Guard Corps (IRGC) would be shipping out. His men had undergone rigorous training in urban warfare for three weeks and were in top condition. And while the city in which they were to fight had not been revealed, Muhtaj now knew it had to be in the oil-rich nation of Bahrain.

Iranian national television was reporting that a civil uprising was taking place on the tiny island off the coast of Saudi Arabia. Shiite youths had first rioted there on May 5, and soon after, it had turned into an insurrection. Bahraini security forces, made up largely of

British and Pakistani mercenaries, were now fighting pitched battles with Shiites in the streets of Manama. For years Tehran had laid
claim to Bahrain as part of Iran. Now, perhaps, the opportunity
existed to act on the claim.

Drinking his tea and looking out the window onto the narrow
courtyard, Muhtaj knew that Iranian intelligence was behind the
uprising. Rumors had been circulating for months that Muhsin
Reza'i, the director of intelligence, had been training Shiite youths
outside the Iranian city of Yazd. Reza'i had, no doubt, then placed the
cadre in Bahrain and established a pipeline of weapons and money. If
the reports from television were true, the Shiite youths were more
than holding their own against a well-armed security force.

By early morning the uprising had succeeded. The young revolutionaries seized control of the parliament building in Manama. On
cue they declared a new Islamic republic and requested immediate
assistance from Tehran to push "mercenary forces into the sea."

The weather was clear and the winds favorable as the Iranian
armada departed the port of Bandar-e Bushehr. Four converted
merchant ships carried Commander Muhtaj and his men out of port
and into the gulf escorted by two Babr destroyers. Four Kilo-class
diesel submarines were supposed to clear the path of any ships that
might try to impede the expedition.

In the command quarters, Muhtaj and his officers reviewed the
maps of Manama and gleaned what they could from the latest intelligence. The IRGC was made up of highly motivated troops driven
by Islamic zeal and passion for the Shiite cause. Yet sometimes this
fervor worked against them. During the Iran–Iraq War, IRGC units
were sent in waves at Iraqi-fixed positions, including machine gun
nests. Muhtaj still remembered well the carnage he saw on the bat-
tlefields near Abadan. From that time forward, the commander had
committed himself to instilling a sense of military professionalism
into the IRGC. He did not want to dampen the fervor but rather
make it more potent and the force more effective.

The 250-mile expedition across the placid waters of the Persian
Gulf went without incident. By late afternoon, the coastline of

Bahrain became visible on the horizon. Muhtaj and the men of the IRGC 2nd Division could see smoke billowing up from Manama. The troops packed their gear and prepared for the assault. Overhead, a group of six Russian-built Backfire bombers streaked south to hit Bahrain's Sheikh Isa air base.

On the only hill in Bahrain, Saudi Arabia had a radar perched as part of her Peace Shield Air Defense System. Within seconds the radar detected the Backfire bombers, and Saudi F-15s were sent to the area. Meanwhile, the American naval base on the southern tip of Bahrain went on full alert. The Bahraini air force tried to get airborne, but the Iranian planes pummeled the air base by using gravity bombs and air-to-surface missiles, shattering the planes in a matter of minutes. Gone too were Bahrain's eight Apache attack helicopters. Two squadrons of RSAF F-16s flew combat air patrol in the distance but with strict orders to attack only if provoked.

The situation on the ground in Manama was tumultuous. The Bahraini armed forces had been organized to deal with a disciplined army on the battlefield, not an insurrection in the capital. Their tank battalion, built around eighty M60A3 tanks and two infantry battalions, dissolved quickly into marauding bands, firing indiscriminately on civilians. When the Iranian armada shot its way into the port of Manama in the early evening hours, it met no organized resistance.

Commander Muhtaj broke his division into three attack brigades and moved toward the parliament building to support the Shiite forces now under siege by a ring of security forces. The IRGC rapidly pierced the circle and finished off the Bahraini units. The few remaining Bahraini forces retreated from the city.

Word that the IRGC had landed sent Admiral John Stevens at U.S. Central Command (USCENTCOM) to the secure phone for consultations with Secretary of Defense Tom Bodine. The U.S. 5th Fleet was based on the southern tip of Bahrain.

"Mr. Secretary, we've now got Iranian forces on the ground less than twenty-five miles from here. Iranian bombers have buzzed us twice. Our forces are on full alert with orders to fire only if provoked. I need to know the rules of engagement immediately."

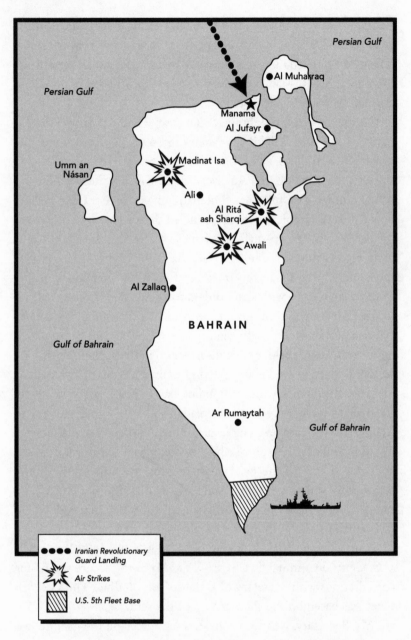

The Iranian Assault on Bahrain: May 6

Bodine cleared his throat and leaned back in the chair behind his desk at the Pentagon. "Admiral, I understand. What exactly is the situation on the ground at this point?"

"I doubt if the government can hold. The Iranian Revolutionary Guards are highly motivated, and the internal Shiite forces are heavily armed. If we don't move swiftly, I believe the government will fall."

"What exactly are you recommending?"

The phone line crackled. "Iran has an enormous advantage in the air. Bahraini forces are getting pounded by their Backfires and fighter-bombers, and, therefore, have a tough time moving. If we get our carrier-based fighters in the air, we can clear the skies in a matter of minutes."

"All right, Admiral. I'll speak to the president right away. He's aboard *Air Force One.*"

As the battle raged in Manama, six hundred miles north in the desolate interior of Iran, the ground rumbled. A crude missile rose to the heavens on a column of flames. Twelve minutes later, a one hundred–kiloton nuclear blast lit up the skies over the desert. Both U.S. AWACS in the Persian Gulf and NSA-eavesdropping facilities in Turkey detected the brilliant light and blinding explosion on their sensors. NSA specialists had never seen anything like it. They immediately sent a dispatch to NSA headquarters in Fort Meade, Maryland. It was marked "Urgent—Priority one."

FLASH REPORT NSA Post 5467
Time: Greenwich 2045
Date: May 6, 1999

Sensors have detected a tremendous explosion and release of energy over Iran. Preliminary determination— explosion of a nuclear device.

In the NSA traffic room, Paula Jameson grabbed the secure phone and contacted the White House, which transferred her call to Jack Fowler, the president's national security advisor, aboard *Air Force One*.

As Jameson spoke with Fowler, Bodine tapped lightly on his cherry-wood desk, waiting for the president to pick up his phone on *Air Force One*.

"Tom?"

"Yes, Mr. President."

"What is it?"

"Mr. President, I want to update you on the situation in the gulf. Iranian forces have moved on Bahrain. I just spoke with Admiral Stevens at USCENTCOM. He is suggesting that we consider throwing our full support behind the Bahraini government."

St. John let out a nervous sigh. "What sort of numbers are we talking about?"

"By our best estimates, the initial Iranian force includes any-where from five to ten thousand troops on the ground, and Bahraini estimates put the number of internal Shiite forces at perhaps another five thousand. Introducing U.S. ground forces would not be a good idea. The best thing we could do at this point is take out the Iranian planes which have hit ground targets on the island."

The President removed his *Air Force One* leather flight jacket and paced in the small space that made up his airborne office. Fowler could see the pained look on the president's face, but the news he was getting would only make matters worse.

After a pregnant pause, St. John returned to his seat and loosened his tie. "Have there been any strikes on U.S. installations or per-sonnel?" he asked Bodine.

"No, Mr. President. At this point they have scrupulously avoided hitting any U.S. targets."

"Well then, Tom, I think this needs more discussion. I don't want to do anything rash. Let's bring everyone in on this." He looked at his watch. "We are supposed to be on the ground in about six hours. I'll have Fowler arrange a full meeting of the NSC for eight o'clock tonight."

Bodine was concerned. "I understand fully, Mr. President. But six hours might be too late. By then the IRGC may have won."

Suddenly Fowler broke into the conversation. "Mr. President, Tom, we have just received two urgent messages from Washington. An NSA-eavesdropping facility in Turkey has picked up what they believe to be a tremendous explosion in the skies over Iran. Their preliminary reading is that this was the detonation of a nuclear device. We have also received a message—or, should I say, an ultimatum—from President Montazeri. He demands the withdrawal of all U.S. military personnel from the Persian Gulf within twenty-one days. Failure to comply will, in his words, lead to the detonation of a nuclear device over a major city in Europe."

President St. John broke into a cold sweat. "Is this possible? Can they have the bomb?"

Chapter Ten

May 7
Bahrain

By the early morning hours, with the sun barely cresting over the horizon, the 2nd Division of the IRGC was in firm control of central Manama. The IRGC 1st Division was en route to reinforce Commander Muhtaj. Ships from the port of Bandar-e Bushehr were bringing a dozen, light Scorpion tanks, multiple rocket launchers, and a few AH-15 attack helicopters. On the heels of the 1st Division were members of the al-Shairqah police. They were being flown in to start the delicate process of building an internal security apparatus. To maintain its grip on the island nation, Tehran would need to keep a tight lid on dissent.

Control of Bahrain gave Iran a door to Saudi Arabia and the rest of the gulf. The King Fahd Causeway, a narrow stretch of road, provided Iran with a land bridge to Saudi Arabia. And IRGC forces were now overlooking the massive Saudi oil port of Ras Tannurah. The campaign could not have gone better for Tehran. The Americans and the potent Saudi Air Force had yet to intervene. That could change. But at present there was a power vacuum, and President Montazeri was all too eager to fill it.

While seizing Bahrain was a critical step in Montazeri's quest to strangle the world's oil supply, it was only the latest action in a decade-long move to dominate the strategic points in the gulf. In 1994 Iran had purchased Kilo-class submarines from Russia, the first by a Persian Gulf country. The double-hulled vessels were equipped with six 533-mm launch tubes and a load of eighteen torpedoes. They represented a dangerous escalation in the Middle East arms race.

Now those subs were patrolling the waters just outside the Strait of Hormuz, off the coast of Oman, serving as a menace to shipping. And the tiny finger islands at the western mouth of the strait—Abu Musa and the Greater and Lesser Tumbs—were under Iran's firm control, occupied by three entrenched divisions of Iranian marines.

Iran and the UAE shared Abu Musa until 1991 when IRGC units seized control of the island, forcing local inhabitants to leave (only a small fishing village was allowed to remain). Construction of a series of fortifications and bunkers began in 1992. A year later Tehran had four thousand Iranian marines, Hawk anti-aircraft missiles, SA-6 SAMs, and 155-mm artillery pieces in place on the barren island. Iran also built underground missile batteries for HY-2 Silkworm and Scud-C missiles on the southwest tip of Abu Musa. Tehran could now hit targets anywhere in the strait.

The Silkworm, a small, slender Chinese-built cruise missile, poses an enormous threat to shipping (it is not unlike the French Exocet missile which struck the USS *Stark* in 1987). The radar-guided sea-skimming missile is a deadly equalizer, giving Iran's small navy a way to draw blood from much larger, better-equipped forces, including the U.S. Navy. Almost impossible to detect, the Silkworm closes in on targets at near-supersonic speeds and projects a cross section the size of a seagull on radar. Once it finds its target, it can inflict serious damage with its payload of two hundred pounds

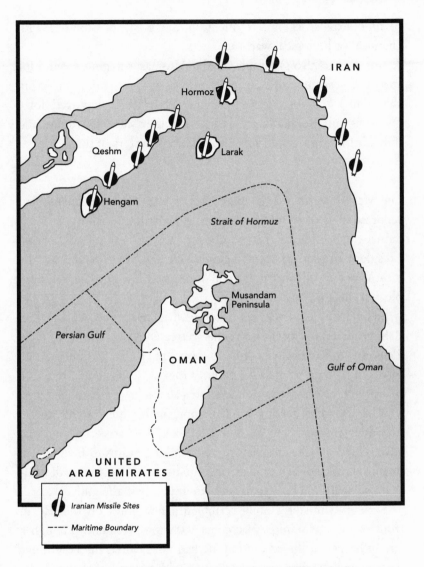

Iran's Stranglehold on the Gulf

of high explosives, not to mention the grisly possibilities with chemical or biological warheads.

But Tehran also saw value in Abu Musa as a staging ground for speedboats armed with antitank-guided weapons (for puncturing ship hulls) and recoilless launchers. The IRGC deployed forty Swedish-built Boghammar Marin boats that were fast, agile, and difficult for large vessels to spot in the blue waters of the gulf.

On May 7 at an NDC meeting Defense Minister Shamkhani reported the latest intelligence from Bahrain. Speaking in long, drawn-out sentences, his pomposity was something to behold. President Montazeri seemed bored. He was there to discuss the future, not dwell on the past. Bahrain was but another building block in his growing empire.

Shamkhani, however, continued. Little resistance remained in Bahrain. Bahraini forces had either retreated across the King Fahd Causeway to Saudi Arabia or had surrendered to IRGC forces. Shiite forces in Bahrain wanted the country to seek admission to Iran as a new province. President Montazeri was all too happy to oblige them.

After Shamkhani's long-winded report on the situation in Bahrain, President Montazeri spoke in a calm, confident voice. "Our forces have achieved a glorious victory, and our long claims to Bahrain can finally be realized. With the expectation that the Americans will withdraw, we will soon be able to act with impunity in the gulf."

Foreign Minister Habibi scribbled a few notes on the pad in front of him, avoiding eye contact with the president. Though a strong backer of the revolution, he had not favored the bold move that Shamkhani had conceived. And with victory in Bahrain, he feared success would breed overconfidence which would only lead to recklessness and then disaster. "What about the Saudis?" he asked Montazeri.

The president looked a little irritated. "Their forces have mobilized, but they have not engaged our forces. Nor are they likely to. Riyadh does not wish to go to war with us."

Habibi persisted with his skepticism. "Have we heard anything from Washington... concerning our demands?"

"No," snapped Montazeri, his irritation yielding to anger with the apparent dissenter on his council. "This is undoubtedly an embarrassment for them. I am absolutely certain that they will comply. What is their alternative?"

Habibi shook his head. "I'm not sure, Mr. President. But it seems unlikely that the Americans would back down in this situation."

The president stood up in disgust as if the celebratory meeting he envisioned had been clouded by the vexing concerns of his foreign minister. "You fool! They have no alternative!" His arms moved in bold gestures like a symphony conductor during a performance. "We have created a weapon they have no defense against. We can bring fire down on Rome, Berlin, Paris, any target in Europe of our choosing! Their hands are tied. Washington knows that they must comply. They will not allow this to happen."

Montazeri settled back into his chair and calmed himself, as if the allowed time for emotion was over. "It is time to chart the path ahead. We must now contemplate our next move. Once the Americans are out of the way, we will have only the Saudis to contend with. And despite their military might, the royal family has built its kingdom on a foundation of sand."

Defense Minister Shamkhani passed out a file to the group. It was an eight-page document drafted by his general staff. "This is our next proposed move."

The plan called for a series of bold strikes on the tiny but oil-rich emirates lining the gulf just off the coast of Saudi Arabia and Oman. The UAE was a loose confederation of states developed in 1971. Abu Dhabi and Dubai were the most enticing targets. They had huge oil reserves but were politically weak. Although the combined armed forces of these two small states numbered forty-five thousand, some 50 percent of the troops were not UAE citizens but rather Omanis, Pakistanis, and Europeans. How reliable they would be under fire remained to be seen. And while their weaponry was advanced, their forces lacked the technical competence to employ these systems to maximum potential.

Abu Dhabi had structured its forces into one armored, one mechanized, and one guard brigade while Dubai had its own mechanized brigade. The attacks on these states, commencing with a series of missile strikes followed by terrorist strikes, would be unconventional and, therefore, difficult for UAE forces to deal with. Once chaos loomed, an assault by IRGC forces would follow. It would be a repeat of the victory in Bahrain. President Montazeri and the NDC embraced the plan immediately. Habibi was the lone dissenter.

In Washington, a worried president sat behind his desk in the Oval Office staring out onto the Rose Garden. Outside it was raining heavily, and the drumming sound of the water broke the unusual silence inside.

With the St. John administration painted into a corner, the president's closest advisors were thin on advice. The CIA had only months earlier reported that Tehran was still three to five years away from building the bomb. The president rubbed the stiff chords running down the back of his neck. "What does intelligence tell us about the Iranian nuclear program?"

CIA Director Mark Unruh fidgeted in his chair. "Well, Mr. President, we have been able to pull together quite a bit on their capabilities and the location of their manufacturing facilities. But most has been culled from satellite intelligence. We have very little HUMINT [human intelligence] concerning Iran, so our knowledge is limited."

"What about our allies? Do they have anything?"

Unruh shook his head. "Mr. President, I've been in communication with Paris, Berlin, London, Moscow, and Tel Aviv. They don't know much more than we do."

"What about their launch sites? Could we take them out?"

There was a long pause. "It's doubtful, Mr. President. Tehran has a mobile-launch capability. And even if we did know the location of

their launch sites, they could be moved. This reminds me of looking for the Scuds during the Gulf War in 1991—but worse. Iran is
a country the size of the United States from the Rockies to the West
Coast. And obviously if we don't get them all—we're sunk."

The president remained somber, swimming in a pool of nervous
emotions. He turned to his defense secretary. "Can we concentrate
enough firepower to hit every conceivable target?"

"Mr. President, it's a little like shooting at a snake in the tall
grass. The more shots you get off the better, but if you have no idea
where it is you have small chance of hitting it."

"Tom, are you suggesting that we comply with their demands?"

Bodine paused to gather himself. "Unless we are prepared to go
nuclear, we cannot know with a certainty that all their launchers will
be taken out. Only if we flattened the country would we be certain."

The president rubbed his forehead. "What are we talking about
if we evacuate?"

"If we pull back," warned Jack Fowler, "the ramifications could be
profound. By virtue of blackmail, Iran will gain a free hand in the Persian Gulf region, a stranglehold on the Strait of Hormuz, and de facto
hegemony over the entire region. The moderate Arab states—should
they survive—will be forced to acquiesce and follow Iran's lead in a
robust, anti-Western bloc. Mr. President, are we ready for ten years
of gas lines, hyperinflation, and unemployment? The markets point
to oil at maybe $100 dollars a barrel during the next six months."

"What about the Saudis? Can't they handle Iran?"

"They simply don't have the population base or military size to
stand up to Tehran alone," cautioned Bodine. "And that is precisely
what we would be asking them to do."

Secretary of State Vaughn Brown wanted to pull U.S. forces out
of the region and try to negotiate a settlement with Iran. To Brown,
a scion of a New England banking family and lifelong business
executive, negotiations were deal-making and everyone had their
price. He likened the Montazeri government to the United Auto
Workers, with whom he had squabbled for decades as head of one
of the Big Three. "If we can give them what they want and live with

it, let's cut our losses. We should negotiate a deal to guarantee access to the gulf."

Fowler didn't like the idea of backing down. "What if they're bluffing?"

The president stood and looked out the window at the gray day, thinking about the sense of relief he would have if he were on the outside looking in. He turned again to his secretary of defense. "What if they aren't?" he asked as he turned from the window and returned to his desk. "I don't want to go down in history as the president who allowed Berlin, Rome, or Paris to be hit by a nuclear strike. I want the CIA to get everything it can on the location of those launch sites. In the meantime, Tom, prepare our forces for an immediate evacuation from the gulf."

Bodine felt weak, as if the weight of the problem was sitting on his chest. "All right, Mr. President. May I suggest that we at least draw up a target list of nuclear facilities and probable launch sites in Iran?"

"Yes, of course."

The meeting broke up, and on his way out Bodine turned to the president. "Sir, I think we also need to be prepared for more such demands. Giving into blackmailers only breeds more acts of blackmail." The president simply nodded as he was left alone in his office.

News of the American pullback from the gulf left the Saudi government feeling vulnerable, even naked. In Riyadh, government ministers realized they would have to face the Iranian juggernaut alone. Sensing the need for a steady hand and real experience in the armed forces, Prince Abudulillah once again took command of the RSAF in addition to staying on as oil minister.

Abudulillah knew full well that Iran would eventually turn and attack the Saudi peninsula. But he also knew that the RSAF's power was unmatched in the gulf. He went to the king and requested authority to strike Iranian military units moving on countries along the southern rim of the gulf. The king agreed. A state of war would soon exist between Saudi Arabia and Iran.

The prince gave strict orders to his pilots to engage Iranian forces on sight. The first air battle took place only a few hours later, just north of Bahrain. Eight Saudi F-15s detected on radar a squadron of Iranian MiG-29s escorting three military transports which were to resupply the IRGC 1st Division. Barely thirty miles south of the Iranian force, the Saudi pilots struck first. It was a devastating blow. The MiGs plunged to the sea, followed by one transport. The brief exchange instantly changed the complexion of the Persian Gulf crisis.

Within days, Prince Abudulillah had complete mastery of the skies. The Iranian pilots were poorly trained, and their Russian fighters were no match for the avionics of the RSAF F-15s, F-18s, and F-16s. The bold move by Riyadh thwarted Iran's plans to strike the UAE. The Saudi rules of engagement were made clear to Tehran: Iranian ships and air transports were in peril if they dared venture across the 25th parallel which divided the gulf.

On May 14 President Montazeri convened a special meeting of the NDC to discuss a countermove. Tehran's strategic position had improved considerably during the past thirty days. Despite Saudi intransigence, the Americans had made clear their intention to leave the gulf, and a large number of forces were already retreating to Diego Garcia. Still, the mood in the room was an explosive concoction of anger and vehemence. As long as Saudi aircraft operated south of the 25th parallel, Tehran's move on the UAE would be checked.

Montazeri was pacing when the meeting started. "We must strike a decisive blow to take control of the gulf as soon as the Americans have left," he told his advisors. "We must take this war to Saudi Arabia itself." It was a puzzling statement. If Iranian forces could not reach the UAE, how would they ever threaten the Saudi peninsula?

There was a new face at the NDC meeting—Intelligence Director Muhsin Reza'i. As head of the dreaded VEVAK, the Ministry of Intelligence and Internal Security, Reza'i cast a dark shadow wherever he appeared. Even the members of the NDC were back on their heels in his presence. Reza'i was a mysterious figure, largely unknown to most of the council. He kept to himself. Strong and heavily built, his shoulders and chest were very broad and his body perfectly proportioned from top to toe. He entered the room with a stiff stride, his neck poked forward. He had a handsome, fresh-complexioned face with remarkably large eyes. The myth was that he possessed the unusual power of seeing in the dark. And his enormous hands were rumored to be so strong that he could poke a finger through a sound, newly plucked apple or into the skull of a boy or young man.

For the past twelve years, Reza'i, a committed revolutionary with real-world terrorist experience, had been laboring quietly to extend VEVAK beyond a capacity for "internal security." His task was to construct a "chain of fire" that would span the entire world. Each link in the chain was a terrorist cell—organized, trained, and equipped by Tehran—that could be mobilized in an instant. For two years Reza'i worked with the terrorist organization Hizbollah at a base in Biqaa, Lebanon. Almost at once he gained a reputation for possessing a unique brutality carried out with indifference. He soon was given responsibility for internal security at the Hizbollah camp and regularly purged the organization of those he deemed unreliable.

The intelligence chief had built his chain by linking preexisting terrorist groups with those he constructed himself. In early 1984, Ayatollah Khomeini established an "independent brigade for carrying out unconventional warfare in every territory." It was another label for terrorist cells, which included a group of suicide fighters called the *Isargaran* (Lovers of Martyrdom). By the mid-1980s, Iran established a set of institutions to conduct infiltration operations against Moslem communities in the West.

Reza'i asserted Iran's control over the existing international terror network in February 1993 when Iranian intelligence officials and three hundred senior terrorist commanders met in Tehran to formulate and define the grand strategy for Iranian-sponsored international terrorism. Many of the terrorist leaders in attendance were friends of the VEVAK chief or old colleagues.

As Reza'i sat down, every member of the NDC took special care to show the greatest respect and decorum. He undoubtedly had a file on each of them, and his sadism was not something to tempt. As he spoke, his mouth was barely visible, covered by a thick brush of heavy beard. "The cells are organized in such a fashion that they can work quite independently of each other. This is to maintain operational security. Members of these units are young and eager but well-trained. On the Saudi peninsula we have a dozen such cells, well-placed and prepared to be martyrs for the cause of Islam."

President Montazeri sat emotionless at the end of the table. "Mr. Reza'i, you have done a great service for our cause. You have provided us with a weapon that can overcome the temporary advantage the Saudis have in the air. These cells must be activated at once, and I want you to take personal responsibility for managing these assets. Our uncounted legions will change the shape and dimension of this war."

Reza'i nodded without uttering a word. He had been away from the ramparts of the terrorist movement for too long and was now set to return to the invisible battlefield in which he felt so at home.

On June 4 the first in a series of powerful car bombs shook the business center of Riyadh. An RSAF office was the first to be hit, a symbolic target demonstrating Tehran's stubborn defiance. The immense concrete and stone structure totally collapsed. Prince Abudulillah was not in the building, but two trusted aides who had trained with him at Sandhurst were not as fortunate.

When news of the bomb reached Saudi ministers, they knew at once who was responsible. In the hours after the explosion, investigators at the scene determined that the culprits used a highly sophisticated device and had inside help. High-quality hexogene and the plastic explosive pentaerythritol tetra nitrate (PTN) were used to achieve an enhanced-blast effect. The bomb used composite-shaped charges to direct the enhanced blast and maximize their impact on the structure. Placed in the back of a Mercedes truck, the bomb consisted of 300 kilograms of hexogene reinforced by PTN. It was a device remarkably similar to the one used in 1983 to kill 245 U.S. Marines in Beirut, Lebanon. The truck reportedly had possessed RSAF credentials and had slipped through the security gate. Several security personnel were now missing and presumed to have fled the country.

Two days after forty-two died in the RSAF building in Riyadh, the main building of the Saudi Oil Ministry was hit, this time by a small red Mercedes truck driven at high speed toward the front entrance. The bomb ignited on impact, leaving an enormous crater. It was expertly made from composition: a delicate combination of 60 percent RDX hexogene, 39 percent strengthened PTN, and a fine wax used to coat and stabilize the sophisticated contours of the charge to enhance the blast. Ninety-four died.

Bombings in Saudi Arabia became a regular occurrence throughout the first two weeks of June, culminating with a spectacular attack on the main Saudi oil refinery, Ras Tannurah. In the early morning hours of June 11, an unmarked Pilatus PC-7 aircraft took off from Shahid Chamran air base in Bushehr, Iran, and flew south for the Saudi peninsula. At the controls was Hani Hassan, a Pasadaran pilot trained by VEVAK for suicide missions. Possessing a fanatical devotion to the revolutionary cause, Hassan had been recruited by the service in 1992 while still a university student. He then underwent rigorous psychological training at a VEVAK facility outside of Mashhad, a city near the Turkmenian border. Using isolation and sleep deprivation, VEVAK commanders were able to brainwash Hani Hassan and two dozen others to be suicide pilots. When they left the facility in 1993, the young men were psychologically equipped to serve as kamikaze pilots. From Mashhad they were taken to Won San air base in North Korea to be trained under the supervision of Korean instructors for suicide missions. Hassan and has classmates returned to Iran in the spring of 1996.

On his mission to Ras Tannurah, Hassan carried out his orders with robotic precision. He flew the PC-7 low over the gulf, just several hundred feet above the water. While Saudi Air Defense Systems detected a weak signal, RSAF assets were concentrated in

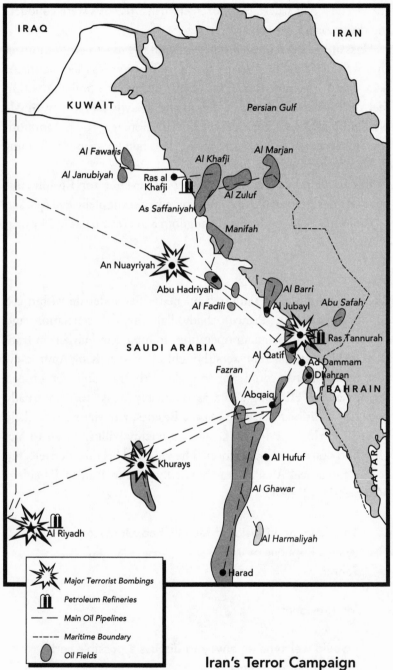

Iran's Terror Campaign

Legend:
- Major Terrorist Bombings
- Petroleum Refineries
- Main Oil Pipelines
- Maritime Boundary
- Oil Fields

the western gulf where two dozen Iranian MiG-29s were conducting diversionary exercises.

Hassan had been briefed repeatedly on the exact point of impact that would maximize damage to the refinery at Ras Tannurah. At 4:11 A.M. he slammed the PC-7 into the massive building within feet of his instructed target. The plane, heavily laden with SEMTEX and RDX hexogene, set off an explosion, igniting a mammoth fire storm which burned for weeks. The flames were visible hundreds of miles from the port.

Ras Tannurah was a major source of revenue for Riyadh. But with one devastating blow, a single man in a scant plane had sparked an economic crisis in the Saudi kingdom and created panic on world oil markets.

The bombing of Ras Tannurah opened a fierce debate within the Saudi government. Prince Abudulillah favored retaliation and wanted to expand Saudi air operations to hit ground targets in Iran. But the king and his ministers thought otherwise. King Amir knew that Saudi Arabia could not grapple with Iran and her unseen legions alone. His kingdom was politically weak, torn internally between traditionalists and radicals. Besides, any victory was likely to be a pyrrhic one in the face of an enemy willing to go to any length to destroy the opposition. The king and his ministers elected to sue for peace. A cable was hurriedly sent to Iranian President Montazeri on June 12.

> The Esteemed President Muhammad Montazeri
> Islamic Republic of Iran
> Tehran
>
> Mr. President:
>
> I would welcome an envoy to discuss a possible settlement of our differences.

Sincerely,
King Amir ibn Abd Abdul Rahman
Kingdom of Saudi Arabia

Two days later, President Montazeri dispatched Ayatollah Morteza'i to Riyadh for consultations. The fact that Foreign Minister Habibi was not handling the mission was a sign of how uncompromising the Iranian position was. Morteza'i had particular disdain for the Saudi royal family. His fervent brand of Islam allowed no room for moderation. Veering from his well-defined, theological path was heresy, and the Saudis, who held the keys to Mecca, were in his mind the most blatant heretics.

Ayatollah Morteza'i arrived at the Royal Palace with two aides. Once in the presence of the king, the modestly dressed ayatollah dispensed with any diplomatic niceties. "My government is not here to negotiate," he informed the king and Prince Abudulillah, who was also present. "We are here simply to make our demands known, and you may choose to either abide by them or reject them. If you choose the latter, you will continue to pay the price for your intransigence."

The prince rose suddenly as fury swelled inside him. "These sorts of insults are barbaric and will not be tolerated!" he shouted, his eyes piercing the surprised cleric.

The ayatollah immediately collected his papers and began to leave, but King Amir hastily intervened. "Sit down, nephew." He turned to Morteza'i. "Tell me your terms, but please refrain from the insults."

The ayatollah returned to his chair and motioned to his aides, who handed two sets of papers to the king and Abudulillah.

Conditions for the Cessation of Hostilities Between the Kingdom of Saudi Arabia and the Republic of Iran

1. Immediate halt to all Saudi air operations over the Persian Gulf and Saudi Arabia proper;

2. Removal of Saudi naval forces from the Persian Gulf for redeployment to the Red Sea; and

3. Saudi oil pricing and production policies in conformity with the wishes of the Iranian government.

King Amir read the demands with interest, concealing his distress. After he digested the proposal, he set the paper aside and folded his hands. "I will need time to consult with my advisors."

Ayatollah Morteza'i nodded and stood from his chair. "Of course." He gestured for his aides to exit and then collected his own papers. "My government will give you twenty-four hours, at which time this current cease-fire will be presumed null and void." He momentarily scowled at the prince and then departed. As the door closed behind him, Abudulillah got up and walked to his uncle's side. "Uncle, may I be frank with you?"

The king smiled, "Yes, you may."

Abudulillah tried to remain respectful. "We must not do this. These terms are unacceptable."

The heavyset king stood and looked again at the demands. "They are not palatable, that is true, but it might have been worse."

"Uncle, they will not allow us to fly our planes over our own territory. They wish to determine where we might put our ships, and they want to dictate our oil policies to us!"

The king began walking slowly toward the large, ornate mahogany doors. The wear on his seventy-four-year-old frame was apparent as he labored with each step. His health had been poor for years. "You may be right, nephew. But with the Americans out of the gulf, we must adjust to the new realities. We are a country of only a few million, and we cannot stand against the might of Iran alone. This agreement might at least save the kingdom or buy us some time."

Abudulillah shook his head. "Tehran cannot be trusted. You know that once they have solidified their hold on Bahrain and the Emirates, their appetite will only grow. They mean to bring us all under their control."

The king did not answer but instead headed to an appointment with his physical therapist. He would meet that evening with his ministers to make the fateful choice.

Chapter Eleven

June 14
the Persian Gulf

Word that Saudi Arabia had acquiesced to Iran's demands sent a cold chill over world financial markets. By the afternoon of June 13, oil futures on the Chicago commodities market jumped to $100 a barrel, setting off a chain reaction, and the New York Stock Exchange (NYSE) plunged nearly one thousand points. The Nikkei Index in Japan dropped 15 percent, and exchanges in Frankfurt and London also went into a virtual free fall. The markets were reacting to Montazeri's so far successful gambit: Tehran was steadily taking command of Mideast oil.

With Saudi pilots grounded, the Iranian offensive against the UAE began anew. Iranian Backfire bombers struck a variety of land targets in Dubai and Abu Dhabi, despite taking casualties from UAE fighters. On June 15 King Abd Allah ibn Al Thani, the nominal head of the UAE, fled his palace for the security of Oman. When IRGC forces landed in Dubai and Abu Dhabi on June 16, they met surprisingly strong resistance from UAE ground forces. The outnumbered UAE troops, however, could not sustain their defensive perimeter for long, surrendering on June 20.

The campaign in the Emirates also brought Tehran its first heavy war casualties. Thirteen hundred from the IRGC 3rd and 4th Divisions were dead and more than 2,100 wounded. Five MiGs had either been shot down or had crashed. But control of the UAE left Iran with control of a significant portion of world oil reserves and the right to control the price of Saudi crude. And Tehran was one step closer in their quest for dominion in the gulf.

By the end of June, the last U.S. forces were out of the region, evacuated by the U.S. 7th Fleet and redeployed to Diego Garcia or the Mediterranean. As the last U.S. Navy ships passed through the strait and into the Gulf of Oman, Iran became indisputably the dominant power in the region.

President Montazeri sat in his usual chair at the end of the conference table on the morning of June 20. The full Defense Council was present, as was VEVAK Director Reza'i. Montazeri had addressed the nation on television the prior evening, proclaiming that a *Ummah* was at hand. But there was still a great deal of work to be done. The next demonstration of Tehran's power would be to exert authority over the sea lanes to the gulf. The critical choke point was the Strait of Hormuz, a waterway only 29 miles wide with an average depth of just 229 feet. Nearly one-half of the world's oil supply was transported through the narrow channel, and Montazeri knew that he had the raw power to control the strait. The coast of Iran bristled with a vast array of missiles and fast patrol boats. And with troops dispersed throughout the islands of Abu Musa, Sirri, Queshem, Khark, Kharku, Larak, Hengam, and the Greater and Lesser Tumbs, closing the strait would not be difficult.

As the meeting began, Montazeri seemed particularly jovial. He had always harbored deep, inner doubts about whether the Americans would retreat. Only now did he realize what he had accomplished. "We have unmatched power in the region. But we must harness this power to serve our ends. If we wish to dictate to world oil markets, we must move at once to exercise authority over the strait. I have asked Defense Minister Akhar Shamkhani to prepare an action plan for the National Defense Council on this matter." The executive summary read:

Closure of the Strait: An Operational Plan
Ministry of Defense June 14, 1999

Our sovereign control over the gulf can best be demonstrated through blockage of the strait. We suggest the
seizure of Kuwaiti oil tankers as an initial step to demonstrate our power. We might also consider enforcing a tax
on those who transit this waterway. The use of Iranian
destroyers and small attack craft, supported by land-
based missiles, should serve as sufficient force to achieve
such a result. This operation should culminate with an
announcement by the president that the strait is not an
international waterway, but part of the territorial waters
of the Republic of Iran.

Foreign Minister Habibi was the only objector, making his case in
his typical, dismal fashion. The rest of the council adopted the
provocative plan uncritically.

On June 22, just off the north coast of Abu Musa, an IRGC attack
craft fired a warning shot across the bow of a Kuwaiti tanker, forcing
the captain to bring the massive vessel to a halt. Iranian special forces
stormed the ship. Once in control of the tanker, Tehran insisted that
Kuwait pay a "tax" for transporting goods across Iranian waters.

News of the seizure led President St. John to convene an emergency meeting of the NSC. He sat stoically at the head of the dark
cherry table in the White House Situation Room, hoping that a
solution might present itself. Since the crisis had begun, the CIA,
NSA, and Defense Intelligence Agency (DIA) had devoted considerable resources to uncovering any information pertaining to the
Iranian missile program. Collaboration with the Israeli Mossad did
yield some results—analysts identified what they believed to be one
or possibly two launch sites southeast of Tehran. But the overall picture was still sketchy.

"Do we have enough to go on?" the president asked Defense
Secretary Bodine.

"We can't know for certain. What we lack is HUMINT, which tells us intentions, capabilities, and the current status of their forces. Satellites can tell us only so much. And while time helps us to get a clearer picture, the picture is likely to remain incomplete."

"What do you recommend, Tom?"

"Mr. President, this most recent move should be only further evidence that there is no limit to Iran's demands. Forcing our retreat from the gulf was not the end of their demands but just the beginning. Their ambitions go far beyond what they have achieved thus far."

By now St. John understood well his defense secretary's position. He might be right, the president thought to himself. But what about alternatives? He turned to his secretary of state. "What do our allies say? Can we do anything up in New York at the United Nations?"

Although Vaughn Brown looked taken off guard, he nonetheless seemed unenthusiastic about what he had to offer. "Mr. President, Europe is screaming that some action be taken, although what sort of action they don't seem to say. We have been working at the United Nations on a resolution condemning these actions. Whether it has any effect on Tehran is another question."

St. John casually flipped his tie with his fingers. "Go ahead and proceed on that front. In the meantime, I want more intelligence before we consider any military action. We need more time." He then turned to his secretary of defense. "Tom, draw up several contingencies. We can't have the Iranians forcing people to pay tolls to go through an international waterway. This is not the New Jersey Turnpike."

Tehran's latest move went beyond asserting sovereignty over the strait. On June 23 in his ornate offices outside Riyadh, Prince Abudulillah received a visit from Iranian Oil Minister Hushang Akbar Mohtashemi. The visit concerned oil pricing and production policies. It was nearly impossible for the prince to retain his civility during the two-hour session. His last meeting with Mohtashemi had been at the fateful April OPEC summit in Geneva when he had felt compelled to leave. Now here was Mohtashemi, issuing orders like a bullying schoolmaster. The vainglorious condescension was insufferable.

"Saudi oil production will be reduced by one-third. This will be in part offset by a price increase of five dollars per barrel. We expect these new figures to be in effect by August first." It was a towering demand which would cut heavily into Saudi Arabia's market share. The king had given Abudulillah strict instructions to comply with Tehran's demands, so he nodded politely at Mohtashemi—what else could he do?

Moments after the oil minister left, the prince placed a direct call to Tom Bodine at the Pentagon in Washington. Dispirited, he sought out the ear of an old friend. The two had become quite close years ago when Abudulillah ran the Saudi air force and Bodine served as secretary of the U.S. Air Force. He was one man the prince knew who would be forthcoming and frank.

"Prince Abudulillah, what a pleasant surprise."

"Mr. Secretary," he began in a forced but upbeat tone, "I hope that you and your family are well."

"Yes, very well, thank you. And you?"

Abudulillah paused. He had never been a good liar and saw no reason to start. "Tom, I was wondering if we might meet in private. I come to you as a friend, not as a representative of my government."

While Bodine tried to read the signals, he was confused. "Yes... of course. Come to Washington. You know that I will be as discreet as possible."

"Yes. There must be no knowledge of this."

"Very well. I will make the arrangements right away."

The next morning Prince Abudulillah flew to an American air base in Turkey. There he boarded a transport plane for a fourteen-hour flight to the States, landing at Pope Air Force Base in North Carolina. On the tarmac, he was transferred to a small jet destined for Dulles Airport just outside of Washington.

The defense secretary finally saw him on the night of June 24 at a private home in McLean, Virginia. While the prince appeared weary and tired at first glance, he seemed to be rejuvenated when they greeted each other.

Abudulillah wasted little time on surface issues. Worried that his country would succumb to Iran within the next six months, he sought solace from his friend. "We are in a very dangerous position. If America does not confront Iran soon, the entire peninsula will fall under their sway."

Bodine nodded. "I understand, Abudulillah. But you must recognize our predicament. I have pushed for a firm policy, but the existence of Iran's nuclear force makes such a policy problematic and risky. The president does not favor confrontation at this time."

Abudulillah did not hear anything that surprised him. Yet, he persisted. "Tom, I understand these realities. But you also know that two-thirds of the world's proven oil reserves are located in the five littoral countries of the gulf, and Tehran's position will only strengthen with time. Right now their nuclear force is small. But we both know that it will grow in the months ahead."

Bodine circled the French sofa in the sitting room, swirling the club soda in his glass. He knew that the administration faced a classic Hobson's Choice: there were no good alternatives. "Abudulillah, we cannot change U.S. policy at this point. But what we can do is lay the groundwork for cooperation if and when war does come."

"Go on."

"We will need complete access to your airfields and a plentiful supply of fuel."

"Done."

"We will also need to consider the Air Tasking Orders [ATOs] for any probable air campaign over Iran. Our boys at the U.S. Central Command Air Forces [USCENTAF] could work with your people."

"Agreed."

They shared a private dinner, and Bodine left around midnight. The prince spent a restless night at the house before returning to Riyadh by the same, circumscribed route the next day.

Diplomatic efforts by Washington failed to temper Iran's aggressive moves. Despite passing a UN Resolution on July 1 condemning Iran's "acts of piracy on the high seas," IRGC units in speedboats and helicopters began boarding every merchant ship and oil tanker seeking passage through the strait, strangling ship traffic. On July 12, a French destroyer and an IRGC attack boat exchanged fire in the Gulf of Oman. A dozen IRGC troops were killed. Paris insisted that the incident was an act of self-defense, but Tehran saw it otherwise. President Montazeri decided to retaliate. Two days later a tanker carrying crude for the French national oil company was fired on and seized. The crew, including a French captain, was imprisoned in the port city of Bandar-e Bushehr. Oil hit $105 a barrel.

For days, President St. John had a gnawing suspicion that war might be inevitable. He tried to bury it deep inside, but Iran's deliberate efforts to take control of the strait meant the crisis was escalating. Intelligence on Iranian missile sites continued to trickle in, but it added very little to the sketchy picture. On July 12 he met privately with Defense Secretary Bodine and National Security Adviser Fowler in the Oval Office. General Mark Chain, chairman of the Joint Chiefs, was also there. The Pentagon had drawn up several contingencies for eliminating Iranian nuclear sites. As the general laid out his plans for hitting Iranian missile sites, the president sat and listened intently. When Chain finished, St. John got up and paced for five minutes without saying a word. He then returned to his seat and crossed his legs. "General, tell me, what are the odds that we get all of their launchers?"

The general adjusted his wire-framed glasses and shifted in his chair. "That's difficult to say, sir. Iran is a large country. We have diverted satellites to give us better coverage in the area, but there is a sizeable risk that we won't find them all."

President St. John shook his head. "When we are talking about nuclear weapons, a sizeable risk makes me skittish. If they get just one off, it could mean hundreds of thousands of casualties. Can't we get any better intelligence?"

"Our intelligence deficiencies can't be corrected overnight, Mr. President. During the past five years we have made cuts in HUMINT, trying to rely instead on national technical means. A good HUMINT service takes years to develop. You need to hire good agents who must be trained and put in the field. And only then can the complex process of cultivating sources begin.

"The neglect has been a disgrace. We have thousands of chicken inspectors working for the USDA [United States Department of Agriculture], but hardly anyone is inspecting the nuclear missile sites of our enemies."

"Will more time make a difference?"

"Mr. President, the decision to retreat from the gulf was a sound one. It bought us precious time to better understand what we are up against. But time may now be working against us. Iran is likely to be producing more systems, and they seem to be getting more bold by the hour."

It was a nightmarish decision, but one that had to be made. St. John dropped his head and turned to Bodine. "Tom, put together what you need for the full implementation of these air strikes. And then await my word for the final go."

During the late night hours of July 14, U.S. Navy Captain Will Peters mindfully piloted the submarine USS *Corpus Christi* through the narrow, underwater confines of the Strait of Hormuz. He navigated the vessel with the delicacy of a surgeon and the precision of a diamond cutter. If the *Corpus Christi* were off course by even a few dozen feet, the massive craft might hit a sandbar and be detected, or worse, be forced to surface. The curvatures in the ocean floor and the jagged coastline made the harrowing task the most difficult that he had ever performed. The nail-biting journey through the strait took one hour. Once the *Corpus Christi* was through, the *Annapolis* and the *Los Angeles* followed.

As the drama below the placid waters of the gulf played out, an enormous collection of American planes was landing at several air bases in Turkey. U.S. Air Force technicians ran checks on American F-117s, F-15s, F-16s, A-10s, B-2s, and B-1s. The planes then took on fuel and ordnance while the pilots received a final briefing in the main bunker at the south end of the runway.

By 1:00 A.M. the final checks and been made, and the pilots had received their ATOs. Now all that remained was the final word from Washington. U.S. Air Force General James Durrance had been in Turkey for two weeks negotiating the use of facilities for possible air strikes on Iran. Although the logistical work had been tremendous, everything had seemingly fallen into place. Sitting in his spartan office, with his feet up on the desk, he placed a call to Fowler in Washington. After a few rings, Fowler snatched up the receiver.

"Everything is in place, Jack. We are just awaiting the go-ahead from you."

Fowler put the general on hold and turned to the president. "They are awaiting your go-ahead, Mr. President. Everything is in place."

The president had not slept much the previous four nights as U.S. forces had moved into place. He had dreaded this moment ever since he authorized the operation. The thought of a war with a nuclear foe made him shudder, particularly since no defense against the missiles existed. But after a momentary pause, he called in his personal secretary and signed the order authorizing the operation. He then took the phone from Fowler.

"General, we will proceed as planned. Commence air operations over Iran in two hours, and godspeed, Jim. We will all pray that they get every one of those launchers."

As the president rested the handset on the phone's cradle, he felt a strange and temporary sense of release. The decision had been made, the die cast. It was the right decision. But in a world of gray choices, it had become clear to him only at that moment.

St. John returned to his chair with some papers while Bodine placed a call to Prince Abudulillah at his home outside Riyadh. The defense secretary had wanted to involve the Saudis earlier, but maintaining operational security had made it impossible. The phone awakened the prince, who was fast asleep.

"Abudulillah, this is Tom Bodine."

The prince rubbed his eyes and collected himself quickly. "Yes, Tom."

"We will be striking targets in Iran two hours from now. We're ready to go, and we would like your pilots to carry out their missions."

By now the prince was standing at his bedside. "I reviewed the ATOs yesterday, and we are ready to proceed."

"Abudulillah, we would also like to begin basing aircraft in your country."

"The bases are ready, as we agreed." The prince paused. "Tom, you made the only correct decision."

Bodine let out a tight sigh, "I hope so."

The USS *Corpus Christi, Annapolis,* and *Los Angeles* soon received word that the operation was a go. The Tomahawk cruise missiles were removed from their storage racks and placed in the launch tubes. Targeting data was relayed to the fire-control officers aboard the submarines via the very low frequency (VLF) satellite uplink with naval officials in Norfolk, Virginia. The targets were chosen and plotted based on the latest satellite intelligence—accuracy was critical. The Tomahawks were expected to take out several important, fixed targets, including Iran's missile command center just west of the ancient city of Qom. If the Iranian command control and communication facilities could be destroyed, perhaps a launch could be prevented.

Once the launch sequencing was programmed into the weapons' computers, the countdown for launch began. Shortly after 3:30 A.M., the Tomahawks burst forth from the ocean surface. Each slender, 21-foot missile unfolded a pair of stubby wings and powered up a kerosene-fueled, pint-sized motor. The 600-pound thrust turbojet engine would push the missile through the air at a subsonic speed of 550 miles per hour. Proceeding inland, the more than two dozen missiles began to bob and weave from side to side as they crossed the shoreline. The Tomahawk guidance system employed a radar altimeter to sample the lay of the land through terrain contour mapping. The digital scene-matching area correlation (DSMAC) then compared what it was seeing with internal reference maps containing topographic scenes gathered by spy satellites.

The tail fins shifted occasionally to make period-course corrections and to match their actual height above the ground with that of the stored terrain scenes in the on-board computer. Skimming the earth's surface at less than one hundred feet, the Tomahawks slinked under Iranian radar and past the numerous air defense sites.

As each Tomahawk approached its target one hour after launch, the strobe light on the nose cone flashed, illuminating the dark scene ahead. The small, digital camera scanned the facility instantaneously, and the guidance system aligned the camera's field of view with a photo image of the target in its memory. In the last few seconds of flight, the missile's trajectory was refined. Each landed a near perfect blow. The one thousand–pound, high-explosive Bullpup warheads rocked their targets, shaking the concrete foundations.

From his F-117A stealth fighter, Colonel George Rudd could see the fires outside Qom as his strike team moved toward their targets deep inside Iran. The F-117A fighter squadron came like a thief in the night. The pilots looked through the darkness and sighted their targets with the help of extremely accurate inertial navigation systems (INS) and a forward-looking infrared (FLIR) device. The FLIR cast a surprisingly bright heat-signature image of the enemy units below on an HUD in the cockpit. As they eyed their targets, the pilots released two thousand–pound GBU-24 smart bombs which used laser-seeking noses, guidance electronics, and movable fins to glide toward the laser light reflecting from the illuminated points on the launch sites below. As the aircraft moved away from their targets, the pilots switched from the FLIR to an underbelly-mounted downward-looking infrared system that let them keep the bomb on course while veering away from surrounding air defenses. As Colonel Rudd banked his black, triangular plane north for the return flight to Turkey, two more attack groups were pounding other probable missile sites nearby.

The Allied Attack Begins

The Tomahawks and stealth fighters, invisible killers that could get into Iran undetected, were only the first wave of the attack. Once they landed the initial blow, a mass of other planes closed in to sustain the assault.

A crafty, visible squadron of F-4Gs were the first nonstealth planes over Iran, flying at high altitude and hoping to be detected by air defense systems. The Wild Weasel crews consisted of seasoned pilots and backseat electronic warfare officers (EWOs), or bears.

Using APR38 radar-detection and homing systems, each Weasel purposely flew near known Iranian SAM sites. Fed with signals harvested by fifty-two antennae sprouting from the aircraft's fuselage, wings, and tail, a black box identified and displayed the locations and types of radar in the area while simultaneously determining which posed the greatest danger. The pilots flew provocatively over the SAM sites, goading the SAM crews into turning on their radar. As they were clicked on, the Wild Weasel pilots released their AGM-88 high-speed antiradiation missiles (HARMs). Once they locked onto the enemy's radar microwave radiation, the HARMs sped toward the antennae, demolishing them with fragmentation warheads.

A few SAM operators did manage to get missiles off, forcing the EWOs to use all the defenses available. The electronic countermeasure (ECM) pods muddied the airplane radar image, and dispensers loaded with tinsel-like chaff were opened. In the front seat, the pilots snapped their jets through missile-dodging maneuvers that would make even seasoned pilots nauseous.

After clearing the air corridor around Tehran and Qom, a plethora of U.S. attack aircraft descended on Iran. B-1 and B-52 bombers from Diego Garcia and Turkey dropped massive quantities of munitions on suspected Iranian missile sites. Meanwhile, Saudi pilots were hitting targets in the gulf and naval installations near Bandar-e Bushehr and Bandar Abbas. It was a desperate, nervous time for everyone. Failure to eliminate Iran's arsenal of nuclear weapons would spell disaster, so nothing was held back.

The air war had raged for more than two hours as Colonel Rudd was making his return flight to Turkey to refuel before flying another raid over Iran. With the lights of the airstrip in sight, he allowed his muscles to relax slightly, releasing some of the tension from his now-cramped body. But as he began his final approach to the main runway, a strange, bright light illuminated the skies above him. Like a shooting star, the object soared across the heavens from east to west. The glow so distracted him that he aborted the landing, choosing instead to make another pass. As he pulled the stick back, the plane started climbing. Curiously he looked upward and followed the light as it continued its path. A few seconds later, his curiosity gave way to horror. "Could it be?" he asked himself.

Twenty-two thousand miles above the equator two Defense Support Program (DSP) satellites in geostationary orbit were observing the object in flight. Infrared sensors had tracked a trail of hot gases as the object rose from the Iranian desert into the sky. Data concerning the rocket's trajectory were relayed to human controllers at the Air Force missile-tracking station in Cheyenne Mountain near Colorado Springs, Colorado, as computers calculated where the missile would land.

Chapter Twelve

July 15
the Iranian desert

It seemed all Italy was sleeping that horrific night when the Italian city of Monza became ground zero of a nuclear nightmare. Technicians in the Iranian desert had followed President Montazeri's orders to launch a Zulfiquar missile at Rome. Relying on incomplete navigational data and an inaccurate navigational system, Rome was spared, but Monza was obliterated. The airburst created an intense blast and suffocating heat, with flash burns causing the most casualties.

News of the nuclear strike made pressing the air war and finding

the remaining launchers all the more important. Satellite and electronic intelligence had failed to locate the entire nuclear arsenal.
Although U.S. pilots had reported direct hits on three launchers,
there had obviously been more. And the ghastly fact was that as
long as Iran's launch capability remained intact, another strike could
occur at any time.

Pilots were dispatched immediately to the area where DSP satellites first detected the launch. A high-stakes game of cat-and-mouse
began. In the clear, dark, early morning skies over central Iran,
American fighters began the desperate search for any sign of Iranian launchers.

Northwest of the Iranian city of Esfahan, Colonel Rudd located
what appeared to be a convoy of heavy-tracked vehicles moving
north. Rudd piloted his F-117A low over the ground and tried to
get a closer look. Using his infrared scope, he saw heavy military
vehicles, perhaps twenty-five or thirty, moving on a dirt road in the
cool twilight. As he made his first pass, he banked over the desolate
plateau and radioed his position to the electronic surveillance aircraft in the area. By now the sun was peaking over the mountains
and visibility was gradually improving. On his second pass, Rudd
saw it—an enormous, oblong, wheeled vehicle with a retractable
launching mechanism. Its configuration conformed to the photos
he had been shown in the preflight briefing: it had to be the Zulfiquar launcher.

Rudd radioed for immediate support. "Scorpion One, this is
Bravo One, over."

"Scorpion One here, go ahead."

"The rat is in sight. I repeat, we have the rat in sight, over."

"Great work, Bravo One. We are on the way, over."

Scorpion One was a squadron of B-2 bombers in a holding pattern
over Turkey. Word that a launcher had been located sent them
streaking eastward toward Iran. Each was loaded with massive
quantities of two thousand–pound bombs: they would make sure

An American B-1 bomber makes a run over the Iranian desert for a strike outside Esfahan.

nothing was left when they were finished. With F-15s in escort, the B-2s were on site within the hour. Each plane took a single pass, dropping their full complement of bombs on the convoy. When they departed, only large, burning carcasses of metal and steel remained on the ground.

Shortly after the warhead ignited over Monza, President St. John was alerted. He was resting at Camp David when he heard about the strike. The news sent a piercing pain through his body. It was unlike anything he would ever feel again in his lifetime. Within a single second, it was as if the screams of thousands were reverberating through his soul. He said nothing for ten minutes as a stream of tears ran down his cheeks.

At the 1:00 A.M. emergency meeting of the NSC, the despondent mood was only slightly broken with word that a launcher, presumed to be the only one remaining, had been identified and destroyed.

The president, who had just arrived from Camp David by *Marine Corps One*, looked worn and weary. Early reports from Italy estimated ten thousand dead, with twice as many facing the grisly realities of radiation sickness. A huge contingent of U.S. medic personnel was en route, but the drift of radiation would make most relief work impossible.

How to respond to the nuclear strike was on the forefront of the agenda. More than a few senior NSC staffers thought consideration should be given to a limited nuclear counterstrike. Paul Baruba, a senior adviser on nonproliferation matters, was paradoxically both circumspect and passionate. "Tehran has breached a clear fire wall. For the sake of deterring future strikes like this, we must respond with a limited retaliatory nuclear strike."

It was a vexing issue. Tom Bodine had wrestled with the question of retaliation since the first Iranian threat was made in April. Baruba's theory made perfect sense in the isolated world of theory. But how would the American people view it? If no Iranian nuclear force existed, what value was a nuclear counterstrike? After a few minutes of questions and rebuttal between staff members, Bodine forced his way into the discussion.

"I agree with Paul in theory, but this is not the time to make decisions purely from the world of theory. The fact is, we are at war, and we have the decisive advantage in the air. We also have the backing of both the American people and world public opinion. But if we choose now to launch a nuclear strike solely for punitive purposes, that could change quickly. Suddenly we will be seen as the aggressor and Iran as the victim."

Jack Fowler nodded in silent agreement. The discussion did not make the decision any easier for St. John. The president rubbed his heavy, dark-circled eyes and looked at his advisers. "Well, gentlemen, I thank you for your input. This is an issue that I will need to reflect on before any hasty decisions are made. I plan to make that decision in the next twenty-four hours."

Attention then shifted back to the ongoing offensive against Iran. The president wanted the tempo of the attack to be maintained.

Any letup could give Tehran an opportunity to use another hideous weapon. The president turned to his Joint Chiefs Chairman, "General, why don't you tell us your plans for the next twenty-four hours?"

In a mammoth underground bunker north of Tehran, President Montazeri gathered with his National Defense Council amid the thunderous explosions. The president was visibly shaken, as if the sand beneath him was being violently washed away by an unstoppable tide. Foreign Minister Habibi was sitting near him, ashen-faced and wide-eyed. Habibi had barely made it to the bunker—the flying shrapnel of a laser-guided bomb had just missed his car. And while Defense Minister Shamkhani and Ayatollah Morteza'i managed to maintain a veneer of confidence, inside they shuddered at the thought of what might happen next. Only Intelligence Director Reza'i seemed unaffected by the apocalyptic events that had unfolded during the past twelve hours.

Although Montazeri opened the meeting with a call for vigilance, it rang hollow. He was uncertain about what to do next, and his hope for victory appeared to be dimming. His mind was fixated on one question: will the Americans retaliate with nuclear weapons?

Muhsin Reza'i was resolute and unbending, yet at the same time calm and collected. His time in Lebanon had served him well. "We should not concern ourselves with this matter. The Americans will choose to respond as they like. Instead, we must concern ourselves with the blows we must bring to bear against this Great Satan. We must take the war to them."

"How so?" asked a tense Montazeri in veiled desperation.

"We deal with the Americans the same way we dealt with the Saudis: our fighters will bring the war to their streets and cities. We cannot strike them from the air, but we can hit them with power from our invisible legions."

The president nodded, encouraged for the first time since the air strike had been launched. "Yes, yes of course. Continue."

Reza'i described in intricate detail the cells in place in the United States. There was Tashayu Sorkh (Red Shiism), a group organized in San Jose, California. Tashayu Sorkh had been formed in 1965 by Mustafa Chamran Savehi, then a student at Berkeley. Chamran was a radical who trained in Egypt, and upon his return in 1965, he established Tashayu Sorkh as a terrorist organization. Presently, it was a tight cadre of well-trained professionals managed by Tehran.

There were also cells built by VEVAK in the United States. In 1984, the Iranian intelligence service started smuggling well-trained Shiite terrorists into the States. They entered through Mexico and were concealed in the Muslim student population in many major American cities. Tehran sustained these terrorists by making them "students" and putting them under scholarship. These cells worked with the Hizbollah, which had independently placed terrorist units on the East Coast. Reza'i brought these groups with him when he left the Hizbollah to join VEVAK.

This network had been used before. In 1989, terrorists struck in San Diego when a pipe bomb exploded in the van of Sharon Lee Rogers, wife of the captain of the USS *Vincennes*, the American navy ship that had shot down an Iranian passenger plane in 1988. The cell was also tangentially involved in the Trade Center bombing.

"We have a network in place, stretching from Boston to San Francisco, Seattle to Miami, which may be activated at any time. Our hidden legions are all prepared to serve as martyrs for the cause. It will take only one phone call to activate them."

President Montazeri scanned the room. With no dissent, he agreed immediately to bring the war to America. "Very well then. Place your phone call."

In the days prior to the air war, the 82nd Airborne and the 1st Marine Expeditionary Force (MEF) had been secretly deployed to Diego Garcia, an island outpost in the Indian Ocean. During the first week of the air war, these units nervously prepared for the pending ground assault against Iranian forces. Tehran's control of the small islands at the mouth of the gulf gave them de facto control over traffic through the strait. Retaking Qesum and Larak was a crucial first step in dislodging Tehran from its grip on Middle Eastern oil.

It would be a complex, perilous task. The Persian Gulf was perhaps the most difficult area in the world in which to conduct an amphibious operation. The landing would have to come at night, preferably several days after a new moon. U.S. night sights required some background or ambient light to function at peak efficiency.

On the night of July 22, a massive naval assault force steamed north into the Sea of Oman and then moved into the strait. The U.S. Marine Corps 1st MEF was aboard a transport, with a collection of cruisers and destroyers in escort. The carrier USS *Nimitz* stayed one hundred nautical miles back, close enough to provide the needed air power but out of range of Iranian missiles.

As the force pressed north, OH-580 Warrior attack helicopters, secretly based in Oman and operated by U.S. Special Forces, attacked the waters around the small islands to eliminate any attack speedboats that might be in the area. Developed under a "black" military program in the 1980s, the Warrior's rotor blades are specially contoured to dramatically reduce noise. It makes achieving surprise a near guarantee, especially at night. Inside the narrow cockpits, the crews wore protection against chemical and biological agents.

Lieutenant Pete Warwick eased back on the stick of his Warrior ever so slightly as he made his first approach on Qesum. The sky was pitch black, and there were no visible lights on the island. As the Warrior hugged the coastline, Warwick spotted three fast attack craft in port. Two Hellfires took out the first craft instantly. As gunfire erupted below him, the lieutenant swung the Warrior back over the island and attacked again, this time from the west. He spotted the remaining two boats on his next pass and shattered them with another Hydra and his .50 calibre machine gun.

For nearly two hours, more than three dozen Warriors peppered Iranian targets with missiles and heavy machine gun fire. The

**Elements of the combined allied fleet move into
the Sea of Oman.**

night-vision equipment gave the crews a perfect view of the targets
below. Iranian forces, using a portable SAM, managed to bring one
of the predators down, but the crew was later rescued at sea.

By 3:00 A.M. the fighter-bombers were set to arrive. Lieutenant
Warwick and the other pilots could hear the warning over the radio.
"This is Big Daddy, we are coming through. I repeat, this is Big
Daddy, we are coming through, over."

The Warriors checked out, flying low over the gulf toward
Oman, and the 23rd Wing now boomed through the night sky.
While the Warriors had opened the attack with precision and
stealth, the A-10s and F-16s out of Pope Air Force Base finished
with raw firepower. Using penetration bombs to break open the
concrete reinforced bunkers, the pilots aimed for the ventilation
shafts and other weak points of the structures. On the first pass, the
Hawk anti-aircraft sites and command post imploded. Soon after,
the Silkworm missile batteries and the communications post were
also gone. Following the 23rd Wing were *Nimitz*-based fighter-
bombers and Saudi pilots.

For two hours the ground shuddered before U.S. Marines stormed the beaches. First onshore were Marines in AAV-7A1 armored amphibious troop carriers. Despite the machine gun fire from IRGC pill boxes, the 30-mm armor offered flawless protection. The first order of business was to establish a beachhead before the M1 Abrams tanks arrived. Peering into the darkness in front of them, the infantry units kept watch for enemy forces. Once the Abrams arrived, the push inland began.

The muscular, 1,500-horsepower turbine engines growled in the early morning sun as a column of tanks attacked fixed-IRGC positions. Using the tank's advanced-imaging systems, the gunners sought out the enemy, firing with precision at targets up to one mile away. The battle for Qesum raged for seven hours until Commander Ali Shah Jilani was compelled to surrender. Of the once-sizeable force of 8,000 soldiers, only 1,400 were still alive. And with the tiny islands of the gulf now in U.S. control, the Iranian strategic position had weakened considerably.

Ghasam Kassar had worked as a trader on the NYSE for two years. Over six and a half feet tall with a dark, thick mane of hair, he was an imposing figure. A loner who largely kept to himself, he was nevertheless well liked by coworkers. Kassar was the son of a wealthy Lebanese merchant living in London and studied at the London School of Economics before moving to the United States in 1995. He had held several management positions with American financial institutions before becoming a trader. But Ghasam lived another life as well, and on the evening of July 23, he received a call from a man named Khalid.

The next morning Kassar walked to Wall Street just as he had every day the previous two years. Only this time he headed straight to the NYSE. Using his pass, Kassar entered the trading floor firmly gripping a thin, tan leather briefcase. As the room hummed with activity, he nervously scanned the crowd to make sure he was not being watched. All of the traders seemed transfixed on the boards which offered signs of a promising rally. Casually and calmly, Kassar set his briefcase on the floor and melded into the crowd. Within minutes, he was back outside walking up a congested, bustling Wall Street.

A violent explosion rocked the trading floor just moments later. As people lay stunned and injured on the floor, a noxious gas filled the room. The deadly substance was a small quantity of *Bacillus anthracis*, an organism that causes anthrax. Lethal in one-thousandth the concentration of nerve gas, Kassar had produced the anthrax spores in his Newark, New Jersey, apartment.

A maelstrom of panicked people and emergency personnel descended on the NYSE. Kassar took a cab across the George Washington Bridge to New Jersey and returned to his apartment. After destroying a few personal papers, he drove north fast, making his way for the small town of Richford, Vermont, on the Canadian border. By evening, he was across the border and in Montreal. The next morning he caught an Air Canada flight to Geneva and then disappeared.

The terror campaign did not end in New York. The following day a bomb rocked the city hall in Chicago, injuring dozens. Similar devices exploded in both Seattle and Richmond, Virginia.

"What will it take?" President St. John asked before drinking some more coffee from a bone china cup. He had passed on breakfast—his appetite was gone. News of the terrorist campaign continued to trickle in. Cities from Seattle to Miami were experiencing random bombings. At the same time, American and Saudi aircraft had been pounding Iran with a fury, and the strategic islands in the strait were now under American control. But Iran offered no sign of buckling.

Bodine scribbled furiously on his legal pad. "Mr. President, we have to remember that the leadership in Tehran does not share our values. When it comes to issues of war and peace, they are willing to sustain much higher casualties than any Western country would.

We need to be prepared for this war to drag on for months... or, dare I say, years?"

"But we have been fighting this war blind. First we lacked the intel to locate Iranian launchers and now we are at the mercy of terrorists—forced to react."

"It's with good intel during peace that you win battles during war."

National Security Adviser Jack Fowler burst into the room with an anxious look on his face. "Gentlemen, I think we have a big problem."

The president slammed down his coffee cup. "What could it be now?"

"Don't have me explain it, Mr. President. Let her do it."

Paula Jameson walked into the room, clutching a loose-leaf binder under her arm. In her mid-fifties and conservatively dressed, her grayish brown hair was tightly pulled back. She looked more than a bit shy as she greeted both the president and secretary of defense.

Fowler pulled out her chair as she sat at the breakfast table. "Mr. President, Paula has worked at NSA for thirty years. She works in the traffic room and analyzes the telemetry and other electronic intelligence [ELINT] we collect. Paula is the official who drew together the data in May from NSA Post 5467 in Turkey concerning the Iranian launch of the nuclear warning shot."

"Well, thank you, Paula. We are deeply indebted to you." She nodded and smiled politely.

Fowler continued, "Paula has been part of the team working continuously to crack the new Iranian codes. They had another breakthrough two days ago, and what she has discovered is quite startling. Paula?"

The matronly woman quietly set her binder down on the table and began in a cautious, quiet tone. "Mr. President, Mr. Secretary, the Iranian codes are quite simple. Despite the fact that they change them fairly regularly, their encryption technology is outdated. So, cracking the codes has not been difficult. Since the air war began, the volume of Iranian communications has decreased dramatically.

I guess we all might expect that, given the targeting by the U.S. Air Force. But Post 5467 has continued to detect telemetry signals emanating from a facility due east of Tehran."

"And what does the telemetry tell us?" asked Bodine with a puzzled look on his face.

"That's not easy to say, Mr. Secretary." She pulled out a sheet of paper and handed it across the table. "It's a series of numbers."

"What could they be?"

Jameson curled her lip. "They could be anything. But this is a military communication, emitted from a bunker north of Tehran. I took the numbers and ran them through a variety of tests." She paused and looked the president straight in the eye. "When I plotted the numbers on navigational charts, they seemed to indicate coordinates for geographical locations."

President St. John squinted his eyes. "Locations? What kind of locations?"

"If you array the figures and treat them as longitude and latitude, they point to a desolate spot east of Tehran in the desert and a downtown block in Berlin, Germany."

St. John caught his breath and sprang to his feet. "Dear God, are you suggesting... ?" He began pacing nervously.

"Mr. President, the numbers are consistent with data that Iran might use to target a Zulfiquar missile."

"That's impossible," said Bodine laying his napkin on the table. "All indications are that we got all their launchers."

Paula Jameson's shyness intensified as she nervously looked down at the notepad in front of her. "That may be, Mr. Secretary. I don't presume to know what our pilots have succeeded in doing. I simply know that Tehran is sending military telemetry to a site out in the desert, and that this includes mathematical data which very possibly could be targeting information for a Zulfiquar missile."

Fowler took another drink of coffee and then injected himself into the conversation. "Mr. President, this requires immediate investigation. I think we also have to consider policy options. If Tehran is preparing for another launch, we need to preempt with a strike of our own. They may have interpreted our inaction to their strike on Monza as weakness."

St. John nodded in agreement. "You're right, Jack. Put everything on this you need to. And work fast. If they are really planning another strike, we will hit them first and hard."

Chapter Thirteen

July 25
the Iranian desert

Colonel George Rudd massaged his leg with one hand as he kept his other hand firmly on the stick of his stealth fighter. The 42-year-old U.S. Air Force Academy graduate was now flying his 12th sortie in four days, and he was rapidly reaching the point of exhaustion. His nerves were frayed, his muscles cramping. But the urgency of the situation in the desert was such that he had little choice but to join his wing to search for the source of the mysterious telemetry that had been reported by Washington. The United States desperately needed stealth aircraft for this mission and there were few available for the task.

Rudd and his comrades were flying escort for two surveillance aircraft taking high-resolution photos of the desert floor. From five thousand feet he could see nothing extraordinary below. The skies were clear, and there was no one in the air. The last Iranian fighter he had seen was on the first day of the air war, and their SAM batteries had been eliminated early on. The modified F-111s made several passes over the area before banking to return to Turkey. Rudd and his group followed, making it home without incident.

The high-resolution photos did not solve the mystery, but they uncovered dangerous signs that there was something to the telemetry. A quick analysis by the Air Force Reconnaissance Office made it clear that something was going on in the desert. There were faint tracks of wheeled vehicles active in the area. Yet the tracks seemed to stop in the middle of nowhere. At the suggestion of Jack Fowler, the president took the intelligence and issued a formal warning to Tehran, sending a sternly worded cable sent to the presidential bunker.

> President Muhammad Montazeri
> Islamic Republic of Iran
> Mr. Montazeri:
>
> Your barbaric act of striking innocent civilians in Monza, Italy, with nuclear weapons has been condemned universally. The United States chose not to retaliate with a nuclear strike on Iran, feeling that such a strike at this point in the conflict would serve no purpose.
>
> However, let me make this clear: any attempt by your government to even prepare for another nuclear strike will be met with an immediate strike by American tactical nuclear weapons. Your governing facility will be our highest priority as a target.
>
> President Michael St. John
> United States of America

Tehran did not respond. On the night of July 25, U.S. reconnaissance aircraft flying over the mysterious sector of desert saw two trucks moving toward what seemed to be a probable missile site. High-resolution photos developed immediately after the planes returned to base suggested the trucks were transporting missile components.

Tehran's next move was foremost in the president's mind when word of the latest intelligence reached him at the White House. Bodine and Fowler were present, joined once again by the methodical Paula Jameson.

Fowler grabbed a cup of coffee. "Paula, tell us the latest you have."

"The telemetry continues. Today there was a new communication—it was again numerical. I'm not certain if they know we are listening, but the same numbers were repeated. And the last communication—which came through barely two hours ago—we are still working on."

Bodine chewed nervously on his pen. Clearly, all intelligence pointed to a launch. "Mr. President, Ms. Jameson has done a tremendous service to our country. It is very apparent to me now that she was correct. All evidence indicates a launch by Tehran. I think we need to hit them hard and fast."

"What do we hit them with?"

Bodine didn't like what he felt he must say. It was a difficult thing for him to spit out. "Mr. President, I think we need to take out that site with tactical nukes. We have no choice." He leaned forward in his chair to emphasize the point. "We need to be certain that underground facility is eliminated. We need to send the unambiguous message that if any more of these bunkers exist, they better not think about another strike."

Jameson looked down at her pad, as if she had heard a secret she would just as soon not know. Jack Fowler said nothing. The silence was not condemnation but recognition by all that Bodine was correct.

The president only nodded as he moved to his desk. "Prepare the orders."

On July 26 at 2:11 A.M. Colonel John Martz and his crew boarded their B-1B Lancer bomber through the narrow retractable ladder built into the nose-wheel well. They went through the preflight checklist just has they had done hundreds of times before. But there was an obvious sense of urgency and concern to this particular flight. Martz had been in the Air Force for almost twenty years, and he was planning to get out at the end of the year. His greatest wish was to return to the family business. And it appeared as if the last months of service would go smoothly—until the crisis in the Persian Gulf erupted.

Based at McConnell Air Force Base in Kansas, Martz and his crew had doubted that they would see much action. After all, they were assigned to nuclear deterrent missions. Things had been pretty quiet since the end of the Cold War. But that all changed forty-eight hours ago.

Martz and his co-pilot, Captain Dale Margolis, tested the thrust on their four 30,000-pound thrust turbofan engines and checked the multi-function display (MFD) to make sure the sensors and the system diagnostic data were working. The screens gave off an eerie glow in the dark night. As Martz and Margolis continued with their tests, Major Bo Bullard checked the offensive avionics systems, including the navigational computer and bomb sites. Underneath the dark, gray, sleek aircraft, munitions experts were loading a large metal cannister into the forward bomb bay. It was a one hundred–kiloton thermonuclear weapon.

Martz taxied the slender plane onto the runway. Pushing on the afterburners, he guided the craft down the runway and into the air. He took one last look at the crop fields below before refocusing his attention on the MFDs. It was a long flight—ten thousand miles to the target. During the trip, few words were spoken.

From McConnell Air Force Base to the East Coast, a quartet of F-15s escorted the B-1. Once Martz and his crew proceeded out over the Atlantic, escort duty passed to four F-16s. The five aircraft were refueled over the dark ocean. When the planes approached the Spanish coast, it was 5:00 P.M. local time, and the sun was shining brightly. Martz was a little claustrophobic in the confines of his cramped seat, and he occasionally got up to stretch his legs. Finally, he grabbed a couple of spare engine covers, laid them in the aisle between the front and rear compartment, and took a short nap. There was plenty of food aboard in the rear compartment, but no one felt like eating.

Over the blue waters of the eastern Mediterranean, the B-1 took on fuel from a KC-135 Stratotanker. As the giant tanker pulled away from the fuel receptacle in the nose of the B-1, Martz knew the mission would not be recalled. They would soon receive final clearance over Turkey and then make their run.

U.S. Tactical Nuclear Strike

Bo Bullard checked the weapons system a third and final time as the Lancer moved into Iranian airspace. Six F-15s were now in escort as were two electronic-jamming aircraft. The group flew high—at forty thousand feet. Martz made the final radio call to Air Force General Karl Lowder at the U.S. air base in Turkey.

"Alpha One, this is Big Bird, over."

"Alpha One here, go ahead."

Martz felt the lump in his throat. "We await final approval, over."

"Big Bird, this is a go. Repeat, this is a go, over."

Martz glanced over at Margolis, and they locked eyes for only a second. Neither said anything. Martz checked the MFDs and then radioed back to Bo Bullard. "We are a go. I repeat, we are a go." Bullard wiped his hands of the thin film of sweat that had formed over them. He looked at his APQ-164 radar, including a terrain-following autopilot and an attack sensor. The computer software for the use of nuclear systems was working perfectly. As the Lancer boomed over the target, Bullard activated the weapons launch system, and the eight-round rotary launcher released a single nuclear device. Seconds after it fell from the sky, an enormous flash pierced the coal-black night. A thundering boom followed. Martz wiped the perspiration from his face and radioed Bullard. "Mission accomplished. Let's head home." He didn't know what else to say.

August 2, 1999

Post-War Strategic Assessment of the Gulf War

Summary: Considerable gaps in the U.S. intelligence system created a situation in which the U.S. government was unprepared to deal with the deployment of Iranian nuclear-armed ballistic missiles.

Military Considerations: The American retreat from the

Persian Gulf, the nuclear strike on Monza, Italy, and the subsequent requirement to resort to tactical nuclear weapons was largely an outgrowth of our inability to restrict Iran's access to critical nuclear-related technologies and to detect with some precision the status of Tehran's nuclear weapons program.

1. The Iranian ballistic missile program is largely based on the transfer of technology by China and North Korea. While diplomatic protests were proclaimed by the Clinton administration in 1993 and 1994 concerning this matter, it was not favorably resolved. Indeed, North Korea, which collaborated with Iran on the production of ballistic missiles, received American foreign aid in 1995 and 1996 in an effort to stifle their nuclear weapons program. At the same time, China sold missile technology to Tehran while continuing to receive unfettered access to American markets. In the future, the U.S. government must be more firm in politically and economically isolating those states that spawn proliferation through the transfer of technologies.

2. Gaps in U.S. intelligence capabilities meant that we were not abreast of Iranian nuclear developments. The human intelligence capabilities in Iran were minimal, largely because the CIA clandestine service has been cut during the past several years, and little emphasis has been placed on the recruitment of agents and sources. America should put priority on enhancing intelligence assets that monitor efforts to develop nuclear weapons.

Long-term Considerations: Conflicts with other rogue states armed with weapons of mass destruction should be expected.

Part Three

Mexico
March 7, 2003

Chapter Fourteen

March 7, 2003
U.S.-Mexican border

Through the lens of his infrared field glasses, Lieutenant James Monroe could see them coming by the thousands, a wandering army in the warm, night-covered desert. The dust storms had died down, so visibility was good on the cloudless night. Perched on a small hill and covered with camouflaged netting, Monroe's eyes followed the still shadowy figures roaming through the dry grass and brush, holding packages or carrying backpacks. The faint cries of babies and murmurs of small children broke up the calm night. Watching them, the irony of the situation struck him. Born and raised in Brownsville, Texas, Monroe enlisted in the U.S. Army to get away from home and see the world. Now here he was, deployed on the U.S.-Mexican border along Highway 281 just nine miles from his hometown.

"Eagle's Nest, this is Eagle Six, over," he radioed to headquarters in a low, hushed voice, breaking the silence.

"Go ahead, Eagle Six."

"I have a large group—eight hundred to a thousand—moving north on foot, approximately one thousand yards in front of me, over."

"Birds will be there shortly, Eagle Six, over."

Monroe set the infrared field glasses down and lit a cigarette. The voices grew louder, the children more audible. But soon they were drowned out by the thump, thump, thump in the distance. Approaching from the north, a quartet of Apache attack helicopters roared directly over his outpost before heading to the flat, rocky plain in front of him. They hovered above the refugees and directed their spotlights to the ground as a voice in perfect Spanish boomed over a loudspeaker, "You have illegally entered the territory of the United States. You are to return to Mexico immediately or face arrest and forcible return to your country." The Apaches' powerful blades whipped up a storm of dirt and sand, sending the confused mass of people to the ground. A few dozen figures—mostly young men—tried to flee, but they were soon snatched up by border patrol personnel in jeeps. From his perch, now barely eight hundred yards away, Lieutenant Monroe picked up his field glasses and watched the whole tragedy unfold. A few minutes later, there was a tap on his shoulder. It was the morning shift.

"Quiet night?"

Monroe laughed. The 7th Division had already been deployed for two months, so he knew better. "Just the usual."

Taking one last look through the glasses, he said with a grin, "You know, I've been in this army five years. I thought I needed to *leave* Texas to see some real action."

Back at the headquarters for Operation Eagle's Nest in Houston, Texas, Colonel Phil Lewis was slowly and methodically reading through the latest reports from the string of observation posts extending from the Gulf of Mexico to San Diego. Lieutenant Monroe's report from Eagle Six was only one of dozens received during the last several hours. He wondered why he continued to read them. Day after day the reports were the same.

For six months now, Lewis and more than 60,000 U.S. troops had been deployed along the U.S.–Mexican line from the Gulf of Mexico to the Pacific Ocean to plug up the flood of refugees and illegal immigrants pouring across the border every hour. But it was a losing battle. "It's like trying to dam the Mississippi River with toothpicks," the Missouri native angrily told his wife one night in frustration. The border that separates the United States and Mexico is the only land border between the industrial and the nonindustrial world, the so-called third world. And the United States had been fortunate in the twentieth century. Trouble in a country with such geographic proximity to America was something new.

A mass exodus of the weary and hungry was driven north by the chaotic situation inside Mexico. The tumult had begun with the assassination of Mexican President Lorenzo Zapata on June 2, 1999. Much hope had followed Zapata into Los Pinos (the presidential mansion). The American-educated economist was hailed as a symbol of political maturity for Mexico, unblemished by the venality and incompetence that had characterized so many previous regimes. This time, the anticorruption drives were carried out with real zeal, and cooperation in eradicating the flourishing cross-border drug trade was substantial. But unfortunately, the promise of change did not go far enough for a radical with a gun. Utopian dreams led the twenty-one-year-old student to a grisly act. The assassin's bullet not only brought down Zapata's body, but also the hopes and dreams of those seeking genuine reform and moderation in Mexican politics. And to add insult to dishonor, the assassin escaped from police custody, apparently with the aid of the Mexican drug cartels.

Amid the ashes of what came to be called the "Zapata affair," a radical populist front emerged headed by Eduardo Francisco Ruiz, a charismatic university professor trained by the Jesuits. Thin and intense with a pointed, balding head, the spectacled Ruiz had entertained the idea of entering the priesthood in his youth. But, as he wrote to his mother, he elected to pursue academics and politics "to bring heaven to this world, not prepare souls for another." A student of both Nietzsche and Hegel, Ruiz was an undistinguished scholar who grew quickly in political stature during the months following the Zapata affair. His National Salvation Front was fueled by a well-financed political organization that included idealistic university students and an enormous reservoir of campaign funds from a mysterious source. His ability to dominate a room or move a crowd came from his aura of controlled tension. He was like a coiled spring.

Ruiz's powerful voice belied his physical condition, in which an unknown ailment forced him to seek constant medical attention. His political message was simple and doctrinaire: Ruiz condemned the "bourgeois paradigm" for failing to solve Mexico's chronic problems. The devil in his political theology was the "gringo" who exploited Mexico "for his own ends." Proclaiming that Mexico was the victim of other peoples' follies, he rode to power on a radical, nationalist agenda by making effective use of power symbols and images from Mexico's past. "Land to the tillers" was his cry in the rural areas.

Installed as the new president in the fall of 1999, Ruiz brought with him to power equally inept advisors who were also wrapped up with his utopian dreams. They came to be called *los cientificos*, the scientists, because they believed in the scientific method for solving problems. The trouble was, street wisdom said, they were using people instead of mice for their experiments. The Ruiz administration acted on impulses, passing a series of radical reforms which shook Mexican society to its core. The result was economic collapse.

The nationalization of the banking and insurance industry annihilated confidence among foreign investors, and repeated attempts by the U.S. banking community throughout the summer of the year 2000 to prop up Mexico's shaky financial structure failed. Promises of "land to the tillers" meant the forcible redistribution of farmland and the devastation of Mexican agriculture, triggering an enormous peso crisis. Much hardship followed.

Rather than correct his mistaken policies, Ruiz made a scapegoat of the United States, blaming his powerful neighbor to the north for food shortages and hyperinflation. In an incendiary speech in front of Mexico City's Museum of Interventions, which retells the U.S.–Mexican War of 1847, Ruiz claimed that America did not want to see Mexico prosper but preferred instead a "brown, suffering, weak neighbor to the south." It was a rhetorical storm that would have made Fidel Castro proud.

Repeated economic crises sparked social unrest in the second half of the year 2000, leading the Mexican president to strengthen his political hand and suppress the opposition. The tools of repression were fine-tuned. The Ministerio de Gobernacion and the federal police received new powers, and opponents of the government were arrested on trumped-up charges. Ruiz also reformed the military. Gone was the complicated, decentralized structure of thirty-six military zones and a fractured command. In its place, Ruiz established a general staff headed by political allies. Troop strength was almost doubled during a nine-month period. The buildup served as both a jobs program and a tool for intimidating domestic enemies.

When the Mexican pot finally boiled over in the spring of 2002, millions of Mexicans began voting with their feet, crossing the border into the United States. Illegal immigration had always been a problem—but this was a massive, if nonviolent, invasion. A population the size of New York City was crossing the border every twelve months.

For Phil Lewis, everything had moved so quickly. He and his family had just settled in for a new assignment at Fort Lewis in Washington. It was likely to be his last. After twenty years and eight different homes, his wife was looking forward to some stability. Instead, the Mexican cauldron brought him to Fort Hood, Texas, and in command of Operation Eagle's Nest. And the latest report from the Immigration and Naturalization Service (INS) indicated he wouldn't be going home anytime soon.

Site Report #234-667

March 5, 2003

Immigration and Naturalization Service Regional Office
San Diego, California

Sector-by-Sector Analysis of Immigration Patterns:
Executive Summary

Data indicate that immigration from Mexico continues to escalate at a dramatic rate. Reports garnered from U.S. Army and INS estimates place the expected number of illegal immigrants for the calendar year 2003 at five to seven million. This figure may increase dramatically given the continued domestic unrest in Mexico and the hardship caused by the December earthquake in Monterrey. The current immigration control effort is insufficient. The deployment of U.S. Army personnel has been effective, but only one-third of illegal immigrants entering the country are likely to be intercepted by U.S. personnel. The crisis is intensified by the fact that the Ruiz government in Mexico City appears to have little interest in tightening the border, apparently in the hopes of "exporting" their problems. The following are the best available estimates of illegal entries into the United States.

January–February 2003

Sector One: San Diego, CA—Phoenix, AZ
Arrests: 94,113
Estimated entries: 300,000

Sector Two: Phoenix, AZ—Ciudad Juarez, Mexico
Arrests: 43,231
Estimated entries: 150,000

Sector Three: Ciudad Juarez, Mexico—Brownsville, TX
Arrests: 118,455
Estimated entries: 200,000

Setting the report on his metal desk, Lewis rubbed his eyes, stood up, took another drink from his coffee mug, and headed for his car. Today, he would tour the "front" to check on morale and security at the observation points from Brownsville to El Paso. Fort Lewis and his wife and kids seemed a world away.

Back in Washington, President Michael St. John was finding little peace in the confines of the Oval Office. During the first two months of the year, more than two million illegal immigrants had crossed the border. And the human river was steadily growing in size and speed.

Between appointments, the president was sitting at his desk and staring off into the distance when his personal assistant walked in. "Mr. Brooks from the DEA [Drug Enforcement Administration] is here to see you, along with Secretaries Brown and Bodine."

"Yes, send them in."

Mike Brooks was built like a pipe organ, solid and straight with nondescript features. He did not fit the image of a Washington bureaucrat. With dark, inset eyes; a thick black mane, and a rich mustache, Brooks was more blue collar than senior executive. He was a solid taskmaster who had been a foot soldier in the drug war for more than twenty-five years. He started in 1975 when the American heroin epidemic had peaked. That year, the DEA estimated that 87 percent of the heroin consumed was coming from Mexico.

His first field assignment had been fighting the heroin trade. Seared in his mind was an incident in January 1986 during his last tour south of the border. For two years he had worked to build a case against Caro Quintero, one of Mexico's most notorious drug kingpins. While Quintero's arrest by Mexican authorities and eventual conviction brought champagne out at the DEA for a celebration, the euphoria did not last long. One night shortly after Quintero's conviction, Brooks saw him dining with friends in the fashionable Zona Rosa District of Mexico City. Enraged, Brooks took his anger directly to President de la Madrid at Los Pinos, but the president appeared powerless to do anything. The lure of *la mordida* (the bite, the bribe) was too strong. Quintero was in prison, but the guards made sure his social life didn't suffer.

Brooks left Mexico bitter and obsessed with destroying the drug cartels. He had almost let go—until Ruiz's rise brought new and troubling rumors. DEA informants reported that the National Salvation Front's "mystery" campaign fund was drug money and that Ruiz was close to some of Mexico's most powerful drug lords. Several billion dollars were being poured into supporting the Salvation Front's coffers. Suddenly, the obsession that had almost died was revived.

As the men settled into their chairs, Mike Brooks began, "Mr. President, I don't need to tell you about the drug problem that is plaguing this country. For almost half a century now, your predecessors have wrestled with the blight of drugs. However, it's about to get a whole lot worse. The street price for cocaine is at an all-time low, so it's cheap and plentiful. The fact is, the Mexican drug gangs are flooding the market. They are shipping the stuff into the country on a scale the Colombians could have only dreamed about. Things are going to spin out of control—and fast."

The president shifted in his seat and took off his glasses, clasping them in his right hand. His words came in a cadence that hinted at a lack of confidence. "What do we know about these gangs?"

"They were a loose group in the 1990s, both cooperating and competing against each other. They called themselves 'The Federation,' but they had their share of turf wars. In 1993 a pretty nasty gang war was waged in San Diego. Twenty people were killed before it was over. But this time the situation will be worse. There is a whole lot more money at stake. This gang war will make San Diego look like a frat party. With prices so low, the leaders of the groups recognize that the only hope they have of bringing prices back up and gaining a larger market share is to drive the competition out of business. And in the drug world that means waging a war until the competition is dead. We already have news that skirmishes have started in San Diego, Phoenix, Albuquerque, Houston, and El Paso."

The president turned inquisitively to Secretary of State Vaughn Brown, who was often lost in the world of geopolitics. "Vaughn, can't we get some more cooperation from Mexico City on this? If we know who these people are, can't they take care of it?"

"Mr. President, they claim to be doing everything they can," he said. He had the puffed face and small, narrow jowls that are typical of bureaucratic inertia. "We give them $300 million a year in drug eradication aid, but frankly, they aren't very effective."

Brooks quickly edged his way back into the conversation, leaving Secretary Brown appearing slightly put off. "And if I may say so, gentlemen, we shouldn't count on them to do much of anything."

"Why not?" asked St. John, turning back to Brooks.

"Our sources in Mexico City make it pretty clear that President Ruiz and much of his cabinet are receiving payoffs from the drug cartels. He is intimately intertwined with the drug lords. And DEA agents in the field have hit a stone wall when it comes to any sort of cooperation from Mexican authorities. In fact, six agents have been shot in the past six months. I wouldn't be surprised if someone in the Ruiz government is passing their names to the drug lords."

St. John turned to his cantankerous secretary of defense. "What does the Pentagon say?"

Silent throughout the first twenty minutes of the meeting, Defense Secretary Tom Bodine cleared his throat and leaned forward with a pained, deliberate look on his face. In his customary, to-the-point tone he began, "Mr. President, we have a crisis brewing on our border. We have deployed sixty thousand troops to stop what is, in blunt terms, an invading civilian army. Even if we strung half a million men along that border, the problem wouldn't go away. We are talking about tens of millions coming across that border during the next couple of years. And what Mr. Brooks has reported confirms what other sources are telling us, that this drug problem is about to get worse and more violence is just around the corner."

President St. John nervously scanned the room while holding an index finger to his lips. "You're right, Tom," he agreed. "The health and welfare problems created by the refugees is already reaching the point of crisis. We have tried to work with Mr. Ruiz, and Vaughn thinks we will get some results. Are you suggesting another course?"

Bodine gently lowered his head, peering over the rims of his glasses. "With all due respect to my friends at the State Department, this is not a problem to be solved by diplomats. The refugees, the drug gangs, these are all symptoms. The real problem is Ruiz. He created the economic mess, and now he offers protection to the drug lords. We need to confront him and make it clear that the present situation is unacceptable. And if he fails to take drastic measures, I think we must consider—and I do not say this lightly—the military option."

Like a heavy fog, silence hung in the room.

Vaughn Brown began, "You're not suggesting—"

"I am."

There was more silence. The president stood slowly and walked over to the window. "Tom, how does a military option solve this problem?"

"If we move into Mexico, there won't be much resistance because the only people who like Ruiz are the party regulars. Most Mexicans fear him. His government will fall immediately, and then we can set up an interim government to run the country and hold elections in six months."

"You make it sound so easy," said Vaughn Brown dryly.

"It won't be easy. But if things go on unchanged, this problem may become unmanageable."

The president broke his gaze from the South Lawn and turned back to his advisers. "Vaughn, take our proposals back to Mr. Ruiz in Mexico City. Tell him that I demand his full cooperation on this. And let him know that we are not ruling out any options for dealing with this crisis."

Chapter Fifteen

March 11
San Diego, California

I n a dark corner of the underground parking lot at Horton Plaza, an upscale and downtown shopping center, two undistinguished figures worked briskly and intently in the back of their windowless van. Occasionally, they peered nervously about. When the job was completed, they left the van in the lot and walked cautiously out of the parking garage. Hugging the perimeter, they evaded the glare of the surveillance cameras and awkwardly avoided eye contact with a professional woman in her mid-thirties who whisked by. Soon the two men were hurrying down Fourth Avenue through the busy Gas Lamp Quarter. They arrived at the corner of Island Avenue shortly after noon and were picked up by a passing car. Within the hour, they were across the border.

Booming thunder and a powerful explosion ripped through the Plaza with a fury and force usually reserved for a war zone. Thousands of people were thrown to the ground by the shock wave, and a shower of plaster and glass fell on the innocent. Forty feet below, amid the parked cars, dozens were entombed in the collapsed garage. As the smoke billowed into the sky, a paralyzing confusion lingered over the Plaza. The first sirens were soon audible in the distance.

In Houston, Texas, Brookhaven had been turned into a war zone. The crackle of automatic gunfire, soon joined by a symphony of guns, rang out during the early morning hours. Rival gangs fighting for control of the lucrative Houston drug market exchanged gunfire, punctuated sporadically by grenades thrown into the narrow houses alongside the streets. Most of the combatants were "enforcers"—poor immigrants paid by drug lords to break the competition. Houston police were outgunned and ill-equipped to deal with the war, so Texas Governor Larry Symington called the White House requesting the deployment of U.S. troops to flush out the gangs. By the end of the day, the president agreed, and the Pentagon assigned Colonel Ron Milsaps to direct the operation.

Having been up most of the night of March 12 planning and preparing for the operation, Colonel Milsaps watched from a command post on the South Loop Freeway as the men from the U.S. Army 7th Division began moving into Brookhaven. A thick mist created a heaviness in the air. The main power lines to Brookhaven were cut, and the troops slowly converged. Using infrared and blinding spotlights from armored vehicles, Milsaps hoped to gain maximum advantage in the darkness.

The area had been sealed off by the Houston police for forty-eight hours, and civilians had evacuated. Colonel Milsaps gave one final verbal warning to the gangs over a bullhorn before the troops closed in. Four platoons, with protection from APCs and armed with small weapons, concussion grenades, and riot gas cannisters crept up Holmes Road. Snug-fitting flack jackets provided some added protection. The storefronts were quiet, and through the infrared glasses, the street looked like a ghost town. Although the guns were eerily silent, occasional footsteps could be heard in the seemingly vacant houses. From the east, a column of three tank platoons proceeded up Cullen Boulevard before turning west onto Mayflower. The two forces converged at the intersection of Independence and Danube.

On the South Loop Overpass, Colonel Milsaps watched nervously through his infrared binoculars for two hours. The thumping of small-arms fire would first echo for a few minutes and then die down only to rise again. Smoke ascended to the sky from burning houses set afire by the cornered gang members. Three police helicopters fluttered overhead, providing occasional updates. Finally, after nearly three hours, Colonel Milsaps received the message he had been waiting for.

"Bravo Command, this is Bravo One, over."

Milsaps picked up the receiver. "This is Bravo Command. Go ahead."

"The sector has been secured, over."

"Good work, Bravo One. What about casualties?"

"First platoon hit a tough spot on Glenrose. We lost nine from the 1st Platoon. Sixteen Army personnel dead, probably fifty from the gangs. We have what I would estimate to be one hundred in custody."

"Any civilians?"

"Negative."

Milsaps rubbed his eyes. "I'll be down in a minute."

Shocked and saddened by events in Houston and San Diego, President St. John convened a special meeting in the Oval Office with his top advisors on the morning of March 14 to discuss options for dealing with the brewing Mexican crisis. Secretary of State Brown's mission to President Ruiz in Mexico City had yielded nothing but more empty promises. And the yawning gap between Ruiz's rhetoric and reality had become so great that it could no longer be ignored by Washington.

National Security Adviser Jack Fowler chaired the meeting. Fowler had worked for decades inside the bowels of the Pentagon on strategic issues. Making a career in the world of arms control, Fowler would probably have preferred analyzing throw weights and command systems instead of grappling with political turmoil and drug cartels.

"Gentlemen," he began slowly, "the president believes we need to take action at once. The latest news from San Diego puts the number of dead at 241 civilians. And there will probably be more. The situation in Houston has stabilized, but the drug war is likely to erupt again." Fowler shuffled in his chair. "The diplomatic route has not yielded the results we expected. We are called here by the president to present him with other options." An aide passed out papers to all the assembled as Fowler took a sip from a Styrofoam cup. "This is a transcript of a phone conversation intercepted by the

NSA. It's a discussion between President Ruiz and Mexican drug kingpin Avila Ortiz Mena."

NSA Intercept Transcript

Mexico City Station
3/12/03

Ruiz: "...I am so glad to hear, my friend, that business has been profitable. Good fortune is always good news to friends."

Mena: "Eduardo, things are profitable for all of us. But the situation north of the border is difficult. It will cause problems for both of us, so I suggest that we meet immediately to address these issues."

Ruiz: "Very well, Avila. I will be in Acapulco tomorrow evening at the private home of our mutual friend Manual Echeverria. Let us meet there at 7:30."

Mena: "That will be fine. Thank you... Mr. President. Until tomorrow."

"I think this speaks for itself," said Fowler setting his reading glasses down.

Tom Bodine cleared his throat. "What do we know about the bombing in San Diego. Anything?"

"As you know by now, the *San Diego Union* received a letter from a group claiming that the Diaz Cartel was responsible. I think Mr. Brooks and his men at the DEA have an opinion on that. Mike?"

"Thanks, Mr. Fowler." Brooks placed a chart on the overhead projector. "The letter to the *Union* is more than likely a crude attempt to get us to turn up the heat on the Diaz Cartel. I think the culprits lie here, with their rivals." He flicked the switch on the projector. "This is our estimate of the organization and structure of the Avila Mena Cartel."

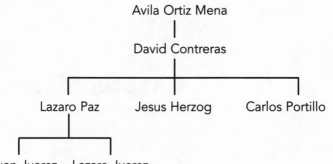

"Senor Paz is responsible for running the operations that bring drugs across the border from Mexicali to San Diego. The Juarez brothers work for Paz and protect Senor Mena's interests in California. Yesterday, one of our most reliable sources struck up a conversation with Juan Juarez in a Mexicali bar. After a few drinks, Juan bragged that he and his brother had orchestrated the bombing."

Vaughn Brown looked skeptical. "How do we know they're not just blowing smoke?"

"Mr. Secretary, Juan Juarez knew details about the bomb that were never reported in the press—its components, its precise location, and the fuse. Either the Juarez brothers did it, or they know the person who did."

After writing furiously, Fowler looked up from the legal pad in front of him. "Well, gentlemen, assuming that these are the men, how do we get our hands on them?"

Bodine tossed his pen on the desk and grunted. "Based on the fine work of our friends at the NSA, I don't think Mr. Ruiz and his government will be of much help."

"Yes," agreed Brooks. "And even a request for help will tip them off, and then we may never find the culprits."

"Any other options?" Fowler asked as he scanned the room and took another drink from the Styrofoam cup.

"I can have the boys at the Pentagon draw up a contingency plan to send in a team and bring them out. It should take only a few days."

"All right, Tom, do that. And then we can forward it to the president."

Chapter Sixteen

March 15
the Pentagon

Georgge Deterrman had been inside the National Security Threat Center at the Pentagon a dozen times or more, yet it always seemed foreign to him. The spartan interior gave it a functional ambiance, and the air seemed stale and cool. It was, however, a room in which he seemed destined to work.

Deterrman was a lanky rail of a man, with thick, reddish hair. As a teenager, he had always planned to attend West Point—just like his father and grandfather. The Army was the family business; olive green the family colors. In the end, poor health kept George Deterrman out of the academy, breaking a long family chain of service. Still feeling the call to serve his country, he attended the University of California at Berkeley and entered the Office of the Secretary of Defense as a civil servant. After twenty-two years, he had about as good a grasp of military planning as anyone, his acumen rivaling even the officer corps assigned to the Joint Chiefs of Staff.

On a large, rectangular desk, he spread out maps and satellite photos for analysis. He was examining the latest photo intelligence from Mexico in search of any potential clues or hints that might provide American forces with an advantage. The Pentagon had taken a U-2 spy plane out of mothballs to get some pictures. Through his small magnifier, Deterrman could see the chaos on the ground. In the photos he saw the swarm of people heading north and what appeared to be mass graves. What a bloody mess, he thought to himself. After several hours of satellite detective work, Determann was interrupted by a short, muscular man who entered the room. Deterrman set the magnifier down and looked him over. The visitor was dark and stern-faced, and there was a deep pride visible in his eyes which made them his defining feature.

"Captain Camacho?"

The young man nodded and walked to the table where the two shook hands. Although Camacho had been born in Mexico, he was 100 percent Indian, priding himself on the fact that there was not one drop of *Gachupines* (Spanish) blood in him. His mother had walked across the Rio Grande in 1974, six months pregnant with what would be her only child. David Jesus Camacho was born in El Paso and, thereby, instantly became an American citizen. His roots seemed to enhance, not deter, his sense of obligation and service to country, so he joined the armed services. With an impressive military record he was rewarded a coveted spot on the Army's elite Delta Force.

"Captain, I've read a great deal about you. Your records are impressive."

"Thank you, sir," Camacho said with a hint of arrogance.

"I've just begun to look over the intelligence. Have a seat."

Deterrman pulled out a stack of reports and handed them to Camacho. "Review this material. You must know everything about the Juarez brothers and the Avila Ortiz Mena Cartel. You will also need to select eight men well-suited for this mission. They will be working in an urban environment disguised as civilians."

"What can you tell me about the mission?"

"The plans have already been approved. Your objective will be to seize the Juarez brothers and return with them to the United States. We have firm evidence that they were involved in the San Diego bombing, and we want to bring them back here for trial. Mexican authorities will not cooperate. In fact, for the purposes of this mission, consider them hostile."

"Where are they located?"

"We are tracking them as best as possible. They were first seen in Mexicali. Further inquiries now place them in Mexico City. We will have something more definitive before you leave."

"When will that be?"

"The president hopes you will be on the ground in Mexico by March 30."

During the next six hours, Deterrman and Camacho went over the Mena file and the DEA reports on the Juarez brothers. Camacho was studious but enigmatic. Deterrman couldn't help but wonder if the captain would complete the mission.

Determined to keep his eyes open, David Camacho drank heavily from a coffee cup. As soon as the cup was empty, he grabbed the pot and refilled it. The eight members of his team tried various other methods to cope with the fatigue on that early morning of March 29. The minus-thirty-degree weather didn't help. Dressed in sports coats and khakis, several tried doing knee bends to circulate the blood. But nothing seemed to provide the answer.

The aircraft hangar at Ellsworth Air Force Base was drafty, and the South Dakota winds were whistling in a nearly constant tone through the narrow cracks of the metallic building. The white, unmarked Gulfstream G5 Jet was receiving a final once-over from technicians. As the team paced and grumbled in the cold, dark hangar, George Deterrman entered through a side door. Dressed in a heavy parka and boots, he looked ready for an arctic tour of Alaska.

"Good morning, gentlemen," he said with a conservative nod. "Be happy, at least you are going south."

A few chuckles ran through the room—but not from Camacho. He was as granite as ever. Deterrman pulled a manila folder out of a soft-carry briefcase. "These are your passports and papers. The folder also includes details of your agricultural delegation. Remember, you are visiting Mexico to attend the Beef Expo in Mexico City and to possibly purchase livestock. An embassy aide will be at the airport to pick you up."

Camacho took the folder with a firm grip and examined the contents.

"Your equipment will arrive by diplomatic pouch. Any questions?"

Camacho shook his head. "No, sir."

Deterrman extended his hand, and Camacho accepted it. "Good luck, Captain."

He wanted to say more, but Camacho seemed detached. No reason to impose on him, Deterrman thought to himself. The Gulfstream G5 left the hangar and taxied through the cold, windy darkness. Once on the main runway, the pilot pushed the throttle, propelling the aircraft into the air. On board, the lights were out, and Camacho and his men settled in for the flight and more sleep.

Deterrman watched as the glow from the aircraft engines slowly faded into the early morning darkness. As he walked back to his temporary office, a knot tightened in his stomach. The team was good—American fighting men were the best in the world. But the intelligence was spotty. The CIA had few assets on the ground collecting information. U.S. intelligence thought they knew where the Juarez brothers were, but it was not a certainty. The Mexican cauldron made Deterrman very nervous.

On the grassy confines of the Bosque de Chapultepec in central Mexico City, a crowd slowly assembled around a series of tables established by the National Salvation Front. The morning commute was proceeding with a fury and cars were tightly packed on the main thoroughfares into the city. But the Paseo de la Reforma, the main east–west boulevard through the metropolis, was closed for the rally organized by party functionaries. Government workers were strongly urged to attend, and party workers had plenty of inducements—food, gifts, and cash—to encourage participation and to give the event a carnival atmosphere.

The sun hung heavy in the morning sky. At the foot of the Monumento a Simon Bolivar, built in honor of the Latin American nationalists, a group of workers was hammering in the last nails on a wooden platform, and sound technicians were erecting loud-speakers. Nearby, President Ruiz sat in the back of his car with his personal physician by his side. The doctor was a soft-looking man with a puttylike complexion and smooth, delicate hands.

"Mr. President, I have another injection for you." Ruiz was lean-ing back in the soft leather seat, his face white and his mouth dry.

"Proceed, Doctor Lopez."

The doctor slowly rolled up a sleeve on President Ruiz's safari shirt. He pulled a syringe and needle from his physician's bag and carefully injected a yellowish substance into the president's arm. After an initial jolt of pain, Ruiz let out a long, deep sigh. "Very good, doctor," he said, closing his eyes momentarily. "Very good."

By 10:00 A.M. thousands were assembled on the Paseo de la Reforma. Many were dressed in red and black, the colors of the National Salvation Front. The crowd milled about, enjoying the dis-pensed gifts. Live music and singing added to the gaiety of the event. But among the revelers, there was a smaller, more somber element—party functionaries moving about in a methodical, even angry, man-ner. They were mostly young men dressed in quasi-military garb, including drab olive green hats and heavy boots. While others danced to the music, the functionaries stood straight without emotion.

After a succession of folk songs, Father Francisco Sanchez ascended the podium. A radical priest who had worked with Presi-dent Ruiz at the university, he possessed a smoldering hatred which could suddenly kindle into a consuming flame. Sanchez began the rally with an angry "prayer." This was not a petition to God but a grand political gesture of defiance. "Lord, we pray that you might vanquish our enemies, that you will pour hot coals on the many adversaries of your people. Protect this revolution!" he shouted. With fists raised in the air, he took his seat.

A string of party functionaries followed, boasting the Salvation Front's victories and accomplishments during their first year in power. The speeches were filled with panegyrics for the revolution and words that were a toxic mix of Marxism and home-grown nationalism. Fed largely by the distribution of food, alcohol, and money, the crowd swelled to ten thousand. At noon, President Ruiz took the stage and the crowd roared.

Although the president was clearly weakened by a worsening medical condition, he was never at a loss for words. Like a heavily laden train, his words came slowly at first, then building in pitch and speed as his oratory continued. By the end of the two-hour address, he seemed incapable of stopping. He concluded with his hands clenched and fists pumping: "Liberacion, si! Yanqui, no! Liberacion, si! Yanqui, no!"

Sweating and fatigued by the ordeal, Ruiz disappeared behind the podium and headed for his waiting car. The crowd continued to cheer. Professional agitators then took over, feeding off the emotions of the moment. With a precise spontaneity that could only have been planned, they herded the crowd to the U.S. embassy just a few blocks away. Clutching their bullhorns, the party activists led the crowd in chants and cheers.

Once at the gates of the embassy, it didn't take long for the festivity to be overshadowed by ugliness, much to the horror of most of the assembled. Bricks were thrown first at the Marine guards and then at several windows. While the crowd quickly thinned to two thousand hard-core functionaries, emotional anger reached its zenith.

U.S. Ambassador Benson Skinner knew a mob when he saw one, and the emotionally charged cabal outside the embassy made him extremely nervous. He frantically began placing phone calls to Mexican officials, requesting police assistance. Promises were made, but the police never arrived. Feeling violence was inevitable, Skinner ordered the staff to prepare for an evacuation. The last call he made was to National Security Adviser Fowler at the White House (they had attended Harvard together).

By 3:30 P.M. the group had reached critical mass, and the agitators made their first push for the embassy front door. Courageous Marine guards successfully fought them off, but their success was only temporary. Just minutes later, a shot rang out, and Marine Sergeant Brian Woods fell to the ground. His compatriots grabbed him and followed the rest of the American staff out the back entrance onto Palaopan Street, fleeing for the nearby Hotel Jardin Amazonas.

The crowd now burst through the embassy's front door and ran through the building in search of booty and papers that might be of interest. Party youth leader Hector Alvaro tucked the revolver back into his belt and pulled out cans of spray paint. With large flowing motions, the twenty-one-year-old university student defiled the embassy's elegant walls with slogans in red and black: "Revolucion, si! Yanqui, non!"

As the others scrounged through the embassy offices, stripping them of televisions and computers, Alvaro forced his way into the locked office of the military attache. Colonel Charles Peyton had been out of town that day, so everything was in its place. In the file cabinet he found a file marked "Camacho, David." He immediately took it to federal police headquarters.

Chapter Seventeen

March 29
Mexico City

David Camacho was waiting restlessly with his men at the commercial aircraft hangar of Benito Juarez International Airport. The civilian pilot, Joe Ross, was smoking a cigarette and standing next to the Gulfstream G5 while the Delta team milled about in anticipation. The bright sun had been out for most of the day. Although the heat was a nice change from the early morning spent at Ellsworth, the hangar was stuffy. The group had cleared customs but was now waiting for a Miss Jennings from the embassy to arrive and provide the necessary paperwork for their business visas.

Camacho checked his watch for what must have been the tenth time in as many minutes. To an officer, schedules were meant to be kept. Traffic, he thought to himself. It must be the traffic. Using a dirty pay phone on the wall, he called the number for the embassy switchboard. As he held the receiver, his left hand tapped a rhythmic beat on the hangar wall. The phone rang for three minutes, but there was no answer. Perplexed, Camacho set the receiver down and headed over to the main terminal to rent a car. After twenty minutes he returned with a white minivan. The affable customs official, who was holding the passports, was sleeping at his desk. Camacho tapped him on the shoulder, stirring him out of his nap. "Sir, if it's all the same to you, I think we'll just find a way to the embassy by ourselves."

The official adjusted his cap and stood. "You may go if you like, gentlemen. But I must hold the passports until Miss Jennings from the embassy arrives. You are part of a business delegation, and she must provide the paperwork for your special visas. I am sorry, these are the regulations I must follow." Camacho shrugged his shoulders and headed for the van with his men.

With a map in hand, Camacho took the wheel and proceeded to Mexico City and the U.S. embassy compound. The route was familiar to him. Twice as a young boy he had come to Mexico City with his mother to visit her family. Now twenty years later, it seemed as chaotic and puzzling as ever. The traffic was light, and before long they were in the heart of the city. As the van proceeded past a standing taxi, Camacho gripped the wheel firmly and saw the appalling sight. In front of him stood a defaced embassy with graffiti now covering much of the outside and a subdued group of young men wandering the grounds. Furniture had been tossed onto the street, and the American flag had been replaced with the black-and-red party flag of the National Salvation Front.

"What's going on?" someone asked from the back of the van.

Camacho didn't answer, but instead stopped the van along the boulevard and removed his sunglasses. The sound of car horns erupted around him, but he could only stare in disbelief. A throng of people continued to fill the boulevard, some in a celebratory mood, others simply curious about the whole spectacle. As the crowd grew, Camacho looked intently for anyone who might be connected with the embassy. Suddenly, a brick smashed through the window, sending glass through the passenger section of the car. The Americans were momentarily dazed, and a band of agitators moved toward the van. "Revolucion, si! Yanqui, no!"

Camacho laid on the horn and punched the accelerator, frantically guiding the van through the human maelstrom that now threatened to engulf him. He raced down the Boulevard Paseo de la Reforma with no particular destination in mind. His immediate instinct was to return to the airport, so he sped up the motorway and headed for the commercial air hangar where the Gulfstream G5 was housed. From a distance he saw Joe Ross in handcuffs and being pushed into a police van and armed guards impounding the plane. With his means of retreat cut off, Camacho was uncertain about what to do next.

George Determan set the receiver down and let out a deep sigh. The knot in his stomach had only gotten worse since the team departed. He wanted confirmation from the embassy that the men had arrived, but no one could be reached. Suddenly, the phone on his desk rang, taking him only temporarily out of his vexation.

"Yes."

"George, it's Jack Fowler at the White House. We need you here right away."

"Yes, sir. What is this about?"

"Things have unhinged in Mexico City. We have serious problems."

Determan swallowed hard. "I'll be there right away."

Jack Fowler's office was a cold, cavelike place. The shades were drawn during even the bleakest days, and the thick, dark, antique English furniture gave the room a mysterious ambiance—the feel of an old library. As Determan entered the office, Fowler was in the corner working the phone. He signaled Determan to sit down, and minutes later, Defense Secretary Tom Bodine rumbled in with Secretary of State Vaughn Brown on his heels. When Fowler hung up the phone, his face was ashen and a filmlike sweat hung from his brow.

"Gentlemen," he said, taking his seat, "thank you for coming on such short notice. George, I've asked you to come because the operation is at risk."

A knot of tension swelled in Deterrman's throat. "Sir?"

"An angry mob just stormed the U.S. embassy in Mexico City. Ambassador Skinner and embassy personnel have taken refuge at a hotel. It is his recommendation that we evacuate all embassy personnel at once."

Deterrman boldly interjected, "Are Camacho and the Delta team at the hotel?"

"No, George. We don't know where they are. We have minimal intelligence as to what is going on down there. It's a disgrace." Shaking his head, the national security adviser pressed on. "On top of all this, the latest INS estimates report that the rate of immigration has tripled in recent weeks. We have had an outbreak of tuberculosis in El Paso, and social services are stretched thin from San Diego to Brownsville. The president has decided that we must act boldly." He paused. "He has asked that we draw up plans for the invasion of Mexico and come up with an action plan for generating a transitional government until elections can be held."

Vaughn Brown glanced around the room, a sour grimace etched firmly on his face. "You can't be serious."

"I am. And the president wants his whole team behind this."

As was his custom, Bodine was leaning back in his chair, his suit crumpled and tie crooked as if he had been wearing them for days. "Well, as you know, Jack, I reluctantly came to that conclusion a month ago. But to move on Mexico, we need to strike with decisive force to break the will of the Mexican army. And I think we need clearly designated political objectives. What does the president want to achieve, and how far does he want to go?"

"The president believes that this crisis cannot be dealt with as long as Ruiz remains in power. The attack on the embassy is just another in a long string of incidents which you all know about. Reports of human rights abuse have increased dramatically in Mexico, and Ruiz is neck-deep in the Mexican drug trade. We have more on him than we ever had on Noriega. The question is, what will it take to get it done?"

Bodine leaned forward, his jaw boldly jutting outward. "You know as well as I do our state of readiness. Cutbacks have put us in a situation where training has been way down during the past four years. Can it be done? Of course it can. What will it take? I'm not sure. Let me put my men on it. But, Jack, we still have the larger question, what follows Ruiz?"

"We will set up a working group including the NSC and State to explore that very question. You get the military plan in shape, and we'll work on the politics."

"Very well, I'll have it for you tomorrow morning." Bodine turned to Deterrman, "George, I want you to come with me."

Deterrman remained seated as the rest of the group stood up. "What about Camacho and his men?"

"Do what you need to," said Fowler, knowing he didn't have much to offer. "You have the president's full backing on this. The embassy's security staff in Mexico says that the phone lines to the Hotel Jardin are being tapped. Skinner did tell me that the diplomatic staff will be on a chartered plane tomorrow morning. I suggest that you make sure those men are on that plane."

Back at his office in the National Security Threat Center, Deterrman's worktable resembled a mosaic with stacks of papers and maps scattered about. Operation Aztec, as it was now officially called, would be a complex operation. Yet his mind was still fixed on the Delta team in Mexico City. The embassy had heard nothing from Camacho, and the staff was now couped up in the Hotel Jardin Amazonas, with a loud mob holding vigil outside. Calls to the commercial aircraft hangar in Mexico City revealed nothing.

Frustrated, Deterrman had to remove the Delta team from his mind as the planning staff worked out a rough military contingency for an invasion of Mexico. Several hours of painstaking analysis with the services yielded a realistic, workable plan. The 2nd Armored Division and 3rd Armored Cavalry Regiment from Fort Hood, Texas, would push down Mexican Highway 85 to Monterrey and then proceed down Highway 54 to Guadalajara. The 24th Mechanized Division from Fort Stewart, Georgia, and the 1st Mechanized Division from Fort Riley, Kansas, would cross the border at Brownsville and proceed along coastal Highway 180. At Tampico, they would move west along Highway 105 to Mexico City. In the west, the 1st Marine Division at Camp Pendleton and the Army's 7th Division at Fort Lewis would pass through Tucson, crossing the border at Nogales before moving south on Highway 15.

Resistance by Mexican forces was expected to be sporadic at best. Fighter-bombers working from Barksdale Air Force Base in Louisiana, Carswell in Texas, and Vandenberg in California would provide the initial strike on Mexican military installations. The most serious problem was readiness. Because of funding shortfalls, several key battalions were about to go into combat with serious training deficiencies. Some platoon leaders had never taken their platoons into the field for training exercises, while others had not been evaluated in live-fire exercises. Defense planners hoped to overcome these concerns with a bold, quick, devastating strike.

Bodine and Fowler would present the plan to the president tomorrow morning. Deterrman thought it was sound, but he wondered if the president would actually go through with it. And even more important, what government would follow Ruiz was still open to question. It was now 10:30 P.M. and the last of the planning staff had gone home. Deterrman rubbed his eyes, grabbed his sports coat and headed for the door. A stack of empty pizza boxes and a pile of soda cans still cluttered the worktables. Just as he was opening the door, the phone rang. While he could have let it go, he felt the need to pick it up. Something drew him to it.

"Hello, this is Deterrman."

Over a crackling line with a slight hiss came the welcome words, "George... this is David."

His pulse raced. "David... where are you?" He wanted to be

more specific, but he had no way of knowing whether Camacho was on a secure phone. That question was soon answered.

"George, the family and I are still in Mexico City… on vacation. Your friends never showed up."

A slight film of perspiration began to form on Deterrman's face. "Oh… that's terrible. David, maybe you should check into the Hotel Jardin Amazonas. That might be where they are staying."

Camacho cleared his throat. "I've already tried that—they're all booked up. No vacancies. Seems as if a crowd of people showed up this afternoon. And they decided to stay the night."

Deterrman began to stutter as a sense of helplessness descended on him. "Well, maybe it's best to just return home. I understand there is a special charter flight tomorrow morning."

"That won't work. There are no tickets… we tried to get some, and the service was very rude."

Deterrman's mouth felt extremely dry, and his head started to throb. "I understand. Let me see what I can do. Can you call again tomorrow?"

"Yes, at ten in the morning."

"Give me more time. Make it noon."

Deterrman set the receiver down. He turned off the lights and went home, but his worries stayed with him.

A light snow fell in Washington as the president met Bodine and Fowler for breakfast. St. John was wearing a red sweater and cracking a hard-boiled egg with a silver spoon. His defense secretary was sipping coffee as Fowler scowled at *The New York Times*. The above-the-fold headline read: "WHITE HOUSE CONTEMPLATES MILITARY OPTION FOR MEXICO."

"So," asked Fowler tossing it on the side table, "who do you think leaked it?"

Bodine set his coffee cup down. The fine bone china seemed ill-suited for his rough hands. "We all know it was the Secretary of State."

St. John carefully salted his egg. "Well, I want him out. On something as sensitive as this, leaks are unacceptable."

"I agree, Mr. President. He's just trying to cover himself." Fowler concluded as he poured himself some orange juice in a small crystal glass. "But we should wait. If we let him go now, he'll be on every talk show with his typical pomposity. I don't think we should risk Operation Aztec."

Bodine returned matter-of-factly to the business at hand. Bureaucratic battles rarely held his interest for long. "Mr. President, we can obviously win a military victory in Mexico. But what about the peace? Once Ruiz goes, who takes his place?"

"The working group has identified four respected citizens from the business community who will work with us. The trouble is, we don't know what sort of reception they will get from the public."

"Jack, if that is the case we can't send our soldiers down there. It's asking for trouble. What happens if we remove Ruiz and the people reject these new guys?"

Fowler was becoming irritated—primarily because he knew that Bodine was correct. "Look, Tom, we'd all like it if there were a better group, but there is no time. This is where the lack of good intelligence really hurts. We had no warning about this pending crisis, forcing us to act in haste. And at this point, we don't have the capability to forge good relations with other likely candidates. We need to go with what we have. The president wants to move now."

St. John nodded. "I do want to proceed as soon as possible. Tom, let me ask you. When can you have the men ready to move?"

"The planning staff tells me we will need fourteen days for the initial force. Mobilizing reserves will take longer, but we can move across the border in fourteen days."

"All right then, in fourteen days."

"Mr. President, there is one other matter. Deterrman called me last night. The Delta Force Team we sent to Mexico City to bring back the Juarez brothers is trapped. With the embassy staff leaving, they are cut off and without passports. George and I would like your authorization to launch a covert operation to bring them home."

His egg finished, the president wiped his mouth and stood up. "Of course, Tom. Do whatever you have to."

Chapter Eighteen

April 4
Mexico City

George Deterrman drank the last drop of water in his plastic cup and then chewed on the ice cubes. Flying always unsettled him. He felt claustrophobic and was nervous about the slightest engine noise. It wasn't so much that he feared death—that could happen in a car or even walking. What he disliked about flying was that if death came at the end of a terrifying plunge, you had time to think about it. Instantaneous death, he thought, would be preferable.

The takeoff from Miami International had been uneventful, and there was surprisingly little turbulence during the flight. Mexico City was now visible in the distance. From his window at ten thousand feet, the city looked partially overcast, cloaked with a gray smog. It had been years since his last trip here, despite his extensive knowledge of the region. South and Central America had received most of his attention since they were supposed to be the hot spots. The crisis in Mexico had erupted without warning, just like so many volcanoes in the region. No one had expected that such profound, complex problems would develop so dramatically and so close to America.

At the airport, Deterrman breezed his way through customs and rented a car. He found the motorway into the heart of the city with little trouble but noticed the tight security along the roadway. Through clandestine contacts at the French embassy, he arranged a rendezvous with Camacho and the Delta team at Parque Mexico, a grassy esplanade at the center of a spider's web of streets and boulevards. He drove past the narrow side streets and ramshackle homes that ringed the city. Once in town, he found ever-present food lines and a wandering mass of unemployed people. It was a ghastly sight.

Parque Mexico was bustling. Even amid the economic misery, people found time to escape with family and sweethearts. While the adults sat placidly, the exuberance of youth brought out a playfulness and laughter in the children that could only make Deterrman smile. He parked the car along the boulevard and got out to stretch his legs and have a look around. The trees were dying and the grass browning, but he could see the appeal of Parque Mexico to weary city residents. There was no sign of Camacho and the Delta team, so he turned on the car radio and waited.

As light guitar music wafted through the air, a commotion across the esplanade broke the tempo of the afternoon. Several dozen uniformed police were struggling with a group of men. A sinking feeling rushed through Deterrman. He began walking across the park until his adrenalin pushed him into a slight jog. As he got closer, he saw David Camacho, unshaven and soiled, being forced into the back of an olive green federal police van. Deterrman clenched his fists but halfway across the grass stopped suddenly. Think clearly, he said to himself. Do you think you can take on a dozen armed police?

By now, a bantam police officer with an ill-defined mustache was staring straight at him, barely twenty yards away. The officer pulled out his revolver and started moving toward him. "Halt!" he yelled in broken English. "I have questions!" Deterrman turned and in a panic began a full sprint back to his car, his giant strides closing the distance quickly. The officer was now running too, his thin legs working like pistons. Deterrman managed to get the car started and off before his pursuer could reach him. Sweating and breathing heavily, he wondered what to do next.

The amassing of U.S. forces along the Mexican border had not been lost on the media. On April 8 CNN reported the movement of the 24th Mechanized Division by rail from Fort Stewart,

Georgia, to a facility outside Brownsville, Texas. For one week, the unit trained in the flat, dry confines of south Texas. The network also reported that the 1st Mechanized Division from Fort Riley, Kansas, had moved south to Fort Bliss, Texas, near El Paso, and the 7th Infantry Division from Fort Lewis, Washington, would shortly be joining the 24th in Brownsville.

In Mexico City, President Ruiz and his advisors had been watching the ominous reports trickle in. The stories on CNN followed *The New York Times* headline disclosing that Washington was contemplating offensive action. In response, the Mexican president called an emergency meeting of his top advisors to discuss alternatives. Ruiz paced in his executive office, smoking a thick cigar and growling, looking for answers.

"What do the reports tell us?" he boomed to his defense minister, General Octavio Rivera. The general was his most brutal and efficient supporter. Trained in the United States, Rivera was a highly political officer who saw military force as a tool not only to protect the country but also to achieve domestic control. His most notorious act was quelling food riots in Hermosillo by using crack troops to fire on civilians. Since he drove the media off at gunpoint, the number of casualties was never determined. He had purged the army leadership of anyone who might oppose the Ruiz agenda and was firmly in control of the military.

Rivera was a squatty man with a fat face and small, marblelike eyes. He was always half-shaven, and a thin scar ran down his left cheek. His loyalty to the cause was unquestioned, even to the point of having his wife imprisoned because she proved politically "unreliable." The other members of the National Defense Council were Foreign Minister Carlos Siquiernos and Army Chief of Staff General Porfirio Madero Cardenas. Siquiernos was by far the most pro-American of the group, and his outspoken advocacy of a compromising policy toward the United States made him suspicious in the eyes of his colleagues. Born into a wealthy family of industrialists, Siquiernos knew deep down the folly that Ruiz and his band were perpetuating on the Mexican people. His hope to moderate their course was the one thing that kept him in an administration that he secretly reviled.

"The Americans have deployed armored divisions and infantry to south Texas," Rivera responded. "It is only a question of time before they cross the border and begin their assault on our country."

Ruiz took a deep drag on his cigar, releasing the whitish-gray smoke that enshrouded him. "We must prepare to defend the revolution. What is the status of our forces? We must resist. The integrity and sovereignty of our people are at stake!"

Calmly, Siquiernos interjected, "Mr. President, the Americans are angered by our seizure of the their servicemen and the sacking of their embassy. But they also have sought cooperation in dealing with the refugee crisis. Some accommodation and flexibility on our part just might prevent this calamity from taking place." The high tone of his voice and the precise nature of his syntax was a sharp contrast to the more common Spanish spoken by the other cabinet ministers.

Ruiz again pulled on his cigar. Turning angrily to his foreign minister, he blew a thick stream of smoke, embellished with contempt, at his face. "I do not need a mouthpiece for Washington in my government." Siquiernos grimaced, the smoke stinging his eyes.

Always unflappable, Siquiernos continued, "I say this only with the interests of this government and our people at heart. We all know that we cannot stand up to the Americans militarily."

Sensing an opportunity to further consolidate his power, General Rivera disdainfully got up from the ornate French sofa. "It is my firm conviction that Mr. Siquiernos does not support the interests of this revolution. Keeping him on this cabinet creates a security risk."

President Ruiz walked over to his desk, pulled another cigar out of a leather box, and placed it in his mouth. He twisted it ever so slightly. Using a crystal lighter, he lit the tip and bursts of smoke soon emerged from his lips. He turned back to Siquiernos. "Carlos," he said softly, "I must ask you to leave the room." Although the foreign minister was not being asked to resign, this request was hardly a vote of confidence.

With a defeated look on his face, Siquiernos got up and left. As the door shut behind him, General Rivera began in a pedantic tone, "We cannot negotiate with the Americans. At the Treaty of Guadalupe Hidalgo our forefathers were forced to cede California and New Mexico to the United States after the war. No, we cannot negotiate with the Americans. And we cannot defeat them in the traditional manner. Head-to-head, they will easily overcome us. However, America has lost one war in her history—Vietnam. We can use the lessons of that war and apply them to our situation. Our country is a crazy quilt of volcanic mountains, cut into a patchwork of isolated areas. It is ideal for guerrilla warfare."

Ruiz was back on the sofa, slouched but listening intently. He squinted his eyes as if in deep thought. "Yes... yes... continue."

"If we move quickly, we can deploy our forces to the Sierra Madres and the foothills of central Mexico. We can create a chain of forces running from the Yaqui River in the north to Oaxaca in the south. With pre-positioned food, ammunition, and other supplies, we can field a guerrilla army that will drive the Americans back over the border, defeated and humiliated."

Ruiz grinned approvingly. "Generals Rivera and Cardenas, do so at once. You have any resources you need at your disposal. We will also need a new presidential headquarters hidden in the mountains. The government will go underground, and we will rally the people." With Siquiernos out of the room, the Ruiz leadership never realized the depths of their folly.

George Deterrman was in a deep valley of depression that he seemingly could not shake. After days of wandering through Mexico City, he still had no information on the fate of the Delta Force team. Detailed intelligence was virtually nonexistent. The agency did not even remotely have the resources it once did in Mexico. It was as if he were blinded, wandering through a maze in search of a moving, silent target. Mindful that the impending invasion was only hours away, Deterrman caught a flight back to Washington.

Chapter Nineteen

April 14
U.S.-Mexican border

During the early morning hours, U.S. forces stormed across the Rio Grande at two points. The 24th Mechanized Division out of Fort Stewart, Georgia, pushed across the Gateway Bridge into Matamoros, Mexico, and the 7th Infantry Division from Fort Lewis, Washington, moved across the McAllen International Bridge into Reynosa. Both units pushed south and met at Highway 180 to advance on the port city of Tampico on the gulf coast. The municipality would serve as a staging base for Operation Aztec, as well as a headquarters and supply route for U.S. forces in Mexico.

The 24th Division was moved largely on heavy equipment transport systems (HETS), heavy trucks capable of carrying armored units long distances. Armored vehicles wear out their tracks and transmissions relatively fast, and the push to Tampico was more than four hundred miles. The terrain, which was mostly flat, irrigated corn and cotton fields, made the advance easier and it had an added benefit: it made it difficult for enemy forces to achieve any surprise. On day one, the 24th met only sporadic resistance from two pre-positioned brigades of Mexican infantry near the small town of Aldama. The firefight lasted fewer than twenty minutes, after which the defending force fled. Nevertheless, U.S. training deficiencies were evident: four soldiers died to friendly fire.

North of Tampico, the 2nd Marine Division out of Camp LeJeune, North Carolina, made an amphibious landing near Lago San Andres. They arrived heavily armed but were also laden with food and other goods to distribute to civilians. Because the Ruiz government was a scourge on Mexico and was highly unpopular with the people, the Marines entered Tampico to cheers.

As American ground units advanced south, U.S. fighters flew sorties from air bases in California, Texas, and Louisiana. Many

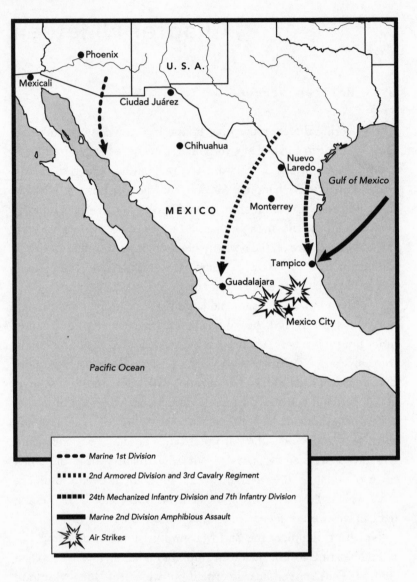

Legend:

- - - - Marine 1st Division

∎∎∎∎∎ 2nd Armored Division and 3rd Cavalry Regiment

∎∎∎∎∎ 24th Mechanized Infantry Division and 7th Infantry Division

▬▬▬ Marine 2nd Division Amphibious Assault

✦ Air Strikes

Pentagon's Operational Plan for the Liberation of Mexico

planes returned to their bases with ordnance because there were so few viable military targets to hit. The first priority was the main military air base housing an almost antique collection of fighters, including F-4s and F-5s. American F-18s took the planes out in less than two minutes, while B-2 bombers and F-15 Strike Eagles hit the Mexican army's communications and command facility outside the capital.

At the same time, a psychological operation (PSYOP) was unveiled to convey America's intentions to the Mexican people. Flying over Mexico City at forty thousand feet, the 193rd Special Operations Group from Pennsylvania activated the main electronic warfare system on Commando Solo, a dull, gray prop plane which moved slowly through the air. Technicians on board jammed the main radio and television frequencies of Mexico's media outlets and replaced government programming with a message from President St. John. "We have only the best intentions in this crisis. The Ruiz regime has caused much abuse, hunger, and suffering in your country. American soldiers have come to Mexico not to harm the Mexican people but to overthrow the Ruiz government and in its place erect a democratic government that can again put Mexico on the path to prosperity. Let me assure you: U.S. soldiers have strict orders to fire only when fired on. If you do not resist, you will not be harmed. If, however, you do fire on American troops, we will respond with overwhelming force."

General Rivera first heard the news of the U.S. offensive at Base Camp Colada in the mountain region of Zacatecas. He had been expecting it for months, so he was not surprised. Now it was time to mount a defense based on what he thought was a fierce guerrilla army made up of young men willing to die for the cause. But the reality was something otherwise; most had joined seeking three square meals a day.

The main guerrilla camp was named Colada after the sword carried by El Cid, the hero who drove the Moors from Spain. "In the same way," he promised his subordinates, "we will drive out the Americans." The small camp was hastily cut from a hillside overlooking a modest valley. With the exception of a few small villages, it was isolated from contact with the outside world. The only way into Colada was via a network of tiny, narrow dirt roads.

A clump of crude, basic structures had been erected in recent months. Dirty tin roofs were covered with netting and vegetation to disguise the facility from the air. Rivera had been to Colada many times during the past several weeks, preparing it for this day. Dressed in camouflage green, with gold stars clipped to his collar, he wore black combat boots and a green beret tilted ever so slightly on his head. Addressing the troops was his favorite task as army commander.

More than 2,500 soldiers, considered the most reliable and loyal men in the army, were crowded into the tight confines of Colada. They appeared to be something less than fierce. Emaciated and sickly, most looked like they had missed more than a few meals in recent months, and their uniforms were a mismatch of colors, some brown and others a faded, palish green. Each soldier clutched an M-16 rifle, a grenade firmly clipped to his belt.

The heavy mist and thick, robust cloud cover seemed appropriate for the grim situation these men now faced. General Rivera walked with a slow swagger through the red mud to the head of the assembly. News of the U.S. attack had worked its way through the camp, and fear soon followed. As he looked over the troops' frightened, hungry faces, Rivera wondered how many were true believers. He shook the doubt from his mind and, with bullhorn in hand, stepped up on a box to address the men.

"The Americans have attacked. Now we must rise! You are the only defense our people have against the Americans. Now is the time for heroism.

"Our enemy's ignorance of obstacles in these hills will be to its great disadvantage. When you see them coming, knowing the path they will follow, observe and count them before they approach. Deploy yourselves along the path out of sight, and when their last man passes your ambush, open fire!

"All direct contact with the enemy should be avoided. Relations

U.S. forces conduct operations in central Mexico.

with local communities should be established, with recruiting and training men as your goal. You are all called upon to recruit your men and bring them into this army. Those who recruit will move up in rank. Strategic targets should be found and sabotaged. These targets should be limited to American military installations and collaborators.

"If you face the enemy once your position is breached, use civilians as a shield and withdraw. Furthermore, search for every new, possible channel of propaganda. We must succeed in explaining to the people the truth about what the Americans are doing.

"The basic structural unit of our armed forces is a group of eleven men. For important ambushes, we might use a group of twenty-two. In the classic eleven-man group, there will always be a political commissar.

"While we will win great victories, there will also be defeats. But the tide of history flows with us, not against us. The Americans fought for their independence two hundred years ago. Today, we fight for Mexico's real independence and freedom!"

For ten minutes Rivera led the men in cheers of "Revolucion, si! Yanqui, non!" the loud cries resonating throughout the valley. Most of the *compensanos* in the surrounding villages were perplexed more than anything else.

Back in the heart of Mexico City, President Eduardo Francisco Ruiz exited Los Pinos through a side door and jumped into the back of a waiting Toyota. His presidential limousine was out in front of the palace, and, on his orders, it proceeded down Parque Lirz with a police escort, a decoy for his many enemies. Meanwhile, the Toyota he occupied raced through the chaotic city streets, heading north for the mountains of Zacatecas and the new presidential offices erected adjacent to Camp Colada.

Foreign Minister Siquiernos was at the Colegio de Defensa (the Mexican equivalent of the U.S. War College) when word reached him of the American move. He had been meeting with a small group of co-conspirators from the officer corps, traditionalists who abhorred the radicalism of the Ruiz regime and the horror it had wrought on their nation. The group agreed to move swiftly on Los Pinos in order to seize power and bring the war to a quick end. The conspirators jumped in their cars and raced toward the palace. Armed with just handguns, they stormed into the executive office only to find it abandoned, stripped bare of anything worth value. "The coward!" Siquiernos screamed in anger. "He talks of fighting but then runs and hides."

With pistols in hand, the junior officers sealed the door to the executive office while Siquiernos went to Ruiz's desk and picked up the phone. Coolly, but with a flutter of nerves, he placed a call to the White House.

Jack Fowler was getting the latest intelligence from the ground units when the call came through. "Yes... put him on," he said awkwardly to his secretary.

After explaining that President Ruiz had fled, Siquiernos said he and a small group of officers from the Colegio de Defensa were now prepared to establish a provisional government to oversee new, open, and free elections. Although the national security advisor was noncommittal and said only that he would raise the matter with the president, he knew instantly that the solid reputation of the Mexican foreign minister would give enormous legitimacy to a provisional government.

Fowler convened a meeting in the Oval Office with the president, Defense Secretary Bodine, and Deterrman. Secretary of State Brown had resigned and had yet to be replaced. "The foreign minister," began Fowler, "is an honest man and one with the stature to bring his country out of this dark period and back into the light of democracy and free markets. I think he is a man we should work with. He will give the transitional government greater legitimacy."

"A good test will be whether he will free Camacho and his men," answered Bodine. "I think that is a good starting point."

Deterrman was concerned also about the fate of the Mexican president. "What about Ruiz? Did the foreign minister shed any light on where he is hiding?"

Fowler shook his head in disappointment. "No. The foreign minister believes that he and the defense general staff might have fled to the mountains. They had talked about a secret presidential headquarters. And there apparently were covert discussions concerning a guerrilla war."

Bodine didn't like things messy. "Don't we have any intel on this?"

"No." This was becoming a familiar word when discussing intelligence. "The NSA will continue to monitor the country in the hope of picking up some electronic intercepts, and satellites might offer some clues concerning the location of the main guerrilla base. But there are no guarantees."

St. John agreed to recognize Siquiernos as president on the condition that he release the Delta Force team and agree to free and fair elections in six months. Jack Fowler went to a phone and placed the call.

In the underground labyrinth at federal police headquarters in

Mexico City, several junior officers were working their way through the cells. Siquiernos had ordered them to locate and free the American prisoners. In a cell reeking of urine, the officers found the Americans—dead. They had been shot through the bars with a handgun. The bodies were still warm.

April 16 was the third day of Operation Aztec, and the Mexican army had all but capitulated. Army intelligence estimated the desertion rate at about 50 percent, and those who remained in uniform either offered light resistance and surrendered or refused to fight altogether. The 2nd Marine Division had established an effective base camp outside Tampico, and cargo ships were bringing in massive quantities of food and fuel. Geographic proximity prevented logistics—always critical in war—from being much of a problem.

The formation of a provisional government in Mexico City meant that U.S. forces would no longer need to push further south and occupy the capital. By now Siquiernos had firm control of the major organs of government and was arresting those officials who had abused state power. But Ruiz and his closest aides were still hiding somewhere in Mexico. President St. John wanted them brought to justice, and U.S. forces would remain in the country until they were found. The war was against the Ruiz government, not the Mexican people. So long as they remained at large, the war was not over as far as Washington was concerned.

Rumors of guerrilla activity in the central Mexican highlands caught George Deterrman's curiosity. The fateful end of Camacho and the Delta team had pushed him deeper into the heart of Operation Aztec. For him it was no longer a job—it had become personal. He somehow felt responsible for the deaths. Guards at federal police headquarters accused General Porfirio Madero Cardenas, the army chief of staff, as the trigger man for the murders. He was presumed to be in hiding with Ruiz and General Rivera.

Deterrman thought the central highlands offered the key. It was unlikely that any of the leadership had made it out of the country.

Secretary Bodine deployed the U.S. Army's 10th Mountain Division from Fort Drum, New York, and some elements of the U.S. Army's 7th Division, already in Tampico, to comb the area.

Chapter Twenty

October 4
central Mexican highlands

The mountains of Zacatecas rose from the earth and stretched to the sky like a jagged stone cathedral. The harsh winds and seasonal rains made for a difficult climate, and the confusing topography frustrated even the most accomplished navigator. Colonel Phil Lewis rubbed the dust off the wallet photo of his family as a humvee took him up the winding, narrow dirt roads to the new forward base camp outside San Juan de Guadalupe. For six months now, Lewis and his men from the 7th Division had been crisscrossing the foothills and peaks of the mountains. Bands of tired, hungry guerrillas occasionally emerged to surrender, but the mission to locate Ruiz or the main camp had so far been futile. Lewis was part of the post-Vietnam officer corps, so dealing with a real-world guerrilla movement was new to him. It was shadowboxing, and without good HUMINT, the shadow would eventually win.

As the humvee pulled up to the base camp, Lewis saw a pair of Apache helicopters in the distance scouring the mountains for any evidence of activity. In tents near the helicopter pad, he found the three platoons from the 7th Division that he would join on patrol. The colonel made a point of going with his men into the field—it was good for morale.

Lewis brought the platoon leaders together for a briefing outside the barracks. Stabbing his finger at a crude topographical map, he pointed to a hill twenty-two miles north. "We're going to move here.

It should take two days of hiking to reach it. Lieutenant Monroe, I want you and your platoon to take the point." James Monroe nodded. By taking three platoons to the interior, Lewis hoped to uncover some clues concerning the location of the enemy's base camp.

The journey was arduous and slow. Guides from Siquiernos's new Mexican army were serving as scouts, and interviews with villagers during the trek revealed some interesting intelligence. Several locals showed Lewis syringes they had found in the woods. Rumors of Ruiz's medical problems gave him hope the dragnet might be closing on the elusive ex-president of Mexico. Following a difficult march the first day, the group camped on a craggy hill with the brush cleared away. Lewis checked with headquarters by COMLINK and then rested.

Day two started out the same way—until a blast of gunfire cut through the early morning calm. "Monroe is down! We need help!" the radio crackled in Lewis's hand. The radio then went dead.

Lieutenant James Monroe was hit in the opening burst of fire. The crack of rifle fire from the right was followed immediately by rocket-propelled grenades. Then came the thump, thump, thump of a heavy machine gun as it cut a swath through the 3rd Platoon and the surrounding brush. Lewis heard gunfire just over a small ridge to his right. The 2nd Platoon was to his left, maybe half a mile off. He bellowed to the men of the 1st Platoon, "Up the hill! Up the hill!" The men raced up the hill, adrenalin pumping and muscles aching. Lewis released the safety on his handgun. The sound of intense gunfire continued, and, in a strange way, it was encouraging: this was not an ambush—the enemy was choosing to stay and fight. The 3rd Platoon had obviously run across something very big.

As the incline of the embankment increased, Lewis and the men dropped to a crawl. It seemed to take an eternity to make it up the ridge, but once at the top, Lewis looked down the ravine and saw the scattered bodies of at least a dozen soldiers. Those still alive were pinned under a hail of bullets, face down on the ground. Three hundred yards north, Lewis spotted a series of crude defensive structures.

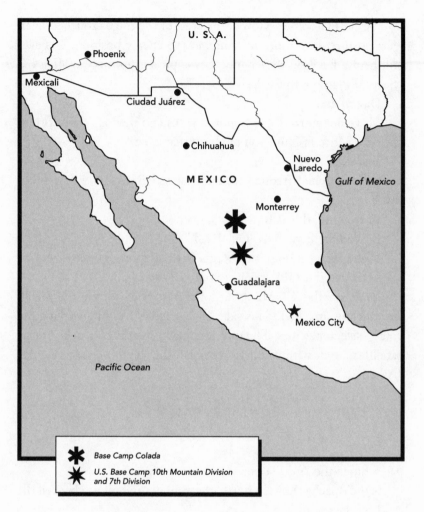

The Guerilla War in Zacatecas

The 1st Platoon was now at the crest of the ridge crouched in an alert posture, firing intermittently at the enemy position. His eyes still firmly fixed on the enemy, Lewis picked up the COMLINK. "Second Platoon, this is Lewis, over."

"Davis here."

"Move due north three hundred yards and then lay cover fire to the east. Move fast and you might outflank 'em!"

"Yes, sir!"

Lewis switched frequencies and radioed Bravo Base fifty miles south.

"Bravo One, this is Bravo Two, over."

"Bravo One here, over. Go ahead."

"We're under intense fire. Request air support at once, over."

"Activate your GPS receivers Bravo Two, over."

Lewis set the COMLINK down and reached for the small, metallic box attached to his side. He activated the unit, working the rotary-selector switch. The tiny antenna inside the box locked on to satellites, and within thirty seconds the liquid crystal display flashed:

LAT 25 40' N

LON 100 19' W

He radioed the 2nd Platoon. "Activate GPS, over."

As the Apaches howled north, the gunners and pilots checked the read on their scanners:

LAT 25 40' N

LON 100 19' W

They then locked onto the coordinates with their navigational computers and quickly moved to the area.

The 2nd Platoon opened up from a small tree line in the west, but the enemy was well-entrenched. Lewis wondered why they were choosing to stay and fight. It could only mean one thing: Base

Camp Colada was not far away. Several rocket-propelled grenades (RPGs) rained shrapnel down on the 1st Platoon. They responded with RPGs, but it was impossible to know if they found their targets.

Ten minutes of heavy fire passed until the Apaches arrived on the scene, flying low to the ground. Colonel Lewis contacted the pilots by COMLINK. "We are ready with LTD [laser target designator], over."

"Go ahead," a pilot responded.

A soldier raised a riflelike device and looked through the range finder. When he had the bunker in the crosshairs, he activated the LTD. "Got it!" he said boldly.

"Got it," Lewis echoed into the COMLINK receiver.

Each Apache pilot had a helmet eyepiece that flashed when the weapons navigational system locked onto the precise point on which the laser was aimed. With the flip of a switch, the gunners sent a half-dozen, laser-guided missiles slamming into the bunker. There was a series of tremendous explosions, and then the enemy position suddenly grew silent.

Lewis ordered the 2nd Platoon to move in slowly from the west. From the ridge, Lewis and the 1st Platoon kept their guns trained on the enemy position. Just two minutes later, a message came from the 2nd Platoon confirming that the enemy position was secure. Lewis picked up the COMLINK and asked the Apache crews to take a look around. "I think we're real close. See what you can find, over."

Colonel Lewis moved his unit down the hill to check on the wounded. He found the contorted body of Lieutenant James Monroe in a clearing at the foot of the ridge. The U.S. Army lost a fine, young officer, the colonel thought to himself. Lewis had picked Monroe because of his first-rate work along the border during Operation Eagle's Nest. In all, eighteen men were down.

As the medics attended to the injured, word came from the air that the Apaches had spotted a series of barely visible structures

A U.S. Army Apache helicopter fires into a guerrilla compound near San Juan de Guadelupe.

only four miles north. Lewis knew it had to be the main compound. He instantly radioed back for more air support and reconnaissance. Ground reinforcements would be helpful, but the terrain made it impossible for airdrops or helicopter landings, and roads were almost nonexistent. Lewis' cautious instinct told him to hold and wait for more ground support, but he had been at this too long to encounter any more delays. If they were going to find Ruiz, it had to be now. Foremost on his mind was his family back in Washington State. "Let's bring this to an end," he said to himself.

Two medics stayed with the wounded while everyone else pushed further north into the remote foothills of the mountains. Achieving surprise was out of the question. The enemy, no doubt, had heard the firefight and would either plan to evacuate or be prepared to stand and fight. The heavy rains made every step more toilsome as the soldiers, heavily laden with gear, sank into the mud. After several hours, the mud-caked units laid down in the brush and waited only a mile from the compound while the four Apaches continued to hover above. When they ran low on fuel, others arrived to replace them.

The Apaches held their fire because everyone wanted to be absolutely certain that the compound was indeed Colada. Lewis sent two soldiers forward to scout the area. They crawled through the undergrowth for almost a mile toward the crude facility. From a quarter mile out, Private Joel Whittle detected a bustle of activity inside the compound. Through his binoculars he saw men scrambling about, placing bundles on packhorses and mules. In the corner he saw General Rivera giving orders and clutching a tattered black and red party flag which had, until recently, flown on the center flagpole.

Whittle reached for his COMLINK. "First Platoon, this is Whittle, over."

"Lewis here, over."

"We got 'em. I repeat, we got 'em."

"Fall back, over."

As Lewis radioed the pilots overhead, a missile fired from the compound burst up through the canopy of trees and was heading straight at the helos. The infrared jammers on the Apaches saturated the incoming missiles' guidance system, sending it aimlessly into the sky. The quartet of helicopters regrouped a mile south of the compound in a half-moon formation, each gunner using his right eye to look through the small, round screen attached to his helmet. The thermal-imaging sight gave him a perfect view of the activity in the compound below, and within half a minute, a full complement of Hellfire missiles were released in unison. Colonel Lewis and his men could hear the pounding in the distance and feel the ground shudder.

Next, the flying metallic hulks closed in, opening up their M230 30-mm chain machine guns just above the compound. The special fragmentation case rounds created a ravaging storm of shrapnel, cutting down anything still erect. Twenty minutes after the last round fell, Lewis and his men walked into Camp Colada. What they found was a wasteland; nothing was moving.

Workers who cleaned up the site during the next several days recovered the bodies of more than two hundred men, including that of General Rivera. President Ruiz and General Cardenas, however, were not among the dead.

On November 11 the president reviewed a Department of State analysis of the conflict.

November 11, 2003

Post-War Strategic Assessment of the Conflict in Mexico

Summary: The lack of detailed intelligence pertaining to the domestic crisis in Mexico left the United States unprepared to deal with this situation.

Military Considerations: The CIA and DIA failed to foresee the emergence of the crisis south of the border. While we do possess substantial satellite intelligence assets and were able to track military deployments and the refugee exodus from Mexico, we failed to have access to critical HUMINT which would have provided details concerning the intentions and future policies of the Ruiz government.

Once the crisis did erupt, we were forced to take immediate military action. This insufficient warning compelled defense planners to use forces that were, in some instances, not at a full state of readiness. The United States suffered only fifty-four casualties in this conflict. Most of these, however, have been attributed to "friendly fire," and investigation reveals that these incidents occurred primarily in those battalions considered subpar in terms of readiness.

Long-Term Strategic Considerations: Ex-President Ruiz and General Cardenas remain at large. Until these individuals are brought to justice, they will pose a threat to stability in Mexico. Again, because of intelligence deficiencies, these individuals and a number of their close aids were able to flee the country to an unknown destination. Several key figures in the drug trade also disappeared and have yet to be captured.

Conclusion: The United States must work aggressively to construct a deep, effective HUMINT network in Latin America and elsewhere.

Part Four

Russia
February 7, 2006

Chapter Twenty

February is the cruelest month of a Russian winter, and the weather in Moscow had been frigid for weeks. A fierce, howling wind and a seemingly endless snowfall had descended on the capital. It was dark by 4:00 in the afternoon, and the streets were empty as even the most veteran Muscovites elected to remain indoors. But to Russian President Aleksandr Dankovich Karashchuk it could just as well have been a pleasant summer afternoon, given the boyish excitement swelling inside him.

A powerful, imposing man, Karashchuk seemed to deny the law of physics by not leaning into the heavy winds as he strode through the courtyard at Russian military intelligence headquarters. He had high, Slavic cheekbones, and a stern look was etched on his face, which appeared immune to the sting of the brisk, winter air. Energy shimmered behind his large, glassy blue eyes. The mink hat atop his head gathered snowflakes.

Karashchuk was a self-made man, and a combination of talent and luck had shaped his destiny. He was neither even-tempered nor open-hearted, neither emotional nor sentimental. Half-Ukrainian, he had managed to make his way through the ranks of the Russian army by carrying out his duties impeccably, with fidelity and enthusiasm. He served in both the infantry and special forces, reaching the

217

rank of lieutenant general at age forty-five. He then resigned his commission and ran for parliament as a staunch nationalist. Through dogged persistence and shrewd maneuvering, he reached the pinnacle of Russian political life to become a modern-day *Vozhd* (an ancient Russian word for leader). His mastery of seizing and holding onto power was a living testament to Machiavelli: Karashchuk was more content to be feared than loved by his people.

The very sound of his name was menacing to Russian ears. Karashchuk was derived from the juxtaposition of the root word "punish" and the root word "pike"—the vicious fish. It served as a mark of warning to potential rivals.

A political storm had been building in Russia since the mid-1990s. With the post-Soviet reform effort faltering, Russia had slowly deteriorated into social chaos. Violent crime, corruption, and the mafia stamped Russian life as powerfully as the Communist party and the KGB had in decades before. Glasnost and perestroika were replaced by *naglost* (brazen insolence) and *perestrelka* (shoot-outs). The economy stumbled under the crushing weight of two pressures—centralized mismanagement from a government that had never essentially gotten over old habits and organized crime trying to establish its own rules. The machinery of government ossified, incapable of reaching decisions as extremist parties began to dominate parliament. A gaping hole now existed where the political center had once been. The few, interim half-measures failed to tame the forces tearing the country apart. In the year 2000 a special presidential election was held, bringing a cluster of candidates to the fore.

It was on the winds of this storm that Karashchuk rode to power. The general ran as a populist, feeding the anger and resentment of the masses and capturing the imagination of millions. He had a charismatic movie-star quality and an unrefined charm that endeared him to the average Russian. An officer much beloved by his men and with a stellar record, his air of authority and forcefulness seemed fitting for the times.

But his popular appeal extended beyond the man to his message. With the social order melting, the Russian people clamored for the iron fist and General Karashchuk promised to deliver it. He ran on a platform that cast aside the trappings of bourgeois liberalism and promised to deal more firmly with crime, disorder, and the mafia. The Russian people readily agreed.

He promised not only domestic stability but also to rebuild the glorious empire of the past. Russians felt a profound sense of humiliation in seeing their country transformed almost overnight from a superpower into a nearly toothless mammoth. To restore Russian greatness, he pledged not to reestablish the empire of the hammer and sickle, but rather to blaze a new, imperial path under the double-headed eagle of the czarist past. A nationalist and a Slavophile, Karashchuk's aim was to bring all Slavs together under one imperial roof.

In the months following his overwhelming electoral victory, Karashchuk forged a so-called red–brown coalition with fascists and communists. The new president understood that his government could not survive moderation, and both of these groups would be powerful foot soldiers in his efforts to destroy the last vestiges of democratic liberalism. The alliance of convenience succeeded. The regular national elections which were to have followed the special presidential election were postponed indefinitely.

On the first anniversary of his government in April 2001, Karashchuk christened a new era of empire at a gala held in the Bolshoi Theatre. Four thousand loyal supporters were on hand as he spoke on the stage beneath the pediment over the Ionic portico surmounted by a colossal group of Phoebus in the Chariot of the Sun. Delivering his address in a soft monotone, he announced a new Slavic alliance with Belarus and the Ukraine, the two neighbors to the west. Russia once again had a geographic route to central Europe.

"The Russian eagle is not an aggressive predator but an intelligent creature," Karashchuk told the audience. "It has a fierce, independent spirit. The Russian eagle is strong enough to defend itself and to keep peace in the wilderness. It has a strong wingspan of almost ten thousand kilometers, reaching from Kaliningrad on the Atlantic to the Kurile Islands in the Pacific. The two heads symbolize a vision split between Europe and Asia. But let there be no doubt, this mighty bird belongs in flight, looking down on the other creatures of the forest. It is more powerful and more cunning than any other animal." Although it was a cryptic speech, it ended with unabated applause which turned to an ovation. Karashchuk then sat down and joined the others to watch a performance of Glinka's *A Life of the Tsar*, a strongly monarchistic opera.

What brought Karashchuk out on a wintery February in 2006 was the anticipation that his five-year quest might finally be realized. With domestic rule firmly in place, he had increasingly turned his ambitions to rebuilding the Russian empire through a variety of exotic military technologies that he believed might revolutionize warfare. Karashchuk thought that military technology—particularly weapons based on "new physical principles"—could propel Russia into a position of strategic dominance in Europe and beyond. He had inherited a military–industrial complex not much different from that which had dutifully produced tanks like sausages for the Soviets throughout the Cold War. Despite military reductions and arms control in the 1990s, three-fourths of the Soviet capability to produce and assemble weapon systems was still in place at the turn of the millennium. Some ninety secret cities remained active, producing weapons and researching advanced technologies.

Karashchuk intensified and expanded these efforts, redirecting resources toward his favored exotica and placing the *Glavnoye Razvedyvatelnoye Upravlenie* (GRU), the Russian military intelligence, at the hub. Enclosed by the Central Airport (the old Khodinka Field), GRU headquarters was surrounded by top-secret science research facilities for rockets and military aircraft and by something called the Institute for Cosmic Biology. High stone walls, guard dogs, and high-tech electronic sensors protected the perimeter. The main building was a nine-story rectangular structure with no external windows; the only sunlight came from the central courtyard. To maintain maximum security, absolutely no one was allowed to drive a car onto the compound. Everyone was required to walk through the main gate, even the president, who now strode through the facility in the frigid February air.

While the KGB underwent a structural transformation after the collapse of the Soviet Union, the GRU was untouched by reform, remaining a strong moving current under the surface of a slow rolling river. Its main task during the Cold War had been to prepare the Kremlin for a future war by providing intelligence and capabilities that they hoped would ensure victory in any conflict. That was still its mission, and to that end, the GRU was unlike any other intelligence organization in the world. The GRU directed thousands of special forces for strategic operations in foreign countries. These so-called Spetsnaz forces were specially trained to assassinate foreign leaders, blow up government buildings, and commit other acts of terrorism. The GRU also trained foreign terrorist organizations at several bases in Russia.

President Karashchuk ambled into the office of GRU Director Grigory Aleksandrovich Platonov, a longtime friend and supporter. The room was an assemblage of books, intelligence reports, and diplomatic cables tossed about in a haphazard fashion. Platonov never seemed to file anything; he relied instead on his photographic memory. The son of Russian farm laborers, he was thin as a reed. At first appearance the general could be quite disarming, but beneath his modesty was a craving for power which drove him to great lengths. Platonov possessed an incredible stamina, sometimes not sleeping for days but instead staying in his office and working single-mindedly. Today, he was in the midst of just such a flourish.

The president and the general had a friendship that began during their youth when they studied together at the Frunze Military Academy and reached its zenith when they served side by side as officers in the tumultuous Poland of the 1980s. When the Berlin Wall fell and the Soviet army was forced to withdraw to Russian soil, it was a humiliating event for every Soviet officer. It had, however, left an indelible mark on both Karashchuk and Platonov. As their units drove east in the retreat to Russia, the future president told his comrade, mimicking the promise Douglas MacArthur made in the Philippines, "I shall return." And the burly, young Colonel Karashchuk did not mean as a tourist.

In the privacy of Platonov's office, the two greeted each other first with a salute and then with a handshake and hug. There was no one Karashchuk trusted more. And it was for that reason Platonov had been entrusted with the military research program.

"Aleksandr, it is so good to welcome you back to my office," Platonov said with a tight but sincere grin.

"Thank you, Grigory," responded Karashchuk, removing his mink hat and placing it neatly on the sofa nearby. He immediately took the seat next to it. Out of the corner of his eye, he noticed a framed verse of poetry on a small table and reached for it with his firm, white hands. It was from Aleksandr Pushkin's "Message to Siberia," an 1827 lyric addressed to revolutionaries exiled to hard labor in Siberia:

> *The heavy-hanging chains will fall,*
> *The walls will crumble at the word;*
> *And Freedom greet you in the light*
> *And brothers give you back the sword.*

"Do you remember this poem, Aleksandr Dankovich?" asked Platonov, now sitting in the ornate, Georgian carved chair near the center of the room.

"Da," said the president softly, nodding with deep emotion.

"You gave this to me in 1995, one of the army's darkest years. But after reading this verse, I knew that one day again the army would be the vanguard shaping the nation and the world. I stayed in the service because of this. And you have, my friend, made this dream a reality."

President Karashchuk grinned, his white teeth contrasting with his complexion still red from the cold. "Yes, Grigory, the army once again has its rightful place, receiving paramount respect from the people. But there is still work to be done. We must restore our tarnished reputation with the rest of the world. The great powers still view us as the country that could not subjugate the rebels in

Chechnya ten years ago." Karashchuk gently set the framed poem back on the table. "But they will know soon enough how times have changed, that we are once again a superpower."

"Yes," affirmed Platonov, "they will indeed."

President Karashchuk crossed his legs and proceeded at once to the business at hand. "Now, Grigory, tell me about the status of Magic Chain."

Magic Chain was one of the most secretive, ambitious plans of the Karashchuk government. Taking its name from the famous fairy tale "Marya Moryevna," in which the hero Koshchei broke the twelve chains binding him to win his freedom, Magic Chain was Karashchuk's best hope of reestablishing Russia as a superpower, perhaps the only superpower. Few in the Russian government even knew of its existence.

"Magic Chain is ready to be activated on your orders," offered Platonov with more than a hint of pride. "We can unfurl the chain, and it will be operable within a matter of weeks."

"Show it to me," the president said eagerly. The two exited the room and headed outside through the falling snow for a large, imposing building just west of GRU headquarters. The enormous structure was a renovated aircraft hangar near the airfield now used exclusively for military research.

The two entered hangar no. 7, where they found military personnel working amid the damp, chilly, and musty environs. Several dozen dark vehicles, approximately the size of large dump trucks, were parked inside. Each carried a heavy payload. General Platonov stood in front of the vehicles with his arm extended, as if he were demonstrating a new car model in a showroom. "These are the some of the components for Magic Chain. They are BMD [ballistic missile defense] launchers, updated mobile versions of Galosh and Gazelle."

Magic Chain was an advanced and dramatically expanded version of the BMD system developed by the Soviets beginning in the 1960s. The original, single-layer Russian BMD system included sixty-four reloadable above-ground launchers at four complexes around Moscow. They were coordinated by battle management radars with the code names Dog House and Cat House. Each complex consisted of tracking and guidance radars and Galosh interceptor missiles, nuclear-armed rockets that could intercept and destroy incoming enemy warheads in space shortly before they reentered the earth's atmosphere.

Under the 1972 Anti-Ballistic Missile Treaty, both the United States and Soviet Union renounced deployment of nationwide Anti-Ballistic Missiles (ABMs) or, as they are now known, BMD systems. But the treaty allowed each country to build one system to protect a single target. The Russians had used that provision to maintain their defenses around Moscow.

Beginning in the 1980s, Moscow modernized the BMD system, adding a second layer which included silo-based Gazelle high-acceleration missiles. If the Galosh failed in the exoatmospheric intercept, the Gazelle was designed to engage targets within the atmosphere (endoatmospheric). Anything the Galosh missed, the Gazelle was expected to kill. Although the one hundred Gazelle silos were reloadable, Moscow also built eleven large ballistic missile early-warning radars around the country with the code name Henhouse. They offered Moscow a thirty-minute warning after any U.S. intercontinental ballistic missile (ICBM) launch.

In addition to the development of this extensive BMD system, the Soviets, in their waning years, were also seriously committed to research on advanced technologies, including laser weapons, particle beam weapons, and kinetic energy weapons. While those research projects continued, even after the collapse of the Soviet Union, Karashchuk had now taken this work to an even higher level.

"By mass producing new versions of Galosh and Gazelle," Platonov said excitedly, "we can today declare the BMD treaty of 1972 null and void. We are now in a position to deploy some one thousand launchers and approximately five thousand interceptor missiles around the country. This will neutralize any foreign nuclear missile capabilities."

President Karashchuk walked suspiciously around the rockets. "Are you certain, Grigory, that this is the case?"

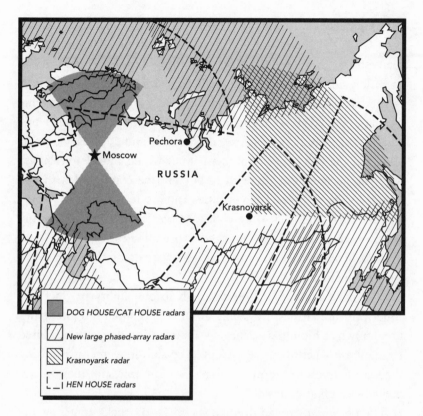

**Russia's Magic Chain: Ballistic Missile Defense
Early Warning, Target-Tracking, and Battle
Management Radars**

"Quite certain, Aleksandr. The START [Strategic Arms Reduction Treaty] II limits the Americans to between 3,000 and 3,500 total strategic warheads. Moreover, they can have only 1,750 SLBMs [submarine-launched ballistic missiles]. And of course ICBMs with MIRVs [multiple independently targeted reentry vehicles] are banned. If we launched a first strike targeting their land-based systems and bomber force of 95 B-52s and 20 B-2s, we could eliminate the vast majority of them. They would choose to retaliate with submarines. But these SLBMs could be countered with our BMD system to protect major cities and a select number of land-based launch sites. The only U.S. weapons left that could possibly get through would be sea-launched cruise missiles."

Karashchuk stared into space, as if he were doing the math. "And what of their submarines?"

"We have achieved a breakthrough in our ability to track the American submarines. By taking advantage of a natural phenomenon known as bioluminescence, an illuminating property exhibited by plankton when they are disrupted by ship movements exposing the sea life to rapid thermal changes, we can now spot their movements with great precision."

The president strolled through the forest of trucks, touching and eyeing them mindfully as if he were handling fine china. After a long period of silence, he turned to Platonov, "Very well. What is next?"

"Follow me."

General Platonov opened the door to hangar no. 7 and led Karashchuk back out into the cold. They walked to another hangar one hundred yards south. As they swung open the huge, metallic doors and entered the building, a thick wall of glass stood before them. Through the glass they could see a box-like armored vehicle with a sizeable microwave antenna on top. Four soldiers sat inside the vehicle, and several dozen dogs wandered aimlessly inside the glass enclosure.

Almost immediately a studious-looking gentleman with wire-frame glasses and a thin face approached them with his hand extended. "Mr. President," he confidently greeted Karashchuk before turning to the general. "General Platonov," said Dr. Mikhail Sergeyevich Lunin, "we are ready to proceed with our demonstration."

"Very well," said Platonov as he and Karashchuk sat in comfortable-looking chairs in front of the translucent wall.

Dr. Lunin turned to the enclosure, putting his cold hands in his pant pockets. "Gentlemen, this is our latest development: an RFW [radio frequency weapon]. Research began in the mid-1980s and has continued nonstop for nearly twenty years. We have finally perfected this as a weapon that can kill silently and efficiently. Production has already begun."

Lunin signaled to the four soldiers inside the vehicle, and they activated the system. For an instant the dogs froze in place—as if seized by an unseen hand—before falling to the ground dead. It happened in a split second, without sight or sound.

Karashchuk appeared genuinely impressed "Very interesting, Dr. Lunin. Tell me exactly how this works."

Lunin pulled out a sheet of paper and began to draw a basic diagram. "It's really very simple, Mr. President. RFWs use complicated pulse shapes and pulse trains involving several electromagnetic frequencies and modulations with a wide spectrum ranging from extremely low frequencies to the hundred-gigahertz range. On all living beings—including humans—they induce an effect called 'biological coupling.' Essentially, the beams destroy the nerve synapses where nerve impulses pass between neurons. The whole system is quite effective. And it is difficult—if not impossible—to defend against. In addition to destroying life, these weapons can penetrate major arms systems and damage the electronics inside."

"How might it be used?"

Lunin set his paper and pen down. "This system has application in all sorts of battlefield scenarios. One-shot, briefcase-size RFW devices can be used in operations by our special forces, while larger devices, with a range of several kilometers carried by large trucks or transport aircraft, can be deployed against intelligence systems, military and civilian electronic data banks, harbors, and other targets of opportunity. They can also be used for disorienting or blinding enemy pilots."

Karashchuk was sparing in his compliments to others, but he liked what he saw. "Very good, General," he said with a slight nod. But the tour was not yet over. There was much to see, the fruits of a decade's labor, soon to be shared with the world.

Chapter Twenty-one

March 15
outside Bialystok, Poland

D mitri Irinarkhovich Zalygin's steely blue eyes stared over a stone fence through the fog-shrouded night at an elegant villa one hundred yards away. The grand house was illuminated by floodlights and guarded by a dozen security personnel who patrolled the perimeter clutching semiautomatic weapons. The Polish government had secretly gathered at the country estate to discuss a disturbing military buildup in western Belarus. Because secrecy was essential, security was relatively light. The local police had not been notified nor any of the Polish military detachments in the area put on alert.

Using his binoculars, Zalygin could see through the villa's full-length windows the assembled cabinet discussing issues over coffee. Zalygin was a colonel in the GRU and a member of Spetsnaz, the elite special forces branch of the Russian army. He checked his wristwatch: it was 10:58 P.M. He signaled his ten-man team, which was skulking in the nearby bushes, to move in.

Four Spetsnaz sharpshooters wielding silenced 7.62-mm sniper rifles picked off the security personnel on the south end of the compound. Seconds later, half a dozen black-clothed figures were over the stone fence and racing across the rich green lawn for the bushes just under the windows of the main house. They waited only momentarily before breaking down the doors and storming inside. Once in the conference room, they sprayed everything with automatic-weapons fire. They then fled as swiftly as they had arrived. In only a matter of several seconds, the Polish cabinet and most of the senior military officers were dead.

Zalygin and his team rushed down a narrow footpath through the dense, dark forest. For more than two miles they dodged branches and sprang over enormous roots while scanning the area for anyone in pursuit. They could hear the faint barking of dogs in the distance but saw nothing. At 11:15 P.M. the Spetsnaz team reached a clearing in the woods where an Mi-24 HIND helicopter was waiting, its rotors chattering menacingly in the night. The commandos jumped aboard and within minutes were flying just over the tree line on their way back to Belarus.

As word of the horror at Bialystok began to spread, a thunderous wave of Russian armor pierced the Polish border under a starless, pitch-black sky just after midnight. At the crest of the wave was Major-General Vladimir Vladimirovich Martov, who was commanding a battalion of T-80 tanks ordered to push west through the rolling plains on a highway running parallel to the Bug River. Martov's force was part of a shock formation that was racing for Warsaw some one hundred miles away. The Russian army wanted a quick victory in Poland, and the fall of Warsaw would deliver a decisive blow to the Poles.

Aside from the growl of the thirty-ton steel animals, the night was quiet and still. Martov's force was fifteen miles into Poland when they encountered the Polish army. Soldiers hid behind craggy rocks and lightly sloping hills as the Russian T-80s closed to within one hundred yards. Then, in a convulsion of fire, the Poles launched several tube-launched, optically tracked, wire-guided (TOW) antitank missiles. While the launches created a spectacular backblast in the night air, the missiles struck their targets without apparent effect. The armored column continued to move forward, aiming their guns and

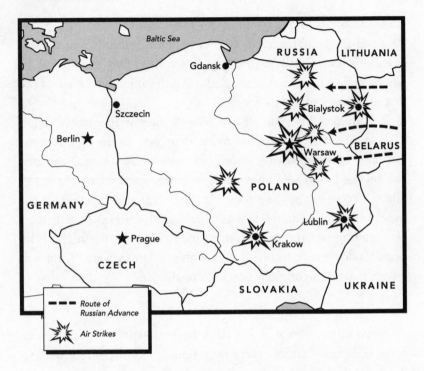

The Russian Offensive Begins, March 16, 2006

firing shells near the Polish position. The T-80s were sporting reactive armor—explosive charges placed on the outside of the turret that blow up missiles before they hit the skin of the tank.

As armor poured across the Polish frontier, Russian aircraft struck airfields and command posts throughout Poland. A horde of Tu-160 Blackjack bombers and Su-34s screamed over eastern Poland, lighting up the sky as they dropped bombs on dozens of targets. Also in the night sky was a sleek, twin-engine aircraft, which seemed to cruise effortlessly at supersonic speeds, making its first appearance ever outside the airspace of Russia. To the few Polish pilots who managed to get airborne, it was not only the speed that was impressive, but also its defined agility. The Russian multifunctional fighter (MFI) had sixteen control surfaces including canards and a twin tail driven by a fly-by-wire system. It could execute remarkable turns and engage two targets at once. The MFIs quickly devoured any Polish fighters in the air.

The ground offensive in central Europe was not confined to Poland. The small, peaceful Baltic republic of Lithuania, a strategic nuisance preventing Moscow from moving west across a broader front, was quickly swallowed by two divisions, supported by air strikes and selective rocket attacks, rampaging across the border.

In Warsaw, pandemonium had overcome what was left of the government. The president, prime minister, foreign minister, defense minister, army chief of staff, and the rest of the cabinet were dead from the spasm of bullets in the villa outside Bialystok. Parliament had been out of session and was not yet gathered. The closest thing the Poles had to a commander in chief under the circumstances was a forty-two-year–old deputy defense minister, Wadislaw Radkiewicz. A diminutive man with a balding head and thick glasses, Radkiewicz was a technocrat who could hardly be considered a likely hand to guide the Polish strategy. But urgency sometimes creates such paradoxes.

British Prime Minister Simon Walton was at Chequers, the country house given by Lord Lee of Fareham for the benefit of British prime ministers, when word of the attack reached him. Awakened by aides at 2:30 A.M., he immediately alerted visiting French President Jacques Lebou who was sleeping down the hall. The prime minister had always maintained a decidedly low opinion of Karashchuk, calling him "a monster coated with a veneer of civility." But even so, he had never expected to see war in the heart of Europe again.

The prime minister notified the defense minister at once, and British forces were put on full alert. Nuclear missile submarines were sent to sea and placed on a wartime footing. One room down, President Lebou was speaking with his defense minister, who was at his vacation home in Burgundy. The French navy was also put to sea, including their nuclear missile submarines. Lebou prepared to return to Paris while Prime Minister Walton made arrangements to meet with his military brass at 10 Downing Street. Shortly after 5:30 A.M., Radkiewicz phoned to discuss the Russian invasion with both leaders. By the time they left Chequers, Walton and Lebou had committed themselves to the immediate defense of Poland.

Since Poland was a North Atlantic Treaty Organization (NATO) member, much of Europe and the United States had an obligation to come to its defense. German Chancellor Heinrich Müller soon followed Britain and France in the commitment to fight for a free Poland with the United States not far behind. Although a strategic session was planned for the NATO command in The Hague, commitment without mobilization meant nothing. Two German divisions were slated to arrive in Poland within twenty-four hours and French paratroopers by mid-morning. But Radkiewicz wondered how far the Russian columns might have advanced by then.

In Washington, President St. John convened an emergency meeting of the NSC in the White House Situation Room to discuss American military contingencies. U.S. forces had pulled out of Europe in 2003, so now it was first a matter of getting units to the continent.

Wearing a heavy sweater and nursing a severe chest cold, the president's voice was raspy and muffled. National Security Adviser Jack Fowler had just completed initial consultations with the Joint Chiefs of Staff concerning the deployment of U.S. forces. He had been up most of the night.

"So, Jack, tell me, what can we get to Poland in the next seventy-two hours?"

"Well, Mr. President, the Joint Chiefs tell me that we can have two wings of aircraft in Europe within forty-eight hours. The 82nd Airborne and the 2nd Marine Division from Camp Lejeune will land in Germany within two days. Two armored divisions should be there within the week." Fowler paused, "But I think we have a larger problem to grapple with."

St. John looked puzzled. "Oh? What's that?"

"I've asked Steve Cramer to shed some light on this matter."

Cramer was a spectacled, assiduous young man with a messy pile of dark hair and a penchant for challenging conventional wisdom. His striking nose and bony cheeks seemed fitting for his dogged search for the unexpected and disconcerting. "Mr. President," he nodded and cleared his throat, "as you know, we have abided by the ABM Treaty for thirty years, as has Moscow, at least officially. It was drafted, of course, on the premise that we wanted MAD [Mutual Assured Destruction] as the strategic doctrine between the superpowers. Unfortunately, this served as a brake on our efforts to develop a strategic defense system. And we assumed that Moscow was also restrained. But now this assumption is no longer valid."

St. John coughed and blew his nose. "Go on."

"Intelligence indicates that Moscow has proceeded during the past two weeks with the rapid deployment of hundreds of launchers and perhaps four to six thousand missiles across the Russian frontier as part of a ballistic missile defense system. They have broken out of the treaty."

"How severely does this affect the current strategic balance?"

Cramer paused. "Essentially, if these systems are capable of what I think they are, there is no longer a strategic balance. The nuclear equation has become entirely one-sided."

A murmur passed through the room, and St. John squinted in disbelief. "Good God! What are you talking about?"

Cramer swallowed hard and pressed on. "Well, Mr. President, if they chose to launch a disabling preemptive strike and we retaliated, the probability is that few of our remaining warheads would make it through their web of defenses and hit critical targets in Russia. We might hit some population centers if we launched enough missiles at them. But we could not do much to hardened military targets. Thus, at the present time, they could fight a nuclear war and face fairly limited damage. In their eyes, it might even be sustainable damage."

The President coughed again. "How come we had no warning of this? How could this happen overnight?"

Cramer looked sullenly at the conference table. "We have known since the mid-1980s that they were violating the ABM Treaty and that they had enough radars deployed to set up such a system. So the infrastructure has always been there. The obvious, covert production of so many ABMs was not something we could have detected with much accuracy. Remember, detection is not as easy as it sounds. It took us over two years to identify the Krasnoyarsk Radar in central Siberia, and that structure was twenty-two stories high and several football fields in length."

St. John shifted forward in his chair, still sniffling. "Cramer, are you telling me that we are sitting here naked, unable to adequately retaliate?"

"Yes... Mr. President." He looked down again. "That is exactly what I am telling you."

President Karashchuk awoke on the morning of March 16 feeling revitalized. The knowledge that his forces were storming across the Polish border had not deterred him from sleeping well at his *blizhny*, or vacation dacha, in Kuntsevo, a village Muscovites had used for weekends since the late nineteenth century. Karashchuk often spent the evening there to escape the confines of the presidential palace.

Before leaving this idyllic setting, he ate the traditional meal of kasha—brown, whole-grain barley with a piece of butter melting on top—for breakfast. He then ordered his driver to take him back to the Kremlin for an early afternoon meeting with his advisers.

The meeting took place beneath the majestic cathedrals of the Kremlin in the Oval Hall, a meeting place for both czsars and Soviets through the centuries. President Karashchuk entered the room triumphantly with inner joy at being present at this great reversal of fate—a reversal he alone had wrought. On this day he took particular notice of the room's splendor. It was decorated with enormous oil paintings depicting great Russian commanders in battle: Peter the Great; General Tshitshagov, who helped expel Napoleon from Moscow; General Ivan Fedorovich Paskievich, who defeated the Turks at Akhalzic in 1828; and Soviet Marshal Zhukov, who pushed the Germans out of Russia in 1944. Karashchuk took his seat and wondered how his portrait might look hanging on the wall.

There was a buoyant, almost giddy, atmosphere in the room. And yet, these were not giddy men. The nine members of the Committee for National Defense (CND), the supreme war-planning body in the Karashchuk government, had a collective three hundred years of military command experience among them. Many had served and been wounded in Afghanistan. They were still hungry for redemption.

Karashchuk sat at the head of the mammoth gilt table inlaid with stones and marble, a vestige from the days of Catherine the Great. General Platonov took the seat to his left, while Marshal Ivan Aleksandrovich Serov took the chair to his right. Serov was from the old school, a patriarch from the armed services who was happy to serve any political master so long as his interests were served. He had enough gold braid on his uniform for all the officers at West Point and was regarded by many in his own officer corps as a blowhard. Yet Karashchuk found him a steady, comforting influence, even if his nuggets of insight came with long-winded sermons.

"Gentlemen," announced Karashchuk to applause and joyous laughter, "I am pleased to report that our forces have reached the outskirts of Warsaw and have begun the occupation of the Lithuanian capital of Vilnius. Major-General Martov reports from the front that our forces might enter Warsaw by tonight." As more applause spilled forth, it was like a heavy curse had finally been lifted from the army.

Karashchuk turned his bearish face to General Platonov. "Grigory, please report to us the latest intelligence concerning the NATO countries."

Platonov bowed his head slightly so his aesthetic, intense blue eyes peered over the rims of his reading glasses. "Our intelligence satellites have detected rapid movement by NATO forces. German units have mobilized and are preparing to move east. American forces will be arriving shortly at air bases in Germany, and a vanguard of British forces has landed at the German port of Kiel. The French army has already moved a division to Strasbourg, and it should be in Poland within two days. We believe that French paratroopers will be landing this afternoon to secure a forward base of operations somewhere in central Poland."

Marshal Serov released a predictable sigh and spoke with sharp, punctuated words. "It is as we expected. President Karashchuk, we must prepare to use our nuclear weapons before these forces cross into Poland. Early use is the best means for achieving success."

"Da," Karashchuk nodded, "I agree." He turned back to General Platonov. "Tell me, is Magic Chain fully activated?"

"Yes, sir. It is now on full alert."

"Very good. I plan to publicly announce this afternoon that we are no longer bound by the ABM Treaty and that the first NATO forces to enter Poland will be subject to nuclear attack." He shifted his posture, looking back to his right. "General, are the missiles targeted?"

General Pyotr Lazarevich Grigorov, commander of the Strategic Rocket Forces (SRF), nodded in affirmation. "Yes, we have three missiles that are currently targeted on the central Polish plain. These are thirty-kiloton warheads. We simply await your orders for launch."

"Very good, General. Be certain that your forces maintain a high state of alert during the next seventy-two hours. We must not be taken by surprise."

General Boris Semyonovich Malinovsky sat at the end of the table, his arms crossed resolutely. The commander of the ground forces had remained silent throughout the deliberations. With a pug nose and firm jowls, Malinovsky had a bulldog look which fit his personality—reserved but ferocious when required. He usually kept to himself and seemed to harbor a deep bitterness. A veteran of Afghanistan, the general had been wounded in combat twice, only to return a third time just before the withdrawal of Soviet forces was announced. Like Marshal Serov, the younger Malinovsky had a vague nostalgia for the Soviet era and blamed the last Soviet leader, Mikhail Gorbachev, for the retreat from Afghanistan. That retreat told the East Europeans that we would not fight for the empire and emboldened them to revolt, he said to Karashchuk in 1993. The government, he felt, had simply lost its nerve.

"General Malinovsky," the president asked, "what is your appraisal of the operation so far?"

Malinovsky curled his lip. "I am very enthusiastic, Mr. President. We should have complete control of Lithuania during the next seventy-two hours and Poland within the week. If we can keep NATO forces at bay, our aspirations will be realized. The weather remains a question. A heavy snow still threatens—which could slow things considerably. Celebration is premature. Thus far, we have conquered nothing."

Karashchuk nodded with a slight grin on his face. "The writer Fyodor Tiutchev wrote 'Homeland of patience, land of the Russian people.' Boris, my friend, the snow might come, but we will wait. We have waited almost twenty years for this day. We can surely wait a few months longer. And after the snow has melted, our armies will be all that remain in central Europe. During the Cold War, the communists sought military superiority to decouple Europe from America. We now have an opportunity to accomplish what seventy years of Bolshevism failed to do."

As the last words poured from his mouth, Karashchuk stood and exited with General Platonov in tow. They proceeded down the long, elegant hallway bejeweled with enormous crystal chandeliers, running carpets, and ornate antiques. Were it not for their modern dress, Karashchuk might have been a czar managing his vast empire as it had been done for centuries.

"Tell me, Grigory," he asked as they walked down the passageway, "did you draft a letter for the NATO countries?"

"Yes I did." Platonov handed the president a sheet of paper. Karashchuk studied it as they continued in stride down another corridor, this one decorated with huge tapestries. He then handed it back to Platonov. "Very good. Send it at once."

French president Jacques Lebou had just returned on an early morning flight to Paris where a short, curt note from Karashchuk was waiting for him. He shook his head as he read it and then flippantly tossed it on his desk. "The Russians," he said scornfully with an air of French superiority. Lebou had always viewed the Russians as ill-dressed, ill-mannered rogues at a party meant for the sophisticates of Europe.

Jacques Lebou
President
Republic of France

President Lebou:

The government of Russia announces that henceforth it will no longer be bound by the Anti-Ballistic Missile Treaty. This agreement was signed by the Soviet Union, a country that ceased to exist in 1991.

We demand that all NATO forces remain off Polish territory. Failure to comply with this demand will mean immediate nuclear attack on any of your forces in Poland.

Sincerely,

Aleksandr Dankovich Karashchuk
President
Russia

Lebou dismissed Karashchuk's threat as typical Russian bluster and hyperbole. Moscow must certainly know that a nuclear strike would be responded to in kind, he thought to himself. The French nuclear force, while small in comparison to that of the superpowers, could still inflict severe damage on Russian cities, not to mention what the Americans might do.

In the event of nuclear war, French military plans called for Lebou to board a La Fayette frigate at the port of La Rochelle. Once at sea, he could manage the war from the stealthy *Courbet*. Its sides were angled, and mooring cables were hidden behind hinged doors. The gun turret was faceted, and there were no walkways along the sides. A retractable radar-protective screen covered the ship's lifeboat. All of these advanced designs made the vessel difficult to detect on radar, helping to ensure survivability.

The announcement from Moscow that the ABM Treaty was now null and void did concern Lebou—enough to warrant an immediate call to Washington. He picked up the receiver on his black, desk-side phone. "Place an urgent call to President St. John in Washington," he ordered an aide.

In recent hours France had agreed to open its air bases and ports to American forces to aid the war effort. It was an important promise that Washington had sought in the first hours of the conflict. Lebou now wanted to extract from St. John a commitment to retaliate for any use of nuclear weapons by the Russians.

"Monsieur President," began Lebou in broken English, "we have received an ultimatum from Moscow."

St. John sighed. "Yes, Jacques, we have as well."

"It remains the policy of France to retaliate immediately for any nuclear launch by Russia. If this does occur in Europe, are you committed to the same?"

St. John hesitated and then collected himself. "Jacques, you must have noticed the reference to the ABM Treaty."

"Oui."

"Our intelligence satellites indicate that Moscow has in place a substantial ballistic missile defense system. Few of our missiles will now get through, and our analysts estimate that our nuclear retaliatory capabilities have been reduced by over 95 percent."

The French president slumped his shoulders as he felt his confidence waning. "Michael, you must not abandon us. You have made a commitment—"

"Jacques, we will stand with France as we will stand with Germany and Poland. But you must recognize that the strategic balance has changed, and we now face new realities."

There was little more to be said. The Russians had done what the Soviets never could—ripped a chasm in the Atlantic alliance.

As the two heads of state hung up their phones, French paratroopers were landing in Poland, including the 1st and 2nd Parachute Brigades and the 13th Dragoons Parachute Regiment. The troops were expected to secure the area and make preparations for the French–German Rapid Reaction Force, which would include more artillery tanks and heavy weapons. But as the troopers deployed, what looked like a star fell from the sky. There was an instantaneous flash, followed by a deep-throated boom. And during the measureless interval in between, there was no color or sound, only a brilliant, piercing light that consumed everything. As the flash dimmed and the thunderous explosion passed, the ground around what was once a French base camp changed from the white of snow to an ashen, forsaken gray. The earth was parched for several miles, and dead French paratroopers were liberally strewn in ash-covered fields.

Word reached Paris almost at once, and President Lebou

immediately took a helicopter to the *Courbet*, which was waiting in La Rochelle. As the ship left port, he ordered a retaliatory strike. French planners identified a Russian military base west of Nizhniy Novgorod as an inviting target. At exactly 4:00 P.M. Paris time, a French M45 missile launched by the strategic submarine *Le Triumphant* punched its way through the cloud cover and slanted east as it began its flight to Russia.

Outside Moscow, Russian missile defense operators picked up the rocket almost instantly after launch, tracking its progress over central Europe. As it began its downward trajectory, two small interceptor missiles streaked to the heavens from a Russian BMD installation west of the capital. Three minutes later they detonated and shattered the French missile above the atmosphere, sending it plunging harmlessly to the earth.

News of the successful intercept reached President Lebou moments after French intelligence detected it. In frustration, he slammed his fist against the metallic desk in his small office aboard the *Courbet*. While his immediate impulse was to seek another way to lash out at Moscow, he knew that his only option was to suspend all French military operations in Poland and to keep his forces deployed in Germany.

The French president dispatched a cable outlining his decision to Berlin, London, and Washington. Only hours after receiving the announcement, German Chancellor Müller and British Prime Minister Walton followed suit, ordering all of their forces to withdraw from Polish soil.

That left only President St. John to make a decision. The United States was now standing alone in its commitment to defend Poland. In light of the emerging strategic imbalance, the president knew that he had little choice. While conceding to blackmail went against every fiber of his being, reason forced him to bend. He convened an emergency meeting with a few, select advisors to chart the next move.

Defense Secretary Tom Bodine sat on the yellow colonial sofa in the center of the room, his leg propped on a nearby chair and his face buried in intelligence reports. Jack Fowler and Steve Cramer were examining several satellite photos fresh from the NSA. Trying to suppress his ever-present cough, the president sat behind his desk drinking hot tea. "Jack, what can we glean from the successful intercept of the French missile?"

"Mr. President, they fired a strategic defense missile tipped with a small nuclear device which destroyed the French missile instantly." He turned to Steve Cramer. "What else do you have?"

"With some help from the NSA, we have been able to determine the location of the most critical elements of the Russian missile defense system—the relevant communications facilities and the command center. That might give us something to target if we want to lobotomize their system."

Fowler looked encouraged. "Can you get us a greater level of detail on this?"

Cramer nodded.

"Good, keep working it."

St. John coughed, feeling impatient and restless. "So then, what do we do? The Russians have us over a barrel. We have to do something."

Jack Fowler shuffled in his seat. "Yes, indeed they do, Mr. President. But we might be able to short-circuit their system if Steve can locate the points of vulnerability. I also think that we need to look at a crash program to develop a strategic defense system of our own."

"That will take two to three years," blurted Tom Bodine. "I agree, Jack, that we need to move in that direction. But secrecy will be of the essence. If the Russians found out we were working on such a system, we could expect a preemptive strike. After all, they are not going to want to give up this strategic trump card. We need a Manhattan Project for strategic defense, the best minds at work on this. But we can't sit still between now and then. Two years from now, Russian generals could be drinking Bordeaux and eating Brie on the Champs-Élysées."

St. John tilted his head. "What do you suggest?"

Chapter Twenty-two

```
March 18
outside Warsaw
```

During the night a heavy snow had transformed central Poland from a blood-soaked plain to a white, velvet dreamland. But it was only temporary. By midmorning the deep cough of artillery and the rumble of armor were heard once again. Russian forces had brought their large-caliber artillery to within ten miles of the capital, and nowhere in the metropolis was safe.

A general's staff car skated down an ice-rutted road toward the front line. The heavy snow restricted the driver's view, but he continued without caution to the first destination. In the backseat of the car was General Andrzej Krynicki who was touring the front to boost morale and check conditions for the expected Russian thrust. The weather had slowed the Russian advance and offered an opportunity to better organize a defensive position. Polish forces had deployed on an ice-glazed slope overlooking an expanse of plains to the east. The peaceful, silver curve of the Bug River was visible from the top of the ridge.

Krynicki was a brilliant officer with a keen, aesthetic face. News that NATO forces had halted at the German border created a deep sorrow in the officer who was now serving as the commander of Polish ground forces. Krynicki had heard from his grandfather how Poland had suffered through the centuries under domination and attack from Germany to the west and Russia to the east. Like most of his fellow officers, the general had staked an enormous amount on Poland's admittance into NATO. But the treaty was meaningless now. Poland would have to stand alone against Moscow's swarming armies, and the military pragmatist in him knew that it was a losing cause. Still he remembered the poignant moments of the Soviet withdrawal in 1990, sixteen years of freedom now no more memorable than another of many similarly brief interludes in Polish history.

Only two Polish divisions were standing between six Russian divisions and the capital. The soldiers were clad in white winter uniforms and clung to the walls of their tunnels and foxholes to stay out of the cold and to avoid enemy artillery. The snow was good news since it had slowed the Russian advance. Yet Krynicki knew that weather alone would not hold back the Russian army.

Russian air power was a huge problem, and as the general reviewed the lines, two squadrons of Russian Su-35 fighters came swooping down through the heavy clouds, flying at five hundred feet. The Polish soldiers ducked for cover as the pilots sent several Kh-31 Krypton air-to-surface missiles screaming at the crest of the hill, the explosions making the ground tremble and shaking snow into the trenches. As the fighters passed overhead dropping KAB five hundred–pound bombs, Polish troops on the ground fired their weapons and several SAMs gave chase. One flew up the tail pipe of a plane, throwing the metal bird off its flight path and eventually sending it careening toward the ground. When it hit the open field in a cloud of white snow, spontaneous cheers erupted. Polish troops had few reasons to celebrate.

Krynicki knew that the air strike was a precursor to a Russian ground assault, and within several minutes his instincts were proven correct as the movement of Russian armor became visible in the distance. The few pieces of available Polish artillery began to boom, but most of the rounds fell short. Only when the advance guard of the Russian force pushed across the valley did these big Polish guns claim any victims.

For more than six hours, the two Polish infantry divisions withstood the blizzard of Russian shells and armor. The supply of Russian tanks moving across the frozen flatlands appeared endless. After their artillery was knocked out of action by Russian aircraft, light weapons, grenades, and a small number of antitank weapons were all the Poles had to hold off six divisions. In the end, the steel of Russian armor proved stronger than the metal of Polish courage.

The defeat of Krynicki's divisions southeast of Warsaw forced the Wadislaw Radkiewicz government to pull out of the city and establish a temporary capital in Szczecin, near the German border. It was there that General Krynicki met Radkiewicz on the night of March 19.

The icy winds were blowing fiercely from the north, coming off the Baltic Sea. The new headquarters for the war effort was an old municipal building at the center of the city. While it was musty and depressing and had little heat, there was no time to be concerned about such things. Krynicki arrived at 6:30 P.M. as aides were placing file boxes on a series of old, oak tables randomly set up in the room. Radkiewicz was at a table in the corner speaking on the phone. He was clearly animated and filled with a futile rage. Finally, he slammed down the receiver.

Realizing that others had witnessed his outburst, he blushed a bit. Yet he was anxious to see Krynicki. "General," he said, offering the beleaguered officer an embrace.

General Krynicki was visibly tired—he had not slept in three days. His physical appearance, however, was as much a reflection of his mental anguish as his fatigue. He knew that only help from NATO could save the country. "Radkiewicz, what is the word from the West?"

"The West," he said with a dismissive laugh, "this is Yalta all over again." He shook his head and reached for a cigarette. "That was President Lebou on the phone from Paris. We have requested materiel aid for our soldiers—food, ammunition, weapons. Materiel, that is all that we request, and Lebou tells me he needs time to think about this matter! We will fight alone, despite the failed promises of our NATO allies to fight with us!" He struck a match and took a drag from his cigarette, sending wisps of smoke into the cool, dank air. He offered one to Krynicki, who declined, and the two sauntered over to a large table with numerous detailed maps of Poland.

"General, we are retreating on all fronts. The Russians have entered Warsaw. And to subjugate the people, they have cut all power to the capital. It's below freezing outside, and they have cut the power!"

Krynicki closely examined the maps, which were marked with

felt-tip pens outlining the Russian advance. A few blue spots indicated the deployment of Polish forces. "What have we heard from General Janowski near Lodz?"

"Nothing in the past twelve hours. We have no communications, and it is impossible to know where our forces are and how far the Russians have advanced." Radkiewicz took another drag on his cigarette.

The general went into a near trance as he studied the map. After a few minutes of silence, he ran a soiled finger over the outline until it rested in central Poland. "There. We must try to hold at the convergence of the Notec and Vistula Rivers near Bydgoszcz. This is our only hope. The rivers might slow their advance, particularly if we can blow the bridges."

Radkiewicz examined the map and nodded in agreement. Yet he felt a cruel futility in the whole exercise. "Yes, you are right. Use what you have to."

Several hundred miles to the east, a black sedan appeared out of place as it traveled over the icy roads of eastern Poland through a main corridor where there had been fighting only a day earlier. In the backseat, General Platonov looked out the window over the North European Plain at the frozen earth and the vestiges of war. A violet glow was descending over the snow as the sun sank behind the wooded hills.

The road snaked its way through a small village that was a ghastly sight for even a veteran of war. Pounded for days by Russian guns and bombed many times from the air, the village was reduced to one great pile of shattered stone. Burned-out tanks littered the nearby fields, and dead Polish soldiers resembled wax mannequins thrown from a show window, lying about in grotesque postures. Platonov could see their faces painted with hints of anger, rage, but mostly fear. Heading west through the village, he came upon a fallen Polish airplane. Screws, bolts, rings, and twisted bits of metal were scattered over an area of fifty square yards. Everything was cloaked with a light blanket of snow. And the snow was still falling.

Following personal orders from President Karashchuk, Platonov was on a special mission to tour the front. While the visible carnage brought back recollections of Afghanistan, the general blotted out the memories, trying to stay focused on his mission. He wanted to get a firsthand view of troop morale.

As the motorcade rolled into Warsaw, the city seemed sullen, even expired. There was no one on the streets, and most of the metropolis was blacked out from cut power lines which had not yet been restored. The new Russian forward command post was in the old Ministry of Defense building, a graying structure that sat solemnly along a major thoroughfare in the heart of the city. General Platonov entered the defense minister's office with its decidedly Gothic decor. There Major-General Martov, the brash tank commander who had stormed the border on the night of March 15, was waiting. Martov's T-80s swept across the North European Plain and into Warsaw with minimal casualties. His was the first unit in Warsaw, and Platonov promoted him to full general on the spot.

The two men sat on a sofa and shared a pack of cigarettes. "You know, Martov, I was in this room twenty years ago," Platonov said reminiscently, his eyes recording the fine woodwork and furniture. "We were organizing the withdrawal of Soviet forces from Warsaw." He chuckled and looked back at Martov. "It is very good to be back." They both laughed, and after a celebratory interlude, Platonov became all business.

"Now, General, tell me the current status on the front."

"The situation appears well-in-hand. But there is still much fighting left. The Polish army has retreated one hundred miles west of Warsaw. We overran many of their forces during the first thirty-six hours of fighting, but they are hoping to make a stand to the west... I would assume near Bydgoszcz. The Poles have established a temporary government in Szczecin, so they intend to continue the fight."

"What about morale and supplies?"

"Both are very good, General. But the snow will slow our advance."

Platonov stood and rubbed his chin. "Martov, I am going to ask you a question I expect you to hold in the greatest confidence. The security of our operations requires complete discretion."

Martov was a bit startled but agreed. "Yes... of course, General."

Platonov paused again. "General, how long till the men reach the German border? And how long until they might be prepared to cross that border?"

Martov looked stunned. Even in the senior ranks, the discussion had always been on obtaining control of Poland, Lithuania, and perhaps the Czech Republic and Slovakia. There had never been any mention of moving further west. But he recovered quickly.

"I am not certain I know the answer to your question, General. I have not thought about it. But I suppose that within fifteen days we will have control of Poland and secure logistical lines." He thought about it another moment. "What I am not certain of is the size of the NATO force across the border."

Platonov nodded silently. "Fifteen days. Fifteen days...," he said softly as he exited the room, leaving Martov astonished.

Along the German–Polish border, the NATO countries had amassed a sizeable conventional force. Germany had seven divisions deployed in the central sector, most to block a move on Berlin. The U.S. Army already had two divisions northeast of Berlin in the lowlands to protect against a Russian armored attack across the North European Plain. And the 82nd Airborne was just beginning to organize behind the American mechanized and armored divisions. Several more divisions would be arriving during the next several weeks. So far France had contributed four infantry divisions and Britain, two. NATO forces were deployed in depth to contain Russian forces if they broke through the front line.

After an all-night flight from Washington, Defense Secretary Tom Bodine arrived in Berlin for consultation with allies. He spent all morning with Chancellor Müller and German military officers, and left the Defense Ministry confident that the combined NATO force could withstand a Russian conventional attack. But if the

Russians resorted to NBC weapons, things would become a bit murkier. Before his return flight to Washington in the late afternoon, Bodine headed for a drab, nondescript house on Unter den Linden Boulevard. Inside he found General Krynicki waiting for him. The general was tall, slender, and dressed in a uniform adorned with several medals for long service to his country. The two shook hands before sitting at a simple pine table with several aides.

"What is the present condition on the ground, General?"

Krynicki looked grim. "It is not good, Secretary Bodine. The Russian advance has thrown our forces into chaos. Our men are well-trained and possess decent equipment. But the lightning attack, combined with the air strikes, missile attacks, and Spetsnaz operations, have made it impossible for us to mount anything resembling an organized defense. Pockets of resistance do remain. General Lech Macharski, a former classmate of mine in the service academy, continues to hold out near Lublin, and there is sporadic resistance near Kalisz. But these islands of resistance will soon be swamped by a sea of Russian forces. We will make our stand near the city of Bydgoszcz where the Vistula and Notec Rivers meet. Since we have blown up the major bridges crossing both rivers, the Russians will have to pass through Bydgoszcz to capture the northwest region of our country."

Bodine wrote a few notes and then looked up at Krynicki. "General, you can understand the dilemma we are under. Moscow has threatened us with nuclear retaliation if we enter this war. They have erected a vast ballistic missile defense system that negates our ability to retaliate with our own weapons. So our hands are tied for the time being. But we do want to be useful." Bodine drank some tea and then pulled out a file folder for Krynicki.

The general put on his reading glasses and scanned several pages—a list of weapons, equipment, and supplies. "What is this, Mr. Secretary?"

"A shopping list, General. You tell us what we can give you to help you fight the Russians more effectively, and I hope to figure out a way to get it over the border. We believe that with the refugees, traffic, and other confusion on the Polish–German frontier, we can funnel some supplies to you."

With his head resting on his hand, the general slowly and methodically went through the list, making marks and writing numbers with a felt-tip pen. After ten minutes, he delicately slid the list across the table back to Bodine. "As you can see, Mr. Bodine, we have a tremendous need for antitank weapons, especially if you have anything that can take on their reactive armor. We also lack artillery shells and land mines, which would make our defensive position more solid. But...," he set his reading glasses back on the table, "I must say something to you, Mr. Bodine, that you already know. Poles will fight subjugation from Russia. Our history has been one of domination by foreign powers. And, having tasted freedom, we will not have it taken from us easily. But we both know that Poland cannot withstand this torrent alone. We will wither under the ferocity of the Russian onslaught. Your support will only allow us to die more slowly, to see our country subjugated at a slower rate. What we need is for you and our allies in NATO to fulfill your commitments and defend Poland from this external enemy."

Tom Bodine hung his head slightly, staring at the table. For the first time in his life he felt ashamed for his country. And yet he knew his president was right. There was nothing else to be done. And tomorrow would be the same. His mind drifted from the moment, and he found himself thinking that the weak must often feel ashamed.

Chapter Twenty-three

April 11
Szczecin, Poland

By early morning the resonant rumbling of artillery had swelled into a cascade. For the second day now, mammoth Russian artillery were thrashing Szczecin, the last outpost of a free Poland, while the inhabitants and soldiers trapped in the city could do nothing but wait for the inevitable march of Russian soldiers.

In the dank, dark basement of the municipal building that had served as the Polish government's headquarters, Wadislaw Radkiewicz stuffed the last of his papers into a leather satchel. Evacuation was a devastating, emotional shock, and deep down he feared that it might be decades before he could return to his country. On his lonely walk to the door, he ran into General Krynicki, his uniform threadbare, his face filthy, and dark rings under his eyes from days without sleep. "Andrzej," pleaded Radkiewicz, "it is pointless to stay. We must return to fight again another day."

Sullen-faced, Krynicki only shook his head and walked toward the scattered communication devices in the corner of the room. The general would stay.

Looking through his field glasses at the scarred city in front of him, General Martov was now two miles south of Szczecin. His men had been waiting thirty-six hours for the final assault. The artillery barrage had gone on for more than twenty-four hours, so long and so heavily that the supply of shells was starting to run low. Yet only in recent hours did the Russian commanders, from a generation who had never faced Poles in battle, begin to grasp the cruel, inescapable fact: with nowhere to retreat, the remnants of the Polish army were preparing themselves not for surrender but death. There was no alternative but to send in Russian ground troops.

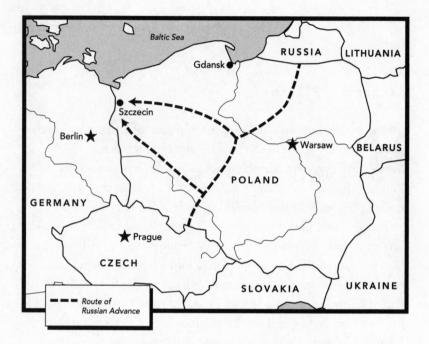

**The Russian March Through Poland,
March–April, 2006**

It was 11:00 A.M. when Russian forces began moving in for the final assault, advancing under the tight-woven noise of war, shells still whistling eerily overhead as the gross rumble of artillery became more insistent. Underneath these sounds, Martov could hear the rapid, staccato bark of machine guns, and the answer of the slower chatter of heavy automatic weapons and the short, sharp boom of the tank guns. The winds were strong, and soon it became clear that much of the city was burning, the smoke billowing over the border into Germany.

As the Russian noose closed, the long bursts of machine gun fire swelled in volume. Many times Martov believed the battle to be at its climax as the guns slowed. But they always rose again, the focus of the noise shifting slightly. In the end it was only the fire that gave the Russians victory in the single, bloodiest day in the history of Russian arms since the Second World War. Just before dark, the guns fell silent. Only then did General Martov's column proceed into the city, down the main road marked for long stretches by the piles of rubble to either side. Free Poland sighed her last breath.

President Karashchuk was at a villa on the Black Sea when word of the fall of Szczecin reached him. Though victory had been a foregone conclusion for days, Karashchuk could not help but celebrate. General Platonov and Marshal Serov were with him, enjoying the soft, westerly breezes coming off the placid waters onto the large, stone patio. Karashchuk proposed a toast, and the three drank heartily. Afterward, they returned to the study for more cerebral pursuits.

Karashchuk was full of verve but restless. The conquest of Poland was a redemption of a sort but hardly sufficient for a twenty-first–century *Vozhd*. On the table in the center of the study was a large map of Europe affixed with labels marking the deployment of Russian and NATO forces. The president perused the map before asking Platonov about the next move.

Clearly, the general had also been thinking about the subject. He ran his finger over the North European Plain. "The NATO armies have deployed themselves along the German border, assuming a thrust westward. If we were to move southwest, through the Czech

Republic, we would force them to redeploy their forces and face attack across a broad front."

Having the same thoughts, Karashchuk concurred with a confident nod. "When can we move?"

On April 25, two weeks after the fall of Szczecin, Russian forces pushed south in a blitzkrieg on the tiny, peaceful Czech Republic. Czech Prime Minister Jan Ripka talked of liberty in cultivated tones. Gentle and thoughtful in small things, he had clearly been out of his depth in dealing with the facts of power. He had tried to appease the Russians by excluding NATO forces from Czech soil. Moscow repaid him by pouring armor and mechanized infantry through the Moravian Gate, the traditional military corridor between the North European Plain and the Danube in central Europe.

Under a light rain in the early morning, Czech forces met the Russians on the field of battle. The Czechs were familiar with the terrain and threatened to at least slow the Russian tide for several days. But Karashchuk had grown impatient, and for a *Vozhd* to play war with the Czechs appeared almost unseemly. By midafternoon, a lone missile was launched from a Russian facility in Belarus, and minutes later a man-made atomic sun exploded over Hradec Kralove, which ceased to exist except as radioactive dust drifting toward Prague.

The destruction of the city had served a brutal purpose—to demoralize Czech soldiers and civilians alike. And when it became clear that NATO would not retaliate, the Czech's will to resist melted like Alpine snow in a hot sun. Within two days Russian tanks were rolling through Prague. Inhabitants of the capital city were in tears as conquering Russian soldiers rode through the narrow streets of the Old Town, across the Charles Bridge with its graceful statues, to Prague Castle. When the Czech flag that had been towering above the castle came down to be replaced by the two-headed Russian eagle, the wailing could be heard on every street corner in the city.

General Ilya Vlasov, the Russian commander, chose Prague Castle as the new military post as much for the pleasure of humiliating the

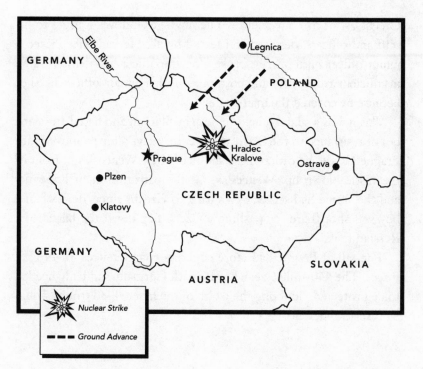

Invasion of the Czech Republic—April 25, 2006

Czechs as for its convenience. The huge general was a brute to his staff and officers, despised and feared by all. He had once kicked a junior officer until his ribs broke after the officer had demonstrated insufficient respect for his position. Another junior officer he shot because he coveted the man's wife.

Vlasov was a staunch believer in pan-Slavism and hated any symbol of resistance to the Slavic empire. Just days after he moved into Prague Castle, he ordered the statue of King Wenceslas in front of the castle blown up. Wenceslas was the patron saint of Bohemia, and the statue had served as a shrine to Czechs since 1968 when a boy was shot there for pushing a Czech flag down the barrel of a Russian tank.

The fall of Prague had more concrete consequences for NATO forces. The 440-mile Czech border with Germany suddenly needed to be protected, doubling the width of the front allied troops would be forced to defend.

Back in Moscow, a throng of people had arrived at the Kremlin's Grand Staircase to cheer and celebrate Karashchuk's victories in central Europe. It was barely above freezing, and a mix of rain and ice was falling. But the weather did nothing to hamper the enthusiasm of thousands of reborn nationalists. Although Karashchuk was preparing for a celebratory banquet inside, he could not resist an impromptu appearance at the top of the Grand Staircase to receive the cheers of the people for their *Vozhd.*

Inside the Kremlin, Karashchuk joined several hundred others in the banquet hall of St. George. The tables were heavy with old glass and silver, sturgeon and caviar. The high-backed, jewel-encrusted chair in which Karashchuk sat had been especially retrieved from the Hermitage in St. Petersburg for the evening. The last man to sit in it in this room had been Nicholas II.

While the evening was committed to celebration, there was also some official business. Bulgaria signed a treaty of military alliance with Moscow and agreed to commit four divisions to the campaign in Europe. Moscow now had twenty divisions in Poland and the Czech Republic, supported by six divisions from Belarus.

Late that night, his head aching from the revelry, Karashchuk returned to his planning room for consultations with Platonov, Serov, and Malinovsky. They all knew that the real prizes in Europe lay further west. Germany was still the political and economic center of gravity in Europe. By now, however, the allies had more than fifteen divisions crowding the border, particularly near Berlin and along the Elbe River. The Americans had six divisions in Germany, though most were in the north, having been deployed there on the mistaken notion that the Russians might attempt to sweep across the North European Plain. Five French divisions were in place outside Dresden, with two British infantry divisions in support. A British armored division was positioned outside Nürnberg near the bank of the Danube. In Germany and eastern France, plenty of allied air power had congregated, and the United States had three fighter wings and two dozen bombers deployed at NATO air bases across western Europe. And while France elected to keep her aircraft on French soil, Britain had shifted several squadrons to the continent, particularly in the Netherlands.

The grim assessment of the current military balance in central Europe was summed up in a report Platonov passed around the room.

STRATEGIC MILITARY ASSESSMENT

SECTOR ONE—NORTH OF BERLIN

NATO ground forces:	Russian ground forces:
Two U.S. Armored Divisions	Two Russian Armored Divisions

In reserve:	In reserve:
German Infantry Division	Belarus Infantry Division

Air power: *Air power:*
Two German fighter squadrons   Two Russian fighter squadrons
One American fighter squadron
Twenty attack helicopters

SECTOR TWO—BERLIN

NATO ground forces: *Russian ground forces:*
Three German infantry divisions   Two Russian infantry divisions
German Armored Division   Belarus Armored Division

In reserve: *In reserve:*
Four German reserve divisions   Two Russian armored divisions

Air power: *Air power:*
Two German fighter squadrons   Two Russian fighter squadrons
One British fighter squadron

SECTOR THREE—SOUTHEAST OF BERLIN

NATO ground forces: *Russian ground forces:*
Two French infantry divisions   Two Russian infantry divisions
Two British infantry divisions   Two Russian armored divisions

In reserve: *In reserve:*
Two German reserve divisions   One Bulgarian infantry division

Air power: *Air power:*
Two American fighter squadrons   One Russian fighter squadron
One German fighter squadron

It was a sobering assessment. Despite the tremendous victories of the past several weeks, Russia was now confronted with an impressive wall of men and materiel that blocked any advance further west. And as the Americans continued to arrive in Europe, the allied wall would only strengthen. "The balance," warned Marshal Serov, "is unlikely to turn in our favor as time goes on."

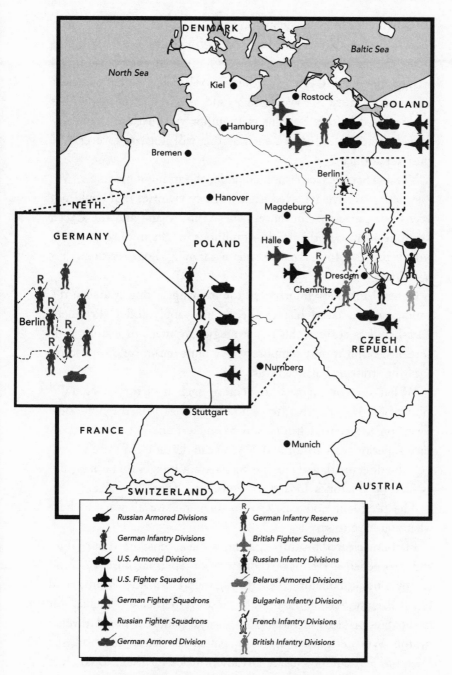

Central European Stalemate

Inwardly, even Karashchuk found the report daunting. But a *Vozhd* must be able to not only cope with reality but alter it. He tossed the paper away dismissively. "Gentlemen, the conventional balance along the German border is irrelevant. We have nuclear superiority against the West and a window of opportunity that has never existed before. But this is a temporary situation, an aberration. A strategic imbalance such as this will not last forever. We must act at once."

Marshal Serov's face crumbled under the strain of his voice. "Mr. President, we have achieved extraordinary victories that could not have been expected. You have achieved in Poland and the Czech Republic what took the deaths of millions for Stalin to accomplish. Now is the time for us to consolidate our gains, not overextend our capacities."

General Platonov interrupted the exchange. "But, Marshal, the limitations we faced historically do not apply today. President Karashchuk is correct: this is a strategic advantage of historic proportions. But it is only temporary. We must maximize our position until the strategic balance returns."

"What do you suggest to achieve such a victory, General?" intoned Serov defiantly. "You know as well as I do the numerical parity on the central front. And to speak frankly, the Americans have superiority in armor and NATO can defeat us in the air."

"The direct path will fail, but we have advantages that can ensure us success." Platonov looked to Karashchuk for reassurance.

The president nodded, "Go on, General, we all want to hear what you have to say."

Platonov cleared his throat, scanned the notepad in front of him, and proceeded. "We have thousands of Spetsnaz forces behind enemy lines, in major cities throughout Germany, France, and Great Britain. Several hundred of these are permanent agents. But in the days prior to the attack on Poland, hundreds more traveled to the West disguised as businessmen, athletes, and tourists. Weapons and equipment are already in place for them to conduct assassinations and bombings. These forces are prepared to act on our orders. They can disrupt the functioning of these governments and the effectiveness of government and military establishments in conducting a war."

"Go on," Karashchuk said in an encouraging tone.

"And then there is our well-developed arsenal of weapons based on new physical principles. These will be immensely helpful in subjugating enemy forces and will allow us to achieve surprise. All this and the psychological advantage of our enemies knowing that we can go nuclear at any time should be sufficient for victory. But in the end, we must be prepared to use weapons of mass destruction. Of course we would rather rule a rich Germany than one reduced to ashes. But as long as we maintain a monopoly on BMD systems, we can use these weapons without fear of retaliation. This will prove to be decisive if we act now."

In the end only Marshal Serov remained hesitant to push west. The prospect of another victorious campaign was simply too intoxicating. As General Malinovsky put it, "The embarrassment of Afghanistan and Chechnya have become a distant memory since the conquest of Poland and the Czech Republic. And with victory in all of central Europe, they will be completely forgotten."

In the days following the meeting at the Kremlin, Platonov and Malinovsky worked with the General Staff to devise an operational plan for the conquest of Germany. Russian forces continued to move west toward the German border. Three Ukrainian divisions joined them, along with two brigades from Bulgaria.

Chapter Twenty-four

April 29
Los Alamos National Laboratory

I t was a small box with a cylindrical tip about the size of a trash can. Tom Bodine had heard about these "Brilliant Pebbles" but had never seen one before. "It weighs less than twenty pounds," offered Dr. Margaret Chase, the chief research engineer on the project. While the mechanical device resembled a small cylinder, it was actually a "killer satellite" which could open several heat-seeking "eyes" and locate attacking enemy missiles thousands of miles away. Upon detecting such a target, the satellite would fire off its own rocket motors and accelerate, rising into space directly in the path of the enemy missile, and destroy it on impact. It was a component of the embryonic U.S. strategic defense system. If the system could be made operational, thousands of such "Pebbles" would be deployed in space to await an enemy launch.

Brilliant Pebbles was nothing new—it had been dreamt up by defense engineers in the 1980s. It was a basic but efficient method of strategic defense that could be upgraded with laser technology. A defense system based on lasers might be more effective, but the United States did not have the time to develop and deploy such an advanced system. The president wanted a strategic defense program off the ground as soon as possible, and Brilliant Pebbles offered the best hope.

Bodine had spent the early morning hours at the U.S. space facility in Cheyenne Mountain in Colorado examining the vast array of advanced computers that could manage and direct the strategic defense system. The U.S. Consolidated Space Operations Center (CSOC) would receive information from early-warning satellites and activate the space systems. The battle for the heavens would then begin.

Working with Dr. Chase at Los Alamos was an army of Ph.D.s

and hard scientists in fields such as physics, chemistry, aeronautics, and electronic engineering. It was a modern-day Manhattan Project tasked with developing a new, advanced military system in the face of a hostile enemy. Yet there were striking differences to this project. One was that Chase and her colleagues would undo the work of Robert Oppenheimer, Hans Bethe, and General Leslie Groves. And there was also the fact that Moscow already had a strategic defense system in place. It was as if the Nazis already had the bomb.

As Tom Bodine walked down the hall for his briefing, he wondered if the massive project, which include four hundred scientists, engineers, and military researchers, would stay secret for long. The Soviets knew of the U.S. atom-bomb project in the 1940s, and he assumed that the Kremlin was equally well-informed today. How they might respond was anyone's guess.

Adjacent to the testing facilities was a nondescript conference room where Bodine and Dr. Chase found a group of eight scientists seated around a sterile, utilitarian table waiting for the secretary of defense. Bodine was anxious to hear about the status of the research. "Tell me, Dr. Chase, when would you expect to have this system operable?"

Chase was petite but full of energy and verve. Her graying hair hung loosely around her face, and her wire-frame glasses seemed to be constantly sliding down her nose. She spoke with slight, matriarchal tones. "Well, Mr. Secretary, you have given us a very difficult task indeed. Since there has been scant research on strategic defense in recent years, we are dealing with technologies that are more than a decade old."

"Doctor, I'm not concerned about how old they are. The question is, will these systems work?"

Chase wrinkled her slight nose. "Well, to be frank, we will not know for a certainty until the system is deployed and used. We cannot engage in actual tests on real missiles at a test range because that would run the risk of tipping off Moscow. And without that testing, we are relying on laboratory tests conducted in ideal conditions." She glanced at the faces assembled around the table. "I think I can speak for all of us when I say that we have complete confidence in this system. The only areas of concern are reaction time and warning."

"How so?" Bodine asked anxiously.

"Well, as you know, an American BMD system will have very little time to attack Russian ballistic missiles as they rise through the atmosphere. The booster stage of the SS-18 Russian ICBM burns out three hundred seconds after launch when the missile is outside the Earth's atmosphere at a height of four hundred kilometers. And their more recent systems have an even shorter booster phase. But the larger problem will come from Russian SLBMs. They will be launched from unpredictable points, and their flight times are typically less than ten minutes, compared with the ICBMs, which can take approximately thirty minutes."

A bearded, professorial gentleman raised his hand slightly to direct attention to himself. He spoke softly. "Mr. Secretary, my name is Jonathan Epstein. I am handling the rocketry portion of our research. A more fundamental problem will be deploying the system in a timely fashion. Despite the advanced nature of our space program, we do not have much of a satellite launch capability. We can deploy this system only piece by piece during a one-year period."

Bodine sat for a moment with his index finger in front of his lips. Looking at the scientists around the table, he then leaned forward for emphasis. "I am sure you all understand the seriousness of this situation. I know the strain you are all being put under. The failure to develop and deploy a strategic defense system was a political—not scientific—blunder. And in retrospect, it was on a magnitude I have never seen before. We are in this predicament because years ago Washington failed to realize that this threat was present. But the country is now relying on all of you to correct this mistake. I don't pretend to understand all of the technological problems you face. But this system not only has got to work, but it also has to be in the heavens as soon as possible. If there is anything you need from me to finish this job, I will get it for you."

Silence hung in the room like a low-lying mist. Dr. Chase again glanced at her colleagues and recognizing her tacit role as spokesperson for the team, continued. "Mr. Secretary, we can build these systems. And they will work. While this will not be a leak-proof defense, based on what we know of the Russian system, it will be very comparable in terms of effectiveness."

Bodine nodded with a reluctant realism. "Yes, I understand. We don't expect perfection. What I do need from you is your guarantee that this system can be fully in place within the next two years."

"That's impossible," an unrecognized voice blurted out. It came from a gaunt, stringy figure with piercing brown eyes and a half-beard. In a snub at the scientific establishment, the man sported a long ponytail and wore turquoise jewelry on his wrists. Bodine scrutinized him with curiosity. "I don't believe we've had the pleasure of an introduction."

"Uh, sorry sir. The name is Tony Gimbal. I am managing the electrical engineering team."

"Why the skepticism?"

"Frankly, Mr. Secretary, we cannot hope to pull all these disparate components together—optics, electronics, navigational—into an effective, cohesive system without testing and more time."

Bodine let out a weak sigh, like a balloon slowly leaking air. "Look, Dr. Gimbal, I understand that these conditions are not ideal. But perhaps you don't appreciate the severity of the crisis. If the Kremlin so desired, they could launch a nuclear strike on this country today and decimate all of our major cities. And they could do this quite comfortably knowing that while our retaliatory strike would cause some casualties, most of the missiles would not get through. So as you can see, deterrence essentially exists in a very, very weak form. We are relying on the generosity of President Karashchuk for our survival. And given the fact that this man is now running through half of Europe with his tanks, I don't think we should tempt him to maintain his generosity for very long."

Murmurs of laughter ran through the room, cutting the tension. Gimbal took a deep breath and began to speak, but Dr. Chase interrupted. "Secretary Bodine, you have my word. The system will be ready in two years."

Bodine looked first at Gimbal and then back at Chase. "Very good. Thank you, doctor." He stood slowly and exited, heading back to his plane for the return flight to Washington.

On the lonely trip back to the nation's capital, Bodine reviewed the latest intelligence reports from Europe. The use of tactical nuclear weapons in the Czech Republic was a frightening omen. Yet Bodine found himself surprised that the Kremlin had not made more use of such weapons, given the present strategic imbalance. If the Kremlin did invade Germany, he expected nuclear weapons to play a central role in the campaign. U.S. forces in Germany were deployed with tactical nuclear weapons and had orders to use them if attacked. While the thought of such a war in the heart of Europe frightened him, he continued to hope against logic that the Kremlin might halt its advance at the Oder River and not proceed into Germany.

As his plane cruised at thirty thousand feet over the Midwest, he received a flash call from Jack Fowler at the White House. "Tom, we have received a cable from Moscow that will require an instant response."

Bodine felt his stomach wrenching. "What does it say?"

"They demand the immediate withdrawal of U.S. forces from continental Europe. Failure to comply will invite a nuclear strike on the continental United States."

Bodine felt his body grow numb with dread. It was not so much the shock of the demand—he had been expecting it—as it was the mortal fear of wrestling with such a vexing issue that made him weak. There was a prolonged silence. "Tom, did you hear me?"

"Yes, Jack, I understand. How long do we have?"

"They want to see movement from our forces within twenty-four hours. The president wants to meet about this as soon as you land."

"I will be there, Jack. Oh, and remember, we have a visit from our special guest."

Fowler paused. "Right, I remember."

As Bodine set the phone down he pondered the alternatives. He had little doubt that Karashchuk would act on his threat. Everything U.S. intelligence had compiled on the man pointed to an individual who placed little value on his own species. Climbing to the top of Russian politics was altogether different from the equivalent in the West. It required a brutality and ruthlessness the West was unaccustomed to. Bodine liked to think that cream rose to the top in the West, at least most of the time. So if America was akin to the creamery, Russia had in recent years become a septic tank: the worst elements of society floated to the top.

It was close to midnight and most of the White House staff had gone home when Tom Bodine walked down the empty corridors. Through the windows he could see the lights of Washington twinkling in the moonless night. It was a lonely feeling.

Reaching the president's residence, Bodine found St. John slumped on the sofa, his feet up on the coffee table and his tie loosened. St. John was a formal person, and Bodine could not recall having seen him in such an insouciant pose. The president waved his arm. "Tom, please come in." Bodine walked casually to the center of the room and took a seat on a yellow, colonial-style chair directly facing the president. Secretary of State Kent Hughes sat in a nearby white wing chair, his legs crossed. Hughes was a rotund man with small black eyes and a thinning mane of gray hair. He was often lost in the subtleties of strategy. National Security Adviser Jack Fowler was in the corner pouring himself a drink.

The room was dim—few lights were on. The president handed the single-page ultimatum issued by Karashchuk to Bodine without saying a word.

President Michael St. John
The White House
United States of America

Dear President St. John:

Russia insists on the immediate withdrawal of all American armed forces from continental Europe. All extra-European powers should leave to allow the continent to determine its own affairs. Failure to comply will compel my government to commence a nuclear attack on the American continent.

We require an answer within the next twenty-four hours.

A. Karashchuk
Russia

Bodine carefully read the note and then set it on the cherry-wood coffee table without comment.

The president sat erect, cleared his throat and began with a solid, granitelike tone. "We know why we are here. I assume you all have seen the letter." Everyone in the room was looking down as in some sort of confession of shame that America was now prostrate in front of her enemies. "I have a very difficult decision to make. And I need to know from each of you what that decision should be." He turned to Fowler who had rejoined the group with a crystal glass in hand. "Jack, give us the latest status on the ground."

"Well, the combined NATO force can match them fairly closely in terms of numbers. In the air, we have superiority."

St. John squinted his eyes, as if in deep thought. "If we were to pull back, what would that do to the balance?"

"It would significantly weaken the NATO force. But if the Europeans move their reserves forward, they should be able to hold. Of course, none of this applies if they use NBC weapons."

"Mr. President," Bodine interjected, "the numerical balance is there. But NATO stockpiles are pretty low. I noticed the wording of the ultimatum. They want U.S. forces out of Europe. If you read this like a lawyer, we will be in full compliance even if we withdraw our troops but leave the weapons behind. Our allies could put these systems to good use, especially some of the Abrams tanks and the antitank systems."

St. John grinned. The thought of complying but still tweaking his nose at Karashchuk had great appeal. "Good idea, Tom. But we know what the reaction in Europe is going to be. They are going to curse at us in four different languages." He looked around the room. "Still, I think we all agree that we don't have a choice. Does anyone here believe that we should not comply with this ultimatum?" There was a long silence. "Very well then. Tom, make the necessary arrangements to pull our forces back to Great Britain."

The president took a drink from a crystal glass and then set it down, the ice cubes chiming inside. "Well, Tom, what did you find out in Colorado and California?"

"As far as the command center is concerned, it will be ready on time. Cheyenne Mountain is already putting the necessary equipment in place. But the system itself is another matter. Several of the scientists have doubts about deploying a system that has not been tested, and secrecy precludes us from doing anything but that. The bottom line is, it will take two years."

Hughes shook his head. "Two years! Two years if we are lucky! The Russians could move in six months, or tomorrow. But even if you get your two years, how do you expect to deploy a foolproof missile defense system in time when we haven't done it in more than two decades—without even testing? What are you going to say when the first Russian missile gets through? Whoops, we missed one?"

"It doesn't have to be perfect. If we get lucky, neither we nor the Russians will ever find out if it works at all. It just has to be credible—credible enough to persuade the Russians that if they risk going nuclear, we'll still be here to shoot back!"

"Oh, great! Now I really feel safe. We can go back to playing head games with the Russians, only this time we're playing against a guy who is unpredictable!"

"Come on, you know better than that," said Bodine growing impatient. "Look, MAD was in some ways an insane policy. And we should have replaced it with a really reliable, foolproof defense a long time ago. But we can't do that now. Instead, what we have to do, unless we just want to surrender, is restore some form of mutual deterrence. We can do that with even a leaky system... and some luck."

"Spell that out, Tom," said St. John calmly.

"Think back to the beginning of the nuclear era. Mutual deterrence worked for decades. Scary, maybe crazy, but it worked because of two simple factors. Both sides were armed to the gills, but neither could deliver its nukes quickly or accurately enough to destroy the other sides before that side had a chance to shoot back. Nobody could deliver a successful first strike, the crippling blow that could win a nuclear war in one launch. So nobody ever pushed the button."

"Sure," concurred the president, nodding his head. "You can't have a gunfight if nobody shoots first."

"But the system was not stable, and toward the mid-1970s it began to break down. Offense threatened to outstrip defense, always a dangerous moment in history. As ICBMs and SLBMs became more and more accurate and as we packed multiple warheads on each one, it began to look possible—just barely—that shooting first would be a winning strategy. If either side ever got to the point at which it was confident that thirty minutes from an all-out launch it could destroy the other side's nuclear forces on the ground, even inside hardened silos, or under the sea, then it might be possible to win a nuclear war."

Hughes scoffed. "You would still have to be nuts to try."

"Sure. Unless the other guy had the same capacity to destroy your missiles on the ground with a first shot. In that case, at a moment of great tension when each side feared the other might shoot first, it might not only make sense to shoot first, but it might seem like the only responsible thing to do. Anyway, by the early 1980s it began to look as if we might one day get to that point, and MAD stopped being just scary but became outright dangerous."

"That's when Reagan announced Star Wars," added Jack Fowler.

"He knew the no-nukers had a point. The world was getting more dangerous as the weapons were changing, throwing the strategic calculus out of whack. We had to change the system before it broke down."

"Precisely, Jack," Bodine agreed. "And you do that by using a ballistic missile defense to cancel out the offensive progress, making the ICBM obsolete or at least unreliable in a first strike. Too many missiles would be destroyed by the defense system, which would bring us back to where no one could risk shooting first. Now, we never got Star Wars, in part, because the threat of it hastened the collapse of the Soviet regime."

Hughes shifted in his seat. "You know, you two probably have wonderful futures as history teachers, but I don't see where this gets us."

"It's simple," answered Bodine. "Even a leaky defense accomplishes the first goal of any strategic defense system: it eliminates the ICBM as a reliable first-strike weapon against our nuclear forces."

"Aren't we missing something obvious here?" asked Hughes. "This whole thing started because the Russians have a defense system, and we can't threaten them. Even if you are right and our own defense system would leave us with enough missiles after a Russian first strike, our missiles wouldn't get through. Isn't that the problem?"

The defense secretary shook his head. "No. While our force is still dangerous this very minute, it's just not a viable weapon of war. But right now theirs is. That's what we have to change. Look, there is a huge difference between being dangerous and being in a position to actually use nukes as part of a winning military strategy. A terrorist strolling up Broadway with a nuke in a suitcase is dangerous. But his suitcase is not a plan for victory. A year ago both we and the Russians were dangerous, but neither of us could use those weapons to win a war.

"When Moscow came up with a defense system, they made nukes part of a realistic war-fighting strategy for the first time since Hiroshima. In the event of a nuclear exchange, the Russians would sustain fewer casualties than they had in the Second World War, Karashchuk would be safe in his bunker, his arsenal would be intact, and he would engulf this continent in unquenchable fire. But if we have a defense too, even a leaky one, then we turn back the clock."

"Give it to us in a sentence, Tom," said St. John, by now painfully tired from the day.

"Sure. No reliable first-strike capacity equals no viable strategy to win a nuclear war. You can kill with second-strike weapons but you can't make war with them. Even a limited defense makes a first strike unreliable. Put up a limited defense and we are back on equal terms with the Russians, and Karashchuk's strategy starts to collapse."

"Will it work?" asked St. John skeptically.

Bodine paused. "Maybe, maybe not. But do we really have an alternative?"

Tom Bodine ran his fingers through his thinning hair as his limousine sped through the cool Virginia countryside, a thin layer of fog cloaking the rolling hills of hunt country. The car headed down a lane toward a large estate located on more than two hundred acres of green pasture. It was a secluded spot, perfect for a covert meeting requiring maximum security.

Armed agents from the Secret Service and FBI wandered the grounds, and a crew of four was establishing a satellite uplink in a small, windowless van. Inside the plantation manor, the secretary found several mid- and senior-level CIA officials unloading a gigantic stack of files and working on laptop computers. Bodine gave them an acknowledging nod before proceeding to the main dining room. Seated at the table were three men drinking coffee and carrying on an animated conversation. One was General Andrzej Krynicki—the Polish patriot who had fought valiantly at Szczecin until the complete collapse of the perimeter. With Russian forces conducting a sweep of the city to arrest and interrogate officers and government officials, Krynicki managed to slip across the border into Germany.

Bodine and Krynicki shook hands, and then the general introduced the secretary to his two colleagues: Major Zbigniew Urban, who had fought in Warsaw; and General Lech Macharski, who had stood up against a mighty Russian assault and held the city of Lublin for six days under constant bombardment. When his forces finally surrendered, Macharski slipped through Russians lines in a disguise and fled for the Czech border. Only hours after he entered Bohemia, Russian tanks stormed the Czech border, forcing the general to escape yet again, this time to Germany. Macharski was a powerfully built man with a heavy face and forceful jaw. Along with his physical strength came an inner peace and confidence Bodine found refreshing.

The four sat at a long, colonial-style table on which there were a coffeepot, cups, and notepads. The window shades were pulled down, and an old, heavy crystal chandelier gave off a particularly radiant light. Bodine went directly to the business at hand. "Gentlemen, the president asked me to summon you to Washington to discuss a proposition with you." He cleared his throat. "There is a very real danger that Moscow intends to extend its grip on Europe by attacking Germany. Russian forces have been massing along the border. And this attack is likely to succeed, especially if they use nuclear, biological, or chemical weapons. So it is essential that we raise the stakes for the Kremlin and begin the process of challenging their hold on central Europe. You undoubtedly know that Moscow has developed and deployed an extensive BMD system, and we are basically powerless to retaliate. In order to deal with this threat, we need time. We are all anxious to fight for the liberation of your country, and I believe that your work will be essential to the freedom of the entire continent."

Urban pulled a cigarette out of the pack in his pocket and lit it without asking anyone. After a few drags, he blew a stream of white smoke into the air. "What exactly are you suggesting, Mr. Bodine?"

"Our intelligence indicates that you have all worked to develop an extensive, underground structure in Poland, and that thousands of your men are trapped behind lines and have built informal cells that can be activated. We will train, equip, and supply your force with the latest technological weapons available."

Urban was not impressed by the suggestion. "This is an interesting proposition, but you cannot realistically think that we can evict the Russians from Polish soil."

"Well, not by yourselves, but it can be part of the unified NATO effort to defeat Moscow."

The major laughed. He took another drag on his cigarette and expelled a cloud of smoke tinged with an air of cynicism. "NATO? Of what use is NATO? Your commitment and that of France, Germany, Italy, and England amounted to nothing."

For the first time in days, Bodine felt his anger directed at someone other than Karashchuk. "Look, Major, I understand your sense of outrage. And believe me, there is nothing I would like more than to blow those Russian divisions off your soil. But we have to deal with the strategic reality. And until this is corrected, we will have to do what we can to fight for a free Poland."

At this point Krynicki entered the conversation with an unspoken authority and respect that had evolved in the wake of his stand at Szczecin. "Mr. Bodine, if you can provide these things to us, we can make life very difficult for Moscow." Urban sat silently, not reacting.

Bodine turned to the general. "I am very glad to hear that, General Krynicki. Now tell me, who can you field in the next several days?"

"We have approximately four thousand men who are presently in refugee facilities in Germany. If you can convince Berlin to allow them to leave the camps, we can begin sending teams across the border. They are eager to fight. We also have several indigenous units in Lublin that General Macharski can activate. And partisans can operate out of the wooded areas in central Poland. To make this force work, we will need communications equipment as well as weaponry, ammunition, and other basic supplies."

"How can we get them in?"

Krynicki gasped. "It will not be easy. We might be able to get some in overland, but this will be difficult and limited. Airdrops I suppose, or perhaps by river."

"Yes, airdrops would make sense," interjected Macharski. "The Russians have placed portable air defense systems only near the bor-

ders. If we know where they are deployed, we can find a weakness—
an entryway—into Poland."

"Gentlemen," offered Bodine, "I would like to bring in several
men from our CIA and the Special Forces. They can help us forge
ahead on this venture right away." They all agreed to the plan. Minutes later four more men entered the room, and they met for
another twelve hours. By early morning, the first in a series of guerrilla attacks behind Russians lines had been planned.

Chapter Twenty-five

May 27
the Kremlin

Dressed in his dark blue dress uniform bedecked with
medals, Russian President Aleksandr Karashchuk walked
stiffly into his office at the Kremlin. He sat down at his
imposing, ornate wooden desk. A seal with the Russian two-headed
eagle was displayed directly behind him, the eyes seemingly peeking over his shoulders. More than a dozen television cameras were
gathered in front of his desk, and the cameramen focused on his
reddish, marblelike face as he began an open address to the people
of Europe. His eyes were steady and his gaze straight as he glared
into the cameras. He was a picture of brash and power.

"Fellow Europeans," he began in a rich, deep tone, reading from a
TelePrompTer. "For decades the Great Powers have placed Russia in
oppressive bondage. We have suffered greatly through major wars,
famine, and economic hardship. But under my leadership, Russia has
been restored to her rightful place as a jewel in the crown of nations.
The Americans have abandoned the continent, having fled across the
ocean, and the myth of a U.S. superpower has been exposed. A new
order is dawning in Europe. This is an important day because we can
now develop and prosper without any interference from external

powers. We mean none of our fellow Europeans harm, except those that hope to hurt the Slavic people. We simply ask for a cooperative, respectful attitude which all countries of the world desire.

"In recent weeks the aggressive designs of the German government in Berlin have become known not only to the Slavic people but the nations of the world. And it is these designs that lead us to offer fraternal assistance to protect the Polish people from German aggression. We have incontrovertible evidence that the brutal murder of senior Polish military and government officials outside Bialystok, Poland, was carried out by German commandos. In light of these barbaric acts, we felt it necessary to protect our brethren in Poland.

"The Slavic people take the German threat very seriously. During the past century, we were attacked twice by German militarists. So the world cannot expect us to sit idly by and allow another such attack to take place. German forces continue to build up along the Polish border, a sign that they have not abandoned their schemes on their neighbor. Berlin must be punished for the barbarous acts outside Bialystok.

"We have also noted the presence of French, British, and Dutch troops on German soil who are either willingly or unwillingly participating in this militaristic venture. Let me say clearly: we have no quarrel with these great nations. However, you must know that if there are hostilities, these countries will not be spared if they continue in any way to support the efforts of German militarists. Let there be absolutely no doubts: Russia possesses a nuclear arsenal against which you have no defense. The American, British, and French nuclear arsenals are impotent against our defensive shield."

Karashchuk sharpened both his tone and his stare as he concluded. "Those countries that resist Russia's efforts to deal with very real threats to its security will not be spared from the nuclear fire that will come." As quickly as he had arrived, he exited, leaving dozens of Western journalists in fearful silence.

A thin line of fifteen men hiked quietly under the cover of darkness through the foothills of the western Czech Republic. It was a clear night, and there was plenty of military activity in the area. Most of the men were Czech nationals returning to their native land to organize a resistance against Russian rule. Among them was Lieutenant Mark Brandt, a member of the U.S. Special Forces, assigned with two other Americans to foment resistance in Bohemia. He carried with him a briefcase-size multimission advanced tactical terminal (MATT), his lifeline to the West. The computer terminal permitted Brandt to receive encrypted intelligence broadcasts on four separate UHF and VHF channels. It weighed about forty pounds and allowed him to transmit in both data and voice through specific data links.

But despite this lifeline to the West, the operation had been launched as a desperate step, with little intelligence to go on. Like most CIA stations overseas, Prague had been reduced in size by one-half during the 1990s. The Directorate of Operations was pared down with budget cuts, and hundreds of experienced operatives were terminated. Most of the new employees at the CIA were designed to track economic trends, not military capabilities, and certainly not to conduct covert and paramilitary operations overseas. And because of these new realities, Brandt and his two colleagues were marching into a situation nearly blind.

While covert operations had been considered "unnecessary in the post–Cold War era," they were one of the few avenues now open to Washington as a means of fighting Moscow's march into central Europe. U.S. forces had retreated across the channel to London. And the Russian invasion of Germany appeared imminent. Yet a guerrilla war, if one could be organized, might severely hamper Moscow's planned military offensive.

Brandt and the fourteen others would march through the mountains for two days and then link up with remnants of the Czech army near the city of Klatovy. More than one thousand Czech soldiers had reportedly taken refuge in the snowy peaks of the mountains. It was hoped these men would form the nucleus of a guerrilla army. But organizing them would have to proceed rapidly. As the weather warmed and the mountains cleared of snow, it would only be a question of time before Russian forces came looking for them.

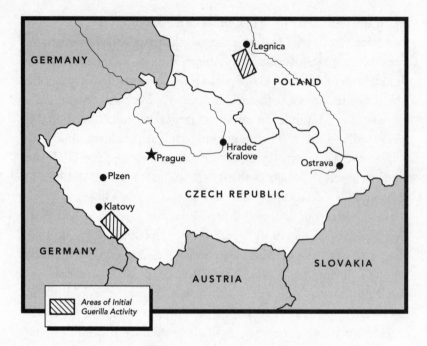

**The Twilight War: U.S. Special Forces Begin
Organizing Guerilla Armies, May 2006**

A similar drama was being acted out in central Poland near Leg-nica where two Americans, along with General Krynicki, were air-dropped into the nearby forests. They at once set about organizing an underground movement that could molest Russian forces and threaten the vital, Russian supply lines running through the region. Using the MATT, the unit would stay in daily contact with a U.S. Special Forces post in London.

These were the first glimpses of a twilight war against Russian occupation. But they were soon eclipsed by the brutality of renewed combat.

"This is Mark One! This is Mark One! The invasion has begun! I repeat, the invasion has begun!" Lieutenant Hans Steigner maneu-vered his tank to the crest of the hill as the last words tumbled from his trembling lips. On the open ground before him he saw a frightful sight. Stretching to the horizon was a logic-defying image of a swarm of menacing, metallic shapes rushing toward his position. Less than two thousand yards away were Russian T-80 tanks traveling abreast in a rough line about two hundred yards apart. It appeared as if the entire North European Plain was full of armor.

Steigner and his Leopards were still undetected, slinking in a heavy growth of trees. He ordered his men to pick a target but fire only on his orders. In the morning air, the tanks continued to rum-ble forward, belching smoke and spitting dirt with their powerful tracks. As they approached one thousand yards, Steigner gave the order to fire. With a momentary clap of deafening thunder, eight shells ripped through the air and struck six Russian tanks on the move. Half a dozen T-80s now sat motionless in the open fields, spewing smoke and fire. But other tanks immediately advanced to take their place in the front line and began firing at the Leopards still perched in the woods. Two of the Russian gunners scored direct hits, sending a sudden flash through the dense forest followed by a great, black cloud of smoke. One shell hissed right over Steigner, hitting a tree and sending branches crashing down on his tank.

By now the German gunners had more Russian tanks on their sights, and they fired off another round, stinging three more T-80s and bringing them to a stuttering halt. Still, the Russian wave continued to move forward, concentrating tremendous fire on the German position. As Lieutenant Steigner prepared to move his Leopard for another shot, a thunderous blast tossed him across the innards of the tank, slamming his helmeted head against the metal wall. The tank came to a halt and the crew cabin began filling with noxious smoke. "Out! Out!" he yelled in punctuated words. "Everybody out!" He popped open the hatch and jumped out on the muddy ground, pulling his crewmates with him. Soon they were all huddled next to the wounded Leopard, dazed and frightened. Steigner noticed the huge indent on his tank's turret. An armor-piercing round had penetrated the shell of the tank but had failed to explode. To that malfunction Steigner owed his life.

As shells continued to fly into the wooded ridge, Steigner led his crew to shelter in a shallow ditch. But the clamor of Russian armor continued to grow, and, clearly, it would be just minutes before T-80s would overrun the German position. The crew covered up with fallen branches and lay dead still as the enemy climbed the ridge.

The ground shook as the Russian tanks passed within fifty feet of the hidden crew. For more than two hours, the German soldiers lay motionless as the tank support units drove by. Steigner let out a deep sigh when the last Russian unit faded into the distance. He was very surprised to be alive, though he could certainly think of better places to be than behind Russian lines.

Overhead, Steigner spotted a squadron of Tornados heading east at approximately one thousand feet. Major Hans Kraemer had been given orders to hit a Russian communications post near the Polish city of Poznan, one hundred miles from the German border. If the strike succeeded, it would seriously impair the Russian offensive by making it difficult for Russian commanders to know the location of other units in the area. The major checked the radar, which indicated a mass of aircraft in the vicinity, both hostile and friendly. He hoped that his squadron would make it through the congestion.

Twenty miles west of Poznan, Kraemer activated the ground attack system and prepared to release his gravity bombs on the fast approaching target. Suddenly, a brilliant light pierced his cockpit. The world went dark. He realized he was conscious and grabbed the flight stick in his right hand. The hum of his engines was still audible to him. But he couldn't see anything, not even an outline of the digital control panel in front of him. "This is Kraemer, over," he bellowed to his squadron. "This is Kraemer. I can see nothing! I am blinded!" Each of his squadron reported the same thing—a sudden, blinding light and an instantaneous darkness had victimized them all.

Try as they might to remain airborne, one by one the men of the German 342nd Fighter Squadron disappeared. With their sight gone, many unknowingly put themselves into slight dives and crashed. Others were shot down by SAMs since they were unable to react to the warning lights flashing in their cockpits. With shafts of intense laser light, Russian ground forces had blinded an entire German squadron in less than a second. This radical weapon was based on technology developed in the early 1990s but never before used in combat.

The ground-based anti-aircraft laser heralded a counterrevolution in modern warfare. Not since the First World War reconnaissance biplane pilot lobbed grenades onto ground troops, firing back ineffectually with their rifles, had ground fire posed a critical threat to aircraft. SAMs at their best posted a moderate kill rate. But each new generation of SAMs had quickly been surpassed by elite pilots backed by the best in ECMs. What ground forces had always needed was a weapon several orders of magnitude faster and more precise than the planes they were targeting. Now they had one, a laser beam traveling at the speed of light undercutting a broad swath of destruction through the air. With one shot, NATO's greatest conventional advantage—air superiority—was devastated.

Back at NATO headquarters, the Supreme Allied Commander Europe (SACEUR) had assembled his staff to review the battle plan for the defense of Germany. With U.S. forces gone, General

Herman Schwartzmann was relying on the combined strength of German, French, British, and Dutch forces to stave off the attack. Italy and Spain had declared their neutrality as had Norway and Denmark. The heart of Europe was at stake, and the next seventy-two hours would be critical.

The Russian attack had commenced along three lines. Russian armor pushed across the North European Plain seventy-five miles from Berlin. A similar attack, including mostly mechanized infantry and a heavy concentration of artillery, had engaged German divisions just east of the German capital. A third force struck from the Czech Republic, moving along the west bank of the Elbe River. To Schwartzmann, the operation appeared simple: Moscow wanted to surround and cut off Berlin to force a German surrender. His greatest worry was the proficiency of the German army. It was made up largely of conscripts who were not entirely familiar with their equipment, and the German army had not conducted large-scale exercises in years. The lines, however, appeared to be holding, at least in the first several hours. Schwartzmann was counting on superior NATO air power to tip the balance in NATO's favor.

But before the end of the first day, the SACEUR was faced with a critical strategic decision. The push of the Russian offensive had become so great that, in order to hold Berlin, he committed his reserves forward. It was a political decision. Militarily, defense in depth made the most sense because it would force the enemy to spread its troops over a large area and maintain momentum while its firepower was sapped. But Schwartzmann knew it was politically unacceptable to sacrifice Berlin—less than one hundred miles from the Polish border—to the enemy. So he would concentrate his forces in the east to cede as little German territory as possible.

The stiffest opposition to the Russians came from British forces deployed outside Dresden. British General Peter Hart had his infantry divisions ready when Russian mechanized infantry began rolling through the valley along the Elbe River's west bank. Though heavily outnumbered, British forces held firm, halting the Russian advance entirely. It was a sobering, embarrassing episode for General Ilya Vlasov, who was commanding the operation from Prague. Impatient as always, Vlasov cabled the Kremlin with an urgent request for the CND.

vn-1   TOP SECRET
no. 442/m   COPY NUMBER ONE
5.28.06

President Aleksandr Karashchuk
Committee for National Defense

Mechanized infantry meeting heavy resistance outside Dresden. Request authorization for the immediate use of nuclear weapons.

General Ilya Vlasov
Prague

Karashchuk felt a fountain of rage bubbling inside him ready to spew forth as he cantered in the Oval Room of the Kremlin, his heavy, black military boots creating a solid thump with each step. He had expected NATO forces to roll over following his televised address. But he now realized that he had not broken their spirit. "We must teach the Europeans," he said in a paternal, authoritative tone, "that we were serious in our pronouncements to their people last night."

The members of the CND looked on quietly, waiting for some indication of where Karashchuk's anger might take him. The silence continued until General Platonov cleared his throat. "We must firmly send a message to all the capitals of Europe," he offered eagerly. "Their resistance must be broken."

Marshal Serov sat stoically, fumbling with his metallic lighter on the varnished table. Finally he grunted, "Yes, well... what are you suggesting, General?"

Platonov first glanced at Karashchuk and then answered Serov. "I think, Marshal, that we must fulfill our promise to use nuclear weapons against those who oppose us."

A look of extreme concern overcame the marshal's face. "You recognize that this will destroy the very areas we are trying to conquer, and that this act will erase any positive view of Russia in Europe for the next thousand years."

Karashchuk rolled his eyes as he paced on the thick, rich carpet. He tried to ignore the marshal as best he could. "General Malinovsky, what are your thoughts?"

"Well, Mr. President," he began reflectively, "I believe we must examine this issue in terms of military effectiveness. We cannot win a long-term, conventional war in Europe. It would cost us too much in blood and treasure. Of course the marshal is right—we want to conquer Germany, not incinerate it. I do believe, however, that the careful use of battlefield or even tactical nuclear weapons against enemy troop formations could decide the matter in our favor, especially if our enemies understand that any nuclear retaliation from them, even on a battlefield level, would provoke a response from us against which they could neither defend nor retaliate.

"Personally, I am not concerned about European public opinion a thousand years from now, or for that matter, a thousand days from now. The Europeans will always be anti-Russian. I am most interested in our men and the glorious tasks they have been asked to perform."

Feeling the emotional pitch rising in the room, Serov lapsed into a solemn silence for the rest of the meeting. After twenty minutes of debate, President Karashchuk authorized the use of five nuclear weapons to be used on NATO troop formations in Germany.

At SRF headquarters General Grigorov sat in the fire-control room with his advisers, plotting the targeting scheme for the missile launch. Russian satellites had pinpointed the major NATO troop concentrations on the North European plain: outside Dresden and east of Berlin. There were also significant NATO air bases through-out central Germany. Grigorov sent a memo recommending the following targets.

plv-1
no. 4532/srf/plv   TOP SECRET
copy—only
5.28.06

TARGETING RECOMMENDATIONS FOR WEAPONS OF MASS DESTRUCTION

Selected nuclear strikes on the following:

1. Target: British troop concentrations outside Dresden, two 20-kiloton warheads.

Objective: Eliminate resistance to four mechanized infantry divisions moving north.

2. Target: German infantry and armor on North European Plain, two 20-kiloton warheads.

Objective: Destroy obstacles to the advance of Russian armor across north German sector.

3. Target: NATO air base outside Bremen, one 20-kiloton warhead.

Objective: Restrict flight activity of NATO tactical aircraft.

When Karashchuk received the memo, he scanned it briefly and then signed it. "Approval, A. Karashchuk." The destruction of tens of thousands of lives had taken but a minute to decide.

May 27, 2006: The Russian Attack on Germany

At SRF command, General Grigorov put his fire-control officers to the task of retargeting Russian missiles onto the selected targets. Within just two hours, the missiles were ready for launch. General Grigorov phoned President Karashchuk one last time to make certain that the launch was to proceed. "Da," he said in a perfunctory way, "at once."

The Russian nuclear strikes on Germany occurred across the expanse of the country. On the North German Plain, two enormous fireballs erupted several thousand meters above the ground, generating an intense heat approaching the temperature of the sun. The flash was visible in Berlin and even parts of France. At the epicenter of the strike, German tanks were reduced to a gray, metallic lava and German soldiers vaporized. Surrounding buildings were shattered by the shock wave that followed and ripped apart by the wind created from the explosion. Within several square miles, nothing survived. Further from the epicenter, the damage was still astonishing and casualties high, more from radiation sickness than from the heat.

A similar fate awaited the British infantry and German civilians south of Dresden. Within minutes after the strike on north Germany, this medieval German city for the second time in its history was engulfed in fire and death. But what had taken hours on February 13, 1945, when the Allies fire bombed the city during the Second World War, now required only seconds. By macabre coincidence, this was Dresden's 800th anniversary. The work of centuries was reduced to rubble in one atomic spasm.

German Chancellor Müller stared blankly out the window onto the *autoplatz* for twenty minutes as he tried to comprehend that his nation was now shattered in a way unimaginable for two generations of Germans. Finally, he turned to an aide and asked to be connected to General Schwartzmann at NATO headquarters. "Herr General, I am asking for an immediate cessation of NATO operations on German soil. It is my intention to negotiate a peace with President Karashchuk in Moscow."

Schwartzmann shook his head in disbelief as he sat at NATO command headquarters. "Chancellor Müller, events make your course of action very inviting. But it will only feed this Russian monster. Karashchuk means to take over all of Europe, and he may do so without so much as a fight if this course is taken."

Müller sighed heavily. "I understand what you are saying, General. But I cannot sit idly by and watch our people succumb to nuclear attack without trying to seek some settlement."

Schwartzmann now rose to his feet in desperation. "But, Herr Chancellor, you know there will be only *diktat*. There will be no discussion. And Europe will look to Germany for leadership. If you buckle, all of Europe will be lost to Karashchuk's savageness."

Müller had no response. What response could there be? He set the receiver down softly and then called Karashchuk at the Kremlin. Müller waited on the phone for twenty minutes while Karashchuk stalled, cherishing the moment of capitulation. Finally, the hum at the end of the line was interrupted by the *Vozhd*'s forceful voice.

"Chancellor Müller," he said in a determined tone, "I understand that you have a proposition."

Hesitatingly, the German chancellor began to outline terms for a possible cease-fire and the cessation of hostilities. "So you see, President Karashchuk," he concluded in a smooth, steady voice, "we are interested in seeing this bloodshed come to an end."

There was a prolonged silence on the other end of the line. Then came the *Vozhd*'s response in terse, punctuated words. "We will accept no cease-fire terms. We will only discuss the terms of your surrender."

An anxious Müller broke into a filmy sweat. In his mind, the alarm of more nuclear explosions now competed with the fear of Russian rule.

"Surely, President Karashchuk, you cannot presume that we would accept occupation..."

"I am willing, out of the kindness of my heart and that of the

Russian people, to propose generous peace terms. But we will accept nothing short of a German surrender. If this interests you, I will welcome you to the Kremlin as my guest to discuss the terms."

Müller laid the receiver back in the cradle of the phone. He sat silently for a moment with his aides. He then rose slowly to his feet, his face painted with a tragic dignity. "Go home and pack," he announced softly. "We will be leaving for Moscow in four hours."

"It's appeasement, pure and simple!" the voice resonated throughout the West Wing of the White House.

French President Jacques Lebou sat in the Oval Office barely ten feet from the president, but he bellowed as if were trying to get the attention of a man in a crowd half a mile away. Seated next to Lebou was an unctuous man with a wide, plump face, high cheekbones, and square, white teeth. He winced as Lebou spoke in his loud tone. Marcel Vaugnot was the director of the Direction Generale de la Securite Exterieure (DGSE), the French intelligence service. He had a reputation for heaping exaggerated praise on his American counterparts while suspiciously trying to purloin secrets from them. The French president was exercised, for he knew that as the Germans sued for peace, he would become the next logical figure to be locked in Karashchuk's vise grip. "You Americans must step in— before it is too late."

St. John knew as well as Lebou that with the German surrender, all of Europe would fall under the shadow of the Kremlin. Yet instinctively he tried to calm the visitor. "Jacques, no one likes this situation, but our hands are tied. We can offer you military support and some theater antimissile defense systems, but I would be lying to you if I committed to anything else. We are as vulnerable and as naked as you are."

Lebou shook his head in mock disbelief. "But you do not face the very real prospect of Russian occupation. We both know that Karashchuk will be satisfied only when Russian troops are garrisoned in Berlin and Paris. And they will be as beastly and horrible in their occupation of the rest of Europe as they have been in the Czech Republic, Lithuania, and Poland." Russian soldiers were raping and looting their way through the cities of newly conquered central Europe, and these activities were tolerated or even encouraged by a senior Russian officer corps.

Jack Fowler sat on the end of his chair as he listened to the French president spell out his concerns. In recent days the National Security Adviser had found it difficult to endure these meetings with pleading allies being abandoned to their fates. Only by achieving the cool detachment of a battlefield surgeon choosing which of the wounded he must leave to die so that he could have time to operate on those with some chance of life could he function effectively. The United States and the Free World had exactly one chance for success, and nothing, no sentimental appeal, no treaty or moral obligation, however powerful or just, could be allowed to compromise that chance. Although Europe would suffer brutally while the American strategic defense system was readied, the United States had no more power to prevent that suffering than a doctor had to bring the dead back to life.

So after Lebou finished, Fowler abandoned the subject of Russian atrocities as if it had never been mentioned and returned to the search for something—anything—that might help the United States overcome the Russian BMD monopoly. "President Lebou and Monsieur Vaugnot, while I understand your concerns, we can only defeat Moscow if we can overcome their BMD system. Moscow's ability to blackmail Europe rests firmly on their strategic defense capability. Perhaps, by working together, our two countries might unravel this mystery and overcome the strategic imbalance."

Vaugnot casually leaned back against his chair, his black, oily hair clinging tightly to his head. "We have very little detailed information on their BMD system. We have an *agent benevole* [unpaid agent] with connections in the SRF. But under these wartime conditions, contact has been extremely difficult."

"Do you have any thoughts on vulnerabilities?" probed Fowler.

"The system essentially operates from a central command post southwest of Moscow. But I have no detailed information beyond that."

President Lebou left Washington empty-handed because the White House had nothing to offer. As he boarded his plane at Andrews Air Force Base for the return flight to Paris, he did so realizing that the Americans were now completely decoupled from Europe.

Chancellor Müller's peace mission to Moscow created a temporary cease-fire on the German front. Russian forces held their positions clothed in NBC protective gear and using antiradiation treatments to reduce radioactivity on their vehicles. For NATO forces, there was the grisly reality of decontamination and dealing with tens of thousands of casualties. Frontline soldiers waited nervously on a hair trigger for word that the war might come to an end and on what terms. They did not know which to fear more: war or a forced peace.

On May 29 German Chancellor Müller, his foreign minister, and a few trusted aides flew to Moscow. Once at the Kremlin, they were treated to a tour of all the imperialist trappings of Russia's past. They were escorted up the Grand Staircase, through the Palace of Facets, and into St. Andrew Hall in the Grand Kremlin Palace. There, General Platonov and Marshal Serov greeted them politely with handshakes. The group sat at an elongated table for several minutes until they were joined by Karashchuk, who made a grand entrance with four military aides, all in rich blue dress uniforms. The Russian president wore the traditional garb of the czar on military occasions.

"Gentlemen," he said with a boisterous tone, "welcome to the Grand Palace!"

Müller had slipped into a cloud of denial since his phone discussion with Karashchuk. He somehow believed that the meeting in Moscow would be a diplomatic conclave to iron out differences and then hammer out terms for a lasting peace. That the jovial man in front of him had the blood of tens of thousands of German civilians on his hands made the entire spectacle all the more garish.

Karashchuk extended his hand, which the German delegation reluctantly but cordially accepted. "Please," he said with a grin, "we will have dinner first and then discuss the relevant issues." He signaled for the chancellor to be seated. But the thought of dining before deciding the fate of his country was unseemly to Müller.

"No, President Karashchuk," he said in soft protest, "we are here to discuss the very serious matters that relate to the German people. I will not sit and dine under these circumstances."

"Very well," Karashchuk replied dismissively, "it will be as you like." The men walked through the palace to the Oval Room and took their places at the gilded conference table. Karashchuk took his regular spot at the head of the table while the others scrambled for a chair. Müller sat at the opposite end of the table staring straight into the *Vozhd*'s face.

"President Karashchuk," began Müller confidently, "I have asked my foreign minister to draft an agreement for the terms of a cease-fire..."

The Russian president raised his hand as if flagging a taxi. "My dear Chancellor, there will be neither a cease-fire nor negotiations." The tension in the room intensified. "Our terms are simple. Number one: the immediate surrender of your forces and the disarmament of those forces by our personnel. Number two: the occupation of Germany by Russian forces to ensure protection from our external enemies. Number three: your immediate renunciation of the NATO Treaty and membership in a new Moscow alliance, joining our allies of Belarus, Ukraine, Bulgaria, Lithuania, the Czech Republic, and Poland. In exchange, we will allow you to remain as chancellor and to govern the internal affairs of your country with all major legislative issues subject to our approval."

To Müller it was an outrage. Karashchuk was demanding the absorption of Germany into a new bloc guided by Moscow. German sovereignty would evaporate and an independent German state would cease to exist. At first Müller was resolute. But his tone of defiance soon melted as the vision of a nuclear horror became fixed in his mind. "President Karashchuk, you must know that these terms are entirely unacceptable..."

Karashchuk again lifted his hand. "My dear Chancellor, you know that the correlation of forces is entirely in my favor. You can either accept these generous terms or face the prospect of greater nuclear destruction in your country." Stunned and silent, Müller was uncertain how to react. There was no nuance in this diplomacy—no stiletto, only the meat cleaver or sledge hammer.

When Müller returned to Berlin the next morning, it was with a deep sense of shame: he had accepted Karashchuk's terms. Germany was now under the Russian umbrella, and the center had just fallen out of NATO.

The initial German television reports of the settlement brought panic first to the streets of Berlin and quickly to the entire country. The optimists began hoarding food while, with Russian troops set to arrive on June 5, other German citizens started a mass exodus that very night, fleeing for France, Switzerland, Italy, and even the United States or Canada if they could get in. Public order was strained and in many places snapped: looting and riots broke out.

NATO forces also began their hastily planned withdrawal. NATO aircraft returned to their bases in Britain and France while British, French, and Dutch infantry started convoying back to their respective countries. German officers began the unpleasant task of rounding up weapons from their troops, to be handed over to Russian soldiers at special collection points on June 5.

The procession of Russian infantry and armor snaking into Berlin on the early summer morning of June 5 was unlike anything even this city with all too much history had ever seen, taking seven and a half hours to pass one point. The formidable 10th Armored Division rumbled in first. The brownish, steel beasts—Russian T-80s—roared down the boulevards of the capital sporting huge Russian-imperial double-eagle flags. The 10th was followed by the

Russian armor prepares for the occupation of Berlin.

3rd Infantry Division, smacking the pavement with the riveting, horrific sounds of the goose step. It was the infantry that made the specter of Russian occupation seem real, and the watching city convulsed in grief.

The procession penetrated through the center of the city to the Brandenburg Gate where General Malinovsky, with tears in his eyes, conducted a military tribute to the fallen Russian soldiers who gave their lives for "peace." Mobile satellite trucks broadcast the ceremony to billions worldwide.

With the army came the Russian secret police. Immediately, senior German military officers were arrested, many of the most capable never to be seen again. Chancellor Müller was given a special "security" detail to protect him from "terrorist attacks." In the days following the Russian occupation, his mind seemed to withdraw, unable to either carry out his part of the charade or to admit what was happening by trying to resist.

In Paris, President Lebou watched what he knew was a dress rehearsal for the conquest of France. As Russian tentacles began to wrap themselves around Germany, a refugee crisis was brewing in eastern France as thousands of Germans were crossing the border into Alsace-Lorraine, childlike, helpless, with lined faces and trembling with fear.

"Expect the worst," warned Jack Fowler as he briefed the president on a series of electronic intelligence (ELINT) communications relating to the political situation in Europe and the Russian BMD. "Lebou will sell out for the best he can get." The two were meeting with Tom Bodine in an office on the third floor of the Pentagon's outer ring, the "E" ring, where the highest-ranking Defense Department civilians, as well as the military's top brass, reside. From the window they could look out over the Potomac toward Washington. The group was reviewing the latest data from a KH-12 Ikon satellite flying in a two hundred–kilometer orbit over central Russia. The optical imaging satellite operated on several wave bands at an approximate sixty-degree inclination, providing a superb look at the Russian BMD system.

As they began reviewing the satellite photos, an aide rushed into the room. "Mr. President, there is something on television that you are going to want to see." St. John clicked on the TV monitor and saw on CNN a live shot from the Kremlin. There stood Presidents Lebou and Karashchuk shaking hands emphatically. The French president took the podium and spoke with uninspired, forced words. "I am pleased to announce a new alliance between the Republics of Russia and France. We believe that this will bring stability and peace to Europe."

"I knew it," snarled Fowler.

Chapter Twenty-six

```
July 6
the White House
```

At Los Alamos Laboratories the crash program to build a strategic defense system was proceeding at a unbelievably rapid pace by scientific standards and yet horrifyingly slow when measured against the rate of Russian expansion. On July 6 the research team forwarded a working paper to the president reporting their findings.

KPN-998-7K
Report to the president
Top Secret—for eyes only

The United States must pursue a layered defense system that will provide a high level of protection against Russian ICBMs and SLBMs. It should be based on the physical principles entailed in the flight of a typical ICBM. The characteristic trajectory of a current ballistic missile can be divided into four phases:

- a boost phase, when the missile's engines are burning and offering intense, highly specific, observable plumes which can be detected by satellites and sensors;

- a post-boost phase, also referred to as the bus deployment phase, during which reentry vehicles and penetration aids are being released from a post-boost vehicle;

- a mid-course phase, when reentry vehicles and penetration aids travel on ballistic trajectories above the atmosphere; and

- a terminal phase, when the reentry trajectories and signatures are affected by atmospheric drag.

For a national strategic defense system to work, it must incorporate the following elements:

(1) Detection. Full-time surveillance of ICBM launch areas is critical in characterizing the composition and intensity of the attack and in determining probable targeted areas for confident battle initiation. The current Defense Support Program (DSP), with the addition of several satellites, will be adequate for detecting missiles in the boost phase.

(2) Tracking, identification/discrimination. Precise birth-to-death tracking of ballistic missiles is necessary for targeting, timely kill assessment, and efficient battle management. We recommend upgraded cryocooler and infrared sensors which will be essential for tracking objects in space. The development of space-based radar systems would significantly enhance the system.

(3) Interception and destruction. We seek the rapid, effective, and discernible kill of ballistic missile boosters, post-boost vehicles, and reentry vehicles along the entire flight path of the ICBM. We recommend the deployment of a team of "Brilliant Pebble" killer satellites in conjunction with several ground-based laser systems to compensate for those missiles which leak through. Several ground sites will be equipped with laser-beam generators; target

acquisition, tracking, and pointing capability; and advanced beam control subsystems. These stations generate a short wavelength beam, condition the beam to compensate for atmospheric distortion, and project the beam onto space relay mirrors. In geostationary orbit these relays redirect the beams from the ground to mission mirrors in lower orbit that guide the beam to target. A free electron laser (FEL) is the most promising approach for this system.

(4) Battle management. Development of an adequate data system for the effective manipulation of information about the defensive battle, the generation of displays to inform the defense commander, and the transmission of his decision to the defense elements can be accomplished by upgrading systems at Cheyenne Mountain.

Proposed Jedi Project Deployment

The overall system will include a dozen satellites at one-half to two times geosynchronous altitude to carry out boost surveillance and tracking. We will proceed with the deployment of several dozen satellites at one thousand kilometers' altitude to carry out surveillance, tracking, and fire control. Then we will deploy some thousand satellites at altitudes of a few hundred kilometers whose main purpose will be to carry kinetic-kill vehicles or Brilliant Pebbles. Three ground-based laser stations will be erected to supplement the work of these kinetic-kill vehicles.

Deployment will occur during a one-year period and will include regular missions already being carried out by space shuttles, in addition to the launch of numerous

Atlas and Delta II rockets. In recognizing the strategic instability this is likely to create, particularly in the mind of the Kremlin which is anxious to maintain its monopoly on strategic defense systems, the final phase of deployment for a basic system could be completed with a massive number of launches during a forty-eight–hour period for final deployment.

As the president received the reports there were now some three hundred thousand Russian troops on German soil and close to one hundred thousand in France. An embryonic resistance movement did provide some discomfort for Russian forces but nothing more than that. U.S. Special Forces Command, still operating out of London, continued to provide intelligence updates through the encrypted uplink to identify targets.

Eventually German Chancellor Müller chose exile in London over the humiliating farce in Berlin. Karashchuk replaced him with Heinrich Schmidt, a sycophant to Moscow who hung onto the Russian president's every word and worked to purge from Germany any shred of independence. The German public had at first tried to resist the tightening Russian grip on their country through widespread civil disobedience. But General Ilya Vlasov, the brute from Prague who was now giving orders from Berlin, lacked that human vulnerability that was the true target of any campaign of civil disobedience—a conscience. Indeed, General Platonov had recommended Vlasov for the post for precisely one reason—he knew that he would never lose his nerve or his taste for killing. Vlasov simply ordered his troops to machine gun any illegally assembled crowd, accepting no surrenders and taking no prisoners once the shooting began.

Russian and Ukrainian troops were being deployed to France to fulfill the terms of the "treaty" signed by Presidents Lebou and Karashchuk in June. Though Russian forces were not yet an army of occupation, French independence and sovereignty were rapidly dissolving. French soldiers were disarmed and the encryption codes and "keys" for the launch of the French nuclear force were turned over

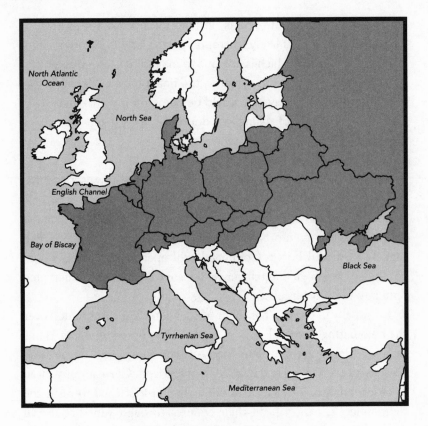

New Russian Empire 2006

to General Platonov. For those old enough to remember, it was a replay of the German occupation during the Second World War.

Moscow not only chose to exert control over the military in Europe, Karashchuk also insisted on managing the vibrant capitalist economies of his newly conquered territories. Within months the fine-tuned engine of production was reduced to a centrally controlled serfdom.

Even more ominous was the growing sense that Karashchuk was turning his gaze toward the United States. He had promised during his speech at the Bolshoi Theatre that he would extend Russian power from the Atlantic to the Pacific. With Lithuania, Poland, the Czech Republic, Germany, and France under his control, and with the remainder of Europe now willing to cede to him whatever he asked, it would soon be time to act on that promise.

The first indication of Moscow's designs came in a request that President St. John receive General Platonov as a special emissary. On November 8 the general strode into the Oval Office wearing formal military dress, including nearly a dozen medals. Accompanying him was a single aide. The president, Secretary of Defense Tom Bodine, and National Security Adviser Jack Fowler rose to greet him. St. John extended his hand and, through an interpreter, calmly greeted his guest. But the general dispelled with any informal exchange of pleasantries and went at once to the purpose of his visit. "Mr. President, I am here to convey the demands of my president." St. John and his advisors were stunned at his boldness. "We have reshaped the power structures of the world in a matter of months. And we now mean to reshape the economic world as well. President Karashchuk believes that in light of historic injustices, the United States and the other capitalist states must pay restitution to the Slavic people for crimes committed. We believe that an annual amount in the order of one hundred billion dollars will be sufficient. We will also seek payments from Japan, the United Kingdom, Canada, and others."

"And if we don't comply?" asked the president coolly.

Platonov grinned, "We will see rejection of this offer as a hostile

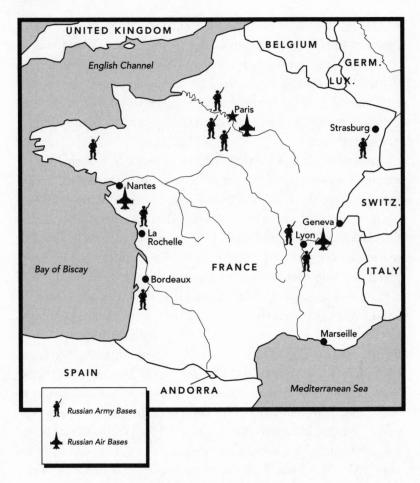

Occupied France 2006

act and will consider all military options." Everyone present knew this was a code word for nuclear blackmail.

"We will need time to consider your suggestion, General Platonov."

"Yes, of course, Mr. President. We will give you forty-eight hours, after which we will establish a payment schedule."

Platonov left as abruptly as he had arrived. Both the general and St. John knew that the payments would be forthcoming.

Chapter Twenty-seven

November 8, 2008
(two years later)
White Sands Missile Range, New Mexico

D eep in the lonely New Mexico desert, a land the conquista-dors called *Jornada del Muento*—journey of death—U.S. government scientists were hurriedly completing their work at the top-secret facility at White Sands Missile Range. A group of four FELs had been constructed during the past eighteen months, and the final tests were now being conducted. All lasers work by creating quick movement among electrons, the tiny particles that normally orbit around the nucleus of an atom. But the FEL goes a step further. The electrons are accelerated by strong magnetic fields and then "wiggled" by a series of powerful magnets that pull electrons back and forth as they move forward. Each time an electron makes a sharp turn, it emits a photon of light. Billions of these combine to create the powerful laser beam. The wavelength varies with the speed at which electrons enter the wiggler, so, unlike most other lasers, the FEL can be finely tuned across a number of wavelengths.

Scientists were testing the laser's high-pulse repetition rates and using accelerating modules with magnetic pulse modulators to maximize the effectiveness of the high-brightness laser for a

A U.S. Air Force F-15 patrols the tense English channel between Russian-occupied France and free Britain.

ground-based component of a strategic defense system. If the beam was too strong, the laser could melt the relay mirrors designed to deflect the beam onto its target. But if the beam was too weak, it would harmlessly bounce off the enemy ICBM, leaving it to continue on its destructive path.

A similar set of tests were being conducted on FEL sites in north Florida and outside Fargo, North Dakota. They formed the ground-based component of the Jedi Project, covertly built during the past eighteen months.

The demands from the Kremlin had become increasingly exigent. Thanks to the despotic, incompetent rule of Karashchuk, a once prosperous Europe was now in economic shambles. And as a result, the Russian president had turned his gaze increasingly toward the United States, which he treated as a wealthy tributary. It had taken Karashchuk nearly two years to digest Europe, and now he was hungry for more. The *Vozhd* no longer simply wanted cash, he was seeking control of critical elements of American foreign and domestic policy. He had also become suspicious that the Americans were up to something, so he began making demands and threats at the slightest impulse. St. John had shadowboxed with Karashchuk for months seeking clarification of his demands, feigning cooperation—anything to buy time and appease the Kremlin. But the *Vozhd's* patience was beginning to wear thin, and during the next seventy-two hours the fate of the United States and Europe would hang in the balance.

A series of space launches began when a space shuttle left launch complex no. 6 at Vandenberg Air Force Base. Another shuttle left two hours later from Cape Canaveral. These were the latest in a series of numerous launches that had taken place during the past six months. More than twenty Atlas rockets and several space shuttles had been carrying tracking satellites and optic relay mirrors into space. And over the course of the next three days, the United States would proceed with the massive and rapid deployment of the Jedi Project's final components. As far as Washington was concerned, deployment was coming not a moment too soon.

At the White House the official word was that nothing out of the ordinary was happening. High visibility was in order. The president had several photo opportunities with Girl Scouts, a Rotary Club, and a group of teachers from Nebraska. Between these highly public and choreographed meetings, St. John received short updates about the launches. Aides occasionally dropped by to pat him on the back and whisper in his ear, "Everything is okay," before moving on.

The number of launches did not go unnoticed by Moscow. Russian satellites tracked the activity, and concerned aides alerted General Platonov. When he saw the dramatic upswing in space launches, he immediately phoned President Karashchuk, who was asleep at his dacha outside Moscow. Within the hour, they met at the Kremlin.

As they sat in Karashchuk's office, Platonov was assuming the worst. "The Americans are attempting to deploy a strategic defense system. The quantity of their launch activity has climbed dramatically in recent months."

Seated behind his desk, Karashchuk held his index finger to his lips and pondered what to do next. "If this is indeed the case, what do you recommend, Grigory?"

Platonov raised his eyebrows. "Frankly, Aleksandr, we must immediately bring it to a halt or they will restore the strategic nuclear balance. We must not stop short of anything, including the use of nuclear weapons to maintain our position."

Karashchuk agreed eagerly. "You are correct, my friend. I will call St. John at once."

An urgent call was placed to the White House where the president was meeting with Tom Bodine, Jack Fowler, and Steve Cramer. An aide handed the president a note. "It's Karashchuk. He's on the phone."

"They know," blurted Cramer visibly worried. "They have been monitoring our launches, and they know something is up."

Fowler checked his watch. "We need another sixty-five hours to complete this launch sequence. If we can last that long, we will be in the clear. Mr. President, you must not take that call. We need to buy time. They will undoubtedly insist that we halt all our launch activities, and that will force you to make a terrible choice."

St. John was worried. "I see what you mean. But if I don't take the call, Karashchuk might get hacked off and then who knows what he might do."

"I'll take the call," offered Bodine in his typical, rapid-fire diction. "I will tell him you are indisposed. It will at least give us a little more time."

Eyes darted around the room, but no one objected. "Okay, Tom," agreed the president, "you take it."

The call began like the dozens of others Karashchuk had placed to the White House during the past twenty-four months. In broken English he bared his customary bravado, issuing threats while making demands. But when he confronted Bodine about the surge in space activity, he raised the tone and pitch of his voice. "Mr. Bodine, we demand that you stop these launches immediately or you will face dire consequences." While such a threat had been made before, this time it seemed real.

"President Karashchuk," answered the defense secretary in a reassuring tone, "I can guarantee you that these space flights pose no danger to you or to the Russian people."

The Russian president answered with a husky laugh. "Mr. Secretary, I do not want your assurances. These launches must end at once. And hereafter, our inspectors will monitor your space launches."

Bodine sat silent for a moment searching for a response, an excuse, more time. "President Karashchuk, I will have to secure the authority of the president to do this. As secretary of defense I have no authority to stop..."

"You need no other authority than that I demand this of you. Your country will suffer immeasurably if you deny me this."

Bodine hung up the phone. A high-stakes game of bluff and bluster would now begin.

Two hundred twenty miles overhead, up in the heavens, the space shuttle *Excelsior* was cruising at more than seventeen thousand miles per hour—several hundred miles faster than a speeding warhead. The shuttle cargo hold was transporting dozens of Brilliant Pebbles to be released over the North Pole, the expected trajectory for Russian ICBMs aimed at the United States. Once the shuttle reached its destination, the cargo bay was opened and the Pebbles drifted off into orbit. From the CSOC inside the Cheyenne Mountains, the satellites were activated by ground controllers and came to life electronically.

Dr. Chase sat in the CSOC behind mammoth, twenty-five–ton doors, two thousand feet beneath the granite of Cheyenne Mountain off Colorado Highway 115. She watched earnestly as the dozens of technicians activated the battle management system that would direct Jedi. Several relay mirrors that would be used to reflect the FEL weapons to their targets were run through a series of rigorous tests to ensure that they would not malfunction or fail during an actual Russian launch. Another group in the fire-control room worked on computer keyboards, running through a series of diagnostic tests on the hundreds of Brilliant Pebbles floating in space.

The American launches continued throughout the afternoon. By 4:00 P.M. they prompted another call from President Karashchuk. St. John took this one.

"President St. John," began Karashchuk in volcanic tones, "I demand that your launch activities end at this moment. Otherwise, we will have no choice but to conduct a nuclear strike on your country."

St. John clung onto the phone in horror. There was a moment of silence until he regained his confidence. "President Karashchuk, I wish to inform you that the United States has completed the full deployment of a space- and land-based strategic defense system. Your threats no longer carry the same sting."

Karashchuk pounded his ruddy fist on the table. "You are lying!" he exclaimed in a wrathful tone. "It is impossible!"

St. John did his best to maintain a calm, steady tone. "You have underestimated American ingenuity, President Karashchuk."

The phone clicked dead. St. John casually laid the receiver back in the cradle. He eyed his advisers and straightened his tie. "Now all we can do is wait and see if he calls my bluff."

Following his exchange with St. John, Karashchuk erupted in a furious rage in his Kremlin office. He immediately pulled together the CND to plot a course of action. While the assembled were weary, having been dragged from their beds by the immediacy of the moment, they were soon aroused from any sense of sleepiness. "There is no doubt," bellowed the president to the council, "the Americans are attempting a flash deployment of a strategic defense system."

General Malinovsky massaged his eyes. "How far along are they?"

"We have no idea," interjected Platonov. "While they have no doubt completed some work, it is impossible that such a system is operational."

"Then we must find out!" exclaimed Karashchuk turning to General Grigorov, commander of his SRF. "I want the immediate launch of two ICBMs. And prepare our submarine force for action."

"The targets?"

Karashchuk shrugged his shoulders. "You pick the targets, General. One civilian and one military."

Marshal Serov had been quietly brooding in the corner. "If they do have a system in place, we can expect some sort of retaliation. We had better be certain that Magic Chain is ready for its own test."

Karashchuk gestured dismissively. "The Americans have nothing; not yet, anyway."

October 2, 2010

To: Miller, Birnbaum, Reese, & Blackwell:
Counsel, The New York Times, Inc.

From: Powell Simpson III, Counsel to the President
RE: Response to FOIA Request

In response to your request of September 15, 2010, the final Executive Office of the President/Strategic Assessment of the events of November 8, 2008, and all other supporting documentation and assessments from all U.S. departments and agencies participating in the strategic review and assessment process remain classified and thus exempt from FOIA disclosure.

Please let me know if I can be of any further assistance.

Part Five

Japan
August 19, 2007

Chapter Twenty-eight

P rime Minister Ishiwara Kawara sat solemnly in his private residence, his mind anxiously racing through what might happen in the next twenty-four hours. As Japan sat on the precipice of war, he felt surprisingly little sorrow. With his thin, angular face resting on his weary hand, his thoughts drifted to memories of the dizzying pace of events during the past seven years.

At the turn of the millennium, the Japanese economic miracle had run into serious difficulty after more than half a century of rapid expansion. Unemployment had reached 18 percent. And while every day thousands more joined the ranks of the jobless, the economic calamity showed little sign of diminishing.

International events generated a major portion of the crisis, putting Tokyo in an unenviable vise grip. A trade war had broken out with the United States, and heavy tariffs had been placed on Japanese exports. The manufacturing sectors of both countries were severely damaged, and many companies in the export-driven Japanese economy had been fighting for survival ever since. In 2003 turbulence in the Middle East sent oil prices through the ceiling, further strangling the economy. The result was fuel shortages, gas lines, and closed factories. It was a serious body blow for Japan, which imported 60 percent of its oil from the gulf and 98 percent of all of its petroleum.

To a generation that had experienced only economic expansion, guaranteed lifetime employment, and rising prosperity, these new realities called for a forceful response. Strikes and labor unrest plagued the large manufacturing centers in Sapporo, Kawasaki, and Yokohama. Rancor and extremism became the bedrock of Japanese politics as moderates were shoved aside.

In the midst of such a crisis there was opportunity for a lowly Parliament backbencher named Ishiwara Kawara. Kawara boldly and convincingly fingered those guilty of these "economic crimes"—foreign powers fed by envy intent on suppressing the Japanese people. He argued passionately in parliament for a new order in the Pacific: "We cannot sit idly by and allow our energy lifeline to be severed. We must act forcefully to deal with these events." Drawing his inspiration from history, Kawara believed Japan's choices were simple: his nation could imitate Venice, the great mercantile power and city-state of its day, which aggressively defended its vast trading empire, or it could follow the path of ancient Carthage, which failed to do so and soon withered on the vine of nation-states. In the eyes of this young, charismatic, vibrant leader, this was no time for moderation.

The culmination of events and fiery rhetoric from the opposition sent shock waves through the body politic, and the Liberal Democratic coalition that had dominated Japanese politics for decades finally fell in October 2003. Soon rising in its place was a nationalist coalition headed by Kawara which included xenophobic factions that romantically embraced Japan's imperialist past.

At a solemn inaugural ceremony, Kawara addressed the nation. "Japan will meet her own needs," he promised. "We can no longer rely on so-called allies or the international community to protect our economic interests." Tokyo's economic vulnerabilities stemmed from a lack of access to critical natural resources. Both the trade war with America and disruptions in the supply of Middle East oil demonstrated that Japan had little control over its own economic destiny. The new prime minister believed, however, that Japan could acquire the resources it needed from its neighbors by securing the supply lines through the most direct method of all—imperial conquest.

There were tremendous oil and natural gas deposits in the South China Sea, Brunei, and Indonesia. Weaker nations in the region, including the Philippines and Malaysia, possessed vast supplies of timber, rubber, and foodstuffs. As conceived in January 2004, the secret strategy called for the creation of a "defensive empire" to guarantee access to these resources through the occupation of the Philippines, Brunei, and eventually Malaysia and Indonesia. Control of these territories would guarantee a supply of cheap energy and raw materials. Indeed, it would turn Tokyo into a net energy exporter, generating billions in revenue. The new empire would be erected in the vacuum left by the United States which had largely expunged any military presence in the region.

To make the prospects of a new economic empire a reality, Kawara embarked on a massive military buildup. Despite the limits in the past that had restricted Japanese defense spending to approximately 1 percent of GDP, the new regime had a substantial military base to build upon. Tokyo claimed the third largest military budget in the world throughout the 1990s. While rather small in size, the Japanese armed forces were technologically advanced. Tokyo could indigenously produce high-tech aircraft, tanks, and warships. The island nation was totally self-sufficient in the manufacture of all major weapons systems and therefore impervious to any cutoff of military materiel.

Kawara casually lit a cigarette as he journeyed through the heady days of his first months in office. He reminded himself of the military buildup and the early plans he had made, plans that might now be finally fulfilled.

Kawara hoped to use Japan's burgeoning military capabilities to fuel his imperial ambitions. As the nation's industrial machine turned increasingly to military production, the prime minister and the armed forces designed a strategy to protect both Japan's national interests and its access to raw materials and markets. The Kawara government hoped the new stratagem would give Japan greater autonomy and control over her economic destiny.

Based on the doctrine *hokushu nanshin*—"defend the north,

advance to the south"—the strategy was basic. In its first stage, the Japanese fleet and air force would attack Taiwanese and Chinese naval and air facilities. Without serious naval capabilities or air power, the ability of Japan's Asian rivals to interfere or challenge Tokyo's move to dominate the Pacific would be minimal. Next they would destroy enemy ships and units and seize essential territory in the central area including the South China Sea, the Philippines, Indonesia, and the islands of the central Pacific including Wake and the Marshalls. As an extension of these operations, the army and navy would set up a defensive perimeter on Japan's larger islands and archipelagos in the western Pacific, denying any other major power, particularly the United States, the opportunity to strike back and challenge Japan's strategic dominance.

The strategy was based on the reality that the eastern Pacific between California and Hawaii is empty ocean, providing no bases or points of replenishment to a fleet or amphibious force based in the United States. In contrast, the western Pacific is a constellation of islands whose forward edge could be fortified to make the whole area impenetrable. Tokyo purposely crafted the strategy to avoid striking U.S. targets in the Pacific, hoping that America's isolationist impulse would keep it off the field of battle and bring it instead to the negotiating table. The long, eastern flank of this island zone could be equipped with advanced SAMs and naval strike forces. These units could inflict such heavy damage on an enemy fleet sailing through the Pacific that no counteroffensive could be mounted.

Stage two of the strategy was to construct fortified bases along a chain running from the Kurile Islands off Russia through Wake Island and the Marshall Islands, to Malaysia. The third and final stage was consolidation: prevent any major power from challenging Japanese control of the newly conquered territories.

Kawara took a drag on his cigarette and stared off into a dark corner of his decidedly old-world study. As he thought about the forces that would soon be unleashed, he felt a few tinges of anxiety. His most serious concern was the role of the United States. Would the two great powers come to blows as they had sixty years earlier?

If armed conflict came, Tokyo was interested in waging a war of attrition. But no great power was likely to seek war with Japan since its claims were limited, Kawara reassured himself. The empire was actually a defensive move, and after time, it would be seen as such by the rest of the world. By claiming hegemony in the western Pacific and occupying energy-rich territories, Japan would no longer be vulnerable to a cutoff of essential resources. Once Kawara consolidated his position, he hoped to strike a bargain with the Americans and negotiate a new trade pact from a more advantageous position.

The prime minister got up from his comfortable dark tan leather chair and walked slowly over to the wood desk in the corner of his study. He began to carefully review the operational maps for the planned move. The proposed perimeter strategy was deeply Japanese, a function of geography rooted in the psyche and history of an island people accustomed to using land and sea forces in concert to preserve the security of the archipelago and to extend national power into adjoining regions. The historical chords were clearly visible: this was the strategy adopted by Imperial Japan in the 1930s that culminated with the outbreak of the Second World War. The Greater East-Asian Co-Prosperity Sphere was being remade into a twenty-first–century system.

Since naval power reigns supreme in the vast expanse of the Pacific Ocean, the first order of business was to eliminate from the Pacific theater all potential challengers to Japan's plans for dominance. A mix of politics and budget cutbacks had forced the closing of U.S. military bases in Korea, the Philippines, Japan, and Guam. Pearl Harbor was America's last outpost, leaving only Taiwan and China as major blue water threats. Japanese war strategists conceived a plan that included a series of quick blows directed at eliminating the naval and air power of both countries. This would immediately be followed by an invasion of the Philippines, as well as two oil-rich areas—the Spratly Islands in the South China Sea and the tiny country of Brunei.

Kawara had already approved the plan two weeks earlier because he had faith in the country's technological prowess. A major element of the attack would be waged in cyberspace—destroying and disrupting computers by using logic bombs and viruses to disrupt and disorient the enemy before the actual military assault began. Specialists would launch a series of debilitating strikes against the enemy's nerve centers, the telecommunications and computer networks that so direct and organize modern life. The strikes would occur in rapid succession and, he hoped, offer Japanese forces an enormous advantage.

With the thoughts of cyberwar racing through his mind, Kawara glanced at the wall clock. It was now 7:30 A.M. He had been up all night.

In the quiet morning hours of August 19, a massive Japanese fleet headed for the blue waters of the South China Sea. Tokyo characterized the armada as part of an extensive naval exercise, something commonly seen in the western Pacific. Neighboring countries took only a minor interest in the movement of the fleet. During the daylong journey south, the armada maintained radio silence, and by noon, as they crossed the tropic of Cancer just north of Cape Engano, the massive fleet split into three task forces.

Task Force I steamed west toward Hong Kong and the Chinese coast. Admiral Hiro Tarayoko, aboard the flagship *Hokkaido*, commanded the armada of sixteen vessels, including four Aegis missile cruisers, five destroyers, and two carriers. A second element of the fleet, designated Task Force II, headed southwest, remaining one hundred miles off the coast of the northern Philippine island of Luzon. Admiral Hiro Nagarito commanded this group, including two carriers, four cruisers, and half a dozen support vessels. The third and final element of the fleet was Task Force III, commanded by Admiral Nagiro Tanaka, which turned west. This force of three cruisers, two destroyers and three carriers, including the flag carrier *Ryoko*, remained on full alert southeast of Taiwan.

Meanwhile, inside a deep bunker beneath Mount Onna on the

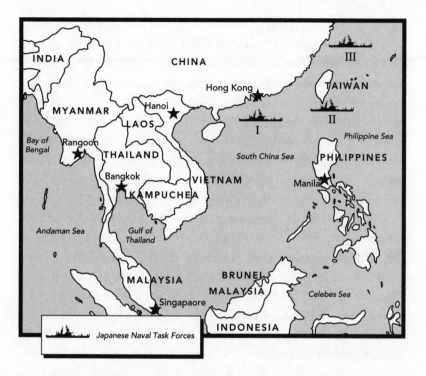

Deployment of Japanese Naval Task Forces:
August 20, 2007

island of Okinawa, Haki Owada and other specialists from the Security and Intelligence Command (SIC) were hard at work at their computer keyboards. Owada was an MIT Ph.D. in computer science, a genius at manipulating computer software and subverting computer networks. He was a leading practitioner of cyberwar, which made him the quintessential 21st-century warrior. Although Owada had never picked up a weapon in anger, he served as the general of a potent, electronic army. His casualties were machines; instead of attacking humans, he destroyed the computer and telecommunication systems that governed their lives.

Owada had been working on a series of complex computer programs for more than eight months. Shortly after midnight on August 20, with the massive fleet almost in place, Owada and his team inserted a series of programs into the telephone switching stations of Taiwan's national telephone company. These highly potent, contagious computer viruses instantly ate the software programs that managed the country's fiber optic and telecommunication networks. Within minutes, telephones and computer networks where thrown into utter chaos. Phone lines went dead, and computers locked into random programs that led nowhere. Owada then detonated eleven logic bombs which at once fried the electronic routers directing the national railway system, air traffic control network, and maritime traffic navigational systems. The first salvos of the Pacific War had been fired, and the results were grave and immediate.

In the air traffic control tower at Taipei Sungshan Airport, controllers saw the entire navigational system suddenly go blank. Incapable of providing any instructions to planes trying to land at the field, airliners were diverted to airports in other countries. Trains froze on their tracks, and traffic lights went dead. The entire nation of Taiwan was paralyzed, prostrate in the face of a pending war.

While the cyberstrikes were the portent of an approaching enemy, the first, audible footsteps came when three Japanese fighters screamed across the night skies of Taipei at 2:23 A.M. These Japanese stealth aircraft were based on the design of the American F-117A, which had been sold to Tokyo in 1999 as part of a co-production arrangement. The S-1 fighter had superior agility and was particularly well-suited for night missions. Along with its radar-negating ability, it also had special night-enhancing features. Painted in light-absorbing black from nose to tail, the pilot's ejection seat and helmet were the color of night. The pilots looked through windows specially coated to reduce glint and light from the cockpit. With its external lights off, the plane blended seamlessly into the dark sky.

The aircraft was equally difficult to detect audibly or with heat-signature sensors. Special exhaust nozzles quieted the roar of the engines which were positioned above the wing, deep within the aircraft's body. The exhaust was first cooled to reduce the heat signature that infrared detectors might pick up. Any engine parts that might warm during the flight were encased inside, hidden from the view of ground-launched missiles that might home in on infrared radiation.

In the lead aircraft was Colonel Kiryo Hamariko, the flight commander and a twenty-year veteran of the Japanese Air Force (JAF). With the lights of the capital visible in the distance, he steadied his plane and then locked the laser guidance system into place. Once over his target, he lined up the crosshairs and released his payload, a small bomblike device the size of a suitcase. It swiftly descended on the city streets below. The device exploded near Taiwan's Ministry of Defense (MoD), erupting with a hollow fury. While it caused little physical damage, it did emit a strong electromagnetic pulse (EMP) which radiated over a large portion of the city. The magnetism from the electric charges effectively destroyed the electronic components of the main government computer system. With his mission complete, Colonel Hamariko and his wing partners banked their black planes over the South China Sea for the return flight to Okinawa.

Several hundred miles to the west another cyberattack was launched, this one against the Chinese mainland. Owada and his team detonated logic bombs in the phone switching stations around Shanghai, headquarters of the Chinese fleet. At the same time, Admiral Tarayoko's Task Force I launched dozens of cruise missiles. Some were armed with special EMP warheads and were bound for Chinese naval headquarters in Shanghai. Others were targeted at the Chinese warships still in port. Over the course of the next hour, the missiles flew along their predetermined flight paths before striking their targets and blacking out communications for most of the Chinese fleet. As the EMP-equipped missiles struck the Chinese Naval Command Center in Shanghai, Haki Owada and his colleagues at the SIC detonated several logic bombs in Beijing, leaving Chinese military command and control at the point of paralysis. The enemy was now blind and deaf, and Japanese offensive military operations could commence.

By 4:00 A.M. the dark skies above northeast Taiwan were filled with seventy Japanese attack aircraft winging their way over the black crystal-like seas. Carrier-based aircraft from Task Force III were joined by several JAF squadrons launched hours earlier from Okinawa and refueled over the Pacific.

Flight commander Hiro Oyzawa slowly manipulated his flight stick and began the descent on Taipei, followed by a cloud of other planes. The combined force of aircraft struck military airfields and several air defense facilities. Meanwhile, four Yuushio-class diesel subs moved toward a group of destroyers and cruisers in Chilung Harbor. Using automatic three-dimensional controls and an advanced digital information processing system that maximizes movement, navigation, and location of targets, the double-hulled, teardrop-shaped subs came to a halt only a quarter mile from their targets. Each immediately fired six torpedoes in rapid succession.

All at once, twenty-four torpedos were cruising toward their targets, traveling at fifty knots just below the waterline. With extreme accuracy, the wire-guided torpedoes found their marks. The warheads erupted in fits of violence, creating a series of luminous flashes that cut through the fabric of the black night.

The crews aboard the Taiwanese vessels tried desperately to contain the raging fires, but it was a futile effort. Although one cruiser, the Taipei, did manage to get under way, it began taking on water and eventually sank just outside the mouth of the harbor.

Japanese forces achieved complete surprise, like the brute who attacks a blinded man. Efforts by Taiwan to organize a coherent defense were stilted by the electronic chaos and paralytic conditions that plagued its command and control system.

The operations were a remarkable, bold display of Japanese military proficiency. Nighttime air operations require pilots to strictly adhere to assigned altitudes and flight patterns in the crowded night skies. Being even a few hundred feet too high or too low can mean disaster. But this strike was a stunning, complete victory. Only three aircraft failed to return from the mission. Although Taiwan possessed a potent air force, the cyberstrikes allowed for complete surprise, and precision bombing destroyed dozens of aircraft on the ground.

With smoke billowing and fires raging in Taiwan, Tokyo turned on the Chinese mainland, hoping to finish off the other main rival for dominance of the western Pacific. The operation began with four Japanese cruisers deployed off the coast of China which launched a cluster of Tomahawk cruise missiles in rapid succession. Within minutes, sixty were screaming toward the mainland. Japanese fighter-bombers then closed in on the coastline, flying just a few hundred feet above the water to avoid detection.

By 9:00 A.M. the entire Chinese coast was trembling as the Tomahawks destroyed targets around Shanghai, Beijing, and Nanjing. Aircraft then pummeled the capital ships of the Chinese fleet and a major air base near Fuzhou. The runway was littered with special munitions the size of tin cans. They exploded vertically, scarring the runway with deep potholes and rendering it useless.

While Japanese pilots reported major success in the disabling first strike, there was some concern about the absence of China's two new aircraft carriers, the *Chiking* and *Xiaping*. Japanese spy satellites immediately went to work, and just shortly after noon they located both carriers off the coast of Vietnam. Admiral Tarayoko sped off in full pursuit, hoping to pin them along the coastline.

Over the course of several hours, the Kawara government had taken an enormous step toward achieving its dream of complete supremacy in the western Pacific. The fleets of both China and Taiwan were mortally wounded and their air power crippled. Although both nations possessed robust ground forces (and mainland China a nuclear arsenal), their ability to project military muscle into the Pacific was now limited.

With his potential rivals now seriously weakened, Kawara turned the full weight of his air and naval power at the Philippines. Astride the major sea-lanes of the western Pacific, the islands were a critical strategic choke point in the theater.

Admiral Tanaka lightly tapped his finger on the steel wall as he stood on the bridge of his carrier *Ryoko* off the coast of the main island of Luzon. His armada proceeded south under a hot sun, and as the massive, gray vessels crossed into Filipino territorial waters shortly after noon, all personnel went on full alert. The admiral's finger now began to tap more rapidly as the urgency of the mission intensified. Success in the Philippines was critical. Luzon was in the middle of the major sea-lanes of communication that linked northeast and southeast Asia, the Pacific and the Indian oceans. It had once served as the site of the U.S. Navy's Subic Bay/Cubi Point Naval Complex and as a logistics hub for the U.S. 7th Fleet. Access to and from these waterways was the lifeblood of commerce for the entire western Pacific and control would give Japan the ability to direct the economies of the region. It could also grant Tokyo a veto over U.S. trade with any country in the western Pacific. If Washington continued to wage a trade war against Japan, Tokyo could restrict U.S. access to important markets in Asia, particularly to those territories it would occupy.

The Philippine Air Force (PAF) tracked the Japanese fleet as it crossed the northern tip of Luzon at Laoag, shadowing Tanaka's armada with six F-5 fighters. PAF pilots were uncertain about what to make of the fleet's presence. They had not yet heard of the attacks on Taiwan and the Chinese mainland. And while the Japanese naval "maneuvers" had been announced, they were not expected this close to the Philippine coast. An uneasy standoff ensued as the fleet moved past San Fernando to the waters off the Zambales Mountains. There it slowly came to a halt, facing the rugged hills of Bataan.

In an instant, the entire assemblage of vessels sprang to life. The cruisers *Sapporo* and *Kirin* radiated the skies with their fixed-array radar systems. Packed with four medium-range SAM systems and more than 160 missiles, they immediately sent a full complement into the calm skies.

The warning lights on the Filipino F-5s began flashing like mad and the pilots rattled their sticks hoping to shake the missiles. Mission commander Major Anthony Sanchez dropped chaff and dove for the ocean, pulling up the nose of his F-5 just fifty feet above sea level. Although the bold, dramatic move allowed him to evade his tormentor, his squadron mates were not so fortunate. As Sanchez expectantly scanned the horizon, he saw five twisting columns of smoke marking the death of as many pilots and their planes.

The tense major steadied his aircraft and let out a deep sigh before radioing back to the main air base on Luzon. "This is Sanchez. We are under attack. I repeat, this is Sanchez. We are under attack!" On the other end he heard only silence. He knew that the war had commenced on land as well.

As Sanchez fled back to Luzon, a massive Japanese assault was unfolding on the island. It came first as an invisible thunder, rumbling from the north. But it wasn't long before the noise grew louder and two dozen JAF stealth fighter-bombers became visible through the hazy afternoon ether. At twenty-five thousand feet the fighter group maintained complete radio silence before splitting into two strike groups. As they dropped to ten thousand feet, the pilots activated the ground attack radars before descending on their targets. On the bridge of the *Ryoko*, Admiral Tanaka broke the hum of radio silence. "Commence the attack," he commanded, giving the final order in a confident monotone.

One JAF strike group descended on Manila Bay, dropping a string of laser-guided bombs on the collection of navy vessels below. Lined up like posts on a picket fence, the ships burst into flames as the bombs exploded, lighting up the aphotic bay. The cruiser *Mindanao* was set adrift, floating out to sea like a ghost ship in a fiery red blaze.

Some seventy-five miles northwest of Manila Bay, the other JAF strike group was pounding the main air base on Luzon. The communications and command posts were leveled first. Next the

PAF was hit. After a few, fleeting moments, the planes were nothing but a pile of white-hot scrap metal. The air strikes on Luzon had come in a rapid fury, and now, with the enemy reeling, Tanaka gave the order to begin the amphibious assault.

Members of the Japanese Special Forces were the first to hit the beaches. Carried inland by transport helicopters, the elite units were equipped with Kevlar helmets, body armor, and laser-sight weapons. Their mission was to secure the perimeter for the main landing. As the units scampered through the thick undergrowth, landing craft were spilling out of the huge transport vessels offshore. With white water curling away from their bows, they rapidly closed on the shoreline.

During the next several hours, the main force came ashore, including tanks, motorized artillery, and armored personnel carriers (APCs). Colonel Takahari Kawasaki, a thin, energetic man whose presence had a power way beyond his size, shouted orders as he walked along the white sandy beaches, pushing his men to pick up the pace. The colonel was under strict orders to move the force of 3,500 men along the Bataan Highway and engage the enemy at the main air base by noon. Once the facility was securely in the hands of Japanese marines, air transports from Okinawa could begin pouring in reinforcements and supplies.

Half a dozen tanks led the charge east on a treacherous road surrounded by a thick brush that greatly reduced visibility. From his command vehicle, Colonel Kawasaki saw a country so thick with jungle undergrowth that it was asphyxiating. And after only a few minutes in the humidity, the colonel felt as if he were standing under a hot shower as sweat poured down his face. He worried about the fatigue of his soldiers.

Nevertheless, the push to the air base went without incident. At 11:48 A.M., barely two miles from the target, Kawasaki divided his force into two prongs. One group, made up of armor and light mechanized infantry, struck from the west, supported by attack aircraft. The second detachment, largely comprised of Japanese marines on foot, pushed from the south. Within two hours,

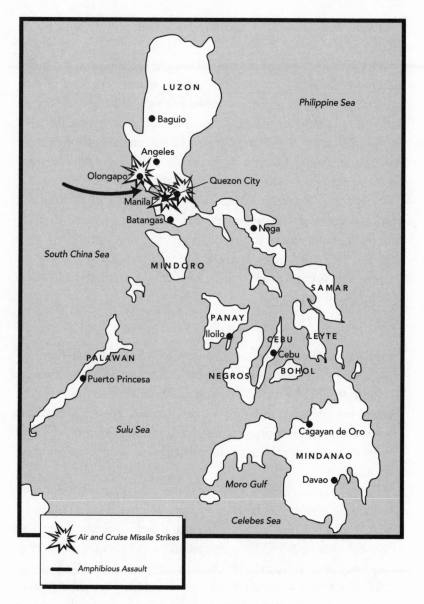

The Japanese Invasion of the Philippines

Kawasaki had control of the air base. Still, victory offered no respite.

The colonel immediately set about establishing a defensive perimeter consisting of twelve "strong points," each with two squads and heavy machine guns. Antitank weapons and rockets dotted the boundary of the air base. Marines then strung portable motion detectors and infrared systems between these strong points to track intruders. The remainder of the force was held in reserve to counterattack should someone try to retake the air base.

Meanwhile, Japanese engineers were fast at work repairing the tower and runway. Transports on Okinawa were prepared to fly in troops, supplies, and weapons to buttress the contingent. By nightfall, the first of dozens of these large aircraft were landing on Luzon. The invading force would now only get stronger and more difficult to dislodge.

In the indigo blue waters of the South China Sea, Admiral Tarayoko was pushing his fleet west in pursuit of the two Chinese carriers skimming along the territorial waters of Vietnam in a frenzied rush back to the mainland with only a single Chinese cruiser in escort. A return to port was critical because air support from ground-based fighters would offer some much-needed protection from Japanese naval forces.

Tarayoko knew that this might be his best opportunity to eliminate the Chinese carriers. As he closed to five hundred nautical miles, he ordered the launch of his FX fighters and strike aircraft. The crews aboard the *Hokkaido* and *Keiyo* proceeded with the launch sequence at a headlong pace, releasing two aircraft every minute. First off was the 524th Attack Squadron, led by Commander Hiro Watanabe, a slight but solidly built man with intense brown eyes. Watanabe was an aggressive pilot who regularly tested experimental aircraft for the government and who relished pushing his plane to the limit. His 524th was expected to deliver the knockout punch to the carriers.

Next off the flight deck was Lieutenant Commander Mishio

Toyoda and his squadron. Toyoda, who was more reserved and conventional, would deliver the first blow to the enemy.

Technicians in the combat command center of the Japanese missile cruiser *Meiji* went to work preparing for the launch of surface-to-surface missiles (SSMs). Scanning the green display screens in front of them, the specialists plotted coordinates based on the speed and course of the Chinese vessels. Just moments after the two attack squadrons disappeared over the west horizon, the first missiles were launched directly at the carriers.

Watanabe and the 524th hung low in the flight toward the carriers, skimming the ocean surface to avoid radar. Toyoda and his squadron remained well back while going into a gradual climb. At thirty thousand feet they launched long-range anti-ship missiles with massive warheads that could inflict immense damage on a carrier. It would then be up to the 524th to finish the job.

The carriers *Chiking* and *Xiaping* were old but sturdy, purchased from a cash-starved Moscow selling off an aging fleet. Despite a functional solidness, both lacked advanced ECMs to deal with enemy aircraft and missiles. (In typical fashion, Moscow stripped the major vessels they sold of most electronics.) That deficiency became apparent as the SSMs crested over the horizon and the missiles launched by Toyoda's squadron closed at Mach 3. Aboard the escorting Chinese cruiser *Nansha*, technicians detected the missiles on radar, sending the electronic warfare officers (EWOs) into a panic. They tried desperately to jam the electronic guidance systems of the closing projectiles. But efforts failed and two radar-guided 20-mm guns aboard the *Xiaping* started banging away. The Gatling gun systems spit out 3,000 rounds per minute at a high velocity—3,600 feet per second. Although the guns claimed three of the dozen missiles en route, the rest slammed into the flight deck and tower, sending fragments of metal into the air. It soon felt like an oven in the hangar as raging fires erupted into an inferno. Hot gases spread throughout the upper deck.

The concussion from the anti-ship missiles was deafening, and the SSMs soon closed on the carriers. Again the guns banged away.

But the missiles came in on a flat trajectory, plastering the tower and deck.

Commander Watanabe and the pilots of the 524th could see the rising black smoke on the horizon. The *Xiaping* slowed to five knots as a great column of smoke poured up amidships, while thinner wisps seeping up from the fires deep in the forward compartments were seen in the hangar. The *Chiking* was still moving, and one flight deck was operable. To make room for the few planes still intact, the crews on the massive carrier began pushing the scattered, damaged aircraft into the sea.

By now the 524th was only fifty nautical miles east and closing the distance fast. Within minutes, the group passed over the *Xiaping*, now dead in the water, her crew members bailing out. The oil-covered sea was alive with bobbing heads, small rafts, and paraphernalia that had slid off the decks or had been blown off by the explosions. Watanabe, however, was after the *Chiking*, which had avoided major destruction while clinging to its course and rushing doublespeed for the Chinese coast. To the beleaguered Chinese sailors on board, it seemed inevitable they would experience the same deadly fate as their comrades.

Suddenly, a massive collection of land-based Chinese fighters appeared on the horizon, including Su-27s and MiG-29s. The hard push north had paid off—the wounded *Chiking* had managed to make it within range of aircraft from the mainland. The scales of battle immediately shifted.

News of the arriving Chinese legions set off a frantic rush aboard the carriers *Hokkaido* and *Keiyo* to put more fighters into the air. But the enormous number of enemy aircraft dancing on radar was not something Tarayoko could hope to match. Commander Watanabe called off his attack and headed east for his fleet. The *Xiaping* was mortally wounded, but the *Chiking* had survived. And while Admiral Tarayoko could claim victory, it was less than total.

The Japanese military thrust startled the world. In Washington, D.C., reports continued to filter in concerning the extent of the offensive.

U.S. forces went on full alert, and the reserves were called up. The nations of the Pacific clamored for firm action from the White House.

Official Washington was stunned by the scope and intensity of the Japanese drive to conquer the western Pacific. Although divisive trade talks had severely damaged relations with Tokyo, no one imagined that war was possible. The Japanese military buildup during the past half-decade had been viewed as a defensive measure and had not generated much concern in Washington. When Tokyo deployed its first nuclear weapons in 2001, most of the powers in the region found it understandable, if only because North Korea had deployed similar weapons in 1998.

The Japanese conventional military buildup had occurred against the backdrop of the continued withdrawal of U.S. forces from the Pacific. By 2004, the United States was out of the Philippines, Korea, and Okinawa, and troop levels in Guam were minimal. Washington appeared all-too-happy to see Tokyo fill the resulting power vacuum. No one believed that the burgeoning Japanese arsenal might be used for a war of conquest. And it might not have been except for the recent major economic earthquake.

At 4:15 P.M. President St. John assembled the NSC in an attempt to grapple with the military storm now raging in the Pacific. Since Japan had scrupulously avoided hitting any U.S. targets, territories, or military facilities, no state of war existed between the two countries. Indeed, Tokyo appeared intent to accomplish its goals without giving the United States a reason to become involved in the conflict. Japanese war aims appeared limited to achieving strategic superiority in the western Pacific. But American allies in the region were desperate for U.S. involvement. President Fidel Ramirez in Manila had wired the president earlier in the day.

President Michael St. John
The White House
Washington, D.C.

Our situation is desperate. The main air base on

Luzon has fallen to enemy forces. Reinforcements are arriving by the hour. The air strikes are unrelenting. We will be forced to move the capital to the island of Mindanao if the advance is not halted. We ask that you honor the defense treaties you have signed with our country and come to our aid.

President Fidel Ramirez
Republic of the Philippines

In a starched white collar and conservative blue suit, President St. John sat quietly behind a cherry-wood table in the White House Situation Room. He listened intently as his advisers debated the merits of involving America in the war.

"The matter is very simple," began Defense Secretary Tom Bodine prosaically. "We have a defense treaty with the Philippines, and we are obliged to come to their defense."

Jack Fowler, the national security adviser, was not so sure and shook his head in disagreement. "Look, Tom, we need to be realistic about this. The American people are going to be very reluctant to send their sons and daughters to die for an archipelago thousands of miles away, treaty or no treaty."

Bodine grunted, leaning forward on his burgundy leather chair. "This is about more than the Philippines. If the initial Japanese moves were as successful as we think, there will be no one in the Pacific theater to challenge their move for hegemony. China, Taiwan, and the Philippines have been hit hard. Russia has been too poor to maintain anything resembling its Pacific fleet of old; they are basically irrelevant. Only Australia and Indonesia remain as naval powers in the region. Although China, Korea, Vietnam, and Taiwan still have sizeable ground forces, the Pacific is quickly becoming a Japanese lake. We need to shift our forces to the region immediately."

The president agreed to that much and ordered three carrier groups to the theater at once. Otherwise, he remained cautious, choosing not to deploy aircraft or ground troops in Asia for fear of provoking a strike by Tokyo.

American military muscle in the Pacific was not what it once was. America's only major military installation in the central Pacific was Pearl Harbor. And due to numerous global commitments, the U.S. Navy was stretched thin, trying to meet a three-ocean requirement with a one-and-a-half-ocean navy. Only 11 carriers were left from the 15-carrier navy of the 1980s. The *Coral Sea* had been retired from the fleet, along with the *Midway* and two other Forrestal-class ships. Of the remaining 11, four were more than 30 years old and past retirement age. The naval attack-aircraft inventory aged as well. By the mid-1990s, annual procurement had dropped below the annual replenishment rate of 330 planes. The American navy was still the best in the world, but the distance between the fleet and potential rivals had narrowed during the past decade and a half. To deal effectively with the Japanese threat, U.S. naval forces would have to be pulled together from the corners of the earth, and that would take precious time.

Tom Bodine left the White House concerned about American capabilities in the theater. His instincts told him that war was inevitable. The 6th and 7th fleets would provide formidable power. But with few U.S. bases overseas, logistics and resupply would be difficult. When he returned to his office on the "E" ring of the Pentagon, Bodine placed a call to Canberra, Australia.

Chapter Twenty-nine

August 21
the South China Sea

Under the merciless glare of the hot sun, dozens of speed-boats and assault helicopters buzzed the waters of a wide, desolate patch in the South China Sea. What brought members of the Japanese Special Forces out were thirty-three rock formations randomly scattered throughout the area. These tiny dots on the map were a cornerstone of Prime Minister Kawara's promised "new era of prosperity." The Spratly Islands are mostly mere rocks jutting from the placid surface of the ocean, many underwater at high tide. The largest isle, Itu Aba, is less than two-thirds of a mile long and one-third of a mile wide—about six city blocks long by three city blocks wide. But below the water's surface were enormous oil deposits—estimated by some to be valued at $1 trillion—ready to be tapped, along with a treasure chest of critical industrial minerals on the ocean floor.

With machinelike precision, members of the Special Forces stormed Malaysian oil production facilities one by one. Facing minimal resistance, the Japanese had control of the oil rigs and mining facilities within hours.

It was a naked grab at natural wealth. Control of the Spratly Islands would give Tokyo the secure source of petroleum it had always desired, setting Japanese industry free from the Middle East cauldron half a world away.

As Washington continued to move cautiously, the Japanese navy was working on extending its reach. Task Force III pushed further south toward Indonesia along the western coast of Palawan Island. Admiral Tanaka was responsible for extending the new empire into the Indonesian archipelago, including the tiny, oil-rich sultanate,

Brunei. Located on the north coast of Borneo, sandwiched between the Malaysian states of Sarawak and Sadah, Brunei is a mere 2,225 square miles (only slightly larger than Delaware) but a major source of world crude. The abundant oil fields in the western corner of the country and offshore rigs were producing 4 million barrels per day.

As Tanaka pushed south, reconnaissance detected heavy naval activity in the Java Sea. The Indonesian government in Jakarta was consolidating its forces as a defensive measure to check any possible move by Japan to push south for Singapore. With a keen eye, Admiral Tanaka watched the force building but with little concern.

Tanaka hoped for a quick victory. The sultanate had invested heavily in advanced weapons over the years and possessed a small but sophisticated air force, including several F-16 fighters with solid avionics and extended radars. Still, the tiny nation was no match for the iron fist of Japan.

As his fleet closed to some two hundred miles off the north coast of Brunei, Admiral Tanaka ordered the attack to commence. Aboard the carriers *Ryoko*, *Meitoku*, and *Amakudari*, pilots rushed from the preflight briefing rooms and headed for their metal chariots as ground crews clamored to prepare the aircraft for takeoff. The lead plane belonged to Commander Akro Ohashi, the flight commander. Seated comfortably in the cockpit, he placed a helmet over his head as the canopy was lowered on top of his FX fighter. He turned on the power to activate the control panel and engaged the engines as he prepared for takeoff. Ten minutes later, he felt the explosive push of the catapult as the engines propelled him into the air.

The skies were overcast and visibility was low. Ohashi and his squadron had the job of clearing the skies of enemy fighters over Brunei. All flight operations had to be conducted over the water and within the narrow confines of Brunei airspace to avoid dragging Malaysia and Indonesia into the war. Ohashi did not like such restrictions. Air combat was an intense art form, and creativity could mean the difference between victory and defeat.

As Commander Ohashi began his journey south, technicians

The offensive begins as Japanese marines invade Brunei.

aboard the cruiser *Kirayo* were staring intently into their green, incandescent screens and furiously working the Tomahawk missile-launch console keyboards. Stored vertically in banks of sixty-one launch cells, the Tomahawks were expected to take out the most sensitive and protected targets in Brunei, including air defense batteries and command facilities. Minutes after the technicians had input the launch sequence, the missiles were on their way, spit out of eight armored boxes in rapid succession. They cruised on a flat trajectory only a few hundred feet above the crest of the ocean waves.

Barely fifty miles off the coast, Ohashi and his squadron were met by a formation of eleven F-16s flying straight at them. At the command was Colonel Akhtar Yousaf, a twelve-year veteran of the Brunei air force and the country's best hope for success in the skies.

As the two forces converged, Ohashi split his group, sending six FX fighters southwest to swing behind the enemy. The move surprised Yousaf, who quickly found himself caught between two forces. Almost at once the warning lights on his Falcon started flashing as a cloud of Sidewinder missiles were closing at Mach 2. Yousaf dropped several flares and put the plane into a deep dive. As the Sidewinders broke off and flew aimlessly into the distance, he let out a brief sigh and steadied his plane. But a glance at radar revealed that the odds had worsened—Sidewinders had claimed four from his squadron.

The colonel immediately banked his Falcon out over the water and climbed to nineteen thousand feet. With his weapons console flashing, he released a medium-range missile. The microprocessors in the radar homing system locked onto a Japanese FX fighter. Just seconds later, Yousaf was able to claim the first Japanese casualty of the operation.

Commander Ohashi spotted Yousaf from a distance as the wily pilot now tried to work his way behind the Japanese squadron. Instinctively, Ohashi peeled off to give chase. Yousaf saw the lone antagonist closing fast and took his Falcon into a mind-numbing 9-g turn at twenty-one thousand feet. Somehow he managed to stay conscious. Ohashi could not stay with him and was forced to pull out of the turn. The Falcon looped sharply and was suddenly behind Ohashi's FX. Within seconds, Yousaf locked onto the plane and released an infrared missile. The planes were now barely a mile apart. Ohashi had no time to evade. The missile flew up the tail pipe of his FX and ruptured the engine, sending the aircraft into a chaotic dive. Reaching desperately to activate his ejection seat, Ohashi was soon riding the wind by parachute. Back on the carrier *Ryoko* a Mayday signal was wailing.

Yousaf again scanned his long-range radar and saw a horrifying sight. During his duel with Ohashi, the enemy had claimed all of his compatriots. He was now alone—the singular, remaining aircraft in the area without Japanese markings. With little time to think, Yousaf elected to stay and fight. He claimed one more FX fighter before meeting a fiery death over the South China Sea.

As the colonel's plane splashed into the rich blue seas, the ground in Brunei shuddered as the first Tomahawk cruise missile arrived. A cloud of Japanese strike aircraft followed, pounding ground units of the Brunei army.

Admiral Tanaka felt a calm overcome him as he gave the order for the amphibious assault to begin. Everything was going as planned. Intelligence revealed that the Indonesian fleet was holding off the coast of Singapore. The seas were calm, and the air war was exceeding expectations. A wave of adrenalin rushed over the thousands of Japanese marines who had been waiting for hours in their landing craft. In an instant, they were thrust into war as their boats sped toward shore. A group of attack helos led the assault escorting a dozen transport helos carrying marine reconnaissance units. Dressed in dark green fatigues, unit members scurried for cover after they were put down several miles inland. Using infrared sensors, they scanned the area before giving the final all clear for the main landing to commence. The first landing craft hit the white, crystal, sandy beaches just minutes later. Mitsubishi Type 90 tanks and infantry began moving inland.

The immediate objective was to secure control of the main road running from Kuala Belait to Seria, the tiny nation's east–west artery. With the road in Japanese control, Brunei would have a difficult time getting into position to engage the enemy.

Two platoons of Japanese marines scampered along the main road east of Kuala Belait, where they constructed a series of small containment lines running perpendicular to the road. Captain Kenzo Fukushima's most serious concern was the unexpected. Was there anything coming down the road?

Fukushima was a hawklike man with a narrow face and intense eyes. He was commanding a forward detachment and had orders to hold the road at all costs. Retreat was not an option for the captain or his men.

By early evening the crude trenches were completed. The sky was lit with an eerie glow, a foreboding luminosity. Fukushima wondered if they would survive the night. Suddenly his COMLINK sprang to life. Air patrols were reporting on the movement of two armored brigades from the Brunei Royal Guard. They were ten miles down the road and moving west. Fukushima knew that this was perhaps the most capable unit he was likely to face. The Royal Guard was well equipped with Chieftain tanks and APCs, while his platoons were lightly armored and outnumbered. The Mitsubishi Type 90 tanks and heavier units were still moving in from the shoreline.

It seemed an eternity as the marines waited along the road, crouched in their trenches. Shortly after 10:00 P.M., there was the distinct sound of grinding gears. The Royal Guard finally emerged amid a blizzard of bullets. The trenches erupted with a flurry of gunfire, but the Chieftain tanks pushed through the blue haze of battle smoke and broke the first containment line almost immediately, forcing a desperate pullback by panicked marines. Fukushima and his trusted aide Lieutenant Hirko Kobe flopped into some thick cover north of the road, and none too soon: a bullet snapped into the underbrush behind them. Fukushima grabbed the COMLINK. "This is Dragon One, Dragon One," he bellowed into his COMLINK. "We need immediate air support. We are being overrun. I repeat, we need immediate air support. We are being overrun, over."

Fukushima then heard the distinct crackle of gunfire and an agonizing moan nearby. He turned to see the crumpled body of Kobe lying in the brush. His face was ashen, and his hands were cold. Fukushima could barely feel a pulse. He looked for a medic—but no one was around.

By now the armored thrust was showing all the signs of becoming a rout. The entire position had collapsed, and most of the marines were either dead or in a panicked retreat for the brush when the drone of helicopters became audible. Suddenly, four attack helos rose above the tree line, hanging menacingly in the air. In a convulsion of fire they drilled the attacking armor with Hellfire armor-piercing missiles. Then a tight formation of fighter-bombers closed from the north. Captain Miyohei Sakaibara brought the squadron in low before dropping a load of laser-guided munitions on the enemy column. In a matter of seconds, the Royal Guard was reduced to limping impotence.

Fukushima and his men emerged from the brush, stunned at what

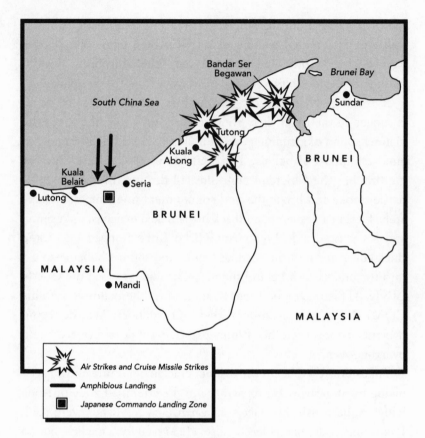

The Campaign in Brunei

they had witnessed. As they rounded up prisoners, the captain felt a tinge of uncertainty. He had been a soldier his entire adult life. But he now found himself wondering whether he could really bridge the vast gap between the comforts of peace and the horrors of war.

Colonel Kawasaki casually slapped at a few mosquitos as he sat in his makeshift office on the main air base of Luzon. His men had performed impressively during the past twenty-four hours—hitting the beaches, moving sixty miles by land, taking over the air base, and establishing a defensive perimeter. As the curtain of night fell on Luzon, the colonel felt at ease for the first time since he had received the order to ship out from Tokyo. The mission appeared to be a complete success. The first transport aircraft were now arriving, bringing troops, weapons, and supplies to the detachment.

North of the air base, Major Fidel Bermudez surveyed the Japanese position through his field glasses. A stout, muscular man who had spent his adult life in the Philippine army, he was confused about just what was happening. Bermudez had been out in the field on exercises with three platoons when the air strikes began. Since then he had been unable to contact headquarters by radio. Something was happening at the air base, and the major was anxious to get a closer look.

A squad was sent out through the tall grass to probe the perimeter of the base, led by Sergeant Miguel Ramos, who was clutching his shoulder-fired antitank weapon. Twelve others followed, mostly young recruits, nervously scanning the brush in front of them. Suddenly, the crackle of small-weapons fire ripped through the calm night air. The men dropped to their bellies as bullets whistled overhead. Ramos detached the safety switch on his weapon and waited.

"This is Post Six, over." The radio in Colonel Kawasaki's office became audible. "Enemy ground units approaching. Infantry and small arms, over."

Kawasaki grabbed the microphone. "All units in the north sector respond to an intrusion, over."

For the next several minutes, Ramos and his men remained face-down in the thick, dry grass. There was a standoff. The squad was afraid to move, and the Japanese marines were unwilling to flush them out.

Then the shelling began. The earth shook and the skies darkened as tons of explosives crashed down on the northern sector of the air base. In a panic, some of the men began to retreat, but Ramos remained still. He could smell the exhaust of an engine, and the trembling ground told him that a tank was nearby. Next he heard the grinding of gears and an external machine gun chattering away. By now the artillery barrage had ended and there was only the constant rumble of the tank.

Ramos did not move for what seemed an immeasurable period of time—until the tank passed within twenty yards of him. Summoning his will, he popped up and steadied his weapon before firing a projectile at the enormous metal animal. There was a huge flash and a thunderous boom. With billowing smoke, the tank lurched forward and came to a halt. Ramos dropped to one knee and reloaded in the cloud of dust and thick smoke. He leveled the firing tube again before sending another rocket straight at the wounded behemoth. There was another flash proceeded by a deep-throated boom. Casting his weapon aside, Ramos dropped to his belly and held his breath. He heard voices from a nearby foot patrol and carefully pulled the .45 from his holster and paused. A minute went by; then two. By now the patrol was nearly on top of him. As his anticipation reached an unbearable pitch, the sergeant leapt up and let loose with his pistol. He winged one marine in the shoulder before being struck a dozen times by automatic weapon fire.

The frantic but thorough search of the northern sector continued. Japanese helicopters hovered above the brush as fighter aircraft gracefully cruised across the clear, dark skies. Major Bermudez, who had witnessed everything through his field glasses, ordered an immediate retreat. The Philippine army sought refuge in the nearby foothills, slinking under a thicket of trees and heavy bushes. With his men both physically and emotionally exhausted, he assigned a squad to sentry duty and he then lay down to catch some sleep.

Back in Tokyo, Prime Minister Kawara was sipping a celebratory saki with his closest aides in the confines of his private quarters. Tokyo's strategic horizon now ran the length of the western Pacific: an arc of power from the South China Sea to the Sea of Japan and the Philippines. And yet Kawara's plans were far from complete. Control of the Philippines and Brunei was only the first step in the overall strategy of conquest of the East Islands—a treasure house of oil, rubber, and nonferrous metal production, as well as rice and timber. Using the combined might of naval and air power, Kawara planned to attack Indonesia in close succession at widely separated points across the two thousand-mile-long archipelago. But first there was one more regional power to reckon with.

Chapter Thirty

August 22
Tokyo

At 5:30 A.M. Prime Minister Kawara awoke from a restful sleep eager for the day to begin. After a small breakfast he met with his military advisers in his old-world–style study overlooking the lush greenery in the garden. Kawara remained firmly committed to the strategy *hokushu nanshin*—"defend the north, advance to the south." Although Japanese forces continued to advance south, a counterattack from the north was not out of the question, and Japanese forces were prepared to deal with just about any contingency that might arise.

Finishing off the last of his morning tea, the prime minister turned to General Murakami Yanaga, his always redoubtable defense minister. "Tell me," he asked softly, "what is our position in the north and east?"

Yanaga shifted his large frame in his chair, his bulldog features apparent to everyone. "On the islands of Tsushima and Iki in the Korea Strait, Japanese army combat engineers have fortified installations with titanium-lined bunkers and thick slabs of concrete. We have built extensive fortifications on Iki, including an advanced air defense system as well as SSM systems. On Tsushima, we have deployed a theater missile defense [TMD] system to intercept any missiles that might hit Japan. The arrayed radar capability and the satellite uplink will give us the ability to deal with any potential missile threat from Russia, China, or South Korea."

Kawara nodded. "What of our naval activities?"

"We have deployed a dozen destroyers in the Sea of Japan to act as a trip wire against any attacks that might come from the west. These vessels are running full combat patrols, guarding the waters from the Korea Strait to the Tsugaru Strait. Following our strikes on China, Taiwan, the Philippines, and Brunei, both South Korea and the Russian Pacific fleet have gone on full alert."

"What about Korea?"

"We have made it clear that we have no designs on their country. It is doubtful they will fight to defend the Philippines or Brunei. If we don't strike at them, we believe Seoul will stay out of the war."

"Do you consider the Russians a serious threat?"

Yanaga chuckled. "Vladivostock is a shadow of its former self. Much of the Pacific fleet has been sold off to foreign nations for much-needed hard currency. Two Russian cruisers were off Sakhalin when war broke out, and they have remained in the Sea of Japan as a show of strength. On August 20 they passed within sight of one of our patrols, but the warships continued on course without incident. Moscow is not interested in entering this war."

Although the overall strategic assessment was positive, the unspoken concern throughout the meeting was the Americans. After a briefing from the navy on the war in the Philippines and Brunei, Kawara finally raised the subject. Yanaga was dismissive. "Prime

Minister, we have extended our reach into the central Pacific. We have missile batteries on both March Island and the Bonin Islands. It will be difficult for them to overcome our fleet." He paused and leaned forward in his chair, staring straight at Kawara. "But if we want to ensure success against the Americans we must strike their facilities on Guam as soon as possible. Without Guam, they will have no forward bases in the theater. Operations would be extremely difficult for them, and victory would be assured."

Sensing the pull of Yanaga's leonine presence, Kawara felt the temptation to strike now as if war with the United States were inevitable. But caution ruled the day. "You offer tremendous insight as always," Kawara said after several minutes of silence. "But I still believe that war with the Americans can be avoided if we act wisely."

Yanaga simply shook his head.

At an isolated missile base in the Gobi Desert, crews from the Chinese PLA Strategic Rocket Forces went through the motions as they had for hundreds of practice drills. This time, however, the launch was for real. The safety locks had been removed from the intermediate-range missiles, and the computer guidance systems were fully operational.

Lieutenant General Lei Pei-hua sat nervously in a nearby command bunker waiting for the launch codes granting final approval. At 8:55 A.M. they came. With his hands slightly trembling, the general typed the final code sequence into the computer keyboard. Next he inserted a small metallic key into the slot on the control panel and gently twisted it. A voice synthesizer then relayed the countdown: "Ten... nine... eight... seven... six... five... four... three... two... one... ignition." An immense cloud of smoke with a heart of flame bloomed inside the silos, propelling two missiles into the air. As they rose through the clouds, they tilted on a northeastward trajectory. Their destination was downtown Tokyo.

But General Lei Pei-hua was not the only one watching the ascent of the missiles. Hanging beneath the stars in orbital space, a

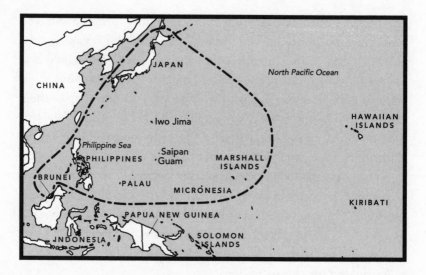

The Growing Japanese Empire

Japanese infrared spy satellite detected the launch moments after ignition and relayed a warning to the Japanese missile defense command facility on Tsushima. Within seconds, the Air Defense Management Computer (ADMC) used the data to calculate launch time, trajectory, speed, and point of impact. It then relayed the information to the proper missile defense interceptor. In this case it was the missile cruiser *Dai-Ichi* patrolling the choppy waters off the Korean coast. The ship's fire-control officers confirmed the data with the ADMC before activating their TMD systems.

By now the Chinese missiles were over the Korean peninsula, beginning their descent onto the island of Japan. There was just one data correction by the ADMC before the *Dai-Ichi* launched a dozen small missiles which cut through the morning sky at Mach 5. Moments later a series of brilliant flashes ignited in the heavens, visible only by infrared sensors. Aboard the *Dai-Ichi*, fire-control officers checked for radar and detected nothing. The intercept had been a complete success.

An intelligence vessel was dispatched to the Korea Strait to search the area for debris. The Japanese military command was interested in answering one very important question: exactly what sort of warheads were the missiles carrying?

While the news of the Chinese missile attack unnerved Prime Minister Kawara, he was preparing for even more bad news as he sat in his comfortable leather chair watching CNN. On TV was President Michael St. John addressing the United States. He was seated behind his desk in the Oval Office dressed in a conservative blue suit and red tie. As he read from the TelePrompTer, he appeared calm but determined.

"My fellow Americans, as you have by now heard, Japanese forces—from the ground, sea, and air—have launched a series of unprovoked attacks on sites throughout the western Pacific. Japanese air units struck targets on the Chinese mainland at Shanghai, Beijing, and Nanjing. There was also a brutal air strike on Taipei, costing thousands of innocent civilians their lives. This was followed by a series of ground attacks in the Philippines and an assault on the country of Brunei. These military operations are wholly unacceptable to the United States. We condemn them fully. Although war is something we hope to avoid, this aggression cannot stand. We have sent a formal note of diplomatic protest to the government of Prime Minister Kawara. After having consulted with our many allies in the region, we are dispatching the U.S. Navy to the region. Let me assure you that as your president, no decision will be made in haste nor will any responsibility be taken lightly. For now that is all. But take heart, we will ensure that the interests of the United States are fully protected."

Kawara attempted to read cryptically between the lines. The mention of "war" had unnerved him. Try as he might, the prime minister could not escape the conclusion that the American president was somehow preparing his people for armed conflict.

Despite the stirring of the Chinese and American giants, the news from the front continued to be encouraging for Kawara. By midafternoon on August 23, government forces in the Philippines were in full retreat. Continued bombardment from the air had bludgeoned the major units that might be able to resist the Japanese advance. Unable to mount any sort of organized defense, let alone counterattack, the most Manila could now hope for was generous peace terms from Tokyo.

Colonel Kawasaki had extended the perimeter around the air base and was organizing several strike battalions to begin the push for Manila. Two other infantry brigades protected the narrow land corridor on the Bataan Highway as the column of supplies continued to arrive by sea. Cargo vessels carrying trucks, foodstuffs, fuel, and ammunition were lined up off shore. Any optimism that Japan might not completely occupy Luzon quickly vanished.

In Brunei the tide of war was flowing the same way. The Japanese army faced only sporadic resistance as it continued its advance in the sultanate. Equipped with advanced night-vision equipment, Japanese armor and marines moved throughout the night. By the early morning hours of August 24, the towns of Kuala Belait, Seria, Kampong Lumut, and Kampong Badas were all under Japanese control. Traffic on the winding Belait River was stopped by Japanese forces outside Kampong Badas. Every major military installation in the country had been destroyed in an intense night-bombing campaign by aircraft from the carriers *Ryoko*, *Meitoku*, and *Amakudari*. And reinforcements continued to arrive.

At the port of Kuala Belait, Japanese transports put ashore units from the regular army. These were the first of what Tokyo expected to be forty thousand regular soldiers who would maintain control of the oil-rich nation. A few days later, the first petroleum engineers and managers arrived to take over production in the oil fields.

A few desperate, but ultimately futile, attempts were made to hinder the invading army. Intrepid combat engineers succeeded in destroying several of the major bridges on the Tutong River, which split the country in two. While it was not much of a victory, it would at least buy a half day of freedom.

Deep worry lines were visible on Admiral Henry Hastings's forehead as he looked through his binoculars at the rough waters ahead. A southerly gale ripped the whole sea white, and the bridge of the *Brisbane* was conspicuously quiet as the fleet proceeded steadily along the Australian west coast. An imposing, resolute figure with a dark tan and robust constitution, Hastings was worried less, however, about the weather than the latest reports from the war in the Pacific. Australian naval headquarters had reported only moments earlier that Brunei was now essentially lost and that Manila would fall in a matter of days. To Hastings that meant that Japan was likely to direct her fury elsewhere, and his Australia was the next probable target.

The latest satellite intelligence from the Americans put Admiral Tarayoko near the Singapore Strait, presumably heading south. Tanaka was already off the coast of Brunei, which meant that five Japanese carriers and a huge supporting armada were only one day from the north coast of Australia.

While Hastings and his fleet had the task of stopping (or at least slowing) any move on Australia, the admiral knew that his fleet would not last long against the enemy tide. The best he could hope for was a showdown in favorable waters such as in the narrow confines of the Arafura Sea, a precarious body of water he knew well. The elaborate labyrinth of reefs and sandbars might provide some sort of advantage. But even under such an ideal set of circumstances, deep down he knew it would not change the outcome of the war.

Plans called for the Australian armada to link up with the Indonesian fleet in the Java Sea. Together, this combined force would face down Tarayoko and Tanaka. But unexpected events quickly changed everything. With a sudden, intense fury, a thunderous explosion ripped through the hull of the *Brisbane*, throwing Hastings four feet across the bridge. It felt like the ship had crashed into a well-rooted dock. As the admiral struggled to his feet, the ship was rocked by another explosion. A thousand yards away, the destroyer *Perth* took a blow port side and began taking on water almost at once.

Hastings picked himself off the floor a second time, and with a solid gash now covering his right cheek, he bellowed to the pilot. "Evasive action! Take evasive action!"

The *Brisbane* began snaking violently in the water. Soon the situation became grave as fires spread and water rushed through the incision on the hull into the belly of the ship. It began listing badly, and Hastings was forced to give the order to abandon ship.

The crew started streaming down ladders, hurrying but not pushing. But the fires continued to rage. The ship began tilting even more severely, and walking ceased to be a form of locomotion. The crew was forced to clamber in order to reach the side.

Meanwhile, on the antisubmarine frigate the *Darwin*, repeated checks of the sonar revealed nothing. Several Sea King helicopters were launched to patrol the area, but their sensors were no more successful. Something had snuck up on the fleet, but it could not be found. In frustration, the *Darwin* launched several antisubmarine missiles, but they disappeared into the dark abyss, never to be heard from again.

The undetected metallic beasts left as quietly as they came, leaving sinking and blazing vessels in their wake. Admiral Hastings boarded the *Darwin* wet but undaunted. He arrived at the bridge just in time to watch his beloved *Brisbane* swallowed up by the water. He had spent six years on her bridge, and now she was gone in what seemed to be just an instant. Only after he bid her farewell did he understand the magnitude of what had transpired. He was the first officer to face the much-reported stealth submarines developed by Tokyo. The cigar-shaped U-boat incorporated some of the same detection-negating principles that had been applied to stealth aircraft. As a twenty-five–year veteran of surface ships, Hastings had never believed that submarines could rule the seas. Now he was not so sure.

Chapter Thirty-one

August 25
northwest of Alice Springs, Australia

A cluster of imposing concrete buildings rose from the desolate floor of the Australian outback, twenty miles from the nearest city. A simple chain-link fence topped with barbed wire ringed the compound while armed guards patrolled the perimeter. The research facility run by the Ministry of Defense included a brain trust of some of Australia's best scientists. Inside the main administrative building, a group of these lofty thinkers had assembled around a simple oblong table to discuss a most-serious topic.

The surprise assault on the Australian fleet meant that a state of war now existed between Australia and Japan. And the fact that the attack had occurred shockingly close to the west coast left Australia vulnerable to a direct assault from Japan. Despite the best efforts of Admiral Hastings, the Australian fleet was badly crippled. The

Perth and *Brisbane* were both lost, and the destroyer *Hobarth* was in dry dock undergoing extensive repairs. After more than a decade of military cutbacks, very little now stood between the enemy and victory. Had it desired to do so, the Japanese fleet could have dropped anchor in Sydney.

It was against this backdrop of urgency that Australian Prime Minister Peter Thurmond had summoned a dozen of the best scientific minds in the country to contemplate the previously unthinkable: how quickly Australia, which had foresworn nuclear weapons for decades, could develop and deploy a nuclear force.

During times of peace, it would have been inconceivable to abandon Australia's nuclear-free tradition. But the desperation of wartime had a way of changing attitudes.

The scientists spent a full twelve hours discussing the technological intricacies of nuclear weapons construction. Following the deliberations, the group recommended that the government proceed at once with the development and deployment of a nuclear arsenal. "The nuclear force should have two components," they advised the prime minister in the secret report, "a strategic capability to strike Japanese soil and a tactical force deployed on aircraft that could target an approaching enemy fleet." Despite the thick air of gloom hanging over all Australia, there was an undercurrent of hope in the report. "The deployment of any such weapons may serve as a deterrent to Japanese aggression and prevent any such attack from occurring."

Prime Minister Thurmond reviewed and pondered the report that afternoon. He approved the research plan but with some reluctance. Minutes after signing the secret directive, he received a phone call from Jack Fowler in Washington. Thurmond took the call with great anticipation. "G'day, Mr. Fowler."

"Hello, Mr. Prime Minister. I am calling because the president has approved the suggestion of a joint operation you discussed earlier with Defense Secretary Bodine. As a gesture of solidarity we would like to bring the 6th Fleet to Sydney and deploy a marine division in your country during the next several weeks."

Thurmond let out a muffled sigh of relief. "Yes, Mr. Fowler, of course. That is precisely what we had in mind. And, Mr. Fowler?"

"Yes, Mr. Prime Minister?"

"Thanks."

Thurmond made no mention of the new research project.

The jungles were hot and muggy, and even the occasional rain offered little relief. Major Fidel Bermudez and the two platoons were resting in the thick undergrowth after an all-night march. After the skirmish at the north end of the air base, Bermudez had moved west, hoping to link up with Filipino units that might still be in the area. But the roads were jammed with Japanese armor and the countryside crawling with infantry. So, Bermudez returned to the hill country.

After a short respite from the march, Bermudez turned on his portable radio. The sullen words of the Philippine president filled the morning air. "...and, therefore, I call on all Filipinos to end the bloodshed. I have received assurances from Tokyo that the rights and interests of the Filipino people will be respected. All units of our armed forces are called upon to end hostilities immediately so that we may guarantee a peaceful, prosperous future for our country."

A dull hopelessness descended on the men as the specter of a future under foreign occupation became real for the first time. Bermudez could sense their will to fight evaporating so he stood atop an old mahogany tree stump and addressed the troops. Though they were simple words, they seemed to resonate with the men. "It's our national duty to fight for our country. I will fight from these hills until I can fight no longer. If you want to lay down your arms and return home to your families, you may do so freely. But if you stay, we will fight together for the freedom of our people and this nation."

A disjointed chatter spread throughout the group, and an informal vote took place: 26 men opted to head for home, but the remaining 183 elected to stay.

Despite the encouragement, Bermudez knew that sheer will

would not be enough to dislodge the enemy. He needed a base of support that could keep his men active. Instantly, his mind flashed to the American embassy in Manila. The capital city was in a panic but he had to take the chance. The military attaché at the embassy was a friend. Perhaps the Americans could be helpful.

Back in Washington, President St. John and his senior advisers were huddled in the White House Situation Room. Few had doubts that the United States was on the path to war. The attack on Hastings' naval forces off the west coast of Australia was the clearest sign thus far of the breadth of Tokyo's ambitions. Kawara's appetite was great—extending from the Kurile Islands in the cold north to Australia in the south. The diversion of the U.S. 6th Fleet to Sydney was America's first material commitment to the allied cause. And now the president wanted to know in greater detail precisely what his military options were.

National Security Adviser Jack Fowler brought the meeting to order, and the president opened with a few words of caution. "This is in all likelihood going to be a naval war. I need to know what our chances for success are and how much it will cost us?"

Admiral Michael Bacon, chief of naval operations, grunted slightly as he cleared his throat. "Mr. President, the strategic situation is quite unnerving, to be frank. We had fifteen carrier battle groups in the 1980s. We are down now to eleven, and four of these are from the 1960s, well beyond the thirty-year safe-operating period. Our naval air power has also been reduced, so we do not have much of a technological edge in the air. We are relying on aviation technologies that in many cases are twenty years old. Japan can match us plane for plane."

"What are you telling me, Admiral?" interjected the president. "Are you saying that we might lose this war?"

Admiral Bacon shook his head. "Mr. President, we still have a larger industrial base, a more substantial nuclear arsenal, and more manpower. But what I am telling you is that this is not going to be a quick, easy victory. And the reason is because we neglected the navy. Whether the American people have the will to sustain a long, difficult war against the Japanese, especially when Japan has not attacked American soil, is a judgment for you to make, not me."

At any other time the president might have dismissed the jab as service politicking, but St. John knew what the data told him. "Admiral, I want a complete assessment of what war might entail and the prospects for success."

"Yes, sir."

Despite his concerns about America's military capabilities, the president inched the United States closer to war when he addressed the nation at 11:00 P.M. eastern standard time.

"My fellow Americans, during the past ten days we have watched with horror as the combined air, land, and sea forces of Japan have attacked the sovereign nations of Taiwan, China, the Philippines, Brunei, and now Australia. It had been our sincere hope that these matters could be resolved by diplomatic means. However, the pattern of aggression has continued unabated and shows no sign of diminishing. I have ordered the deployment of U.S. ground forces to the region. Although it is still our hope to resolve these matters by peaceful means and pull the world away from the precipice of world war, there should be no doubt in anyone's mind that we will not, and cannot, seek peace at any price. This blatant, aggressive conquest of East Asia cannot stand. While it threatens our fundamental security and economic interests, it also overturns the stable order of the Pacific, something that has immense implications for the future of our country. America has always stood for the twin pillars of peace and freedom as the essential supports of any humane society. Let the world know that my commitment is to these same two principles."

Japanese Prime Minister Kawara was seated inside a simple temple shrine drinking tea when an aide handed him a translation of the president's address. Like many of his countrymen, Kawara often came to the island of Shikoku, a holy place for those seeking spiritual solace, to walk its famed trail of tears. After Kawara studied the note, he softly set it down on the shrine's teak-wood plank floor. Amid the peace of the island, Kawara knew that the speech could mean only one thing—war with America.

The peace of Shikoku was an already-fading memory as Kawara immediately boarded a helicopter bound for Tokyo and war. Less than an hour later he was sitting with his cabinet reviewing the news from the front, which was universally promising. Tokyo's grip on the Philippines was firm. And with the exception of sporadic guerrilla activity, there was no armed resistance on the island.

In Brunei the opposition was dimming, like a fire waning for lack of fuel. Most of the army had surrendered; the sultan had fled for the safety of Indonesia. A chain of enormous Japanese transports was bringing what would eventually be seventy thousand troops to manage the sultanate. Oil was beginning to flow from the rich fields in the west, and crude was arriving in Tokyo.

But this review of good news was perfunctory. "The Americans are preparing to enter the war," intoned Defense Minister Yanaga, speaking what everyone knew. "It is only a matter of time. Our best hope is a preemptive strike, to try to knock them out of the Pacific and then negotiate terms."

Finally, Kawara had to agree. All indications were that American forces were positioning for war. Reluctantly, but firmly, he turned to Yanaga. "General, ready the plans."

By the first week of September, the entire Pacific theater was alive with allied activity. At ports in the western United States, from Seattle to San Diego, American soldiers crowded into the bellies of huge troop transports already heavy with supplies and war materiel. Hickam Air Force Base in Hawaii became the hub of an air bridge which ferried troops and equipment from the continental United States to Australia. But despite the activity, moving the troops was a slow, laborious process, far too slow under the circumstances.

America had dramatically reduced its overseas presence in the years following the end of the Cold War. By the year 2000 more than 90 percent of its military power was based in the continental United States which meant that America would have to rely on air and sealift capabilities to project power and deal with strategic threats. Unfortunately, U.S. "lift" budgets had been slashed so more hardware now had to be moved with fewer transports.

On September 4 the first elements of the British fleet docked at Sydney, Australia, and Wellington, New Zealand. Britain's rich, deep historical ties with both countries had evoked a strong sense of duty at 10 Downing Street. A British armada on duty in the Indian Ocean had been diverted to the Pacific in the earliest hours of the conflict. The force included three destroyers, four cruisers, and the carrier HMS *Ark Royal.*

But most eyes were on the progress of the U.S. 6th Fleet, diverted from its regular assignment in the Mediterranean to the Pacific. After taking on supplies at Diego Garcia, the fleet pressed on for Australia to bolster the Anglo-Australian fleet symbolically as well as militarily.

In the late afternoon of September 5, commanding officer Admiral Donald Swarsky sat on the bridge eagerly consuming the latest satellite intelligence, the coast of Sumatra just visible in the distance. The photos were an ominous warning to the 6th Fleet. Digital imagery from a KH-11 satellite launched into polar orbit a week earlier placed Admiral Tanaka and his fleet in the nearby Java Sea. The admiral was probably positioned to finish off the remnants of the combined Malaysian and Indonesian navies. Sixth Fleet reconnaissance aircraft now put the Japanese fleet barely four hundred miles away, far too close for comfort.

Tactical intelligence indicated that Tokyo was taking a keen interest in the movements of the U.S. fleet. The USS *Ticonderoga* had detected several faint sonar signals that could be underwater vessels shadowing the fleet. Still no state of war existed with Tokyo, and the official opinion from the Pentagon was that Japanese forces were unlikely to strike American vessels.

The several thousand-mile-long journey had sustained a predictable tempo since the fleet left the Mediterranean. But off the coast of Indonesia, everything changed in an instant.

"Incoming!" a voice bellowed over the intercom on the *Eisenhower*. First Lieutenant Mike Walters activated the alarm as sonar detected the launch of several torpedoes three thousand yards away. The tin fish closed rapidly before slamming broadside into the *Ticonderoga*. With four more torpedoes soon on the way, the cruiser *Yorktown* was the next victim. The United States and Japan were at war.

A flock of U.S. Navy helicopters were dispatched to the area and hovered only a few feet above the crest of the waves while dropping sonar buoys. They detected a slight pulse just north of the fleet and half a dozen antisubmarine torpedoes were released, plunging into the dark abyss. A few minutes later, two distant thumps were audible. The sonar images then faded just as suddenly as they had arrived.

Aboard the *Ticonderoga* and *Yorktown* the situation was desperate. Crews shut down compartments to contain the damage. Though the *Yorktown* began taking on water, the leaks were finally plugged. The *Ticonderoga* suffered a worse fate, eventually slipping underneath the surface of the water to rest on the ocean floor.

Admiral Swarsky immediately went to the COMLINK to issue an emergency report to PACOM headquarters in Hawaii. As he began his urgent message to Admiral Bacon, he was interrupted by a report from an EC-2A reconnaissance plane flying off the coast of Java. The crew reported that three Japanese strike wings were flying south. Swarsky sounded the alarm at once. The race was on to get as many navy fighters in the air as possible. With the *Ticonderoga* at the sea's bottom and the *Yorktown* limping behind, nearly everything now rested on the pilots aboard the carriers *Eisenhower* and *Theodore Roosevelt*. Admiral Tanaka now had what he hoped for: a straight air war with the Americans.

Commander Graham Pierson and the WSO behind him felt the force of the catapult and the thrust of the engines as the eighty

thousand-pound aircraft was propelled into the air. His F-14 Tomcat was the first off the deck of the *Eisenhower*. Though the F-14
was weighed down with AIM-120 AMRAAMs and Sidewinders,
the twenty thousand-pound thrust engines kept the iron chariot
sprinting through the air. Tactical intelligence updates from the
EC-2A aircraft indicated that the size of the Japanese force continued to grow. Even with the entire compliment of fighters from
the *Theodore Roosevelt* and *Eisenhower*, American pilots would be
outnumbered by more than 3 to 1.

Pierson's 52nd Squadron took the lead of the interdiction group.
One hundred sixty miles south of Java, they picked up the enemy on
air-to-air radar. As the two forces closed to thirty-five nautical
miles, Pierson wanted to make sure he got the first shot, ordering
the launch of AMRAAMs. The terminally active radar guided the
projectiles toward their targets at Mach 4.2. In the cockpits of the
Japanese FX fighters, the threat warning indicators (TWIs) began
wailing like mad and the ECMs were activated. Like startled birds,
the planes veered off in radically different directions. Yet, evasive
action failed to shake the predatory missiles. As they hit their
targets, the laser-proximity fuses ignited, lighting up the sky with a
series of flashes and clap explosions.

The American Tomcats continued to rise in the twilight and prepared for close-range combat. Japanese aircraft regrouped.

Since air combat is about predicting the enemy's future position,
Pierson took his plane into a slow climb and banked south in lag
pursuit of an FX fighter. The commander selected his angle perfectly and closed to within a mile before his WSO launched several
Sidewinders. One connected, sending another plane into the sea.

As another Japanese fighter flew directly in his flight path,
Pierson kicked on his afterburners and closed quickly. Now only
four thousand feet away, the 20-mm Vulcan cannon sprang to life,
spitting one hundred shells every second at the enemy fuselage.
There was a wisp of smoke as the plane leveled off before diving
into the ocean.

But in the zeal of the hunt Pierson failed to notice that the odds had considerably shifted against him. Half the Tomcats had been hit, and the enemy now had him in its sights. With his TWI buzzing, the commander glanced over his shoulder and caught a fleeting glimpse of an FX fighter closing fast. Once the hunter, he was now the hunted. Instinctively, he manipulated the stick slowly, putting the plane on a flat trajectory. He then jerked the stick back while pushing on the afterburners, which offered a whopping twenty-five thousand pounds of thrust in each engine. In an instant he was inverted and flying in the opposite direction. The aircraft gracefully rolled upright while Pierson centered the stick. The perfectly executed Immelman Turn had put the FX fighter right in his crosshairs.

The two planes rushed headlong toward each other with cannons blazing. Pierson banked to the left and saw his nemesis skid toward the ocean. But as he checked the HUD, he saw his fuel gauge plunging. He looked out the west side of the canopy and saw the fuel tank in the wing leaking badly. Calmly, he calculated the fuel supply and distance. He knew he would not make it home, so he headed north for the island of Sumatra, where he landed his plane in a green field.

The battle in the skies over the empty ocean south of Indonesia was the most intensive air war in fifty years. From the ground it appeared as if angry swarms of bees had turned on one another, pulsating and striking with blind fury. When it was over, the skies were clear of American planes. Although five heavily damaged F-14s made emergency landings in Indonesia, most of the Tomcats descended like fiery comets into the sea. Japanese casualties were also high. Barely a dozen aircraft remained. But Commander Hiro Watanabe now had a clear path to the U.S. 6th Fleet, and he wanted to claim an American carrier.

Admiral Swarsky witnessed the entire drama on radar courtesy of data supplied by American reconnaissance aircraft. He prepared the crew for the looming assault and wondered how much damage the huge carrier could sustain. Fire- and damage-control crews were fully mobilized, waiting for the worst.

As the Japanese force closed to within one hundred miles of the 6th Fleet, Commander Watanabe led his squadron into the descent, leveling off at four thousand feet and ordering release of their long-range stand-off attack missiles. What had been a contest of human courage and pilot cunning was now an electronic war. The missile guidance systems used radar to home in on the massive carriers, while the 6th Fleet activated the full complement of ECMs in an attempt to jam the guidance systems. Although most of the projectiles fell harmlessly into the choppy waters, seven found their target, the flight deck and hangar of the *Eisenhower*. The explosions shattered the metallic ligaments of the ship.

Over the course of the next several hours, the *Eisenhower* became a torrent of smoke and fire. Major portions of the carrier were shut down to contain the damage as courageous crew members fought to keep the inferno from spreading. Swarsky stood on the bridge in clothes grimy with smoke, determined to make it to Australia and avenge his defeat. Three hundred miles away aboard the Japanese carrier *Hokkaido*, Admirals Tarayoko and Nagarito celebrated with saki as they greeted the returning pilots from the strike group.

Tokyo had elected to move decisively against the Americans. As Japanese fighters pummeled the *Eisenhower*, Admiral Tanaka's fleet closed in on Guam, the last remaining American outpost in the central Pacific west of Hawaii. The admiral held his carriers south of Guam as a detachment of landing craft and escorts proceeded along the western coast. As the landing force reached its staging area, Tanaka ordered the carriers to launch their planes while the missile cruisers released a salvo of Tomahawks aimed at the limited American air defense systems. The aircraft were expected to deal swiftly with a small American air group at Agana Naval Air Station and Andersen Air Force Base. The redoubtable Commander Ohashi, who had commanded the air war over Brunei, was again the flight commander.

Ohashi led two squadrons of fighter-bombers along the eastern shore of Guam before banking west at Catalina Point and proceeding to Andersen Air Force Base. Meanwhile, the Tomahawk missiles slammed into Agana Naval Air Station, destroying a fighter group of half a dozen planes. The 1,200 U.S. Marines on Guam would now have to fight alone.

From the ground, American Marines could see the Japanese fighters dodging in and out of the towering cumulus clouds, occasionally diving down over the island to drop their ordnance. The drone of the planes became almost mind numbing but was soon broken by the echo of naval guns and the rumble of landing craft. A large contingent of Japanese marines was hitting the beaches off Ritidian Point.

Colonel Akir Ashara and a group of 2,500 men were put ashore just north of Andersen Air Force Base. This was the vanguard of what was expected to be the nearly 10,000 troops Tokyo expected to deploy in Guam during the next several weeks. Ashara had strict orders—seize control of northern Guam and hold it at all costs.

The amphibious force moved inland under the cover of Japanese fighter-bombers. By nightfall they reached Andersen, where the U.S. Marines had deployed in recent weeks. Strike aircraft dropped ordnance on troop positions throughout the night. The Americans fought valiantly for two full days, taking 80 percent casualties. On September 6 they surrendered.

Chapter Thirty-two

September 8
the White House

S hort of sleep for days, President St. John sat half-awake in a wing chair in the Oval Office reading the latest intelligence report, his feet propped on the ottoman and a large cup of coffee in his right hand. His tie was loose.

Japanese forces had stormed Guam four days earlier, and the island was now firmly under their control. A formal state of war existed between Tokyo and Washington.

NIE 82-F-909
9/7/07 am

JAPAN: TROOP DEPLOYMENTS

Philippines
Ground forces

28,000 regular army
6,000 marines
60 artillery pieces
32 tanks

Aircraft

30 attack helicopters
32 FX fighter aircraft
18 F-15 fighter aircraft

Brunei
Ground forces

21,000 regular army
3,000 marines
120 artillery pieces
41 tanks

Aircraft

33 FX fighter aircraft
21 F-15 fighter aircraft

Guam
Ground forces

2,200 marines
50 artillery pieces

| Aircraft | 4 FX fighter aircraft |

Bonin Islands

Ground forces	700 marines
	6 SSM sites
Aircraft	4 vertical takeoff and landing
	(VTOL) fighter aircraft

March Island

Ground forces	300 marines
	4 SSM sites
Aircraft	2 VTOL fighter aircraft

Spratly Islands

| Ground forces | 600 marines (offshore) |
| Aircraft | VTOL carrier in vicinity—12 fighters |

The president casually laid the report on the side table and swallowed some coffee. The loss of Guam changed things considerably. The United States now had no forward bases in the Pacific theater. In the early stages of the war, the country would have to rely on naval power until a new foothold could be gained somewhere in the Pacific. The U.S. Navy would need to take command of the seas before establishing a permanent forward base of operations, something critical to sustaining the war effort. St. John took one more sip before heading to a special meeting with his military advisers in the White House Situation Room.

The room was a beehive of activity as admirals and generals talked with each other and by telephone with their offices to get the latest update on the Pacific War. As the president entered the room, the chatter subsided and those assembled took their seats. St. John greeted Admiral Roger Hitchcock, the commander in chief, Pacific (CINCPAC), and then took his place at the head of the table.

"All right, gentlemen," urged Jack Fowler as he convened the meeting. "Thanks for coming—let's get started."

Hitchcock began in a calm monotone, laying out PACOM's proposed strategy for executing the war. He went through a series of charts and maps about logistics in the Pacific and the current

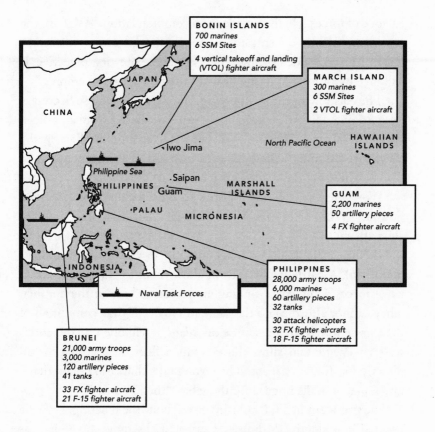

BONIN ISLANDS
700 marines
6 SSM Sites

4 vertical takeoff and landing
(VTOL) fighter aircraft

MARCH ISLAND
300 marines
6 SSM Sites

2 VTOL fighter aircraft

JAPAN

CHINA

HAWAIIAN
ISLANDS

North Pacific Ocean

·Iwo Jima

Philippine Sea

·Saipan
PHILIPPINES   Guam

MARSHALL
ISLANDS

GUAM
2,200 marines
50 artillery pieces

4 FX fighter aircraft

·PALAU   MICRONESIA

INDONESIA

⚓ Naval Task Forces

PHILIPPINES
28,000 army troops
6,000 marines
60 artillery pieces
32 tanks

30 attack helicopters
32 FX fighter aircraft
18 F-15 fighter aircraft

BRUNEI
21,000 army troops
3,000 marines
120 artillery pieces
41 tanks

33 FX fighter aircraft
21 F-15 fighter aircraft

Deployment of Japanese Forces

balance of forces. He then made his recommendation. "We have the capability—if we concentrate our sea and airlift assets—to retake Guam," he concluded firmly. "This should be our first objective. It will give us a foothold in the heart of the new Japanese empire."

"The Australians think otherwise," interjected Defense Secretary Tom Bodine. He had returned only two days earlier from an official visit to Canberra. "They suggest we move against the fleet in the Singapore Strait as a prelude to an invasion of Brunei. Success in Brunei will bring down the entire house of cards."

"Won't that stretch our logistics to the breaking point?" asked Fowler. "What does the MAC [Military Airlift Command] say about Brunei?"

Hitchcock shook his head, his thin lips curled. "It will in all likelihood fail. A battle in Brunei will allow them to concentrate their naval forces while also bringing air power to bear in the conflict. They cannot afford to do the same in Guam. If they commit all of their naval forces to the defense of Guam, it will open up the entire western Pacific and allow the combined fleet in Australia to sail directly for Tokyo's harbor. They won't take that risk. Guam first," he said jabbing his finger into the table, "then Brunei."

The president had sat stoically throughout the meeting. Now he nodded confidently. "Admiral, I agree. Let's move on Guam as quickly as possible. I want to hit them hard and fast."

Hitchcock concurred. "Yes, Mr. President. But before we act we need to take out their photoreconnaissance satellite over the central Pacific. As long as they can track the movement of our fleet, they will be able to counteract our moves. If we blind them, we gain a tremendous strategic advantage."

The president noticed Jack Fowler shaking his head skeptically. "Jack, what are you thinking?"

"That makes me very nervous. Taking out their satellite is a serious escalation. They may interpret it as a prelude to launching a debilitating nuclear strike. At the very least they will retaliate by attempting to take out our satellites."

"We need to do this, Mr. President," pleaded Hitchcock. "If we don't, it's as good as telegraphing our next blow. We are talking about dooming perhaps thousands of our soldiers to a needless death."

The president sat back and reflected. "Let me get back to you on that, Admiral."

Three cigar-shaped submarines crept ever so slowly below the surface of the dark, tempestuous Philippine Sea. Just minutes earlier, the USS *Atlanta* had received an encrypted very low frequency (VLF) radio transmission, via satellite, from naval command in Pearl Harbor. It was the latest intelligence on the movement of a convoy of Japanese supply ships bound for Guam. The leviathan cargo ships sat low in the water packed full of men and materiel.

The VLF transmission was decoded by an onboard computer and printed in plain English on a Teletype machine. It included data on the predicted course of the convoy culled from satellite intelligence. The U.S. Navy subs *Atlanta*, *Corpus Christi*, and *Annapolis* were lurking just forty miles west of Ritidian Point, waiting to pounce.

In the sonar room, which was bathed in blue light to enhance the cathode-ray tube displays, sonarmen tuned out the world and concentrated on the video screens in front of them. Sonar is a tricky matter. The average speed of sound in water is about 4,757 feet per second, or four times faster than the speed of sound in the air. But it can vary greatly depending on the precise combination of temperature, water pressure, and salinity. Finding and tracking the enemy is both science and art.

The sonarmen waited patiently for the slightest indication of ship activity in the area. After what seemed an eternity of stable pinging sounds, Navy Ensign Patrick James was the first to hear it: the distant murmur of propellers churning on the surface. With pen and paper in hand, he began gauging the turncounts (the number of turns of the shaft per knot of speed) of the first vessel to determine what sort of craft he had discovered. The number was low—it was probably a transport. He then gauged the other acoustical readings, including several ships with rapid turncounts. The experienced Ensign James found what they had been searching for—a procession of cargo vessels with warships in escort. It had to be the Japanese supply convoy.

James swiveled in his chair and, with his large fingers, rapidly typed into the keyboard. He relayed the information to Mark Short, his executive officer. A few minutes later "Man the battle stations!" boomed over the intercom.

Off-duty sailors who were resting in their bunks awakened immediately and jumped into blue coveralls before rushing to their stations. Using preliminary data from Ensign James, the plotters in the fire-control room began determining the range, course, and speed of the armada. They then established the angle of the ships' bows, ocean current, and speed on their own navigational computers. Twelve minutes later, the "fire solution" was complete and the launch sequence could begin.

Confidently, Short gave the order to prepare for launch. Within seconds the hydraulically operated racks in the firing tubes sprang to life, whining as the Mark-48 torpedoes were loaded into place. He then gave the final order to fire. The keys were turned, and in an instant six Mark-48 torpedoes were spit out of the launch tubes and gliding through the cold, black water toward the enemy fleet. In the sonar room, Ensign James continued to listen cautiously. The torpedoes swam leisurely at first as the guidance systems searched for their targets. But after a few minutes, they picked up speed, and with the target identified, closed for the kill. James could hear the turn of the torpedo screws, which sounded a lot like a commuter train. Next he heard a series of deep, rich thunderous crashes as the Mark-48s slammed into the hulls of the enormous Japanese transports. Amidst the desperate cry of ripping steel, he counted six explosions in all. The dramatic sneak attack had succeeded.

Short was not content with sounds, he wanted to see exactly what had transpired on the surface. Peeking through the periscope, he saw four transport ships ablaze in the early morning light. But he also spotted two Japanese cruisers shifting course, straight for the

Atlanta. With the torpedo tubes reloaded, a quartet of Mark-48s were sent forth, claiming two more transports just minutes later.

While the second launch had succeeded, it further revealed to the Japanese cruisers the location of the *Atlanta*. Commander Short took the massive U-boat into a deep dive, but the cruisers were closing fast. Meanwhile, the *Corpus Christi* and the *Annapolis* had been waiting for precisely this moment. Both sonar rooms had been tracking the faster turncounts and knew the location of both the *Akiro* and *Feiji*. As the cruisers closed, both subs sent four Mark-48s straight at them. Thirty seconds later, they scored direct broadside hits.

For the next thirty minutes, the three American subs prowled the night waters of the Pacific for the remnants of the convoy. When the engagement was over, the entire enemy convoy had slipped underwater and was resting at the bottom of the sea.

American subs were active not only off Guam but also near the Philippine island of Luzon. The USS *Cavalla*, specially equipped for sensitive special operations, had slipped into the waters off Luzon in the calm, still night. A mile offshore and thirty-five feet below the surface, the *Cavalla* released several swimmer delivery vehicles (SDVs). They hummed quietly through the ebony waters, barely disturbing the surface as they traveled underwater toward shore. The vehicles carried two dozen men and equipment. Twenty feet from the beach in a rough, white water surf, the men detached themselves from the SDVs and ran for a thicket of bushes along the sandy shore.

First into the bushes was Captain Tom Brown, a twelve-year veteran of the Navy Sea, Air, and Land forces (SEALS). He climbed out of his rubber suit and collected his gear from a large water-resistant pack. With the others from the team, he slipped into the wilderness.

The SEALS were expected to link up with Filipino guerrillas who reportedly had been operating from the mountains. Working together, they were expected to harass the occupying army and collect vital intelligence. If war plans went according to the blueprint, allied armies might be landing on Luzon by Christmas.

The United States had begun a counteroffensive in small, guarded steps. The Japanese resupply convoy to Guam had been intercepted, and special forces were now establishing a base camp on Luzon. But the most serious blow of the day had not yet been landed.

At Hickam Air Force Base in Hawaii, Air Force Colonel David Mattox sat in the cockpit of his modified F-15 Eagle staring at an empty runway. Although the Eagle looked normal otherwise, it was carrying a single missile on its belly. It was also specially equipped with sophisticated communications equipment that allowed the pilot to maintain a computer data link not only with PACOM in Honolulu but with the North American Air Defense Command (NORAD). Feeling restless, Mattox gave the instruments a visual once-over and inspected the fuel, hydraulics, and navigational systems. He then ignited the massive engines for takeoff.

As the engines propelled the plane into the lonely night sky, a bright plume was visible in the distance. Mattox gradually climbed to fifteen thousand feet, where he checked the computer data link. The system gave him the clearance to proceed, and he put the plane into a steep ascent. Pushing the bird through the clouds, he was flying nearly vertically before leveling off at sixty thousand feet.

The WSO seated behind him now went to work on the weapons console in front of him. Strapped to the belly of the plane was an air-launched miniature vehicle (ALMV), a satellite-killer consisting of a terminal homing warhead boosted into space by a two-stage rocket. The first stage was a modified short-range attack missile (SRAM) to propel the missile into space. The second stage was an Altair III booster to direct the warhead to its final destination. The warhead was a complex device consisting of eight cryogenically cool infrared telescopes, a laser gyro, and sixty-four small computer-controlled rockets to make the final course adjustments. The warhead would home in on the heat emitted by the satellite and then slam into the satellite, destroying it.

Timing, however, was everything. The WSO would have precious few seconds to ensure that the missile was launched at the proper time. The missile's guidance system required liquid helium and nitrogen to cool it during flight. These compounds depleted during the mission. If the plane was off course and the missile launch delayed, the guidance system would probably overheat. The margin of error was close to nil.

It was Mattox's job to make sure he found the precise navigational point at which the WSO would launch the missile. The colonel took one final reading from the high-frequency data link on the aircraft wing tips for any last-minute corrections. There were none. Mattox watched anxiously as he crossed into the launch point, activating the launch indicator. With the singular twitch of his finger, the WSO sent the missile on its way. Looking through the canopy, both men saw it rocket into the darkness of space.

Mattox began a slow descent for the trip back to base. An hour later, approaching Hickam at ten thousand feet, he received a radio message from the ground. "We confirm one kill, over."

Tokyo was now blind, at least in one eye. The Japanese armed forces no longer had a window on events in the central Pacific.

Chapter Thirty-three

September 22
Guam

As night turned to twilight in the skies over Guam, Captain George Gordon tugged one last time on his standard T1OB dorsal pack. The drone of the jet engines on the transport had been constant since the force had left the continental United States—now more than twenty hours ago. The captain was anxious to get out into the open night air. Gordon and his unit from the 82nd Airborne would be the first group to directly engage the enemy, the lead echelon in the bold counterstrike against Tokyo. Success in the operation was critical. If the battle for Guam was lost,

**U.S. Marines hit the beaches in an effort to liberate
Japanese-occupied Guam.**

the allies would have a difficult time mounting any serious offensive
in the Pacific.

A day earlier, U.S. submarines had fired Tomahawk cruise missiles at Japanese planes deployed at Andersen Air Force Base. None
of these aircraft were now operational. The U.S. 7th Fleet had been
moved into the area, and a team of Navy SEALS had been secretly
dropped on the island to serve as reconnaissance. Now it was up to
the soldiers to finish the task.

Two minutes from the drop zone, Gordon gave a silent nod to his
men. When the order came to jump, the troopers spilled out of the
Starlifter into the cool air. From the ground they appeared as specks
in the sky, like birds gliding on white silk toward the earth. They
descended four thousand feet before touching down on the rich,
reddish clay soil in central Guam.

Gordon detached from his chute and checked his wristwatch: it
was 5:37 A.M. An ambient light was visible in the east. He had only a
few hours to organize his men and march north to link up with a
Marine Expeditionary Force (MEF) that was landing twenty miles
away at Catalina Point. The rendezvous had already been staked out

by the reconnaissance unit. It was the small town of Yigo, a provincial village that seemed wholly unaffected by the occupation. Moving by truck and foot, the troopers arrived promptly at 9:20 A.M.

The village would serve as the base of operations for the campaign. Captain Gordon created a crude command post inside a concrete municipal building to serve as headquarters. A satellite uplink was established, and he began to review the latest intelligence data provided by PACOM. In the distance the captain heard several rumbles and then three booming explosions in rapid succession. He moved to the window just in time to hear the scream of a jet fighter overhead. He checked his wristwatch and looked out the window, where he caught the glimpse of a U.S. Air Force F-22 fighter banking elegantly over Yigo.

During the past twenty-four hours, the U.S. 7th Fleet had been harassing Japanese forces at Andersen with Tomahawks and fighter-bombers. Now the heavy stuff had come. The F-22s and a stealth bomber squadron had taken off from Hickam and had been refueled at forty thousand feet for the more than three thousand–mile, one-way flight. They had arrived on schedule to begin the job of softening up the entrenched marines.

Air operations gave the United States a tremendous advantage because Tokyo had no operational aircraft in the vicinity. And satellite intelligence put Admiral Nagarito and his carriers six hundred miles west of Guam in the Philippine Sea streaming east, presumably to relieve the embattled marines.

Admiral Bo Curtis and the 7th Fleet had the responsibility of making sure that Nagarito's planes never got there. The fleet began air operations with two ATOs in place. The first consisted of supporting the ground offensive. But the fallback ATO provided for an air strike on Nagarito's fleet. Admiral Curtis would make the call as to which ATO would be in operation and when.

For two hours the admiral watched planes take off from the flight deck for strike missions over Guam and then return for more ordnance and fuel. Although the air operations were inflicting serious damage on Japanese ground positions, satellite intelligence indicated that Nagarito was continuing to push east and was now only 550 miles west of Guam. Curtis had a critical decision to make: should he continue air operations to support the ground attack on Guam, or was it better to throw everything at Nagarito to destroy his fleet? He wrestled with the decision for only a moment. The prospect of knocking Nagarito out of the war was simply too inviting. Curtis wanted to avenge the attack on the *Eisenhower* and also ensure that Nagarito could not intervene in the battle for Guam. He calmly but urgently ordered the second ATO be put into operation.

Two hours of heavy air activity had allowed U.S. forces on Guam to make substantial progress. With the enemy pinned down, they had moved along the main road from Yigo to Andersen. Several miles from the enemy position, troopers from the 82nd headed west through the scrub grass as the U.S. Marines proceeded north.

The core of the Japanese defensive position was a series of hastily built trenches running along the southern edge of the air base. There was little armor or artillery. And what had been deployed was knocked out by aerial bombing. The task for U.S. ground forces was to evict the enemy from their fortified trenches.

The U.S. Army and Marine artillery units rapidly prepared their systems for operation and then began placing fire down on enemy positions. Several squads from the 82nd moved forward, carrying the seventy-eight–pound M252 81-mm mortars and setting them up in the brush. The baseplate, barrel, mount, and sight—each carried by one man—were locked together, and within moments a dozen were adding to the chorus of artillery. The artillery and mortar barrage heralded the initiation of the ground war. The tempo of mortar fire was slow at first—hardly four rounds per minute. But when the full attack commenced, they reached their zenith with the mortar teams firing thirty shells per minute. While the rapid fire generated an immense amount of friction on the barrels, the exterior casing had been helically grooved to dissipate the heat.

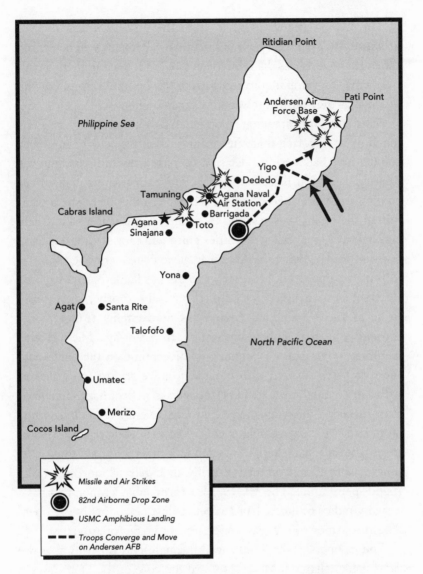

U.S. Operations for the Liberation of Guam

The U.S. Marines closed in from the east, spearheaded by a group of M60 tanks. (These old reliable war-horses weighed thirty thousand pounds less than the formidable M1, making them a realistic tank for amphibious operations.) The tanks grunted and groaned as they pushed toward the Japanese line.

An enemy outpost radioed Colonel Ashara at headquarters, alerting him to the fact that the ground offensive had begun. The colonel now had a critical decision to make: should he commit the reserves to his left flank to blunt the move, or was the main attack coming from elsewhere? Fearing a breach in the line, Ashara committed the bulk of his reserves to counter the initial attack. Using antitank weapons, heavy machines guns, and mortars, the Japanese position held, slowing the American advance to a crawl.

But by committing his reserves to his left flank, Ashara exposed the right flank to direct attack from the 82nd Airborne, which swept in from the west. Four Armored Gun Systems (AGSs) burst through the chain-link fence lining the runway. The vehicle's aluminum-alloy hull was augmented by ceramic on the flanks, and the turret was covered with modular passive armor—one layer to withstand frontal cannon shots, the next to deflect hand-held antitank rockets. Following the AGSs were several APCs. Positioned atop the large, boxy vehicles were soldiers sporting Mk-19-3 automatic grenade launchers. The gunners pummeled anything that moved with 40-mm grenades, firing in bursts of more than 375 rounds per minute. The Mk-19-3 is a formidable weapon that has a casualty radius of more than 16 feet against personnel in the open. The anti-armor rounds can penetrate two inches of armor.

The troopers of the 82nd roved through light opposition as the right flank collapsed. Moving toward the core of the line, Captain Gordon and his men approached the skeletal remains of a collection of buildings at the center of the air base. There the enemy resistance stiffened. Near the control tower, Lieutenant Joe Price and his platoon traded heavy gunfire with a half-strength company holed up in the crumbled remains of a supply building. Price used the breach-loaded grenade launcher attached to his M-16 to fire several 40-mm explosives into the building. Yet the unseen enemy continued to resist.

There was a strong odor of cordite in the air, and a grayish-white smoke was now drifting through the area. The rattle of machine gun fire was interrupted by the steady thump–thump of the grenade launchers. Price was mystified as to how he might draw the enemy out when suddenly, fifty yards to his left, a Bradley Fighting Vehicle rolled forward, banging its way through the debris. Since the Bradley could survive direct hits from light antitank weapons and heavy 30-mm cannons, it led the push forward, the Coaxial machine gun firing a burst every few seconds. It rumbled toward the building as the gunner went to work with the 25-mm Bushmaster cannon. Price and his men followed in behind the Bradley, firing into the building's dark corners.

Several miles to the east, U.S. Marines were still pinned down as the tottering enemy continued to stubbornly resist from foxholes and crude fortifications. Company C surreptitiously moved north through the undergrowth in a effort to outflank the enemy line. When the company finally closed in from the north, the line shattered. Dispersed small units fled west, only to be met by the troopers of the 82nd Airborne which had worked its way across the airfield. Now overwhelmed and encircled, more than 200 weary Japanese marines dropped their weapons and surrendered. As the last of the guns fell silent, Lieutenant Joe Price let out a sigh. Guam was once again an American outpost, and Tokyo had suffered its first territorial defeat of the war. But 261 American soldiers died in the assault.

Two squadrons of the U.S. Navy screamed over the island of Guam during the most brutal phase of the fighting. The F-14s were pushing west at one thousand feet. Commander Bill Bergstram and the attack group had a straightforward mission—clear the skies of enemy fighters to make room for strike aircraft. For Bergstram this was a mission of uncertainty. How capable were the Japanese pilots?

How would their aircraft match up against the aging but still robust F-14s?

About twenty miles west of Guam he scanned the instruments through his helmet-mounted sight, jostled the stick on the quad-redundant fly-by-wire flight control system, and let out a deep sigh of anxiety. "Waiting," he told his WSO, "is the most difficult part."

The enemy was lurking just over the horizon as satellite intelligence put the fleet only three hundred nautical miles west of Guam. The skies were rainy and overcast, so visibility was a problem. Suddenly, there was a flash on Bergstram's long-range air-to-air radar. A group of enemy aircraft was eighty miles due west and closing fast. He alerted the other pilots before clicking his air-to-air radar to the multiple-target tracking mode. Since it was unclear whether the enemy had detected the American Tomcats, Bergstram split the squadrons in the hope of giving someone a superior angle of attack.

The 367th Squadron banked south and leveled off five miles south of Commander Bergstram's 244th. The Japanese squadrons appeared to have stayed on course, indicating they were ready for battle. As the distance between the opposing forces narrowed, Bergstram ordered the activation of the AMRAAMs. Although they were the most potent air-to-air weapons in the world, timing was everything. The AMRAAM has a range of forty nautical miles. If you launch too soon, the enemy can turn and fly out of range. But if you wait too long, the AMRAAM is less capable and the enemy might put you in his crosshairs first.

When his distance from the American Tomcats closed to forty nautical miles, Commander Hiro Kyto sent the 57th Squadron into a climb, rising rapidly into the thick cumulus clouds at twenty-five thousand feet, hoping to sow confusion and gain the high frontier in the pending air war. But Bergstram was watching the move on radar and countered by doing the same. Then, at twenty miles out, he ordered the launch of AMRAAMs in a single spasm of pyrotechnics.

Bergstram and his 244th banked slightly to the north, anticipating evasive action by Kyto. The guess was a good one. As they came within visual distance, they saw the AMRAAMs crashing into enemy aircraft with tremendous force. Bergstram and two other Tomcats immediately went into a low yo-yo—a tight, curving dive to increase the closure rate on survivors.

Kyto withstood the opening volley and screamed north in a desperate effort to flee. Bergstram rolled into his bank and dove slightly to keep up his speed. It was a perfectly executed move as he climbed back onto Kyto's geometrical plane. The Tomcat spit out two Sidewinder missiles which found their target. Kyto went into a whip stall before falling into a steep dive toward the ocean, his fuselage consumed by flames.

For twenty-eight minutes, men and their machines waged a deadly duel over the Pacific. When the last gasp of battle was breathed, the entire Japanese squadron of twenty-one planes had been lost. Twelve American planes were claimed by enemy fire.

Bergstram and the remaining pilots of the 244th and 367th regrouped and began a patrol of the area. The carriers with the 7th Fleet began launching fighter-bombers packed with heavy anti-ship ordnance packages. Vengeance was very much on Admiral Curtis's mind. The 7th Fleet was now northwest of Ritidian Point, pushing westward at twenty-five knots.

Shortly after 3:00 P.M., an EC-2A reconnaissance aircraft located Nagarito's fleet. Bergstram and the Tomcats were dispatched to the area. They noticed only one carrier—not the expected two, which meant the fleet was without air cover and wide open to attack. Nagarito's second carrier had been dispatched to the Java Sea to prepare for an expected allied push on Brunei.

Bergstram radioed the strike aircraft and soon a squadron of F-18 Hornets was on its way. Cruising toward the fleet at 10,000 feet, a quartet of Hornets concentrated their efforts on the air defense cruisers *Kirin* and *Sapporo*. Sensors in the cockpit warned that the vessels had their phase-array radars switched to a higher pulse rate to develop target solutions on the enemy aircraft. But before the technicians could fire their SAMs, the Hornets released a quartet of HARMs, which descended on the fleet at Mach 2. Seconds later, the 146-pound blast fragmentation warheads exploded, scarring both vessels. But more important, their radars were silenced. Nagarito's once powerful fleet lay defenseless against enemy aircraft.

The American pilots fully pressed their advantage as they dove toward the fleet before dropping anti-ship ordnance. It was essentially a one-sided affair—a defenseless behemoth harassed by enemy aircraft attacking with a vengeance. The carrier eventually stopped dead in the water, killed by what seemed to be dozens of cuts. The U.S. Navy had won the first major naval battle of the Pacific War, and Tokyo had lost its first carrier.

Chapter Thirty-four

September 29
Tokyo

From the old-world confines of his private quarters, Prime Minister Kawara was pouring over the intelligence reports and navigational maps arrayed on his desk. It was just after midnight, and a burning, passionate pride was pushing him to requite the defeat in Guam. But beneath his anger, something else was taking root. For the first time since the outbreak of the war, he felt self-doubt. If the war was fought conventionally, time would be decidedly against him. America had a larger gross national product (GNP) and population base and could outlast Japan in a protracted war. The question was, would the United States have the will to fight a prolonged conflict?

What Kawara yearned for was a decisive battle at the location of his choosing. He wanted to so humiliate the Americans that they would negotiate a settlement. Better still, he wanted to shift the war onto a different level. Victory would not be achieved by attacking the enemy's strength, but by exploiting its weakness. This, for Kawara, was the critical ingredient.

The war effort was now seriously complicated by the destruction of the photoreconnaissance satellite which had been covering the central Pacific. The General Staff was reduced to playing a dangerous guessing game, hoping to locate the true position of the American fleet by speculation. A flash intelligence report from the Foreign Ministry suggested the Americans were engaged in a massive buildup in and around Guam. Presumably, this was to mount an assault on the Philippines. If the report was accurate, it would be exactly the sort of information Tokyo would need to spring a trap for the enemy fleet. But if the report was incorrect, the shift in Japanese naval forces might be a monumental blunder, leaving the growing allied armada in Australia an open path to Brunei or Japan.

Kawara laid the intelligence report on a stack of papers by his side and then reviewed the memo from the General Staff on proposed offensive action against the Americans.

Top Secret
98-J-45622
29 September 2007

1. Missile and aircraft strikes on the allied fleet

Objective: Dramatically reduce the offensive naval capabilities of the allied powers aligned against our country.

Proposal: Use of land-based missiles from Okinawa and mainland Japan, as well as naval aircraft from the fleet, to converge on the allied fleets to substantially weaken the capabilities of their navies. The use of thermonuclear warheads should not be dismissed.

Probability of success: Minimal. Targeting of systems on the moving fleet will be difficult absent the ability to use satellite data. The allied fleet is presently out of range from land-based air assets.

2. Counterattack on Guam

Objective: Remove the American foothold in the central Pacific by retaking the island of Guam.

Proposal: Retaking Guam would significantly weaken the American geostrategic position in the Pacific. By moving Task Force I and III, currently in the South China Sea, to the Philippine Sea, sufficient naval and air power would exist to evict U.S. forces.

Probability of success: Mixed. The United States is likely to continue reinforcing the island, so time is of the essence. The movement of Admirals Tarayoko and Tanaka out of the South China Sea, as well as the reequipping of our forces for an assault on Guam, would take several weeks. The U.S. presence on Guam may have grown considerably by that time.

3. Cyberstrike on United States

Objective: Raise the costs of war for America and hamper the war effort on the home front by disrupting major electronic systems on the continental United States.

Proposal: Generate logic bombs, computer viruses, and other cyberweapons through the Security and Intelligence Command to be activated in the United States.

Probability of success: Substantial. The United States lacks the ability to deal with such a threat, and it will likely demoralize the American people to the point of encouraging a negotiated settlement.

4. Limited nuclear strike on United States

Objective: Force America into a negotiated settlement by launching a limited nuclear strike on select targets in the United States.

Proposal: Launch Japanese ICBMs at militarily significant targets in the United States as a demonstration of our power, compelling Washington to negotiate a settlement.

Probability of success: Mixed. America lacks a BMD, ensuring the complete success of our strike. However, whether such an attack will simply provoke American retaliation and strengthen U.S. resolve is an issue of serious concern.

5. Limited nuclear strike on Australia

Objective: Force Australia to seek a separate peace by launching a limited nuclear strike on targets in Australia.

Proposal: Conduct a limited nuclear strike on Australia and offer an end to hostilities in exchange for exiting the war.

Probability of success: Mixed. How Canberra chooses to respond to a selective nuclear strike remains open to question. The attack may drive a wedge between Canberra and Washington. But it may also strengthen Australia's resolve. The possibility of an American retaliatory strike should not be dismissed entirely.

Kawara set the memo on the table and carefully reviewed the options in silence. In two hours he would meet with his military advisers and make two critical decisions that would fundamentally determine the outcome of the war.

Somewhere above the desolate Pacific in the penetrating darkness of night, a lone U.S. Navy EC-2A reconnaissance aircraft was patrolling the skies in search of enemy aircraft. The twin-turbo-prop Hawkeye was loud and rough, the constant drone of the engines breaking the stillness. Navy Lieutenant Paul Stern was behind the controls of what had been a routine mission. Radar pointed to no enemy activity. The only presence in the waters near Guam was a U.S. convoy moving cargo. Running low on fuel, Stern turned his aircraft for the journey back to the *Nimitz* when a streak of brilliant light pierced the black sky. Stern jerked his head toward the illumination. Soon there were several more flashes racing across the horizon like shooting stars.

Stern immediately radioed back to headquarters. Admiral Curtis, clearly alarmed by the report, dispatched a group of Tomcats and Hornets to investigate.

The reports provoked a frenzy of activity aboard the *Nimitz*. Bleary-eyed and emotionally worn, Commander Bill Bergstram, along with the equally tired members of his squadron, were pulled from their beds. Within an hour, a band of Tomcats and Hornets were in the air trying to uncover the enigma.

At Andersen Air Force Base, the spears of light were no mystery. U.S. soldiers had been sleeping soundly when six white phosphorus warheads exploded near the main runway, generating a cyclone of hellfire and candescence. Dozens of soldiers died instantly. The survivors suffered severe burns and would spend a lifetime dealing with the pain and disfigurement from what had been visited upon them that night.

News from Guam added a sense of extreme urgency to the flight mission. Bergstram led the group north to where the arcs of light had first been detected. After one hour, he detected several unusual structures on a small chain of islands on his air-to-ground radar.

The commander was trying to get a closer look when suddenly a quartet of SAMs burst through the cloud cover. With the TWIs flashing, members of the flight group dropped flares, throwing the heat-seeking missiles off into the blackness. A bit shaken, Bergstram radioed back to the *Nimitz*. "This is Boxer One, Boxer One. We have come under fire. I.D. the location below, over."

In the flight control room aboard the carrier, technicians cross-referenced the coordinates of the Tomcats with computer navigational charts and then radioed back to Bergstram. "Boxer One, Boxer One. We put you near the Bonin Islands, over."

"What do we know about it. Over," he asked calmly, having collected himself.

"We have poor intelligence, Boxer One. Possible Japanese military installation. That's it, over."

Bergstram sighed. Where was good intelligence when you needed it?

The Tomcats rolled to the east, and with radar warning receivers (RWRs) still active, they released several HARMs to take out enemy radar sights. The missiles plunged through the carpet of clouds before erupting below. From ten thousand feet, Bergstram could see the dazzling flashes. The RWRs suddenly went silent.

Bergstram radioed the F-18 Hornets flying nearby. "Boxer Two, Boxer Two, this is Boxer One, over."

"Boxer Two here."

"The highway is free and clear, over."

The Hornets passed over the islands at ten thousand feet, releasing a payload of BLU-109/B bombs. Fashioned with a sharp nose designed to cut through concrete, dirt, or armor, the two thousand-pound bombs exploded after burrowing into fortifications— the perfect device for leveling bunkers. On the first pass the bombs landed with precision on the rooftop of the main bunker. And on the second pass the roof of the headquarters collapsed.

Bergstram and the flight group patrolled the area for twenty minutes, waiting for SAMs as a sign of life below. But Bonin remained quiet, so the weary flight crew headed back to the

Nimitz, their mission complete. At daylight, a reconnaissance aircraft would take pictures to confirm that the guns on Bonin would remain silent.

At 7:00 A.M. General Yanaga strode confidently into the teak-wood meeting room in the prime minister's office. The general had become increasingly vocal in recent days, issuing public statements about certain victory, some of which appeared to be veiled criticism of Kawara. "Defeat will come only if we lack the resolve to make courageous decisions in the execution of the war," he had said on national television.

The general took his place at the conference table as the prime minister began deliberations. "You have all seen the options memo presented by the General Staff. I have made some preliminary decisions about our next step. But I would like to hear from my advisers first."

Since the beginning of the war, Foreign Minister Kazio Nukazawa had purposely and scrupulously avoided injecting his views into major discussions over military strategy. A cultured, polite man with occidental tastes and mannerisms, Nukazawa felt he could no longer be silent. He spoke in clipped words and a brutally efficient syntax. "Any of these steps represents a dramatic escalation of the conflict. We must remember that our national goals were limited, our security interests legitimate. If we carry out these plans, we lose all hope of victory on the battlefield or in the court of world public opinion."

General Yanaga grunted and shuffled in his seat. To the stern general this was treason. "The dynamics of this conflict are such that this war is a test of nerves. The leader who demonstrates a superior political will is the leader who will ultimately prevail."

Nukazawa shook his head in disagreement. "If we exercise these options, there will be no victors. An attack on the American financial system will destroy our financial markets as well. We initiated this war because we felt it necessary to serve our economic interests in a time of great distress. Do you now suggest that we destroy our economy to save it?"

"This is foolish!" Yanaga bellowed. "Wars are not fought in isolated circumstances. Victory comes at a high price. As I advised before we made our decision to initiate this war, you should only commence aggression if you are prepared to do what is necessary to win. The Americans are soft and the Australians nervous. Our people are already experiencing economic hardship. If we lead our nation to defeat, our failures will visit future generations. The SIC is confident that a cyberstrike on American financial markets can be launched with minimal effect on our economic interests."

The prime minister listened to the animated debate for the next thirty minutes and then, finally, playing the referee, raised his hand to halt the exchange. The room fell silent. "All of these points are quite interesting. I find myself in a quandary, somewhere between your two positions. Foreign Minister Nukazawa, you are correct in pointing out that we must not destroy ourselves to win. The general, however, is also correct in that we can only win this war by carrying the struggle into new areas. Therefore, we must take drastic measures."

In the hushed room he delivered two simple directives.

Amid the stiff winds and heavy rains in the early morning hours of October 24, the massive combined armada of British, Australian, New Zealander, and American ships began their slow passage north with the hope of reaching the Singapore Strait in two days. From the serene ports of Sydney, Brisbane, and Melbourne, the enormous machines of war cranked their main turbines and lifted anchor, turning their bows west for the journey along the majestic Australian coast. The Royal Australian Navy would spearhead the move north with Admiral Hastings in command. His familiarity with the waters was a crucial asset, something no one wished to squander.

Following the Australians was the American 6th Fleet, including the carriers *Carl Vinson* and *Eisenhower*. The *Eisenhower* bore the scars of war but was otherwise operational. A new collection of aircraft was parked on the patched flight deck, and Admiral Swarsky was on the bridge. The U.S. fleet was supplemented with heavy cruisers, particularly air defense specialists capable of striking enemy aircraft 100 miles away, and antisubmarine specialists who could better deal with Tokyo's sonar-evading subs. Sailing with the 6th Fleet was a flotilla of transport ships carrying 12,000 marines. In formation with these vessels were British transports carrying 1,500 marines and an Australian ship loaded with 2,000 troops.

Six miles behind the American armada flew the colors of the British Royal Navy, which included more than a dozen destroyers and frigates along with the carrier HMS *Ark Royal.* The British fleet was nuclear-capable but would resort to using nukes only if the enemy fired first. Bringing up the rear of the international armada were four destroyers from New Zealand.

Satellite intelligence put the bulk of the Japanese fleet off the Philippine coast in anticipation of an American move from Guam to retake Luzon. Admiral Tarayoko along with the carriers *Hokkaido* and *Keiyo* was holding to the south, while Admiral Tanaka was positioned barely fifty miles north of Luzon.

The true allied objective was oil-rich Brunei. But U.S. forces on the Philippines were highly active, the Navy SEALS aggressively promoting the guerrilla uprising in the remote foothills of the Zambales Mountains. The SEALS had linked up with Major Bermudez and his men several weeks earlier. U.S. submarines specially outfitted for special operations ensured a steady supply of weapons, ammunition, and other equipment. Under the cover of darkness, the small vessels would fire torpedolike cannisters at the shoreline. The SEALS would unlock the cannisters on the beach and transport the supplies over the mountains. The cargo was often high tech, including advanced third-generation Stinger missiles and a number of other exotic systems.

On the morning of October 24, SEALS Captain Brown received a specially coded message from PACOM over the burst communicator. The orders called for the newly formed ragtag army to engage the enemy in two days. The message was Priority One, Alpha One, which meant a specific set of orders had to be executed at all costs. Brown reviewed the Alpha One operational plans before taking them to Bermudez.

In room 3J of the Security and Intelligence Command Haki Owada sat slumped in his chair. The room was a simple structure with concrete walls, fluorescent lighting, and tan carpeting. It looked like any other nondescript government room except for the fact that it was part of a bunker several hundred feet underground.

For days, Japan's leading cyberwarrior had been grappling with his most daunting challenge yet. The General Staff had ordered the SIC to launch a series of selective cyberstrikes on targets in the United States. Shortly, Owada would be carrying out those orders. Some would do nothing more than cause a nuisance while demonstrating Tokyo's power and reach. But one target worried him. While he could pull the operation off, he worried about what destructive forces the attack might unleash.

The General Staff had ordered several logic bombs be detonated on the Fedwire, a network operated by the twelve Federal Reserve Banks in the United States. This network kept track of bank balances, liabilities, and assets for various banking transactions, and its destruction by logic bombs could cause a financial meltdown in the United States, plunging the New York Stock Exchange into disarray and causing a run on U.S. banks. In the realm of cyberwar, it was the equivalent of a massive thermonuclear strike.

There was also the additional problem of blowback: once the financial house of cards began to tumble in America, it was also likely to pull down Japanese financial markets.

Owada glanced at the wall clock. It was 3:14 A.M. He sighed and slowly rose to his feet. By now one hundred yards away in the combat center his subordinates had carried out their orders. He could feel the anguish of events unfolding halfway around the world.

U.S. Navy SEALS conduct special operations.

President St. John was meeting with the Joint Chiefs of Staff reviewing operational plans for the liberation of Brunei when reports began trickling in. First came word that massive power outages had occurred along the West Coast, from San Diego to Bellingham, Washington. Soon afterward there was an urgent call from Fed Chairman Winthrop Hamilton.

"Win," St. John asked, paying only half attention, "what's the problem?"

"The Fedwire is frozen, Mr. President."

St. John looked puzzled during a long, tension-filled pause. "What exactly does this mean?"

"The Federal Reserve Banks and the Clearing House Interbank Payments System [CHIPS] have been thrown into chaos. The flow of assets between banks has been frozen. And currently there is no way bank assets and liabilities can be transacted between institutions. If things are as bad as I think they are, we could be facing a financial meltdown."

The president urgently leaned forward in his chair. "A what?!"

"Something or someone has sabotaged the heart of our financial system. Billions upon billions of dollars float across the Fedwire every day. Now suddenly it has ceased to function. This wreaks havoc not only on the Fed system, but is likely to destroy faith in banks nationwide as this information becomes public. I expect a run on the banks during the next several days, not to mention a plunge in the stock market."

St. John sat stunned, as if he had been completely blind sided. "Win, what can we do?"

"Mr. President, I want to meet with you and the Treasury secretary at once. We will probably have to declare a bank holiday tomorrow. That will buy us some time to figure out how to put our house back in order."

Chapter Thirty-five

October 26
off the Malaysian coast

A squadron of dark, uniformly gray aircraft broke the morning stillness as they rumbled 500 feet off the Singapore Strait. The sleek B-1 bombers were cruising at more than 550 knots guided by the plane's autopilot and terrain-following radar. As they crossed the coastline of Brunei, the formation split. Two planes headed for the main Japanese air base near Bandar Seri Begawan, another for the Japanese army's main command post. The fourth screamed toward a major troop installation near the capital. Each dropped more than 125,000 pounds of ordnance—including eighty-four 500-pound bombs—over the targets in less than two seconds. It was an ephemeral but awesome display of power. At the main air base more than a dozen FX fighters were cast about like toys, the army's main command post was leveled, and a substantial portion of the Japanese troops in Brunei lay under rubble. The

Japanese command and air defense systems were shattered. The four sleek aircraft headed back out over the ocean for their return flight to Indonesia.

Allied ground crews had been very active in Indonesia during the past forty-eight hours. American, British, and Australian workers had been secretly brought into the country to establish makeshift air bases in Jakarta and Unjungpandang. The government had turned over two commercial airports so the teams could establish fuel sites and ammunition depots for strike aircraft. On the night of October 25, dozens of planes were flown in. These land-based aircraft would offer critical support for allied air operations in and around Brunei.

Reports of the successful first strike by the B-1 bombers reached the massive allied fleet as it moved along the Malaysian coast at twenty-five knots. Now two days from Australia, the fleet was very much on course. Satellite intelligence located a Japanese armada some six hundred miles north of Brunei. It was distant but moving into range. Carrier-based aircraft could seriously disrupt allied amphibious operations and put the entire operation at risk.

In light of the approaching threat, Admiral Swarsky elected to split the allied fleet. The bulk of the strike power would proceed north—including the carriers *Eisenhower, Carl Vinson,* and HMS *Ark Royal*—to engage the enemy. An assemblage of destroyers and cruisers would remain with the amphibious group to support the landing in Brunei.

The carriers steamed north, cutting a wake in the choppy South China Sea. By 10:00 A.M. reconnaissance aircraft were reporting that only five hundred miles divided the opposing navies. Swarsky hesitated—he did not want to commit his forces too early. The fate of the entire operation hinged on success in the air war. If the Japanese fleet broke through, it could stifle the landing and set back the allied cause for months. After a few minutes of wrestling with the options, Swarsky determined the time was right and ordered the immediate launch of all available aircraft. The largest air war of the conflict was about to begin.

As the carrier flight decks hummed with activity, fire-control officers aboard the Aegis cruiser *Valley Forge* analyzed the latest satellite data on the location, movement, and course of the Japanese fleet. The analysis was then relayed via encrypted communication to all allied cruisers and destroyers in the strike group. Launching sequence instructions were also included. The British vessels HMS *Minerva*, *Penelope*, and *Dante* were laden with Exocet and long-range cruise missiles. The American cruisers were carrying Tomahawks. Admiral Swarsky wanted a well-coordinated missile strike, one that might shatter the Japanese fleet in a single blow. He gave the order to commence the barrage, and together the cruisers and destroyers thrust dozens of cruise missiles into the air, targeted on the enemy formation.

The Japanese fleet possessed a variety of countermeasures that could prevent the missiles from finding their targets so the allies had programmed the cruise missiles to close on the enemy fleet by two distinct paths. Some missiles closed on their targets several hundred feet in altitude. As they approached to within two miles of their targets, the missiles would suddenly rise into the air to out-maneuver enemy defenses before diving down on the ships below. Others would simply skim the surface of the sea on a flat trajectory, striking their targets just above the waterline.

Allied aircraft flew due north in a triangular formation. Two squadrons of F-14 Tomcats took the lead, with a squadron of British Harriers four miles back flying in reserve. Further south were two more allied squadrons which had departed from makeshift bases on Indonesia.

It was in the early afternoon that Commander Bill Davis first detected the enemy formation on air-to-air radar. There were three Japanese squadrons cruising in a split formation. He radioed his fellow pilots and braced himself for the orgy of violence.

Enemy squadrons were flying in a loose formation. Commander Kashiwagi, the flight commander, flew with his 211th Squadron in the middle of the formation with Lieutenant Commander Hiro Shirohawa's 58th ten miles off to his starboard side and Lieutenant

Commander Miyohei Sakaibara and the 42nd to his port side. Sensing that his formation was too tight, Davis split his force. One squadron would engage the 211th, while his group would grapple with the 58th. The Harriers would have to contend with the 42nd, and Davis knew that the British pilots would be seriously outmatched by the superior Japanese planes.

As the planes converged at twenty thousand feet, a frenetic air war erupted. Davis and his squadron aggressively hunted the enemy, claiming three planes on the initial pass. The British Harriers, however, went quickly, lacking the power, agility, and avionics to match the FX fighters. The intense air war appeared to be at a standoff until additional allied aircraft suddenly arrived. U.S. Air Force F-22s and British Tornadoes joined the fray. Since the planes had been refueled over the Singapore Strait, they could execute difficult maneuvers and use afterburners without much concern about the volume of fuel they were burning.

The JAF had also planned to join the air war by using fighters based in the Philippines. When word reached the air base that the enemy was closing, JAF fighters on Luzon began preparing for departure from the main runway. But only two managed to get off the ground. The first plane up was shot down by Navy SEALS using Stinger missiles from the brush. After a second plane experienced the same fate, Japanese marines were sent into the brush in a desperate bid to locate the culprits. Some were found—and paid with their lives. But others remained concealed, creating a six-hour standoff which critically altered the outcome of the air war hundreds of miles to the south. The JAF reinforcements from Luzon never arrived.

During the height of the air war, a tempest erupted on the water's surface two hundred miles to the north. Allied cruise missiles began pounding the Japanese fleet with a vengeance, and enemy countermeasures managed to deflect only a handful of projectiles. The strategy of employing dual trajectories—some missiles skimming the surface and others climbing before diving at the target—had brought success. By the time the last missile struck the cruiser

Asayuki, the water had become a lake of fire with bobbing heads, small rafts, and an assortment of debris floating in the dark, oil-covered water. Remnants of the wounded fleet were forced to retreat to their home port.

Victory both at sea and in the air sent a wave of enthusiasm through the allied amphibious force now off the coast of Brunei. Intelligence indicated that the beaches near Tutong would provide an ideal setting for the landing. It also helped that no Japanese forces were deployed in the immediate area.

The tide was low and the waters rough as the allied force landed unopposed. The assemblage of landing craft carrying men, equipment, and ordnance slid up to the shoreline. U.S. Marines hit the beaches first. Next were the Australians and British, followed by heavy equipment. It was not until 8:00 P.M. that the combined forces were snaking their way down the road inland from Tutong.

Amid the fading daylight, allied pilots were reporting the movement of a Japanese army column, a mix of infantry and light armor, due east from the allied force. Allied command elected to build a defensive line to confront the approaching enemy. U.S. Marines were to the middle of the line with the British marines on the right flank, the Australians on the left.

Several hours passed and by now everything was covered by the veil of night. The roar of allied aircraft was audible in the distance, punctuated by the far-off concussion of exploding munitions. Next came the murmur of enemy armor through the thick, humid air. The center of the allied line was dotted with M-60 machine guns. The gunners steadied their weapons while their colleagues checked the stock of one hundred–round ammunition clips.

Then the enemy column appeared, turning on the bend in the road and moving methodically down the highway. Allied artillery and armor instantly sprang to life, laying down a bombardment. Japanese infantry rushed into the brush for cover. The M-60s began chattering wildly as the gas-operated, air-cooled guns spit out two hundred rounds per minute. Although the enemy countered with tank and small-weapons fire, it was pinned down.

During the next several hours a fierce battle raged. While the main Japanese force on the road was stalled, infantry were slinking through the brush toward the allied position. By early morning, allied and Japanese forces were fighting in the close confines of a labyrinth of bushes and trees. On the right flank, however, the British marines were making steady progress. As the sun crested over the horizon, they overran the end of the Japanese line. Eventually the line collapsed, and Lieutenant General Misio Nikkyoso issued a formal surrender.

In the United States, President St. John had shut the banks for three days to deal with the financial storm which had engulfed the country. The giant flywheel of the American economy had almost become unhinged. The electronic sinews that ran between the major financial institutions had been seriously damaged by logic bombs. Although the Fed had been able to rebuild the system to a minimal level of operation, the disruption had created panic in the American public and shock in the financial world. The closure of American banks and the NYSE spawned similar actions by the governments in Britain, Germany, France, and Japan. And while a complete meltdown had been temporarily averted, the creditworthiness of U.S. financial institutions was called into question. U.S. Treasury Secretary Michael Pipes and Fed Chairman Win Hamilton headed for an emergency meeting with European finance ministers in London. The war was now as much about averting financial collapse as defeating the enemy on the battlefield.

President St. John turned his attention to the vexing issue of how to retaliate for the cyberstrike on the Fedwire. He met with his advisers on October 30 to discuss both this sticky issue and the mounting problems with the military offensive. While the tide of war seemed to be shifting inevitably toward the allies, the advance was beginning to falter. Stocks of spare parts for aircraft and other major systems were running dangerously low. Ground crews had to resort to cannibalizing airplanes to keep others flying, therefore reducing the available number of fighters. There was also the problem of a naval force stretched unbelievably thin. The United States had entered the war woefully short of capital ships. The naval battles and continued harassment by Japanese subs was taking a toll. The Joint Chiefs were now recommending that offensive operations be suspended until allied forces could be replenished.

St. John began the meeting in an irritable tone. "Gentlemen, we can't stop now. Every day the Kawara government remains in power we risk another attack. Their last cyberstrike almost succeeded. And let's remember, they have a nuclear arsenal."

Tom Bodine nodded in agreement. "Mr. President, while I agree with everything you said, the realities are such that our stocks of weapons and ammunition are nearly depleted. We don't have a choice in this matter."

"Tom's right," added Jack Fowler. "The latest report from PACOM calls the situation 'dire.'"

St. John pounded his fist on the table and stood up. He began pacing with his hands folded behind him. "We need to do something to bring a quick end to this war. What about a cyberstrike retaliation?"

Bodine sighed uneasily. "The boys in our information war department have drawn up a list of targets. The trouble is, anything we do is likely to exacerbate our domestic economic difficulties. If we hit back at their financial markets, it will send everything around the world crashing down like a house of cards. And the smaller targets are not likely to yield much in the way of results. This is a war that we are going to have to win on the battlefield." The defense secretary stood and handed the president an unmarked manila folder. "We have been researching some advanced military technologies during the past two decades, and that work has yielded some results. The boys at DARPA [Defense Advanced Research Projects Agency] have come up with something that might help."

Chapter Thirty-six

February 7, 2008
the Sea of Japan

The eerie and unseemly standoff had lasted for four months. Both sides used the opportunity to solidify their positions and prepare for renewed fighting. The crippling of the American financial system had generated a worldwide economic downturn, with markets all over the world terrified that another cyberstrike might unhinge the system completely.

The allied offensive began anew in the Philippine Sea in the early hours of February 7. During the past two days a silent fleet of dark, sleek submarines had worked its way through the Japanese naval line before settling off the coast of Okinawa. These twelve Los Angeles–class subs represented an immense concentration of American naval power. It was hoped that a successful mission might bring an end to the war.

Shortly after 4:00 A.M., the subs received a VLF radio transmission via satellite. The coded message included revised targeting data and final instructions. The orders confirmed that the operation was to proceed as planned. Right away, the submarine crews began preparing for an immediate launch.

At promptly 8:30 A.M. a group of cruise missiles burst forth from the ocean surface, leveling out until perfectly horizontal. Just a few seconds later, another bunch erupted from the water, followed by a third. In all, the subs spit fifty Tomahawks into the morning air. The cruise missiles were destined for the largest JAF air base on Okinawa and an air defense installation outside the city of Kagoshima. Others were directed at the JAF base on Luzon.

During the one-hour passage to their targets, the cruise missiles made periodic adjustments to stay on course. By 10:00 A.M. they were closing on their targets. At the last minute they climbed to one thousand feet before erupting and spreading a foul gas.

The warheads contained "calmative agents" mixed with DMSO, which quickly delivers chemicals through the skin and into the bloodstream. These powerful, airborne narcotics numb the senses and stunt aggressive impulses, ultimately triggering a deep sleep. Those who manage to resist the full sensation still suffer severe motor skill difficulties. It was the perfect nonlethal gas agent for war.

The effect was almost instantaneous. Ground and flight crews at the main air base on Okinawa were immobilized. The air defense facility near Kagoshima was anesthetized. And in Tokyo, thousands of civilians fell in the streets, swimming in a state of lethargy.

Next, a squadron of American B-2 bombers swept across the afternoon skies above Okinawa. With the enemy docile and deadened, the planes flew in low over the main air base. Each released a full load of 16 MK-84 two thousand–pound bombs on JAF aircraft on the tarmac and runway. The entire fleet of planes was shattered into thousands of splintered fragments.

On Luzon, Navy SEAL Lieutenant Ron Estes and five of his compatriots were squatting in the brush as the cruise missiles began to rain down on the air base. Each was covered head to toe in protective gear and clutched a shoulder-fired rocket launcher. When Estes gave the word, each man steadied his weapon, looked through the scope, and programmed "direct flight path" into the small computer attached to the launch tube. One-by-one they pulled the trigger and released their missiles, which went screaming off toward the air base. Each rocket was equipped with a warhead containing more "calmative agents."

The SEALs methodically detached the thermal-imaging sights and control units from the launch tubes and tossed them into the brush. They then slipped back into the dark under a heavy canopy of trees, working their way to base camp. Estes remained behind to watch through his infrared scope Japanese soldiers staggering from their bunkers in a weakened daze. He reached for his COMLINK and reported what he saw back to base. Overhead, the hum of aircraft was audible as a squadron of B-1 bombers closed in on the compound.

As the lightning strikes shook the Japanese garrison on Luzon, the allied navies were converging in the waters off the coast. Admiral Curtis and the 7th Fleet had streamed west from their position near Guam, and the international armada that had won the great victory in the South China Sea in October had moved north. Tokyo still had four carriers and ample naval power to cause the allies serious difficulties. But the combined force hoped to pin the bulk of Tokyo's fleet between Taiwan and the Philippines.

Allied forces landed on Luzon by early afternoon. U.S. Marines were put ashore west of Manila along with British and Australian forces. U.S. Army Rangers were airdropped in the central plains 50 miles north of the capital. The first wave of landing craft took about 25 minutes to hit the shore, and the next three arrived at 2-minute intervals. Within six minutes, more than 3,000 men and 150 armored vehicles and artillery had landed. Six destroyers and 2 cruisers remained several miles offshore to support the operation.

The amphibious force pushed inland under light resistance. Guided by Captain Brown and the embattled unit of SEALS, the Rangers moved in to seize the air base. Only eleven of twenty-four members from the Navy Special Forces lived to see the liberation of Luzon.

While the combined force continued to move inland toward the capital, Japanese forces retreated to Manila and formed a defensive perimeter in the suburbs. They held their position and dared the allies to evict them.

Despite relative success on the battlefield, for Prime Minister Kawara the fruits of war had been bitter. The economy continued to falter, and protests mounted with the casualties. Japanese public opinion had never supported the war. In the days following the allied counterstrike, Kawara began fearing assassination and ordered his closest aides searched before meetings.

On February 9 he convened a special meeting with his war cabinet. With his hopes for conquest of the Philippines dashed and the allies employing a highly effective new weapon against his soldiers,

U.S. Forces Strike Japan

Kawara had come to the painful realization that the longer the war continued, the more likely it became that Japan would lose outright. His chief concern now was the nature of the postwar peace he hoped to forge, in a world in which the United States would accept Japan as an equal and as the unrivaled power in Asia.

"We underestimated our adversaries from the beginning," he told his war cabinet, the pain evident in his eyes. "We did not think the Americans would fight, but they showed resolve. We did not believe they could stomach a prolonged conflict, but they demonstrated no desire to compromise with us. We doubted they could absorb a serious blow to their economy, but they did. By these miscalculations we have nearly destroyed our nation."

Defense Minister Murakami Yanaga rose to his feet in apparent disgust. "If the war is lost, it is because of a lack of will! We have failed to use the ultimate weapon in our arsenal. America cannot sustain a nuclear missile strike. America is decadent, and its society is weak. A nuclear missile strike will force America to negotiate. Our failure to use this weapon will condemn two generations of Japanese to international servitude and dominance by foreign powers which seek only their benefit at our expense, the same servitude that was thrust on us because the Americans were willing to use the bomb in 1945!"

The low hush that ran through the room quickly collapsed into a deafening silence. The prime minister set his glasses on the table. "The Americans know that we are willing to use these weapons. Everything about their response suggests this. There are once again TWO superpowers. It is enough. I will contact Washington and discuss peace terms as *EQUALS!*"

As Kawara spoke these words, Yanaga turned his back and strode forcefully out of the room, flying through the open double doors without so much as a glance back at Kawara. No one else in the room ever knew whether Kawara, as he shouted the last word *EQUALS!*, raised his voice in triumph and in defiance of Yanaga, or in surprise, because at that precise moment six men dressed in black from head to toe strode in through the double doors.

National Security Council

May 19, 2008
Post-war analysis
EYES ONLY

Summary: The origins and results of this war can be tracked to a series of misguided policies.

Origins of the War: The United States pursued an aggressive trade war with Tokyo which exacerbated economic and political tensions in Japan at the turn of the century. This seriously damaged the health of the Japanese economy and strengthened extremist political forces within the nation. When energy prices jumped dramatically in 2003, the Japanese economy was sent into a tailspin.

Domestic political considerations, which were ultimately damaging to American economic and political interests, drove U.S. trade policy. The resulting nationalism and political extremism in Tokyo might have been averted had the United States pursued a more free-trade policy. Failure to maintain a solid security relationship with Tokyo compounded the internal problems.

Conduct of the War: The continued builddown of American forces in the Pacific created an opportunity for an expansionist power to fill the resulting vacuum. It was, after all, the American retreat from the Pacific and the deployment of nuclear weapons by North Korea that compelled Tokyo to develop and deploy similar systems. The reduction of the American aircraft carrier presence and the reduction by 50 percent of the American submarine and surface ship fleet committed to the region led Tokyo to believe that hegemony over the western Pacific was a viable option. In addition, American withdrawal from bases on the Korean peninsula, Japan, and Guam reduced our air and ground forces in the region. This came at a time when such a presence might have deterred aggression by Tokyo. It is likely that the American retreat from the Pacific was interpreted by Japanese nationalists as evidence that the United States was indifferent to events in the region.

Military Considerations: Military deficiencies were exposed in the serious damage the American economy sustained as a result of Japanese "cyberstrikes" against U.S. economic and financial targets. Clearly, we failed to take adequate steps to ensure the secure operation of the most fundamental information and telecommunications networks in the country. While the American investment in information warfare during the 1990s was substantial, there was not an adequate effort to generate defensive systems guaranteeing that American information links were secure.

Other military shortcomings were revealed during the war. The closing of American military installations overseas during the past twenty years was enormously shortsighted. Repeated assurances that U.S. military air and sealift capabilities would allow for the projection of our forces into foreign conflicts were simply not borne out. There is no substitute for a strong overseas presence through bases which provide a secure location for supplying and reinforcing U.S. forces during war.

Appendix A

**INTERCONTINENTAL RANGE BALLISTIC MISSILES
IN-SERVICE AND IN-DEVELOPMENT**

Weapon	Re-entry vehicles	Maximum Range in miles	User countries
JL-2 (SLBM)	1	5,000	China
DF-31	1	5,000	China
CSS-4	1	6,850	China
DF-41	1	7,500	China
M5 (SLBM)	10	6,850	France
H1	1	7,500	Japan*
H2	1	9,300	Japan*
SS-11	1	8,080	Russia
SS-13	1	5,842	Russia
SS-17	4	6,215	Russia
SS-18	10	6,837	Russia
SS-19	1 or 6	6,215	Russia
SS-24	10	6,215	Russia
SS-25	1	6,526	Russia
SS-X-26	n/a	n/a	Russia
SS-X-29	1	6,215	Russia
SS-N-8	1	4,848	Russia
SS-N-18	3	4,040	Russia
SS-N-20	4 or 10	5,158	Russia
SS-N-23	4	5,100	Russia

SS-NX-26 (SLBM)	n/a	n/a	Russia
SS-NX-27 (SLBM)	n/a	n/a	Russia

key: SLBM= submarine launched ballistic missile

n/a= not available, system currently in development

* Japan has the capability to develop these systems but has elected not to at this time

INTERMEDIATE-RANGE BALLISTIC MISSILES IN-SERVICE AND IN-DEVELOPMENT

Weapon system	Payload in lbs.	Maximum Range in miles	User countries
Iran 700 (SCUD C)	1,340	435	Iran
Al Fatah	1,340	590	Iran, Libya
Labor 1 (No Dong)	2,681	622	Iran, North Korea
Labor 2 (No Dong)	2,681	932	Iran, North Korea
M18	1,072	622	China, Iran
DF-25	5,362	1,057	China, Iran
Taepo-Dong 1	2,681	1,243	North Korea
Taepo-Dong 2	2,681	2,175	North Korea

(source: Jane's Defense Weekly, U.S. Department of Defense)

Appendix B
Aircraft and Helicopters

The following appendices include the specifications and capabilities of a number of weapons featured in this volume. Keep in mind that in many cases these systems are being continuously updated. We have assumed some level of enhancement particularly as it relates to scenarios past the year 2000.

APACHE (AH-64A)

Manufactured by the United States of America

Owned by the United States of America, Egypt, Greece, Israel, the Netherlands, Saudi Arabia, the United Arab Emirates, the United Kingdom

Mission:
Attack helicopter used for ground support

Performance:
Maximum range: 300 miles

Maximum speed: 227 mph
Rate of climb: 2,500 feet per minute

Specifications/Features:
Engine(s): 2 General Electric T-700 turboshafts (1,696 horsepower), some equipped with LONGBOW millimeter-wave radar system; crew compartment and other key areas protected by Kevlar armor and electro-slag remelt steel

Armaments:
4 underwing hardpoints for up to 16 Hellfire missiles or Hydra rockets, 2 wingtip hardpoints for Sidewinder or air-to-air Stinger missiles, 30-mm Chain Gun with 1,200 rounds of varied types of ammunition

B-1 LANCER

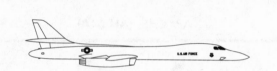

Manufactured by the United States of America

Owned by the United States of America

Mission:
Strategic penetration bomber

Performance:
Maximum range: 7,455 miles
Maximum speed: Mach 1.25 (825 mph)
Ceiling: 50,000 feet

Specifications/Features:
Engine(s): 4 General Electric F101s (30,000 lbs. of thrust each), Doppler radar altimeter with forward-looking and terrain-following capabilities

Armaments:
3 internal bays for up to 75,000 lbs. of weapons and 8 underfuse-lage stations for 59,000 lbs. Weapons include: air-launched cruise missiles, nuclear bombs, and conventional bombs

Notes:
Capable of extremely high speeds at low levels (600 mph+ at 200 feet!)

B-2 SPIRIT

Manufactured by the United States of America

Owned by the United States of America

Mission:
Low-observable strategic penetration bomber

Performance:
Maximum range: 7,595 miles (with full weapons load)
Maximum speed: 600 mph
Ceiling: 50,000 feet

Specifications/Features:
Engine(s): 4 GE-F118-GE-110 non-afterburning turbofans
Radar: Hughes AN/APQ-181 low probability of intercept covert strike radar with 21 modes for bombing missions; aircraft mostly built with compositions (especially graphite and epoxy). It is encased in a radar-absorbant covering

Armaments:
Maximum weapons load of 40,000 pounds can include 16 air-launched cruise missiles, eighty Mk82 500-pound bombs or 16 B83 strategic freefall nuclear bombs

Notes:
A combination of stealth and precision bombing capability make this the most effective deep-strike weapon available

F-14 TOMCAT

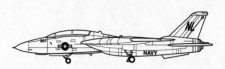

Manufactured by the United States of America

Owned by the United States of America

Mission:
Fighter and tactical strike

Performance:
Maximum range: 2,000 miles
Maximum speed: Mach 2.4 (1,564 mph)
Ceiling: 56,000 feet

Specifications/Features:
Engine(s): 2 General Electric F110s (29,000 lbs of thrust each)
Pulse Doppler radar

Armaments:
Sidewinders, AMRAAMs, Phoenix missiles or up to 14,500 lbs. of bombs, 20-mm Vulcan cannon

F-15 EAGLE

Manufactured by the United States of America

Owned by the United States of America, Israel, Japan, Saudi Arabia

Mission:
Dual role attack/air superiority fighter

Performance:
Maximum range: 2,762 miles
Maximum speed: Mach 2.5 (1,650 mph)
Ceiling: 62,000 feet

Specifications/Features:
Engine(s): 2 General Electric F110s (29,000 pounds of thrust), AN/APG-70 I-band Pulse Doppler radar; body constructed out of titanium, aluminum honeycomb wingtips, graphite/expoxy composite skin

Armaments:
Carries a maximum weapons load of 24,500 pounds including wing pylons for AIM-9 Sidewinders, AIM-120 AMRAAMs (maximum load of four each). Air-to-ground weapons include 26 Mk20 Rockeye, 7 GBU-10s, or 15 GBU-12s; 20-mm gun on starboard wing

F-16 FALCON

Manufactured by the United States of America

Owned by the United States of America, Bahrain, Belgium, Denmark, Egypt, Greece, Indonesia, Israel, the Netherlands, Norway, Pakistan, Portugal, Singapore, South Korea, Taiwan, Thailand, Turkey, Venezuela

Mission:
Tactical fighter

Performance:
Radius of action: 852 miles
Maximum speed: Mach 2 (1,320 mph)
Ceiling: 50,000 feet

Specifications/Features:
Engine(s): 1 General Electric F110 (29,588 pounds of thrust), Westinghouse AN/APG-60(v) Pulse Doppler range and angle attack radar with track-and-scan capability for up to ten targets; body made of light alloy, primarily aluminum

Armaments:
Mounting on each wing-tip for an air-to-air missile (AIM-9L Sidewinders), also carries AIM-120A AMRAAM, Sparrow and Sky Flash air-to-air missiles. Can carry HARM and Harpoon anti-ship missile

F/A-18 HORNET

Manufactured by the United States of America

Owned by the United States of America, Australia, Canada, Finland, Kuwait, Malaysia, Spain

Mission:
Carrier-borne and land-based attack/fighter

Performance:
Combat radius: 340 miles
Maximum speed: Mach 1.8 (1,185 mph)
Ceiling: 50,000 feet

Specifications/Features:
Engine(s): 2 General Electric F404 low bypass turbofans (16,000 pounds of thrust), Hughes Aircraft AN/APG-65 multimode digital air-to-air and air-to-ground tracking radar with track and scan capability for 10 targets; body constructed with light alloys, graphite/epoxy skin panels

Armaments:
Nine external weapons stations including 2 wingtip stations for AIM-9 Sidewinder, 2 outboard for air-to-air or air-to-ground weapons— AIM-7 Sparrow, Sidewinders, AMRAAMS, AGM-84 Harpoons, 2 inboard wing stations for air-to-ground weapons, 3 fuselage stations for Sparrows or laser-guided bombs; nose-mounted 20-mm cannon

F-22

Manufactured by the United States of America

Owned by the United States of America

Mission:
Tactical fighter

Performance:
Maximum range: 1,300 nautical miles
Maximum speed: Mach 1.7 (1,120 mph)
Ceiling: 60,000 feet
G limit: +9

Specifications/Features:
Engine(s): 2 Pratt and Whitney F119s with two dimensional convergent/divergent exhaust nozzles with thrust vectoring (35,000 pounds of thrust each), Westinghouse/TX AN-APG-77 radar

Search range: 150 miles
Tracking range: 80 miles

Low observables technology including aluminium/titanium and steel construction including thermoset and thermoplastic composite structures

Armaments:
Three internal bays for AIM-9 Sidewinders and/or four AIM-120A, 6 AIM-120C AMRAAM, internal barrel M6/A2 20-mm cannon

Notes:
Perhaps the most impressive feature of this aircraft is the supersonic cruising speed of Mach 1.58 (1,040 mph)

F-117

Manufactured by the United States of America

Owned by the United States of America

Mission:
Precision attack

Performance:
Mission radius: 656 miles
Maximum speed: Mach .9 (646 mph)
Ceiling: 60,000 feet
G limit: +6

Specifications/Features:
Engine(s): 2 General Electric GE F4-4-F1D2 non-augmented turbo-fans (10,800 pounds of thrust), designed to optimize radar energy dispersion and low IR emission.

Armaments:
Two 2,000-pound bombs—free-fall or laser-guided, AGM-65 Maverick, or AGM-88 HARM air-to-surface missiles

MIG-21 (CHINESE JIANJIJI-7) FISHBED

Manufactured by North Korea

Owned by North Korea, China, Cuba, Iraq

Mission:
Interceptor and ground attack

Performance:
Maximum range: 1,180 miles
Maximum speed: Mach 2.05 (1,350 mph)
Ceiling: 59,710 feet
Maximum rate of climb: 35,435 feet per minute

Specifications/Features:
Engine(s): One Chengdu WP7B turbojet (13,448 pounds of thrust)
GMAv Type 226 Skyranger radar

Armaments:
Two hardpoints under each wing, capable of carrying PL-2, PL-7 missiles or one 18-tube pod to carry Type-57 air-to-ground rockets. The Fishbed can also carry four 500 lb. or ten 200 lb. bombs.

MIG-25 FOXBAT

Manufactured by Russia

Owned by Russia, Algeria, India, Iraq, Libya, Syria

Mission:
Interceptor

Performance:
Maximum range: 1,491 miles
Maximum speed: Mach 2.8 (1,865 mph)
Ceiling: 67,900 feet
G limit: +4.5

Specifications/Features:
Engine(s): 2 Soyuz Tomansky R-15BD-300 turbojets (24,675 pounds of thrust each), Sapir-25 fire control radar in nose

Search range: 62 miles
Tracking range: 46 miles

Airframe is 80% welded/tempered steel, 8% titanium, and 11% heat resistant aluminum alloy

Armaments:
Air-to-air missiles on four underwing attachments

MIG-29 FULCRUM

Manufactured by Russia

Owned by Russia, Belarus, Bulgaria, Cuba, Hungary, India, Iran, Iraq, Moldova, North Korea, Poland, Romania, Syria, Yemen, the Ukraine

Type:
All-weather single seat counter-air fighter, with attack capability

Performance:
Maximum range: 810 nautical miles
Maximum speed: Mach 2.3 (1,520 mph)
Ceiling: 55,775 feet
G limits: 9

Specifications/Features:
Engine(s): 2 Klimov/Sarkisov RD-33 turbofans (18,300 pounds of thrust), coherent pulse Doppler lookdown/shootdown engagement radar

Search range: 62 miles
Tracking range: 43 miles

Approximately 7% of airframe is made of composites; remainder out of aluminum-lithium alloys and other metals

Armaments:
Three pylons under each wing for six close-range R-60MK infrared air-to-air missiles, or four R-60MK and two medium-range guided R-27R1

The platform can also carry FAB-250 bombs, KMGU-2 submunitions dispensers

MIG-31 FOXHOUND

Manufactured by Russia

Owned by Russia, China

Type:
Two-seat strategic interceptor

Performance:
Radius of action: 447 miles
Maximum speed: Mach 2.83 (1,865 miles)
Ceiling: 67,600 feet
G limits: supersonic: 5

Specifications/Features:
Engine(s): 2 Aviadvigatel D-30F6 turbofans (37,170 pounds of thrust each), Zaslon radar enables the aircraft to track 10 targets and engage four simultaneously, including targets below and behind its own location

Search range: 124 miles
Tracking range: 75 miles

Airframe is 50% arc-welded nickel steel, 16% titanium, and 33% light alloy

Armaments:
Four R-33 (Amos) semi-active radar homing long-range air-to-air missiles in pairs, under the fuselage; two R-40T (Acrid) medium-range infrared missiles on inner underwing pylons; four infrared R-60 (Aphid) air-to-air missiles on outer underwing pylons; GSh-6-23 six-barrel 23-mm gun inside starboard side of lower fuselage

SU-27 FLANKER

Manufactured by Russia

Owned by Russia, China, Syria, Vietnam

Type:
All-weather air superiority fighter

Performance:
Maximum range: 2,485 miles
Maximum speed: Mach 2.4 (1,550 mph)
Ceiling: 49,350 feet

Specifications/Features:
Engine(s): 2 Saturn/Lyulka turbofans (27,557 pounds of thrust each),
track-while-scan coherent Pulse Doppler look-down, shoot-down
radar

Search range: 150 miles
Tracking range: 115 miles

All-metal construction with titanium components

Armaments:
Ten air-to-air missiles in air combat role on tandem pylons, GSh-301
30 mm cannon

SU-34

Manufactured by Russia

Owned by Russia

Type:
Long-range theater bomber

Maximum range: 2,485 miles
Maximum speed: Mach 1.8 (1,185 mph)
Ceiling: 60,000 feet

Specifications/Features:
Titanium cockpit armor, dielectric nose to house navigational /attack and terrain-following radar

Armaments:
The aircraft can use a variety of laser-guided and gravity bombs, air-to-surface missiles and can carry underwing a number of rear-facing infrared homing air-to-air missiles developed from the Vympel R-73 (Archer)

TORNADO

Manufactured by International Consortium

Owned by Germany, Italy, Saudi Arabia, United Arab Emirates, the United Kingdom

Mission:
All-weather close air support/battlefield interdiction, or counter-air strike

Performance:
Radius of action: 863 miles (with heavy weapons load)

Maximum speed: Mach 1.4 (920 mph)
Ceiling: 70,000 feet

Specifications/Features:
Engine(s): 2 turbo-union RB 199-34R turbofans (14,840 pounds of thrust each), multi-mode forward-looking, terrain-following, ground-mapping radar

Detection range: 115 miles
Track several targets simultaneously at 75 miles
Made with aluminum alloy and integrally stiffened skins, titanium alloy

Armaments:
May carry a wide array of weapons including Sidewinders, AGM-88 HARMs, Paveway II and Paveway III, 1,000-pound bombs, cluster bombs, etc.; two 27-mm IWKA Mauser cannons

TU-160 BLACKJACK

Manufactured by the Ukraine

Owned by the Ukraine, Russia

Type:
Long-range strategic bomber

Performance:
Maximum range: 4,740 miles
Maximum speed: Mach 2.05 (1,380 mph)
G limit: +2

Specifications/Features:
Engine(s): 4 Samara/Trud Nk-321 turbofans (55,115 pounds of thrust each)

Armaments:
Maximum weapons load: 88,185 pounds
Rotary launcher can carry 12 Kh-15P (Kickback) SRAMs or 6 Kh-55MS (Kent) air-launched cruise missiles

HARRIER II (AV-8B USMC DESIGNATION)

Manufactured by the United States of America and the United Kingdom

Owned by the United States of America, Italy, Spain, the United Kingdom

Mission:
Close support, battlefield interdiction

Performance:
Maximum range: 684 miles
Maximum speed: Mach .98
Ceiling: 50,000 feet

Specifications/Features:
Engine(s): 1 Rolls-Royce Pegasus 11-61 vectored thrust turbofan (21,450 lbs of thrust); Fuselage is made from graphite epoxy (carbonfiber) and other composites

Armaments:
Two under fuselage points mounted portside to carry 2-4 Sidewinders or up to 16,540 pound free-fall bombs or 10 Paveway laser-guided bombs; 5-barrel 25-mm cannon on starboard side

Notes:
Short and vertical take-off capability offers valuable support for ground operations but is seriously outmatched by most in a dogfight.

Sources:
Jane's, U.S. Department of Defense

Appendix C
Missiles

AMRAAM (AIM-120)

Mission:
Medium range air-to-air missile

Specifications/Performance:
Guidance system: the missile is launched and cruises on a preprogrammed course until it reaches the vicinity of the target where it activates its active radar seeker

Warhead: 50-lb. proxity delay and impact-fused blast fragmentation

Range: 45 miles
Speed: Mach 4

Notes:
This missile can receive mid-course updates from the launch aircraft's radar so it can literally follow an enemy

HARM (AGM-88)

Mission:
Air-to-surface anti-radiation tactical missile

Specifications/Performance:
Guidance: Passive radiation seeking
Warhead: 145-lb. proximity-fused blast fragmentation
Range: 46+ miles
Speed: Mach 3 + (1,975 mph+)

Notes:
This system keys in on enemy radar; however, even if the enemy has shut down the radar emitter it can continue to home in on the target. The software for this missile allows adjustments in the guidance system for a wide variety of radars that are likely to be encountered.

HARPOON

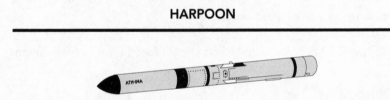

Mission:
Medium range tactical anti-ship missile

Specifications/Performance:
Guidance: Radar altimeter for midcourse phase, active radar for terminal phase

Warhead: 488-lb. impact-delay blast fragmentation
Speed: Mach .9 (645 mph)
Range: 68 miles

HELLFIRE (AGM-114)

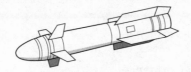

Mission:
Air-to-surface tactical missile

Specifications/Performance:
Guidance: Autopilot for midcourse phase, and semi-active laser homing for terminal phase
Warhead: 20-lb. hollow charge high explosive
Speed: Mach 1.17
Range: 5 miles

Notes:
Used primarily as a tank-killer; this is considered the most advanced anti-tank missile in the U.S. Army's inventory

MAVERICK (AGM-65D)

Mission:
Air-to-surface multi-role tactical missile

Specifications/Performance:
Guidance: Imaging infrared
Warhad: Can be fitted with 120-250 lb. warheads, including shape-charged high explosive or blast fragmentation, depending on target
Speed: Supersonic
Range: 13 nautical miles

Notes:
A fire-and-forget weapon that carries a punch, it is capable of destroying most ground vehicles, and can inflict damage on small ships

PHOENIX (AIM-54)

Mission:
Long-range air-to-air missile

Specifications/Performance:
Guidance system: semi-active homing for the cruise phase and active radar for the terminal phase
Warhead: 132-lb. high explosive
Speed: Mach 4+
Range: 2.4-125+ miles

Notes:
Has the ability to engage six targets simultaneously by using a time-share system which can lose touch with the radar for fourteen seconds before failing to reacquire the designated target

SIDEWINDER (AIM-9)

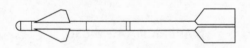

Mission:
Short-range air-to-air missile

Specifications/Performance:
Guidance: Infrared homing, with close-cycle cooler for improved seeker sensitivity
Warhead: 22.5 lb. blast fragmentation with laser-proximity fuse
Speed: Mach 2.5 (1,646 mph)
Range: 6 nautical miles

Notes:
This steady workhorse has been continuously upgraded since it first appeared in 1972

SILKWORM

Mission:
Short- to medium-range anti-ship missile

Specifications/Performance:
Guidance system: Mid-course flight phase is by autopilot with a terminal phase using one of six available I-band radar seeker head frequencies
Warhead: 1,130-lb. high explosive or chemical
Speed: Mach .85
Range: 3-24 miles

Notes:
Can be fired from a fixed or mobile launch site; flight cruise altitude for approach to target can be preset in multiples of 50 between 100 and 300 meters. In use by Iran, China, and North Korea

STINGER (FIM-92A)

Mission:
Portable air-defense surface-to-air missile

Specifications/Performance:
Guidance: passive infrared homing
Range: 3.1 miles+
Speed: Mach 2

TOMAHAWK

Mission:
Long-range surface-to-surface or anti-ship missile

Specifications/Performance:
Guidance: Radar altimeter with terrain contour mapping
Warhead: 1,000-lb. high explosive
Speed: 550 mph
Range: 1,400 nautical miles

Appendix D
Tanks and Armored Vehicles

BRADLEY FIGHTING VEHICLE (M2A1)

Manufactured by the United States of America

Owned by the United States of America

Specifications/Performance:
Crew: 3 (6 in transport)
Combat weight: 49,000 lbs.
Maximum speed: 41 mph
Maximum range: 300 miles

Armaments:
1 x 25-mm cannon
1 x 7.62-mm machine gun
1 x anti-tank guided weapon (5)

Armor:
5083 aluminum

CHIEFTAN (MK5)

Manufactured by the United Kingdom

Owned by the United Kingdom, Iran, Iraq, Jordan, Kuwait, Oman

Specifications/Performance:
Crew: 4
Combat Weight: 121,275 lbs.
Maximum road speed: 29 mph
Maximum range: 312 miles

Armaments:
1 x 120-mm (64 shells)
1 x 7.62-mm (machine gun)
1 x 7.62-mm (anti-aircraft)

LEOPARD (A1A3)

Manufactured by Germany

Owned by Germany, the Netherlands, Sweden, Switzerland

Specifications/Performance:
Crew: 4
Combat weight: 93,392 lbs.
Maximum speed: 40 mph
Maximum range: 375 mph

Armaments:
1 x 105-mm gun (55 shells)
1 x 7.62-mm machine gun
1 x 7.62-mm machine gun (anti-aircraft)

Armor:
70-mm—front
25-mm—rear

M1A2 ABRAMS

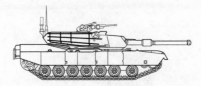

Manufactured by the United States of America

Owned by the United States of America, Egypt, Kuwait, Saudi Arabia

Specifications/Performance:
Crew: 4
Combat weight : 126,024 lbs.
Maximum speed: 45 mph
Maximum range: 310 miles
Armaments:
1 x 105-mm (40 shells)
2 x 7.62-mm machine gun
1 x 12.7-mm

Armor:
Classified

MLRS [MULTIPLE-LAUNCH ROCKET SYSTEM]

Manufactured by the United States of America

Owned by the United States of America

Specifications/Performance:
Crew: 3 (can operate with two)
Maximum speed: 40 mph
Range (rocket fire): 20 miles+

Armaments:
Two rocket containers, each with six pre-loaded tubes, primarily use warhead packed with 644 M77 dual-purpose submunitions

Notes:
A computer fire control system, which includes a Global Positioning System (GPS) satellite navigation suite, allows the 12 rockets to be targeted in under a minute with pinpoint accuracy.

T-54/5

Manufactured by Russia

Owned by Russia, Afghanistan, Algeria, Angola, Bulgaria, China, Cuba, Czech Republic, Egypt, Hungary, Iran, Iraq, Libya, North Korea, Poland, Syria, Vietnam

Specifications/Performance:
Crew: 4
Combat weight: 79,380 lbs.
Maximum speed: 31 mph
Maximum range: 287 miles

Armaments:
1 x 100-mm gun
1 x 7.62-mm machine gun

Armor:
97mm—front
46mm—rear

T-62

Manufactured by Russia

Owned by Russia, Afghanistan, Algeria, Angola, Cuba, Egypt, Ethiopia, Iran, Iraq, Libya, North Korea, Syria, Vietnam, Yemen

Specifications/Performance:
Crew: 4
Combat weight: 88,200 pounds
Maximum speed: 31 mph
Range: 280 miles

Armament:
1 x 115-mm gun

1 x 7.62-mm machine gun
1 x 12.7-mm machine gun

Armor:
102mm—front
46mm—rear

T-80U

Manufactured by Russia

Owned by Russia, China, the Ukraine

Specifications/Performance:
Crew: 3
Combat weight: 101,430
Maximum road speed: 44 mph
Range: 275 miles

Armaments:
1 x 125-mm gun/missile launcher with laser rangefinder
1 x 7.62-mm machine gun
1 x 12.7-mm machine gun (anti-aircraft)

Appendix E
Ships

Australia

ADELAIDE CLASS FRIGATE

Specifications/Performance:
Displacement: 4,100 tons
Speed: 29 knots
Range: 4,500 miles

Armaments:
Surface-to-surface missiles: 8 Harpoon (70 nautical mile range)
Surface-to-air missiles: 2 launchers
Guns: 1 x 76-mm, 1 x 20-mm
Torpedoes: 6 x 324-mm tubes

China

LUDA CLASS DESTROYER

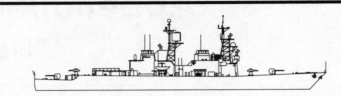

Specifications/Performance:
Displacement: 3,730 tons
Speed: 32 knots
Range: 2,970 miles
Crew: 280

Armaments:
Surface-to-surface missiles: 8 C-801 launchers
Surface-to-air missiles: 8 Crotale launchers
Guns: 4 x 130 mm, 8 x 57 mm, 8 x 37 mm, 8 x 25 mm
Torpedoes: 6 x 324-mm tubes

Great Britian

INVINCIBLE CLASS AIRCRAFT CARRIER (ARK ROYAL)

Specifications/Performance:
Displacement: 20,600 tons
Speed: 28 knots
Range: 7,000 miles
Crew: 685 (plus 366 aircrew)

Armaments:
Fixed-wing aircraft: 9 Sea Harriers
Surface-to-air missiles: Sea Dart twin-launcher
Guns: 3 x 20-mm, 3 x 30-mm

BROADSWORD CLASS FRIGATE

Specifications/Performance:
Displacement: 4,800 tons
Speed: 30 knots
Range: 4,500 miles
Crew: 296

Armaments:
Surface-to-surface missiles: 4 Exocet inertial cruise or 8 Harpoon
Surface-to-air missiles: 2 Seawolf launchers
Torpedoes: 6 x 324-mm tubes

Iran

BABR DESTROYERS

Specifications/Performance:
Displacement: 2,388 tons
Range: 3,740 miles
Speed: 32 knots
Crew: 290

Armaments:
Missiles: 4 SAM launchers, semi-active radar homing with range of 25 nautical miles
Guns: 4 x 127 mm, 2 x 23-mm
Torpedoes: 6 x 324-mm tubes

KILO SUBMARINES

Specifications/Performance:
Displacement: 3,076 tons
Speed: 17 knots underwater, 10 surfaced
Range: 6,000 miles
Crew: 53

Armaments:
Torpedoes: 6 x 21-inch tubes, 18 torpedoes with 8.1 nautical mile range
Mines: 24 (in lieu of torpedoes)

Japan

YUUSHIO CLASS SUBMARINE

Specifications/Performance:
Displacement: 2,450 tons, underwater
Speed: 24 knots underwater, 12 surfaced
Crew: 75

Armaments:
Surface-to-surface missiles: Sub-Harpoon (active-radar homing to 70 nautical miles)
Torpedoes: 6 x 21-inch tubes, active/passive homing to 27 nautical miles

KONGO CLASS DESTROYER (AEGIS SYSTEM)

Specifications/Performance:
Displacement: 9,485 tons
Speed: 30 knots
Range: 4,500 miles
Crew: 300

Armaments:
Surface-to-surface missiles: 8 Harpoon launchers, active homing radar to 70 nautical miles; surface-to-air missiles: total of 90
Guns: 1 x 127-mm, 2 x 20-mm Vulcans
Torpedoes: 6 x 324-mm tubes

Taiwan

WU CHIN CLASS DESTROYERS

Specifications/Performance:
Displacement: 3,500 tons
Speed: 32.5 knots
Range: 5,800 miles
Crew: 275

Armaments:
Surface-to-surface missiles: 5 Hsiung Feng launchers
Guns: 2 x 127 mm, 4 x 40 mm
Torpedoes: 6 x 324-mm tubes

United States

NIMITZ CLASS AIRCRAFT CARRIER

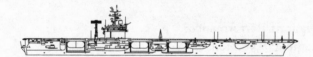

Specifications/Performance:
Displacement: 102,000 tons
Speed: 30+ knots
Range: n/a (nuclear powered)
Crew: 3,184 (plus 2,800 air crew)

Armaments:
Fixed-wing aircraft: air wing composition depends on operational
task; standard 50 TACAIR configuration includes: 20 F-14s and 36
F-18s

Surface-to-air missiles: 3 octuple launchers
Guns: 4 x 20-mm
Torpedoes: 6 x 324-mm tubes

TICONDEROGA CLASS GUIDED MISSILE CRUISER
(AEGIS SYSTEM)

Specifications/Performance:
Displacement: 9,466 tons
Speed: 30+ knots
Range: 6,000 nautical miles
Crew: 358

Armaments:
Surface-to-surface missiles: Tomahawk (range: 400 nautical miles)
TASM anti-ship (range: 250 nautical miles)
Harpoon (70 nautical miles)
Surface-to-air missiles: 68
Guns: 2 x 127-mm, 2 x 20-mm
Torpedoes: 6 x 324-mm tubes

LOS ANGELES CLASS SUBMARINE

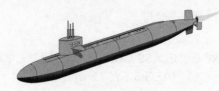

Specifications/Performance:
Displacement: 6,927 tons (underwater)
Speed: 32 knots
Crew: 133

Armaments:
Submarine launched cruise missiles Tomahawk (1,400 nautical mile range)
Surface-to-surface missiles: anti-ship Tomahawk
Torpedoes: 4 x 21-inch tubes

Sources:
Jane's Fighting Ships, U.S. Department of Defense

Bibliography

BOOKS

Abrahamian, Ervand. *Khomeinism: Essays on the Islamic Republic* (Berkeley: University of California Press, 1993).

Alexander, Bevin. *The Future of Warfare* (New York: Norton, 1995).

Allen, Kenneth W., Glenn Krumel, and Jonathan D. Polack. *China's Air Force Enters the 21st Century* (Santa Monica, Calif.: RAND, 1995).

Barnaby, Frank. *The Automated Battlefield* (Oxford: Oxford University Press, 1987).

Baxter, William P. *Soviet AirLand Battle Tactics* (Novato, Calif.: Presidio Press, 1986).

Bermudez, J. S., Jr. *North Korean Special Forces* (London: Jane's Publishing Company, 1988).

Blackwell, James. *Thunder in the Desert: The Strategy and Tactics of the Persian Gulf War* (New York: Bantam Books, 1991).

Bodansky, Yossef. *Target America: Terrorism in the U.S. Today* (New York: Spi Books, 1993).

———. *Crisis In: Korea—the Emergence of a New and Dangerous Nuclear Power* (New York: Spi Books, 1994).

Bradin, James W. *From Hot Air to Hellfire: The History of Army Attack Aviation* (Novato, Calif.: Presidio Press, 1994).

445

Brzezinski, Zbigniew. *Out of Control: Global Turmoil on the Eve of the Twenty-First Century* (New York: St. Martin's Press, 1993).

Carus, Seth. *Ballistic Missiles in the Third World: Threat and Response* (Westport, Conn.: Praeger Publishers, 1990).

Chaliand, Gerard, and Jean-Pierre Rageau. *Strategic Atlas: A Comparative Geopolitics of the World's Powers* (New York: Harper-Collins, 1992).

Chubin, Shahram. *Iran's National Security Policy: Capabilities and Intentions* (Washington, D.C.: Carnegie Endowment for International Peace).

Clancy, Tom. *Armored Cav: A Guided Tour of an Armord Cavalry Regiment* (New York: Berkley, 1994).

———. *Fighter Wing: A Guided Tour of an Air Force Combat Wing* (New York: Berkley, 1995).

Cohen, Eliot. *Gulf War Air Power Survey Summary Report* (Washington, D.C.: U.S. Government Printing Office, 1993).

Cohen, Eliot, and John Gooch. *Military Misfortunes: The Anatomy of Failure in War* (New York: The Free Press, 1990).

Creel, Herrlee G. *Chinese Thought: From Confucius to Mao Tse-Tung* (Chicago: University of Chicago Press, 1953).

Curtis, Gerald L., ed. *The United States, Japan, and Asia* (New York: W.W. Norton, 1994).

Dunnigan, James F., and Raymond Macedonia. *Getting It Right: American Military Reforms after Vietnam to the Gulf War and Beyond* (New York: William Morrow and Company, 1993).

Dupuy, Trevor. *The Evolution of Weapons and Warfare* (Fairfax, Va.: Hero Books, 1984).

———. *Future Wars: The World's Most Dangerous Flashpoints* (New York: Warner Books, 1991).

Eikenberry, Karl W. *Explaining and Influencing Chinese Arms Transfers* (Washington, D.C.: National Defense University Press, 1995).

Evangelista, Matthew. *Innovation and the Arms Race* (Ithaca, New York: Cornell University, 1988).

Fotion, Nicholas. *Military Ethics: Looking Toward the Future* (Stanford, Calif.: Hoover Institution Press, 1990).

Freedman, Lawrence. *The Evolution of Nuclear Strategy* (London: Macmillan, 1989).

Friedman, George, and Meredith Lebard. *The Coming War with Japan* (New York: St. Martin's Press, 1991).

Godson, Roy, ed. *Intelligence Requirements for the 1990s: Collection, Analysis, Counterintelligence, and Covert Action* (Lexington, Mass.: Lexington Books, 1989).

Hahn, Walter, and H. Joachim Maitre, eds. *Paying the Premium: A Military Insurance Policy for Peace and Freedom* (Westport, Conn.: Greenwood Press, 1993).

Harries, Owen. *America's Purpose: New Visions of U.S. Foreign Policy* (San Francisco: ICS Press, 1991).

Henriksen, Thomas H., and Kyongsoo Lho. *One Korea? Challenges and Prospects for Reunification* (Stanford, Calif.: Hoover Institution Press, 1994).

Hughes, W. P. *Fleet Tactics: Theory and Practice* (Annapolis, Md.: Naval Institute Press, 1986).

Ishihara, Shintaro. *The Japan That Can Say No* (New York: Simon and Schuster, 1989).

Joss, John. *Strike: U.S. Naval Strike Warfare Center* (Novato, Calif.: Presidio Press, 1989).

Kelly, Orr. *Hornet: The Inside Story of the F/A-18* (Novato, Calif.: Presidio Press, 1990).

Kinzey, Bert. *The Fury of Desert Storm: The Air Campaign* (New York: McGraw-Hill, 1991).

Lehman, John. *Making War* (New York: Scribners, 1992).

Leonard, Robert R. *The Art of Maneuver: Maneuver-Warfare Theory and AirLand Battle* (Novato, Calif.: Presidio, 1991).

Lind, William S. *Maneuver Warfare Handbook* (Boulder, Colo: Westview, 1985).

Luttwak, Edward. *Strategy: The Logic of War and Peace* (Cambridge, Mass.: Harvard University Press, 1987).

Mazarr, Michael J. *North Korea and the Bomb: A Case Study in Nonproliferation* (New York: St. Martin's Press, 1995).

Norris, Robert S., Andrew Burrows, and Richard Fieldhouse. *British, French, and Chinese Nuclear Weapons*, vol. 5 of *Nuclear Weapons Databook* (Boulder, Colo: Westview Press, 1994).

Odom, William. *America's Military Revolution: Strategy and Structure after the Cold War* (Washington, D.C.: American University Press, 1993).

O'Sullivan, Patrick, and Jesse W. Miller. *The Geography of Warfare* (New York: St. Martin's Press, 1983).

Parker, Geoffrey, ed. *Cambridge Illustrated History of Warfare* (Cambridge: Cambridge University Press, 1995).

Potter, William C., and Harlan W. Jencks, eds. *The International Missile Bazaar: The New Suppliers' Network* (Boulder, Colo: Westview Press, 1994).

Richelson, Jeffrey T. *A Century of Spies: Intelligence in the Twentieth Century* (New York: Oxford University Press, 1995).

Ripley, Tim. *The New Illustrated Guide to the Modern U.S. Army* (London: Salamander Books, 1992).

Sanders, Sol. *Mexico: Chaos on Our Doorstep* (Lanham, Md.: Madison Books, 1986).

Santoli, Al. *Leading the Way: How Vietnam Veterans Rebuilt the U.S. Military* (New York: Ballantine Books, 1993).

Sharpe, Captain Richard. *Jane's Fighting Ships: 1994–1995* (London: Jane's Publishing Company, 1995).

Simpkin, Richard. *Race to the Swift: Thoughts on Twenty-First Century Warfare* (London: Brassey's Defense Publishers, 1985).

Smallwood, William L. *Warthog: Flying the A-10 in the Gulf War* (Washington, D.C.: Brassey's, 1993).

———. *Strike Eagle: Flying the F15E in the Gulf War* (Washington, D.C.: Brassey's, 1994).

Snyder, Jed C., ed. *After Empire: The Emerging Geopolitics of Central Asia* (Washington, D.C.: National Defense University Press, 1996).

Sullivan, Gordon. *America's Army into the Twenty-First Century* (Cambridge, Mass.: Institute for Foreign Policy Analysis, 1993).

Summers, Harry G. *The New World Strategy: A Military Policy for America's Future* (New York: Simon and Schuster, 1995).

Suvorov, Viktor. *Spetsnaz: The Story of the Soviet SAS* (London: Grafton Books, 1987).

Swaine, Michael D. *China: Domestic Change and Foreign Policy* (Santa Monica, Calif.: RAND, 1995).

Taylor, Charles W. *A Concept for a Future Force* (Carlisle, Pa.: Strategic Studies Institute, Army War College, 1990).

———. *A World 2010: A New Order of Nations* (Carlisle, Pa.: Strategic Studies Institute, Army War College, 1992).

Toffler, Alvin and Heidi. *War and Anti-War: Survival at the Dawn of the 21st Century* (Boston: Little, Brown and Company, 1993).

Trachtenberg, Marc. *History and Strategy* (Princeton, N.J.: Princeton University Press, 1991).

Uhlig, Frank. *How Navies Fight: The U.S. Navy and Its Allies* (Annapolis, Md.: Naval Institute Press, 1994).

Ullman, Harlan K. *In Irons: U.S. Military Might in the New Century* (Washington, D.C.: National Defense University Press, 1995).

Van Creveld, Martin. *The Transformation of War* (New York: The Free Press, 1991).

Waller, Douglas. *The Commandos: The Inside Story of America's Secret Soldiers* (New York: Simon And Schuster, 1994).

MONOGRAPHS AND GOVERNMENT DOCUMENTS

Codevilla, Angelo. "American Security: Back to Basics," *Essays in Public Policy* (Stanford, Calif.: Hoover Institution, 1994).

International Institute for Strategic Studies. *The Military Balance: 1994–1995* (London: Brassey's, 1994).

National Military Strategy of the United States of America (Washington, D.C.: U.S. Government Printing Office, 1995).

Robinson, Roger. *Economic Security and Global Defense* (Washington, D.C.: Center for Security Policy, 1992).

U.S. Department of Defense. *Joint Warfare of the U.S. Armed Forces*, Joint Pub. 1, November 11, 1991.

Whitehurst, Clinton H. *The Last Clear Chance for an Enduring Maritime Policy* (Clemson, S.C.: Strom Thurmond Institute, Clemson University, February 1996).

ARTICLES

"Air forces update: quality to rule over quantity," *Jane's Defense Weekly*, April 16, 1994.

Auchincloss, Kenneth, "Friend or foe?" *Newsweek*, April 1, 1996.

Auer, James E., "The Imperative U.S.-Japanese Bond," *Orbis: A Journal of World Affairs*, winter 1995.

Banks, Howard, "Parkinson's law—military style," *The National Times*, December/January 1995.

Belkin, Alexander A., "Needed: a Russian Defense Policy," *Global Affairs*, fall 1992.

Bickers, Charles, "Sting-in-the-tail AAMs for Russian fighters," *Jane's Defense Weekly*, April 23, 1994.

Bracken, Paul, "Risks and promises in the two Koreas," *Orbis: A Journal of World Affairs*, winter 1995.

Brick, Andrew B., "The Asian giants: neighborly ambivalence," *Global Affairs*, fall 1991.

Bruce, James, Jacques de Lestapis, Carol Reed, and Barbara Starr, "Country briefing: Saudi Arabia," *Jane's Defense Weekly*, May 6, 1995.

————, "Civilian is appointed as Iran's top soldier," *Jane's Defense Weekly*, May 20, 1995.

Bullard, Monte, "U.S.-China relations: the strategic calculus," *Parameters*, summer 1993.

Carus, W. Seth, "Missiles in the third world: the 1991 Gulf War," *Orbis: A Journal of World Affairs*, spring 1991.

Chase, Robert S., Emily B. Hill, and Paul Kennedy, "Pivotal states and U.S. strategy," *Foreign Affairs*, January/February 1996.

Clark, Mark T., "The future of Clinton's foreign and defense policy: multilateral security," *Comparative Strategy*, no. 1, 1994.

Codevilla, Angelo, "Missile defense: A case of self-denial," *Wall Street Journal*, November 15, 1994.

Cohen, Eliot, "Please action," *National Review*, October 10, 1994.

————, "The meaning and future of airpower," *Orbis: A Journal of World Affairs*, spring 1995.

"Critical mass," *U.S. News and World Report*, April 17, 1995.

Cropsey, Seth, "The only credible deterrent," *Foreign Affairs*, March–April 1994.

Dane, Abe, "America's 'invisible' warship," *Popular Mechanics*, July 1993.

Day, Dwayne, "Soviet military space programmes in the 1980s," *Spaceflight*, April 1995.

Dobriansky, Paula, "Ukraine: a question of survival," *The National Interest*, summer 1994.

Farmer, Mark, "Fire of the dragon," *Popular Science*, August 1996.

Foley, Thomas C., "An armored force for the future 2000 and beyond—technology," *Armor*, September/October 1991.

Foss, Christoper, "Kornet rides the beam," *Jane's Defense Weekly*, November 26, 1994.

Fulghum, David A., "Pilots to leave cockpit in future air force," *Aviation Week and Space Technology*, February 5, 1996.

Gaffney, Frank, "Clinton must approach missile defense as D-Day of the '90s," *Defense News*, June 6–12, 1994.

"Glosson: U.S. Gulf War shortfalls linger," *Aviation Week and Space Technology*, January 29, 1996.

Gormley, Dennis M., and K. Scott McMahon, "Who's Guarding the Back Door? The neglected pillar of U.S. theatre missile defense," *Jane's International Defense Review*, May 1996.

Gourley, Scott, "Digitizing the battlefield," *Jane's Defense Weekly*, November 5, 1994.

Gray, Colin S., "Back to the future: Russia and the balance of power," *Global Affairs*, summer 1992.

Gregor, A. James, "China's shadow over Southeast Asian waters," *Global Affairs*, summer 1992.

Hall, Ivan P., "Japan's Asia Card," *The National Interest*, winter 1994/5.

Hasenauer, Heike, "Glimpsing the future soldier," *Soldiers*, November 1992.

Henriksen, Tom, "The coming great powers competition," *World Affairs*, fall 1995.

Herring, Thomas A., "The Global Positioning System," *Scientific American*, February 1996.

Howarth, Mike, "Japan's ready for a longer military reach," *International Defense Review*, September 1994.

Ikle, Fred Charles, "The second coming of the nuclear age," *Foreign Affairs*, January/February 1996.

"Iran's submarine fleet increases by the 'Kilo,'" *Jane's Defense Weekly*, May 7, 1994.

Kagan, Donald, "World War I, World War II, World War III," *Commentary*, March 1987.

Karniol, Robert, "Guam set to reclaim land from U.S. military," *Jane's Defense Weekly*, September 10, 1994.

"KDX combat system finalized," *Jane's Defense Weekly*, June 11, 1994.

Krepinevich, Andrew, "Cavalry to computer: the pattern of military revolutions," *The National Interest*, fall 1994.

Kristof, Nicholas D., "The Real Chinese Threat," *The New York Times Magazine*, August 27, 1995.

Lennox, Duncan, "Ballistic missiles hit new heights," *Jane's Defense Weekly*, April 30, 1994.

de Lestaspis, Jacques, "Regional briefing: the United Arab Emirates," *Jane's Defense Weekly*, March 18, 1995.

Lin, Chong-Pin, "Red Fist: China's army in transition," *International Defense Review*, February 1995.

Lok, Joris Janssen, "Assessing the fangs of Cobra," *Jane's Defense Weekly*, June 10, 1995.

Luttwak, Edward, "Toward Post-Heroic Warfare," *Foreign Affairs*, May–June 1995.

Macgregor, Douglas A., "Future battle: the merging levels of war," *Parameters*, winter 1992–93.

Mahnken, Thomas G., "Planning U.S. forces for the twenty-first century," *Strategy Review*, fall 1992.

McNaugher, Thomas L., "A stronger China: is the United States ready?" *Brookings Review*, fall 1994.

Meacham, James, "Clouds over the Gulf," *International Defense Review*, December 1994.

"MiG-29SE Gets Refueling Edge," *Aviation Week and Space Technology*, February 26, 1996.

Morton, Oliver, "Defense Technology: The information advantage," *The Economist*, June 10, 1995.

Mylroie, Laurie, "The World Trade Center Bomb," *The National Interest*, winter 1995/6.

"New eyes in space," *Technology Review*, November/December 1995.

Nixon, Richard, "How to live with the bomb," *National Review*, September 20, 1985.

North, David, "A Ride in the B-2," *Popular Mechanics*, October 1995.

Novichkov, Nicholay, "New Russian MiGs set for flight test," *Aviation Week and Space Technology*, January 1, 1996.

"Nuclear non-proliferation: between the bomb and a hard place," *The Economist*, March 25, 1995.

Oberg, James, "Soviet space secrets," *Spaceflight*, August 1995.

Payne, Keith B., "The Iron Laws Confront the 21st Century," *Global Affairs*, fall 1991.

———, "Post-Cold War deterrence and missile defense," *Orbis: A Journal of World Affairs*, spring 1995.

Peters, Ralph, "The movable fortress: warfare in the 21st century," *Military Review*, June 1993.

Pipes, Richard, "What to do about the CIA," *Commentary*, March 1995.

Ratliff, William, "China asserts itself in the South China Sea," *Orange County Register*, May 8, 1994.

Schweizer, Peter, "The Soviet military today: going high-tech," *Orbis: A Journal of World Affairs*, spring 1991.

Sciolino, Elaine, "CIA report says Chinese sent Iran arms components," *The New York Times*, June 22, 1995.

Seay, Douglas, "The defense of Europe," *Global Affairs*, spring 1992.

Sharpe, Richard, "World's navies: treading water," *Jane's Defense Weekly*, June 10, 1995.

Sherr, James, "Russian Orthodoxies," *The National Interest*, winter 1992/3.

Sincock, Peter, "Moving along, but not yet in step: Southern Gulf states are trying to improve their defenses and operate more as a team," *International Defense Review*, December 1994.

Snider, Don M., "The coming defense train wreck..." *Washington Quarterly*, winter 1996.

Sobel, Cliff, and Loren Thompson, "The readiness trap: U.S. military is failing to prepare for the next big war," *Policy Review*, spring 1995.

"South China Sea squabble intensifies," *International Defense Review*, May 1995.

Starr, Barbara, "Super sensors will eye the new proliferation frontier," *Jane's Defense Weekly*, June 4, 1994.

———, "No Dongs may soon be nuclear, warns USN," *Jane's Defense Weekly*, June 18, 1994.

———, "Economics could undermine North Korean capability," *Jane's Defense Weekly*, June 25, 1994.

———, "Covert proliferation solutions studied," *Jane's Defense Weekly*, July 9, 1994.

———, "U.S. missile defense set for a journey into space," *Jane's Defense Weekly*, August 20, 1994.

———, "Iran gets 'Scud' TELs from North Korea," *Jane's Defense Weekly*, May 16, 1995.

Starr, S. Fredrick, "Making Eurasia stable," *Foreign Affairs*, January/February 1996.

Stix, Gary, "Fighting future wars," *Scientific American*, December 1995.

Stover, Dawn, "The coming food crisis," *Popular Science*, August 1996.

Sullivan, Gordon R., "Doctrine: a guide to the future," *Military Review*, February 1992.

Sweetman, Bill, "Bear Arms," *Air and Space*, October/November 1994.

Swinburn, Sir Richard, "Future armored warfare: the case for the tank," *RUSI Journal*, June 1992.

Tajiri, Tadashi, "Russia and the New World Order," *Global Affairs*, fall 1992.

Thatcher, Margaret, "Why America must remain number one," *National Review*, July 31, 1995.

Thies, Wallace J., "A twenty-first century army," *Parameters*, spring 1991.

Timmerman, Frederick W., "Future warriors," *Military Review*, September 1987.

"Tiny receiver aids special ops," *Aviation Week and Space Technology*, February 26, 1996.

Tguchim, Robert, and James Hogue, "The battle of convergence in four dimensions," *Military Review*, October 1992.

"Treaties fail to stem the threat," *Jane's Defense Weekly*, July 16, 1994.

Truver, Scott, "Budget squeeze blurs the long-range vision," *Jane's Navy International*, June 1996.

Vuono, Carl E., "Desert Storm and the future of conventional forces," *Foreign Affairs*, spring 1991.

Waldron, Arthur, "China's Coming Constitutional Challenges," *Orbis: A Journal of World Affairs*, winter 1995.

Waller, Douglas, "Onward cyber soldiers," *Time*, August 21, 1995.

Wohlstetter, Albert, and Gregory S. Jones, "'Breakthrough' in North Korea?" *Wall Street Journal*, November 4, 1994.

Wolfowitz, Paul, "A bomber for uncertain times," *Wall Street Journal*, June 12, 1995.

Wood, Perry, "Storm clouds over the South China Sea," *American Legion*, July 1995.

Woolsey, R. James, "Missile Blackmail Exists Today," *Wall Street Journal*, April 8, 1996.

Xiaowei, Zhao, "The threat of a new arms race dominates Asian geopolitics," *Global Affairs*, summer 1992.

Yost, David S., "France's nuclear dilemmas," *Foreign Affairs*, January/February 1996.

Zakheim, Dov S., "A top-down plan for the Pentagon," *Orbis: A Journal of World Affairs*, spring 1995.

Zhan, Jun, "China Goes to the Blue Waters: The Navy, Seapower Mentality and the South China Sea," *Journal of Strategic Studies*, September 1994.

Index